Medical Negligence: Cost Effective Case Management

Medical Negligence: Cost Effective Case Management

Iain S Goldrein QC
MA (Cantab), Barrister, Northern Circuit,
Visiting Professor in Litigation (The Sir Jack Jacob Chair), Nottingham Law School,
Companion of the Academy of Experts,
Fellow of the Royal Society of Arts

Margaret R de Haas
LLB (Hons), Barrister, Northern Circuit,
Fellow of the Royal Society of Arts

With contributions by
Sarah Brennan
LLB (Hons), (Qld)
Partner, Russell Jones & Walker, London

Keith Haynes
M Sc, LLB (Hons), Dip HSM, MHSM
Medical Protection Society
Scheme Managers for the
Clinical Negligence Scheme for Trusts

Foreword by
**The Right Honourable
Lord Justice Otton**

Tottel
publishing

Published by
Tottel Publishing Ltd
Maxwelton House
41-43 Boltro Road
Haywards Heath
West Sussex
RH16 1BJ

ISBN: 978-1-84592-661-8

© Reed Elsevier (UK) Ltd 1997
Formerly published by LexisNexis Butterworths

This edition reprinted by Tottel Publishing Ltd 2007

British Library Cataloguing-in-Publication Data.
A catalogue record for this book is available from the British Library.

Typeset by Kerrypress, Luton, Bedfordshire
Printed and bound in Great Britain by
Marston Book Services, Abingdon, Oxfordshire

Foreword

All who are engaged in personal injury litigation in whatever capacity are aware that over the last two decades this area of activity has not only increased but become more complex and specialised and none more so than the speciality of medical negligence claims.

There was a consensus of opinion that the procedural status quo could not continue which resulted in the Lord Chancellor inviting Lord Woolf to address the problem.

This book sees as its task the orientation of the conduct of medical negligence litigation to accommodate the reforms proposed by Lord Woolf in his Report, 'Access to Justice'.

Iain S Goldrein and Margaret de Haas bring both scholarship and experience to that task. These distinguished authors rightly identify that the future of Personal Injury (and in particular Medical Negligence) Litigation inevitably requires the 'reduction of orality'.

From their professional perspective they have already seen the momentum increase in the generation of paper which is meant to achieve or at least assist this reduction. Judges have for some time witnessed this increase from the Bench with alarm. They, like the authors, divine that the shift and emphasis in presentation does not inevitably result in expedition, elucidation and reduced cost. Indeed there is abundant evidence that the departure from a predominantly oral presentation results inexorably in delay, obscurity and increased expenditure. There is a growing perception that the change is counter-productive, the outcome a mere chimera.

This need not necessarily be so. The authors are to be congratulated in addressing the trend and in identifying means whereby, with proper case management, the ideals of Lord Woolf can be achieved and the merits of his reforms can be assimilated into our Civil Justice System.

The authors modestly claim that their approach to file management is 'radical' — I respectfully suggest 'pragmatic' might be more apt. Their thesis is that the approach of all concerned must be focused on efficient courtroom presentation. They see litigation as a highway and chart the optimum route for the litigator. The hazards of each stage of litigation are identified, analysed and constructive proposals put forward, in order to ensure a smooth and safe journey.

Although primarily (and inevitably) concentrating on the position of the Plaintiff there is abundant material within these pages to assist all of those engaged in this kind of litigation. It will be a fool-hardy litigator in any capacity who omits to study this book, to absorb its message, to have it at his elbow and put it into practice if he wishes to achieve Cost Effective Case Management.

The learned authors deserve to be congratulated for their foresight, imagination and practical guidance.

The Right Honourable Lord Justice Otton
Royal Courts of Justice
Strand
London

To: Our Children
Alastair and Alexandra

Preface and Introduction

Readership

This book is written expressly for those directly involved in medical negligence litigation, namely:

- **The lay client** (and the style of writing is intended to render complex legal concepts susceptible to analysis by the lay person).
- **All litigators** (barristers, solicitors, legal executives and managing clerks).
- **All medical personnel** (including doctors, midwives and nurses) who may in their daily practice become exposed to medical negligence litigation.
- **Health Trusts and hospital risk managers**.
- **Insurance brokers** involved in conditional fee agreements.
- Members of the Association of Personal Injury Lawyers (**APIL**), Action for Victims of Medical Accidents (**AVMA**) and the Forum of Insurance Lawyers (**FOIL**).
- **Citizens Advice Bureaux**.
- **Community Health Councils**.

This Preface, and the book, are to be read against the backdrop of this range of people with a direct interest in the **cost-effective** and **fair** management of medical negligence cases.

Issue!! *Issue*!! Or We All Fall Down

Hitherto, **funding** for medical negligence litigation (whether for Plaintiff or Defendant) has been 'demand-led' and paid by reference to an hourly rate.

Case management in this field has become established against that backdrop.

It is no secret, however, that there are to be radical changes in the money supply to litigators in this field. Assuming Legal Aid is the nationalisation of the funding of litigation, then **conditional fees** and **budgeted tendering** are the **privatisation** of the funding of litigation.

Industries which are privatised tend to experience a dramatic shake out in manpower and a much more cost-effective product.

It is submitted that such changes to funding demand that case management has to change, or litigator insolvency beckons.

This book is designed to address that challenge, and is to be read in the context of:

a   Restrictions in funding including conditional fee agreements.
b   Lord Woolf's Reforms.

c   Lord Taylor's **Practice Direction** (the implications of which for case management are explored in Appendix 2 at p 227 under the title *'Tayloring'* **Case Management to *Woolf's* Litigation Highway**).

d   The **Practice Direction** of 1 November 1996 regulating *Medical Negligence Litigation* in the Central Registry.

Lord Taylor's Practice Direction uses the words **'issues'** seven times. The central importance of **'issues'** in our system of dispute resolution was explained by Lord Salmon in a paper he delivered in 1964 entitled: **'Some Thoughts on the Traditions of the English Bar'**. He inter alia said:

> *'You must familiarise yourself with all the facts and documents of any case in which you are engaged and the law applicable to it. You must consider all the many points that could be made. But remember this, in few cases, however complex, is there usually more than one point that matters. Very seldom are there more than two and never, well hardly ever, more than three. Discover the points that really matter. Stick to them and discard the rest. Nothing is more irritating to a tribunal than the advocate who takes every point possible and impossible. To do so is a very poor form of advocacy because the good points are apt to be swept away with the bad ones. Stick to what matters.'*

This was a paper delivered to young barristers. But it has very real practical implications for litigators today, as explained by Rose LJ *Re Freudiana Holdings Ltd* (1995) Times, 4 December:

> *'Whether there should be a wasted costs hearing was clearly a matter for the judge's discretion. In his Lordship's judgment, unless the proceedings could take place in summary form on or very soon after judgment they were unlikely to be appropriate.*
>
> ...
>
> *... Wasted costs orders were an imperfect means of seeking to control excess by the legal profession. They provided the courts with a tool which in some cases was equal to the task but which in many cases was inadequate.*
>
> *However the real remedy lay in the hands of the legal profession itself. The proper conduct of litigation did not require every point to be taken, it required all those involved to concentrate on the vital issues in the case.*
>
> *The legal profession must relearn, or reapply, the skill which was the historic hallmark of the profession but which appeared to be fast vanishing: to present to the court the few crucial determinative points and to discard as immaterial dross the minor points and excessive detail.'*

One of the aims of this book is to enable litigators to come up to the standards set out by Lord Salmon and Rose LJ, and to explain that if there is a failure to match those standards, the financial consequences fall onto the balance sheets of the litigator, not the Legal Aid Board.

Because the *issue* is so overwhelmingly important as a tool in our system of dispute resolution, the word is highlighted throughout the book wherever it appears.

Funding/Access to Justice

We seek to demonstrate that by stricter application of the Rules of Court, a medical negligence case can be run with more focused case management which in turn reduces the money needed to finance it.

If the cost of litigating is too high, litigants will not litigate even if the claim is strong. They will not be able to afford the premium for the insurance policy linked to the conditional fee agreement. Thus **cost-effectiveness** is a key to **Access to Justice**. Our aim is to demonstrate that it lies within the power and ability of all litigators to run **major claims** in the field of medical negligence less expensively. The grounds for this assertion are set out in Chapter 1.

The book is not targeted at the new 'fast track' — that may be expected to have its own tight and dedicated protocols.

The Litigation Highway: A Route Map

To further the aim of cost-effective litigation, this book takes an approach to legal writing perhaps entirely different from anything previously published: Chapters 1–4 set out the *'litigation highway'* — **starting in the courtroom**. They explain at the beginning what the judge needs. The chapters then work backwards along the **'litigation highway'** until finally there is covered the client coming through the door of the solicitor's office for the first time.

In other words, the legal principles and the requirements of the Judge predicate the organisation of the file and the management of the case.

The purpose of looking at litigation through this matrix is to avoid the contemporary problem of the creation of enormous quantities of paper, most of which is subsequently screened out with Counsel's Advice on Evidence after setting down for trial and more particularly, with the Skeleton Argument. Such screening out connotes waste.

When irrelevant material is funded on demand at an hourly rate, the creation of such material has been at the account of the Legal Aid Board or the Health Trusts. With conditional fee agreements, the creation of irrelevant material will (if the action loses) be at the exclusive account of the Plaintiff litigator. This is where litigator insolvency rears its head.

Chapters 1–4 are based upon a series of Papers delivered by Iain Goldrein in the major Cities of England and Wales in 1994 and 1995, under the aegis of Butterworths.

Despite these Papers explaining the need for a very radical overhaul of established case management, Butterworths' tele-marketing revealed that the audience response was overwhelmingly positive, and generated the encouragement to develop the theme further.

Subjecting the *Bolam* Test to *Rational Analysis*

The **micro-processor** of this book deals with the **'Bolam'** test. This test of a **'Responsible Body of Medical Opinion'** is explored. The thesis is developed that one can explore whether a body of opinion is **'responsible'** by focusing on the balance to be struck between the risk of injury and the precautions to be taken to reduce or avoid that risk.

Our motivation in researching '**Bolam**' is simply expressed. If the '**Bolam**' test is not susceptible to rational analysis then how can a 'risk analysis' be made for the purposes of a conditional fee agreement?

Our articulation of this approach to the **'Bolam'** test was first published (after some years' research) by the New Law Journal as a series of articles in 1994 **'Bolam — Problems with Ancestor Worship'**. In revised form, it constitutes **Chapter 5**, at p 57.

This thesis in turn has a bearing upon the approach to Case Management to be found in **Chapter 1** and in particular the Model Letter of Instruction to an Expert to be found in **Chapter 2** at p 16.

The primary case law underpinning **Chapter 5** is embraced in the decisions in the following cases: *Hucks v Cole, Bolitho v City and Hackney Health Authority,* and *Joyce v Wandsworth Health Authority*. They are set out in full in **Appendices 4–6**, to facilitate, in particular, a barrister's research prior to running an argument in the courtroom.

Risk Analysis in the Health Trusts

The mirror image of **'risk analysis'** in the context of litigation, is quality control in the work-place: in the Health Trusts. Thus there is covered in **Chapter 6** the operation of the **'Clinical Negligence Scheme for Trusts'**, penned by **Keith Haynes** of the Medical Protection Society.

Case Digest — Speedy Research Tool

Since speed of access to the relevant data is critical to the making of a legitimate margin in the context of restricted funding and medical negligence litigation, there is set out in **Chapter 7** a comprehensive **Case Digest** (prepared by solicitor Sarah Brennan of Russell Jones & Walker) covering medical negligence case law for about the last six years. The purpose of the Digest is not to provide a comprehensive glossary of judicial dicta. Rather, it is to enable the litigator readily to assess whether there is a relevant case on the **issue** he or she has to address, where that case is to be found, who the medical experts were and (where appropriate) whether their opinion was accepted by the Court.

Understanding the Medical Terms

Because medical reports are so regularly replete with complex medical terminology, there is set out in **Appendix 7**, a **glossary of medical terms** which has been compiled in reference to many years of specialist practice in this field.

Expressions of appreciation

This book does not pretend to embrace all the answers to the challenges which beckon with restrictions in funding and the Reports of Lord Woolf. What it does seek to achieve, however, is radically to challenge the way we think about case management.

We are indebted to Mr Justice Latham and James Badenoch QC who triggered the thought process which led to this book, by their Chapter in *Medical Negligence* edited by Powers and Harris (2nd edn) Butterworths. They explain how counsel should open the case to the Judge and in so doing, set out what the Judge needs. It is that approach, what the Judge needs, which sets the template for this work.

This preface would not be complete without expressions also of gratitude to Daniel Brennan QC, Robin de Wilde QC and David Body (of Irwin Mitchell). They have held high the torch of a more analytical examination of the **'Bolam'** test. We are in their debt, not only for helping to create case law to direct our thoughts, but also for their guidance and assistance in our researches into **'Bolam'**.

None of our efforts, of course, would have borne fruit without the assistance of Butterworths.

The assistance we have received does not of course excuse our errors. If anything, it compounds them. For such errors as may have crept into the text, we crave forgiveness and invite the reader's attention to a precedent from 'Dryden':

'Therefore, our Poet as he thinks not fit
T'impose upon you what he writes for Wit
So hopes that leaving you your censures free,
You, equal judges of the whole will be;
They judge but half who only faults will see.'

Iain S Goldrein
Margaret de Haas
Valentine's Day 1997

The Corn Exchange Chambers   12 King's Bench Walk
Fenwick Street   Temple
Liverpool   London

Contents

Table of statutes

References in this Table to *Statutes* are to Halsbury's Statutes of England (Fourth Edition) showing the volume and page at which the annotated text may be found.

Table of cases

Chapter 1

Explaining the need for a litigation highway

PART 1 THE FRAMEWORK OF THIS BOOK

Few areas of litigation generate cost and delay more than medical negligence litigation. Chapters 1–4 inclusive endeavour to address the following **issues**:

Firstly, 'Why cost and delay?'

Secondly, How cost and delay appear to be the creatures of funding which is *demand-led* and calculated on the basis of an *hourly-rate*.

Thirdly, given *conditional fee agreements*, cost and delay must dramatically reduce, or the litigator may face insolvency.

Fourthly, as to case management, there is proposed:

- a different approach which is radical;
- what is 'radical' is that this proposed system of case management is tied in strictly with the rules of evidence, advocacy and the court. This is radical because the artificial split between the Bar and solicitors has resulted in a fundamental anomaly: those charged with case management (solicitors) have traditionally had little formal training in procedure, evidence or advocacy while those charged with the duty of advocacy, knowledge of procedure and evidence (the Bar) have no formal responsibility for case management.

This anomaly – the hiatus between the responsibilities of the legal professions – generates a thrombosis in the arteries of access to justice.

Fifthly, the book then seeks to do the following:

- show how the whole approach to case management must be focused on efficient courtroom presentation;
- provide a '*model*' opening to the court at trial;
- show how that model opening can only work effectively by reference to the '*Agenda for Trial*' — ie the pleading;
- explain the template of a model pleading in medical negligence litigation;
- demonstrate how that model pleading dovetails with the medical reports on liability, causation and damage, which in turn flow from a letter of

FOCUS AND FILE MANAGEMENT

A piece of litigation must from its inception anticipate the courtroom. If it does not, it has no focus.

1

instruction which is legally (not medically) focused; and

- explain what should (and more importantly, should not) go into the lay witness statements.

PART 2   WHY COST AND DELAY?

A   Contemporary case management

Cost and delay is the inevitable result of the following fairly typical sequence of events:

- The client comes into the office. The first stage is the taking of a statement. That (first) statement can often run into a dozen or more pages, even in a case of relatively limited proportions. What is being explored is every avenue of enquiry, irrespective of the fact that so often there is no template for the enquiry.

- The medical records are obtained from the hospital authority. The litigator goes through them carefully, not just to put them into order, but to seek in minute detail to understand them. He or she then brings in the client to go through them again for the client's comments. *Result:* Voluminous explanation of the notes by the litigator by way of file memorandum, and a further statement from the client.

- The medical experts are instructed. Often several are instructed contemporaneously. The litigator may write very lengthy letters, trawling through all the medical records, including much medical theorising.

- The experts respond with medical reports, often at very great length. Almost invariably each expert records the notes in very great detail, additional to the litigator's own researches. Each expert will also set out 'The Facts' often at very great length, leading to alarming duplication.

- The file is now vast. Counsel is instructed. The cost of the preparation of such instructions is correspondingly vast; a cost which hitherto has been underwritten by the Legal Aid Board. When this vast bulk lands on Counsel's desk, one look at it tells him he needs to set aside several hours. That may take weeks to fit into his diary commitments. He has other cases marked urgent and court appointments.

- Counsel advises there may be a case. Legal aid is extended and, some months later, back come the papers to draft a statement of claim. The file is now

TEAMWORK

If solicitor and counsel work as a team from the beginning, and work more strictly within the rules, the consumer secures speedier and cheaper access to justice.

STATEMENT TAKING

When the client first comes into the office, what does the solicitor know of the medical matrix? How much does the client truly remember? How can the client be expected to remember it, 'on the hoof' as it were, in the pressurised atmosphere of a legal environment?

☞ *Letters of instruction can readily run into six or more sides of medical theorising.*

**AMENDING THE
STATEMENT OF CLAIM**

- *Counsel interviews the experts in conference.*
- *He or she makes notes in Counsel's Notebook.*
- *Other commitments prevent the early re-drafting of the claim.*
- *By that time, Counsel has forgotten the fine tuning of the case and amends the pleading to the best of his or her recollection of the conference. The pleading is then sent to the solicitor.*
- *The solicitor has forgotten the fine tuning of the case.*
- *The solicitor then sends the pleading to the experts for checking (who in turn have forgotten the fine tuning of the case).*
- *The experts check the pleading, suggest further alterations, and the papers are returned to Counsel.*

'VETTING' AGENDA

- *Distilling the issues from the pleadings and schedule of loss.*
- *Assessing what evidence there is in relation to each issue.*
- *Screening out all hearsay material, and all material which is not relevant to the issues.*
- *Making sure that every matter in issue is covered with relevant and admissible evidence.*

even bulkier. Counsel drafts the statement of claim many weeks later, when he can set aside the time. The delay probably generates a 'supply failure' for Legal Aid Franchising purposes.

- The statement of claim is served. A defence comes in and Counsel is asked to advise in conference. The file is now back-breakingly substantial, and the conference is organised for some months hence.

- At the conference, the case is explored with the experts. It becomes apparent that the Statement of Claim is in need of very substantial amendment. Counsel undertakes to do this. This brings into play a protocol all its own (see box).

- Months later, an Amended Defence is served. The Plaintiff litigator takes out a summons for directions for hearing (say) three months hence. Waiting for the summons for directions, the client comes into the office and gives another statement, on the Amended Defence.

- The lay evidence is then compiled, often in a startling number of separate documents. Counsel is then asked to 'vet' the witness statements. This can take many weeks. There is another 'supply failure'. The instructions to counsel are now in several lever arch files (the metal clips of which have bent in the DX defying one's ability to read through the files and warranting the need to remove all the documents and insert them in new files). 'Vetting' witness statements invariably means going through every piece of paper in the instructions (see box). This generates a further problem: the statements for 'vetting' are frequently inadequate and **issues** have not been covered. Counsel asks for these **issues** to be covered, and is met with the response:

  'We have already had these statements signed by the witness; he/she lives hundreds of miles away and we cannot on Legal Aid justify re-interviewing.'

- On exchange of witness statements, the following documents are frequently generated:

  a statements from 'our' lay witnesses in relation to the statements of the other side.

  b reports from 'our' medical experts as to the evidence as to fact from the doctors on the other side.

  c instructions to Counsel to advise in conference — the number of experts and the bulk of the case resulting in the timing being several months hence.

- At this conference with experts (after exchange of lay evidence) much further medical opinion is forthcoming. This generates more *'supplemental'* medical reports and a need to re-amend the Statement of Claim. This takes a further several weeks (or even months). Another 'supply failure'? The new draft is circulated to the experts, who in turn make alterations, which are then referred to counsel, who finalises the Re-Amended Claim. This exercise takes a further several months.

- There then follows the instructions to counsel to vet the experts' reports prior to disclosure. This involves going through every word and checking every cross-reference (so often there is a cross-reference to a document which is not to be disclosed). In a substantial case, the exercise of counsel going through the medical reports, identifying the passages which should not be in, advising on the passages which should be in (but are not), etc results in a flurry of correspondence with the experts which generates more reports. The exercise on average seems to take about a year, in a piece of substantial litigation.

  ☞ *Sometimes, the medical experts become confused as to the legal standard of proof and insist on using the word 'could' rather than 'would' irrespective of their intention to support 'causation' on the balance of probabilities.*

- On exchange of experts' reports, there should as a rule be at least one further conference with experts, to review all the evidence now disclosed by both sides. This in turn usually generates the following:

  a a further statement from the client on the other side's reports;

  b further reports from experts on the reports of the other side.

  At this stage, if counsel asks for a rationalisation of the expert evidence (eg one 'Stand-alone' comprehensive report for each expert and one agreed statement of fact to be incorporated by reference into each report) he is probably going to be told that this will not be capable of justification on taxation. This argument holds strong despite remonstration that the judge will take much longer to get a grip on the case because of the state of the documentation: there will be a 'myriad' supplementals from a variety of experts.

- Shortly before trial, an offer is made which (for whatever reason, including attrition) the client accepts.

B   Due process

This approach to case management is now so entrenched that it can readily be perceived as being *'due process'*.

☞ *Any suggestion that this 'due process' can be altered can be met even with incredulity.*

A parallel with English military history can perhaps be drawn. In his work *On the Psychology of Military Incompetence* Dr Norman Dixon writes at page 113:

> '... Over the years Liddell Hart produced a number of articles and books on mechanisation, on new infantry tactics, and on the strategic and tactical use of armour. His efforts encouraged extreme hostility and resistance from the British General Staff. When he submitted his essay on "Mechanization of the Army" for a military competition, it was rejected in favour of an entry on "Limitations of the Tank". The judges were a field-marshal, a general and a colonel.'

C   The significance of public funding

The Legal Aid Board is primarily a financier, not a legal auditor. Thus the Legal Aid Board cannot change case management by edict.

D   The significance of conditional fee agreements

For reasons explained below, conditional fee agreements can vindicate the restriction of legal aid in areas of legal activity covered by those agreements. Without demand-led public funding at an hourly rate, the approach to case management set out above would speedily render the litigator insolvent. A litigator could not afford to lose a case with such costs and disbursements running on the file.

E   What does the client want?

It is frequently said that the client does not want money, but only to find out what went wrong and if appropriate, an apology. Medical negligence litigation is a curious route to achieve that result. If the client only wants to find out what went wrong and an apology, then more vigorous use of the hospital complaints procedure is a more compelling route. It is certainly cheaper than an adverse order as to costs.

F   Underpinning everything: the size of the core bundle

Once the core bundle is subject to a vigorous discipline, the issues will be clear.

It is suggested that case management should be conducted on the premise that if the core bundle for the court (including pleadings, witness statements, medical reports and the core case notes) generates more than 150 sides of A4, there has been an error. In this way, electronic mail/disc transfer becomes a much more viable option. **Issues** could then more readily be clarified with experts by use of a video conferencing facility (rather than the solicitor having to pay for the experts, as they travel around the country for conferences in the Temple or otherwise).

G   Hazards of litigation

Before considering how demand-led public funding can be legitimately restricted in the field of medical negligence, it is a useful exercise to examine the phrase *'Risks of Litigation'*.

PART 3   RISKS OF LITIGATION

A   Rationale

This is a 'catch-all' phrase. It is used (if not invariably) in the following situations:

- to discourage a client from running an action;
- having commenced an action, to discourage him from continuing it;
- having continued it, to discourage him from fighting to trial (thereby to achieve a settlement).

B   Traditional risks of litigation?

Since the courtroom has been the primary forum for the finding of fact until the 1980s all evidence as to fact and expert opinion was privileged until disclosure in the courtroom. Thus witnesses volunteered their factual evidence to the other side, for the first time, in court. Facts could surface which had not been anticipated therefore undermining the case or, alternatively, a client's case could collapse under cross-examination by a skilled advocate on the other side. The same hazards could arise when experts exchanged their opinions for the first time in the courtroom.

C   The consequences of 'cards on the table'

The new procedural rules as to *'cards on the table'* are explored in the next section. Suffice to say the traditional 'Risks of Litigation' (arising as they did from a lack of 'openness') no longer apply. But the phrase is still used. Why?

D   The present risks of litigation?

They include:

- failure to have recorded in the relevant witness statements, the correct information;
- failure to retain an expert of the correct calibre in the relevant discipline;
- failure to achieve tight dovetailing between the pleadings, the lay and expert evidence;
- failure to retain a barrister of the appropriate calibre in the relevant discipline, and of sufficient forensic expertise;
- failure to have recorded in the experts' reports, the relevant opinion on the **issue** to be proved;
- failure to recognise the heads of past and future loss capable of being recovered;
- failure to exercise a proper judgment in relation to the information revealed by the other side's cards which are face up on the table; and
- *failure to realise that the 'go for it mentality' seduces the client with a false prospectus if then confronted with a shrewdly pitched payment-in;*
- failure to think through with sufficient focus, succinctness and clarity the 'Skeleton Argument'.

E   Cards on the table and legal aid

? *Why cannot the litigator himself or herself underwrite that risk of losing?*

☞ Once all the cards are on the table, there is opened a challenge to the litigator: why should the public purse underwrite the risk of losing?

PART 4   CAN THE CONTINUING PROVISION OF DEMAND-LED FUNDING BE LEGITIMATELY QUESTIONED?

The pecuniary reward of consummated case management has in the past been achieved upon receipt of a Legal Aid Certificate rather than upon securing a satisfactory judgment.

☞ Hitherto, the Legal Aid Board has underwritten the bulk of medical negligence litigation. The Plaintiff litigator has been in a *'win-win'* situation. If the Plaintiff has won the action, his or her litigator has been paid out by the defendant; if the Plaintiff has lost, the litigators have been paid out by the Legal Aid Fund.

This has in turn distorted the market, resulting in health authorities volunteering some compensation even in claims lacking merit.

All that is about to change. The quiet revolution in the changes to court procedure predicate 'cards on the table'.

The Rule changes enabling 'cards on the table' are:

a **More particularity in defences** — to prevent trial by ambush and to apprise the plaintiff of the issues and the risks before trial rather than at trial.

b **Reciprocal disclosure of lay witness statements** This means that the evidence-in-chief is presented prior to the hearing.

c **Reciprocal disclosure of expert evidence before trial**.

d **Service of the medical report** with the statement of claim together with a statement of the special damages claimed thereby to enable the parties in good time to apprise themselves of the extent of the claim and the issues between them.

e **Greater use of the 'split-trial' procedure** to speed up the trial of **issues** such as liability in cases where the question of damage/prognosis is unclear. The 'split trial' also enables a litigator to reduce his exposure to the risk of losing if there is a real issue on liability.

f **Greater use of interrogatories**. This technique enables each party to learn more about the other side's case before reaching the door of the court, thereby clarifying the **issues** earlier.

☞ *Interrogatories are a means of discovery which reach parts of the other side's case which ordinary documentary techniques of discovery cannot reach.*

g **Greater use of the 'notice to admit facts'** to prevent facts having to be proved expensively at court which are not contentious and which can readily be admitted inexpensively before trial.

h **Without prejudice meetings of experts** to enable experts to liaise and achieve if possible a consensus long before trial rather than in some smoke-filled conference room or corridor adjacent to the trial courtroom, with all the attendant expense of readiness for trial.

i **The lodging with the court before trial of the agreed bundle of documents** and an agreed list of **issues** thereby focusing the attention of the parties on the **issues** before reaching the court door rather than at the court door.

These rule changes secure '*openness*' and result in the following:

a The courtroom is not the primary fact-finding forum.

b The capability of making an informed risk analysis of the merits of winning/losing is accessible to the litigator who knows how to exploit openness.

c *'Exploiting openness'* includes knowing which facts and expert evidence are required to be adduced, when the relevant document should be created and at what cost.

The alternative to cost effective file management is insolvency.

☞ d Knowing what facts and expert evidence to adduce are intrinsic to cost-effective case management.

e Cost-effective case management predicates a 'product' which is not defective. 'Openness' forecloses the use of the courtroom as a repair workshop for a defective litigation product.

Why insolvency? Because:

Why cannot the Legal Aid Board withdraw its safety net, and require the litigator to underwrite the risk of losing? Once the litigator can make an informed judgment of the risks of winning or losing, why should the Legal Aid Board underwrite the risk of losing?

☞ a The Litigator underwrites the risk of losing in the regime of 'Conditional Fee Agreements'.

b Thus the thesis is: Conditional Fee Agreements are the privatisation of the funding of litigation (just as Legal Aid is the nationalisation of the funding of litigation).

If the risk analysis of the Plaintiff litigator is wrong, he goes without his fees. If his risk analysis is consistently wrong, he will fail to make an overall margin.

Synthesis

1 Case management should be predicated by Court Management.

2 The ultimate expression of Court Management is trial.

3 Understanding 'trial' is critical to understanding case management.

4 The 'key note' of the trial is the *opening speech.*

Pages 10–44 below cover the following topics:

a structure of the opening speech;

b organisation of documents for trial;

c proposed framework for a pleading in the field of medical negligence;

d initial letter of instruction to experts;

e the primary lay evidence.

It is proposed to show that the template struck by what the Court requires in an opening speech can properly predicate the template for the pleadings together with the lay and expert evidence. This must have the effect of very substantially cutting down cost and paper and correspondingly highlight the **issues**.

Chapter 2

The nuts and bolts of the litigation highway

PART 1 STRUCTURE OF THE OPENING SPEECH

The following is a suggested structure flowing from the Chapter of Mr Justice Latham and James Badenoch QC, contained in Chapter 19 of *Medical Negligence* (2nd edn) Butterworths at p 493 et seq. Note that:

- it must not be rigid;
- it will accommodate most claims; and
- it must be tailored to the individual action.

- **Plaintiff's present condition** 'Describe the condition of the plaintiff today, in respect of which he/she claims damages.'
- **Identify the individuals allegedly to blame** 'Explain who is said to have been to blame for the suffering complained about, and what their status and duties were at the material time, briefly setting out the basis for vicarious liability, if any.'
- **What was the problem which warranted treatment?** 'Set out how, when and why the plaintiff came to be in the care of the allegedly negligent staff — with an account of the disease/condition if any from which he was suffering, and for which he required their attention.'
- **What should have happened, given correct treatment?** 'Propound, with clear reasoning, what the plaintiff had a right to expect by way of outcome, if correctly treated (eg restoration to ordinary physical fitness and capability, and to his pre-treatment employment).'
- **Pleadings** 'Now advert to the pleadings. These may be, as in the modern way, very full and detailed. It is to be hoped that the judge will indicate that he has read and digested them.'
- **What should have happened?** 'Explain step by step the care/treatment which the plaintiff needed, and why, and which it is alleged should properly have been given to him if the duty of care had been discharged.'

- **Treatment in fact given** 'Detail the care/treatment in fact given to the plaintiff, which is said to have been negligent, doing this where possible by way of juxtaposition so that the alleged shortcomings are individually and tellingly highlighted, in chronological sequence.'
- **Experts** 'Now advert to the expert's reports, and discover whether the judge has (*a*) read them, and (*b*) understood them.'
- **Clarify the issues between the experts** 'Subject to the judge's indication, and/or counsel's perception of the need, now present a concise summary of the arguments between the opposing experts as they emerge from the reports, and give an explanation of the crux of the dispute or disputes which require to be judicially resolved. This is obviously the opportunity which must be taken by the plaintiff's counsel to highlight and fix in the judge's mind the merits and persuasive force of the plaintiff's case, as they are perceived to be, and to attack, undermine and diminish the defence case so far as possible. Remember that with the burden of proof on the plaintiff the opportunity provided by the right to open the case should be exploited as efficiently and effectively as possible.'
- **Do not exaggerate** 'Beware at all times during the opening of hyperbole or exaggeration, and of emotive or excessively colourful language. The media, especially the tabloid press, have the habit of latching on to counsel's more vivid excursions and turning them into headlines ('Mother left dying in pool of blood', or 'Patient fled in terror from the dentist's chair'). Unless what you describe is strictly accurate, and also a necessary part of the case, any excesses may return to haunt you. Even if they do not, they may cause considerable unnecessary pain to the professionals thus publicly pilloried, and/or give the impression (rightly or wrongly) to the judge that counsel is improperly playing to the gallery. This could prove extremely damaging to the plaintiff's case.'
- **Quantum** 'Obviously, where quantum is in issue it is necessary to deal as clearly and shortly as is reasonably possible with the matters which remain to be tried. It will have been everyone's proper concern to reduce to the irreducible minimum the areas of dispute, and wherever possible to confine the triable issue to the matters of principle rather than mathematical disputation.'

The template struck by this 'opening speech' dovetails into the template (immediately below) for organising the documents at trial.

PART 2   ORGANISATION OF
DOCUMENTS FOR TRIAL

A   Strategy for each bundle

- On the spine and the face of each bundle:
  a 'legend' to explain contents;
  b number;
  c colour code (eg 'red' for clinical notes).
- Absolutely accurate, clear and consistent pagination and indexation.
- Name and firm of solicitor preparing it (preferably towards the bottom of the spine).
- Ensure that it is *not* so full as to result in either of the following:
  a inability properly to turn the pages; or
  b distortion of the rings/lever which secure the documents (aim for no more than two-thirds full).

B   Documents which should be in
entirely separate bundles

- **Pleadings:** Suggest blue ring binder (*note: pagination and indexation are essential*).
- **Plaintiff and defence expert evidence:**
  a The plaintiff expert evidence relating to separate issues (such as liability, causation, damage, etc) should be compiled together in the file — *each issue separated from the next with a coloured card divider.*
  b In a separate file, but in the same way — the defence expert evidence.
- **Core medical case notes and related documents:**
  a These should almost always fit into a *ring binder* (rather than a lever arch file).
  b They should be accompanied by any drawings (*colour is particularly desirable*) provided by experts on either side which clarify the medical opinions.

☞ *In this way, the court can, in relation to each **issue**, contrast the respective fields of expert evidence by having both files open alongside each other.*

It is essential to screen out from this binder all the separate supporting documentation. That can be decanted into lever arch files, which are available to the court if needed but which should not block the arteries of forensic concentration and discussion.

c Any handwritten documents should face immediately opposite a typed-up copy of them (the typing must be absolutely accurate). Thus handwriting can be rendered immediately susceptible to understanding without interrupting the judge's increasing grip on the detail of the case.

- **All the medical case notes:**

*The notes may take many lever arch files. They are **not** to be given 'centre stage' in the courtroom. This is because it is very rare for there to be more than 50 actual sheets of notes to be relevant in any case, and they constitute the core bundle.*

a Coloured dividers to segregate each category of note.

b Page numbering and indexation (which should have been agreed long before with the other side) to be absolutely accurate and consistent.

- **Medical literature:**

a This is the literature upon which experts seek to rely to buttress their opinion.

b The literature should be *page numbered* and *indexed*.

It would assist to have agreement between the parties on this colour coding to avoid misunderstanding at trial.

c Each article/treatise should be separated from the next by a numbered coloured card divider.

d The passages in the literature *central to the case* of each party should be highlighted in fluorescent pen (say 'red' for plaintiff and 'blue' for defendant).

- **Schedules relating to damages:**

a In a form whereby the court has a column to add its own comments.

b In a separate ring binder.

- **Core correspondence:**

a But only if absolutely essential to the **issues**.

b Edited to an absolute minimum.

Note: Trial and document preparation runs primarily to the agenda struck by the pleadings, and particularly the Statement of Claim.

PART 3 · PROPOSED FRAMEWORK FOR A STATEMENT OF CLAIM IN THE FIELD OF MEDICAL NEGLIGENCE

IN THE HIGH COURT OF JUSTICE
QUEENS BENCH DIVISION

1998 D No...............

Writ issued the ..... day of 1998

Between:

JOHN DOE

Plaintiff

and

BARCHESTER HEALTH AUTHORITY

Defendant

<u>STATEMENT OF CLAIM</u>

1   Introduction: The Defendant at all material times pursuant to the National Health Service Act 1977, managed and administered the ...... Hospital ...... and provided medical specialist and other services including .... services at and for the purposes of the hospital.

2   Chronology: The chronology of events is set out as a schedule to this pleading.

3   Matters to be set out in brief, as agenda for opening speech to the Court:

a   *P's condition*: The condition of the plaintiff today, in respect of which he or she claims.

b   *The condition requiring treatment*: How, when and why the plaintiff came to be in the care of the allegedly negligent staff with an account of the disease/condition if any from which he or she was suffering, and for which medical attention was required.

c   *What happened (the 'occurrence')*: Set out as an exercise in succinctness:
   i   What factually was the treatment actually administered?
   ii   How did that treatment (as a matter of 'mechanics') cause the damage?
   iii   With what result to the plaintiff?

d   *Which individuals to blame:* Who is said to have been to blame for the occurrence, and what were their duties at the material time, briefly setting out the basis for vicarious liability.

e   *What should have happened:* Explain what treatment should have been administered, when and by whom?

4   The said occurrence was caused by the negligence of the Defendant by itself, its servants or agents:

<u>PARTICULARS</u>

A   The risk of the said occurrence was reasonably foreseeable. The grounds for that averment are:

a ....

b ....

c ....

B   Precautions capable of being taken which would have averted such occurrence were:

a ....

b ....

c ....

d ....

C   Such precautions ought to have been taken because:

a ....

b ....

c ....

d ....

5   Because of the occurrence, the Plaintiff who was born on the .... day of .... 19 .... has sustained pain, suffering and loss of amenity and has suffered loss and damage:

<u>PARTICULARS OF PAIN AND SUFFERING AND LOSS OF AMENITY</u>

....

<u>PARTICULARS OF LOSS AND DAMAGE</u>

Please see Schedule of Loss served herewith.

And the Plaintiff claims damages and interest thereon pursuant to section 35A of the Supreme Court Act 1981.

Etc

Note (1): This 'Model' pleading is to be adapted to the needs of the individual case.

Note (2): Until the Defence is served, the **issues** will not have crystallised. Until the **issues** have crystallised, there is no purpose in drafting full statements from the lay witnesses.

Note (3): Central to an effective claim is the quality and focus of the expert evidence. See Part 4 immediately below.

Note (4): For a legal justification for the template struck by this model Statement of Claim, see p 57.

Note (5): This 'Model' is intended to guide and *not* to be a substitute for thought and judgement.

Note (6): Warning: No amendment (however small) should *ever* be made to a pleading without the *express* approval *in writing* of the person who originally drafted it.

PART 4   INITIAL LETTER OF INSTRUCTION — A TRAINING MODULE FOR EXPERTS

Model letter of instruction from a solicitor to a medical specialist in a proposed action for medical negligence

Note: What follows is not intended to constitute a letter to be sent without more to the medical experts. Rather it provides a 'training module' to experts in the field of medical negligence. They learn the legal matrix and the need for their report to dovetail with overall case management and presentation of their evidence at trial. This training module is intended for use by any expert (plaintiff or defence) but for ease of presentation is expressed in terms of plaintiff orientation. Prudence may dictate that litigators will ensure their experts are trained in the theory and practice of expert evidence (including mock trials) before risking their profit margins on untried/untested forensic expertise.

Dear Sir
Re: ....

Introduction

1   We would be grateful if you would advise us on a matter of suspected medical negligence. The circumstances in outline are contained in the client's statement (document X in these papers) and (General Practitioner/hospital — *delete as appropriate*) medical records, copies of which we enclose.

2   Before we explain how we wish the report to be drawn up, we would be grateful if you would confirm that the issue falls within your field of expertise.

3   With regard to the preparation of your report, could we refer you to the Notes for Guidance which are attached to this letter as a separate schedule. Could we advise you particularly to note the following:

First: It is critical that you keep the creation of documentation to an absolute minimum. The proposed legal action will be run under a conditional-fee agreement. That means for the lawyers: 'No-win, no-fee'. This in turn means that our case management must be accurate and cost-effective. The creation of documentation which is not absolutely necessary for the action, has to be avoided. Could we invite you to approach this letter with that in mind?

Secondly: An absolute minimum means this: — sufficiently succinct to explain your conclusion and the grounds for your view. Please record in a separate letter the time taken.

Thirdly: If the case comes to trial, the report from each expert will be divided into parts, namely (as appropriate):

- *Part one:* Your primary opinion on the issue on which you are retained.
- *Part two:* Your opinion on the Defence pleading; including any requests for '*particulars*' and '*interrogatories*'.
- *Part three:* Your opinion on the evidence as to fact of the other side's staff who dealt with the plaintiff.
- *Part four:* Your opinion on the expert evidence adduced by the other side.

- *Summary:* Thus your final report in the courtroom will be a stand alone document. Please do not create any documentation which will be more than absolutely necessary to achieve that result. Please note that at the first conference with experts, there may be prepared with counsel an agreed statement of facts which can then be incorporated by reference into every report from each expert.

Fourthly: Whenever preparing further documentation, please do so by revising your initial report. Do not create new and separate reports. In this way we can build up your expert evidence in one stand-alone document rather than several. Ensure that the date of your report for exchange with the other side corresponds with the date when you made your last revision to the document.

Liability

4   As to the format for your opinion; could we ask you to adopt the following approach (which will then dovetail with Counsel's opening speech, and the pleadings):

If mis-treatment:
- Set out clearly *when and why* our client came to be in the care of the allegedly negligent staff with an account of the disease/condition, if any, from which he was suffering, and for which he required their attention.
- Identify and itemise clearly the *treatment* which was in fact administered to our client.
- As a matter of 'mechanics' — *what went wrong*: the 'occurrence'.
- As to the risk of that damage resulting:
  a   what was the likelihood of it occurring, and
  b   how serious was the damage which would result if that risk materialised?
- What measures were in fact available to reduce that risk of damage so that it would not have materialised?
- Should such measures in fact have been taken, balancing the magnitude of the risk of injury/damage against the disadvantage arising from taking such measures (eg the effort and expense of taking such measures, the possible frustration of important other activities in the hospital/surgery, and the possibility that the precautions would be futile etc)?
  Note: If your view is that measures should have been taken, then could you set out with precision (because this will form part of the pleading):
  a   what measures;
  b   by whom;
  c   when; and
  d   on what grounds do you so advise?

If failure to diagnose:
- As to the diagnosis actually made:
  a   Was it incorrect?
  b   If yes, what were the factors (assuming this is clear from the medical case notes) for the making of that actual diagnosis?

- As to the symptoms complained of:
  a What were they?

  b Should they have prompted further questioning to elicit information about other symptoms of which the patient did not complain, or other history?

  c If further information should have been elicited, *what* information and on what grounds is that contended for?

  d Given the information which either was or should have been available to the diagnostician, *what* potential diagnoses beckoned?

  e In relation to each particular diagnosis which did so beckon, *what* was the risk of harm to the Plaintiff if that diagnosis was not made and what were the steps available to make such diagnosis?

  f What in fact was the correct diagnosis, and why?

  g Should steps have been taken to make that correct diagnosis and if yes, on what grounds do you so advise and when should they have been taken?

- If a 'wait/see' approach is adopted:
  a Why was it adopted?

  b What were the *risks* to the patient of so waiting?

  c What were the *advantages* to the patient in so waiting?

  Balancing risk against advantage, was the balance properly struck? If no, on what grounds (as precisely as you can) do you so advise?

  (If relevant) Informed consent:

- Was our client warned as to the *risks* inherent in this operation?

- If yes:
  a In what terms?

  b Were those terms *sufficient*?

  c If yes — on what *grounds* do you so advise?

- If no — or if inadequately informed — on what grounds do you say he/she should have been better informed and in what terms should he/she have been so informed?

- Was our client told of non-surgical alternatives to the treatment proposed? If not, should he/she have been informed? In this respect, is there a body of responsible medical opinion which would have acted as the medical personnel in question?

Resulting damage/causation

If you are of the view that the treatment/diagnosis was negligent, please go on to cover the following:

- State in relation to each failure of medical care, what injury/damage was sustained by our client as a result including:
  a the pain and suffering and loss of amenity flowing from that failure;

b   the pain, suffering and loss of amenity our client would have endured had the medical men *not* fallen below the standard of care; and

c   the condition and prognosis resulting from the failure of medical care.

- If it is not possible to advise as to whether or not such failure actually caused the pain/damage, can you advise as to whether or not it materially increased such pain/damage? If yes:

a   On what grounds do you so advise?

b   By what proportion was there such contribution?

  - What is the condition of the plaintiff today, in respect of which he/she claims damages?

  - What did the client have a right to expect by way of outcome, if correctly treated (eg restoration to ordinary physical fitness and capability, and to his pre-treatment employment).

  - Can failure of the medical personnel (if any) be rectified? If yes — when, how and to what extent will such medical intervention help the client? Would private treatment (as opposed to treatment under the NHS) be beneficial? If yes, why and at what cost?

Conclusion

In conclusion, we would be grateful if you could, on each continuation sheet of your report, ask your secretary to type your name, the date of the report, and the fact that it is a preliminary report to be finalised for disclosure.

Yours faithfully,

....

Note: See Appendix to this letter, below. This appendix forms part of the 'Training Module for the Experts' which is the additional role of this Model Letter.

Appendix to model letter

1   Standard of proof:

- The plaintiff lawyers can plead as a certainty, what can be proved on the balance of probabilities.

- *Please note:* We are not looking for scientific certainty. Thus, if you can show that a particular disability would probably have been avoided given correct treatment, then the barrister can plead:

    'Had that treatment been administered, the following injury would have been avoided.'

2   Guidance for the physical construction of the report: You should prepare your report as follows:

- It should be well spaced out with margins, on *A4 sized* paper.

- The *Heading* for the report should include:
  a The *title* (ie type of report) 'Report in respect of a complaint of alleged Medical Negligence in relation to (eg brain damage arising out of failure of orthopaedician to be put on enquiry as to brain damage following vehicle accident ... etc)'
  b The *name* of the *client* in *full*.
  c The *date of birth* of the client.
  d The *date* of preparation of the report.
  e That it was prepared on instructions from *our firm*, giving our firm's name, address and reference.
- *Sources of information:* All sources of information used for the compilation of the report should be recited, including:
  a *All medical or other case notes,* X-rays and medical case records (if you require records which we have not provided, please tell us by return what further records you require).
  b *Physical examinations:* Where an examination has been performed, the date and persons in attendance should be noted. Please also set out briefly in your report the nature and extent of the examination (to avoid imputations of inadequate assessment).
  c *Interviews* upon which the opinion is based.
- *Curriculum vitae:* The report should (preferably by way of appendix) give your full name, qualifications, appointments and annex as a schedule your relevant publications.
- *Complex medical terminology:* If using complicated terminology, please put in brackets afterwards a layman's explanation, with a glossary at the end as an appendix.
- *Diagrams:* If referring to parts of the anatomy, please use recognised medical drawings.
- *Supporting literature:* The report should, in a schedule, recite any publications, etc upon which you rely in support of any opinion which you advance with sufficient notation to link such material to the relevant part of your opinion. For preference, please use the *Vancouver* system.
- *Chronology:* Please set out in a schedule annexed to your report, a chronology of the dates and times *central* to your opinion (whereby the date is set out first, and immediately afterwards, a short explanation as to its relevance).
- *Conclusion:* For the sake of clarity, please summarise conclusions clearly, with focus and succinctly.

3   **As to individuals concerned:** If you are able to identify an individual's conduct as responsible (in whole or in part) for the damage complained of, please:

- identify that individual; and
- explain why you are of the view that such individual was the cause of the damage, in whole or in part.

4   The relevant standard of care:

- *First:* In the event that the matters complained of happened some time ago, the relevant standard of medical care is that prevailing at the time of treatment, not that which prevails now. If possible, please support your opinions with contemporaneous case references in respect of any failure on the part of the medical men which you have identified.

- *Secondly:* The courts compare *like with like*. Thus if the relevant medic was a senior registrar, the standard of care is that reasonably to be expected from a medic of that status rather than of a consultant.

5   Check on sources of information: Are your views based on the history in the case notes or on what the client says or both? In this regard:

- Do the case notes contradict what the client says? If yes, could you help us by identifying the contradictions or inconsistencies?

- If there are contradictions or inconsistencies, can they be reconciled? If yes — how and on what basis?

- If the contradictions or inconsistencies cannot be reconciled what evidence have you relied upon in your report and why; that of the case notes *or* that of the client? *In either event, please tell us the reason for your so relying on one as opposed to the other.*

6   Visual aids: In the event that the treatment involved equipment, would the court be assisted in understanding how the medical accident occurred by seeing the equipment and/or by having a video film as to how the treatment ought to have been administered?

7   Relevant decisions of the courts as to expert evidence: Please note the following two cases which assist in focusing your attention on how your evidence will be tested in court:

- *National Justice Cia Naviera SA v Prudential Assurance Co Ltd (Ikarian Reefer)* [1993] 2 Lloyd's Rep 68. Mr Justice Cresswell inter alia said:

    '1 Expert evidence presented to the court should be, and should be seen to be, the independent product of the expert uninfluenced as to form or content by the exigencies of litigation ....

    2 Independent assistance should be provided to the court by way of objective unbiased opinion regarding matters within the expertise of the expert witness .... An expert witness in the High Court should never assume the role of advocate.

    3 Facts or assumptions upon which the opinion was based should be stated together with material facts which could detract from the concluded opinion.

    4 An expert witness should make it clear when a question or issue fell outside his expertise.

    5 If the opinion was not properly researched because it was considered insufficient data was available then that had to be stated with an indication that the opinion was provisional .... If the witness could not assert that the report contained the truth, the whole truth and nothing but the truth then that qualification should be stated in the report.

    6 If after exchange of reports, an expert witness changed his mind on a material matter then the change of view should be communicated to the other side through legal representatives without delay and, when appropriate, to the court.

7   Photographs, plans, survey reports and other documents referred to in the expert evidence had to be provided to the other side at the same time as the exchange of reports.'

- *Loveday v Renton* [1990] 1 Med LR 117 at 125 per Stuart-Smith LJ:

'In reaching my decision a number of processes have to be undertaken. The mere expression of opinion or belief by a witness, however eminent, . . . does not suffice. The court has to evaluate the witness and soundness of his opinion. Most importantly this involves an examination of the reasons given for his opinions and the extent to which they are supported by the evidence. The judge also has to decide what weight to attach to a witness's opinion by examining the internal consistency and logic of his evidence; the care with which he has considered the subject and presented his evidence; his precision and accuracy of thought as demonstrated by his answers; how he responds to searching and informed cross-examination and in particular the extent to which a witness faces up to and accepts the logic of a proposition put in cross-examination or is prepared to concede points that are seen to be correct; the extent to which a witness has conceived an opinion and is reluctant to re-examine it in the light of later evidence, or demonstrates a flexibility of mind which may involve changing or modifying opinions previously held; whether or not a witness is biased or lacks independence. Criticisms have been made by Counsel of some of the witnesses called on either side and I shall have to consider these in due course. ...

There is one further aspect of a witness's evidence that is often important; that is his demeanour in the witness box. As in most cases where the court is evaluating expert evidence, I have placed less weight on this factor in reaching my assessment. But it is not wholly unimportant; and in particular in those instances where criticisms have been made of a witness, on the grounds of bias or lack of independence, which in my view are not justified, the witness's demeanour has been a factor that I have taken into account ....'

Note:

a   This letter sets a framework for the medical report. That framework dovetails with the template for the 'opening speech' (see p 10). It also dovetails with the Model Statement of Claim.

b   In the more complex case, the Statement of Claim will not be drafted until there has been a conference with Counsel and the expert(s). For the relevant Agenda, see p 24.

c   Underpinning the Statement of Claim and the letter of instruction to the expert is the factual basis of the case. That will be refined by the medical experts in conference. However, the raw material initially at least, comes from the lay client. Thus one cannot focus on the Statement of Claim without first focusing on the primary lay evidence — *the statement from the client.*

Summary: The aim is to achieve dovetailing/compatibility between the following: opening speech, documents, pleadings, expert evidence and lay evidence. To adopt the language of industry, it is to provide for the components manufactured by the machine tools, to be compatible, and dovetail with, the requirements of the ultimate product.

PART 5   THE PRIMARY LAY EVIDENCE
— THE STATEMENT FROM
THE CLIENT

As to the purpose of this statement and the relevant legal principles, please turn to Chapter 4, p 40.

The client should be given a template, in the following terms:

Economy before screening the 🎞 case is essential.

Because the client has an immediate financial interest, he or she may be expected to undertake the drawing up of the initial statement seriously.

'Please tell me about your complaint of medical negligence. Tell the story clearly. Do give dates, the names of any people who are relevant to the story and the names and addresses of doctor's surgeries and/or hospitals.

If you can get the statement typed up, so much the better. If you cannot, please write neatly, so that I can easily read it.

When you have done that, could you answer the following questions also. I will need that information in order to get information which I need to run the claim:

a   Name and address of each GP whom you have had.

b   Name and address of any hospital at which you have ever had treatment and the name of any doctor at the hospital whom you remember dealing with you.

c   What was your condition prior to the medical treatment you now complain of?

d   What medical treatment do you complain of?

e   Who administered the treatment?

f   Where was it administered and when?

g   What result did you expect from the treatment? Why did you expect that result?

h   What in fact is the result from the treatment?

i   Have you complained already to someone? If yes, to whom, when and with what result?

j   Do you want to claim money compensation, or are you really looking for an explanation of what happened and an apology?

There is a parallel with 'day-in-the-life-of' video films: Experience frequently shows that when the family is asked to use the video camera, with an agenda provided by the solicitor, the result is a very effective product at a fraction of the price of a professionally produced product.

k   When did you first think that the medical treatment had gone wrong?

l   What made you think it had gone wrong?

m   When did you first think of going to a solicitor and why?

n   Has anyone said anything to you which makes you think that something has gone wrong? If yes — who, when, where and in what words?'

Chapter 3

Agendas for conferences

PART 1 AGENDAS FOR FIRST CONFERENCE WITH EXPERT(S) BEFORE THE DRAFTING OF PLEADINGS

A Preamble

It is submitted that Counsel only *needs* the following material for this conference:

- the *medical case notes* disclosed by the other side;
- a *statement* from the relevant lay witness (eg the client) on the issue on which the case turns (but only if the case turns on his or her oral recollection); and
- *'skeletal' reports* from the key expert or experts retained by the solicitor.

Please note:
- Anything more is surplus to what is strictly necessity.
- Any more information will have to be paid for.
- Counsel should be instructed before the conference to draft a skeletal pleading. That pleading should be circulated to the experts prior to the conference.
- Only those experts essential for the conference should be asked to attend.

☞ *The solicitor may be paying for all the information out of his or her own professional pocket.*

☞ *That draft skeletal pleading is the basic agenda for the first conference with experts.*

B What does 'skeletal reports' mean?

It means nothing more than:

- **Firstly**, those facts central to the case (and no more).
- **Secondly**, a firm opinion that:
  - a there is no case, or
  - b there is a case, or
  - c the expert cannot decide and is equivocal. (This also has to be spelled out just as firmly as a positive or negative opinion.)

Any one of these three options must be accompanied by a succinct expression of opinion and no more.

☞ *The use of prolix experts spells, as a matter of regular case management, nothing less than long-term insolvency for the solicitor working in a regime of conditional fee agreements or budgeted fundholding.*

- **Thirdly**, in relation to any fact upon which the medical opinion turns, the source of that fact:
  a If it derives from the client or other lay witness, identify precisely the page on which it is to be found, and schedule a photocopy of that page to the report *(or if oral, when the fact was elicited, where and when with identification of any contemporaneous note)*.
  b If it derives from medical case notes, precisely the case notes relied on, with copies of **only** the relevant pages, scheduled to the report.

C Why only 'skeletal'?

The rationale is:

- **Firstly**, the initial conference with counsel draws a legal comb through the matrix of the medical opinion on the facts. Almost invariably this conference bears witness to a significant revision of medical opinion around the table even if only in the form of finer turning.
- **Secondly**, every minute spent by solicitors and counsel reading passages in reports is time which is wasted if the reading of such passages is not immediately necessary. For this conference, Counsel does **not** '*need*':
  a Extensive summaries of the medical notes as a preamble to the report.
  b Lengthy discussion as to fact.
  c Convoluted expressions of medical theories which gradually distil themselves to a conclusion.

Note: The word '*need*' (mentioned above) is to be contrasted with words and phrases such as '*desirable*' or '*in the interests of completeness*'.

- **Thirdly**, this conference with counsel is the cornerstone to the litigation. It predicates all future case management. Thus until this conference, the file should be kept as slender as is feasibly possible.

D The Agenda

A copy of the following should be given to each expert attending the conference, at the time of his instruction to attend:

- **Firstly** — preliminary check — is the expertise of those experts in attendance at the conference precisely what is required?

- **Secondly**, counsel must critically assess the expert's view:
  a Do the experts come over as poor witnesses (however good their medical skills)?
  b If the report is negative, counsel has the opportunity to test the grounds for the opinion.
  c *Most importantly*: counsel rigorously to explore with the experts, the grounds for their view. The conference should be the opportunity for a firm cross-examination (as if in court, and acting for the other side). Counsel should have the experts argue the other side's case, to establish the potential strength of the defence and the potential flaws in the claim.
  d Check with the experts the CV/credentials of the treating doctors whose conduct is challenged. *Note:* The *Medical Directory* is now available on CD Rom.

  ☞ *Not infrequently, a critical analysis of the medical opinion by reference to legal principle causes a medical expert (quite legitimately) to change his mind.*

  ☞ *It is highly desirable — it is tempting to say 'essential' — for the experts to have experience of acting for both plaintiffs and defendants in medical negligence litigation.*

- **Thirdly**, counsel should ensure that the experts understand the following strategy:
  a to ensure that the other side see the strength of the expert evidence, via the content of the pleadings; and
  b to foreclose the opportunity to defend by plugging up potential gaps in the case.

- **Fourthly**, as to the issues:
  a Counsel to identify the real medico-legal issues.
  b Identify whether on any *issue*, a further expert is required and if yes, why.
  c *Note:* If there is more than one expert already retained, it is essential as far as possible for the experts to cross-reference and appreciate the viewpoint of the other and how the other arrives at it.

  ☞ *The calling of a number of experts inevitably affords to the other side the potential opportunity of trying to drive a wedge between their respective opinions.*

- **Fifthly**, medical literature — check with the experts what literature is available to support their views. As E Anthony Machin QC explains in *Medical Negligence* (2nd edn) (Butterworths), at pp 393–4:

  'The value of carefully researched studies by acknowledged medical experts, some of whom may hold academic posts which permit greater opportunity for reflection than that afforded to the busy consultant practitioner, cannot be over-emphasised. If a medical expert witness puts forward a thesis which cannot be supported from the corpus of extant studies it runs the risk of being belittled as idiosyncratic. Thus, the medical experts forming part of a team should be asked at an early stage to research the literature in support of views advanced by them which are likely to prove controversial. This procedure should be repeated at a later stage, when reports from the defendant's experts have become available.

Medical literature, such as standard textbooks and articles in learned journals, is not of itself evidence but may be used by experts in support of their views, or in cross-examination of opposing experts to destroy their opinions. The relevance of such material is discussed in *H v Schering Chemicals Ltd* [1983] 1 All ER 849, [1983] 1 WLR 143.'

In summary: Identify the number and discipline of the experts the plaintiff currently intends to rely on, when their reports will be available and the issues to which they will be directed.

What the Plaintiff says should be accurately recorded. This is the first opportunity the legal team will have had to identify what facts from the client are relevant to the medico-legal framework.

● **Lay evidence** At this conference, assuming the proposed plaintiff is present, the experts should interview the plaintiff to elicit such facts as are material to their opinion. As to which facts are relevant for the drafting of the Claim, see Chapter 4, p 40. **Note:** At this conference identify the initial list of potential witnesses as to fact.

Evidence on commission can be taken by way of video film, and should be if the character of the Plaintiff is relevant and substantial sums in compensation are at issue.

● **Life expectation** If relevant, this is an opportunity to consider the life expectation of the plaintiff. Are his or her statements signed for Civil Evidence Act purposes? Should there be evidence on commission?

E   A new approach

Use of the *portable notebook computer:*

● Notebook computers are increasingly sophisticated. In addition to word processing they can come equipped with a pentium/200 mhz processor and 8 speed CD Rom. This facilitates the use in conference of sophisticated anatomy software programmes with virtual reality animations. Such aids can be invaluable for a speedy and accurate analysis of the medical matrix of a case. This technique also helps avoid the risk of only understanding the full picture in the courtroom (with the potential for severe financial consequences if working under a conditional fee agreement).

● Counsel can at the conference type the allegations of negligence in the presence of the experts.

● Counsel should then confirm point by point their agreement.

Once the experts have absorbed what is happening, they may be expected to take particular care over the wording; it is after all effectively their wording in the witness box.

● When the pleading is complete, counsel should print it out (portable printer, or disc transfer to computer at solicitor's office etc). A copy should be given to each expert. **Note:** Do the core allegations in the pleading ever have to be more than 250 words. See the Practice Direction of November 1996 on p 238 and the Commentary at p 239.

- Each expert should then draft his report by reference to the *issue(s)* for which he or she is retained. He should keep the length of the opinion to a minimum. All that is required is a medical opinion which explains and underpins the allegations of negligence already pleaded with the experts' assistance.

Note:

- With the *'cards on the table'* technique, it is absolutely essential to seek to ensure that the lay evidence, the pleading and the expert evidence dovetail. This can be secured by a contemporaneous finalised drafting of the pleading.

☞ *Dovetailing is ensured if the pleading is drafted with the experts present.*

- A carefully pleaded claim also opens the door to the other side properly to plead a Defence which raises the real issues between the parties.
- The most careful consideration should be devoted to ensuring that only such allegations are made as are relevant *and* can properly be supported by the evidence.

☞ *By Counsel's use of the notebook computer at the conference with experts, the litigator can go from preliminary enquiry to virtual readiness for trial in one step.*

F   What should be in the covering letter which accompanies the claim?

To avoid the complications which arose in *Bergin v Wickes* [1993] PIQR P167 the covering letter should include the following phrase:

> 'You will appreciate that the pleading of a defence now requires full particularity. For the avoidance of misunderstanding henceforth, we invite from you a fully particularised Defence. We want to know precisely:
>
> 1   What allegations of fact are and are not admitted.
>
> 2   Similarly, what allegations pleaded under *'particulars of negligence'* are and are not admitted including any allegation as to causation and consequent damage.
>
> 3   If you intend at any stage to raise positive averments, please do so now in the Defence.
>
> In the event of you seeking at a later stage to raise positive averments which could have been asserted in the original Defence, we will refer the Court to this letter.'

Note (1): The purpose of the Statement of Claim is to generate a Defence which is sufficiently focused as to reveal the real issues in the case. The issues will be of fact and/or expert evidence and/or law.

Note (2): See the Practice Direction of November 1996 at Appendix 3 on p 238. Check that all steps necessary to secure compliance have been taken, *before* this first conference is over.

PART 2 AGENDA — WHAT TO DO WHEN THE DEFENCE IS SERVED

A The significance of close of pleadings

On close of pleadings there should be separately recorded, paragraph by paragraph, exactly what is and is not in issue. Issues of fact should be recorded separately from issues of liability, causation and damage.

Subject to service of a Reply, pleadings are closed 14 days after service of the Defence. Pleadings do *not* remain open even if there is an outstanding request for particulars. The close of pleadings marks the time to draw back and take stock and also triggers the requirements (for litigation pending in the Central Registry) of the Practice Direction set out in Appendix 3, at p 238.

B Take stock of what?

- The *issues* are identified from the pleadings once they are closed.
- The *issues* as distilled from the pleadings should be typed up, one by one, and set out on the front of the file for future reference.
- What is *in issue* constitutes the agenda (subject to review by Counsel) for the lay witness statements and experts' reports.
- Thus the answer to the question — what should be decanted into the lay evidence — is: all the evidence which is required to prove the *issues* of fact thrown up by the pleadings, *and no more*.

C The lay witness statements

These should follow the agenda for trial:

- The agenda for trial is the Claim: *Southport Corpn v Esso Petroleum* [1954] 2 QB 182 per Morris LJ.

The relevant lay evidence must also deal in detail with the matters raised in the Schedule of Loss.

- The Schedule of Loss is as much part of the Pleading as the Particulars of Negligence.

D Check-list for drawing up lay witness statements

- Title as in action.
- Date.
- Signed by the intended witness including a statement by him that the contents are true to the best of his knowledge and belief.

- Clear identification of any documents referred to in the body of the statement.
- Language of the witness — *not* the artificial language of, eg, affidavits.
- Chronological order.
- Divided into paragraphs each numbered.
- Dates and sums/figures should be expressed in numbers and not in words.
- Paginated.
- The statement should contain *no hearsay* unless:
  a what is quoted is an admission of the Defendant by itself, its servants or agents acting in the course of their employment; or
  b what is quoted is relevant not for the truth of what was said but the fact that the words spoken were said (that would be relevant if, for example, an issue in the case was whether anything at all was spoken).
- Does it cover all issues of fact thrown up by the pleadings to which the deponent can give evidence?

Note:

a As to 'litigation technique' and the compilation of lay witness statements, please refer to Chapter 2 Part 5 and Chapter 4, Part I.

b Once the lay evidence is exchanged, there has to be a further file review.

PART 3   AGENDA — FILE REVIEW AFTER EXCHANGE OF LAY EVIDENCE

A   Introduction

By this stage:

- The *Defence* will have been served and
- By reference to the *'Model Directions'* there will have been:
  a discovery; and
  b the exchange of the lay witness statements.
- The new material forthcoming will probably justify a *further conference* with counsel, the relevant experts and the client.

Note:

a *Prior* to the conference, the experts have to report on the pleaded Defence and the lay evidence from the other side.

☞ *Such a conference will enable the experts to review the pleadings, the further documents (if any) disclosed on discovery, the lay evidence and (most importantly) consider whether their opinions are suitable and final for exchange.*

AGENDA FOR EXPERTS

Their opinion on the Defence pleadings should be 'Part 2' to their initial report. Their opinion on the lay witness statements from the other side should be 'Part 3' to their initial report.

b In relation to the other side's witness statements, the opinion should follow the paragraph numbering of each witness statement, for ease of reference.

c Any such opinion should be expressed with clinical succinctness.

B   The Conference with Experts and Counsel

The proposed check-list is set out below. It should be sent to the experts prior to the conference.

C   What happens after this conference?

The experts finalise their reports for disclosure. To recapitulate, those reports will (depending on the facts of the case) be divided into the following parts (paginated and with a brief index):

- **First** — primary opinion on the *issue* for which the expert was retained.
- **Second** — expert's opinion in relation to:
  a defence;
  b any Request for Particulars from the other side;
  c any interrogatories which he has assisted in answering.
- **Third** — his opinion on those parts of the lay evidence he is able to comment on, *statement by statement* and *paragraph by paragraph*.

Note:

Leave should if necessary be asked to serve it, and it should be included in the document which contains the other three parts.

- A 'Fourth' part to be prepared after exchange of expert evidence is desirable. This 'Fourth' part will be his opinion in respect of the report of his opposite number for the other side.

After exchange of expert evidence, there is a final opportunity to review the case as a whole. *This is the Pre-Trial Conference*, and is explored below in Part 4 of this Chapter, at p 35.

Checklist for the conference with experts and counsel after exchange of the lay evidence

1 **The *issues*:**
- Are all the *issues* covered by those sufficiently skilled in relation to those *issues*? *Note:* The primary issues are liability, causation and damage.

- Has the Defence raised any positive allegations and/or blamed any other party? If yes:

  a What is the riposte to the counter-positive allegation?

  b Have all the potential parties to the action been properly identified? Should another party be brought in as a defendant?

2   Lay evidence:

- Do the lay witness statements from the other side throw up a matrix of fact different from that advanced by 'our' side? If yes:

  a Where are the differences?

  b Can they be reconciled? If yes, how? If not, why not?

  ☞ *Is there any means (eg corroborative evidence from another source) whereby 'our' factual matrix can be supported and/or that of the other side weakened? Will interrogatories help?*

- If the other side's factual evidence is believed by the Court, what difference does that make to 'our' expert opinion?

  ☞ *Is the prejudicial material relevant to any expert opinion to be advanced? If no, is there any reason for it to remain in the statement?*

- Does our lay evidence constitute a proper basis for the expert opinion 'we' are calling? Is there any material in any of the statements which might prejudice 'us'. If yes, is that material relevant to any of the issues in the pleadings?

- The experts should (if they have not already) identify precisely upon which parts of which lay witness statements they seek to rely in support of the opinions they have already volunteered. Similarly the experts should identify what material is missing from the lay evidence which should be included and without which their expert opinion is not properly founded.

- Have all discrepancies and inconsistencies between the lay evidence for the plaintiff and the medical case notes been identified? Can such discrepancies be reconciled?

  ☞ *How relevant are such discrepancies to the expert opinion? (Eg a client may mistake a female doctor for a nurse and say in his statement that he was seen by a nurse when in fact he was seen by a doctor.)*

3   Expert evidence:

- Are there any *inconsistencies* in 'our' medical expert evidence? If yes, what? Why are they there? Can they be ironed out? If not, does this disclose a weak link in the armour?

- Does 'our' *expert evidence* dovetail with the *lay witness statements* and the *pleaded* case. Check this point by point in the pleading in relation to each *'issue'* in the list.

- Have the experts expressed their views in the way they intended? Does 'our' pleading express the expert opinions in a way which they are content to support in the witness box?

- Have the experts restricted their opinions to advising within their own fields of specialisation? *(This is the opportunity to identify whether other fields of expertise should be brought into the expert team.)*

It is no use just annexing reams of medical literature — lawyers are not medics. The literature has to be set out in a way in which its relevance is immediately apparent. Red highlighter pen is ideal not least of all because unlike yellow, it photocopies clearly.

- Have the experts identified the medical literature on which they wish to rely (for the purpose of exchange under '*Model Directions*') see p 51, explaining its relevance and cross-referencing the relevant passages with their reports?

- Check that the experts have appreciated where the boundaries of the *relevant standard of care* lie (to take an extreme example: alleged General Practitioner mismanagement in 1985 should not be judged by reference to the standards of a consultant in the relevant speciality in the context of the standard applying in 1997).

- Draft preferably on screen with the assistance of the experts any amendments to the Statement of Claim which may be warranted in the light of the other side's Defence and/or lay evidence.

- Draft (again, preferably on screen) with the experts the answers to any Request for Further and Better Particulars which may have been served with the Defence.

- Check that the reports of the experts do not refer to *privileged* material which has not been seen by the other side. For example:

  a earlier statements which are not to be disclosed;

  b earlier reports of experts which have since been revised or are to be revised.

If there may be such further information available to the other side, draft (with the assistance of the experts) interrogatories to reach that information.

- Enquire of the experts whether there is any information which the other side may have which would not be revealed on ordinary documentary discovery (eg if there is a hiatus in the medical case notes such as a gap in the chronology of events).

Under RSC Ord 34, r 10 the case notes should be indexed and paginated with a view to their being lodged with the Court before trial.

- Enquire of the experts what facts in the case, presently thrown into issue by the pleadings, cannot be disputed by the other side. In relation to those facts, again assisted by the experts, draft the *Notice to Admit Facts*.

- Check that the experts' reports for disclosure to the other side tie in with the pagination of the case notes.

Ensure that the significance of the date as per the expert report dovetails with the significance of the date as pleaded.

- Check that the *chronology* (which should be scheduled to the Statement of Claim when drafted by counsel) is accurate. Any references by any expert to any date should be cross-referenced with the date in the chronology as scheduled to the pleading.

- Are all the medical terms contained in the reports readily explicable? Schedule to the report of the lead medical expert a glossary of the medical terms used in the case (to perform the role of 'mini-medical dictionary').

☞ *It is all too easy to lose sight of the fact that the medical reports are primarily for the benefit of the Court. It should not be assumed that medical principles and terminology will be understood without explanation or definition.*

Note: This conference must take place to allow sufficient time for the experts to revise their reports before any deadline for exchange.

D　Efficient file management

Remember that at this stage 'our' expert evidence has not yet been disclosed. Thus the following is suggested:

- With the experts around the table, draw up a statement of fact. This statement will contain the factual information upon which is based the expert opinion as to liability, causation and damage (if not a split trial).

☞ *This statement of fact must be sufficient to provide a basis for the expert opinion of each of the experts, however disparate their fields of expertise.*

- This agreed *Statement of Fact* can then be incorporated by reference into the report of each expert.

Rationale

- All parties and the judge read, time and again, the factual background as expressed by all the individual experts in the opening pages of their reports. Sometimes, these opening pages are voluminous.

☞ *Very considerable time is wasted pre-trial and at trial in the course of a medical negligence case because of a repeated reading of 'the facts'.*

- This approach to case management has grown up with the Legal Aid Board paying the bill, if the claim failed.
- But with the individual litigator now underwriting the risk of losing, this new approach will achieve a substantial saving in costs and disbursements, if the claim fails (and will pre-empt an attack on the case management if the claim succeeds but the defendant calls for a taxation).

Note (1): In the not unrelated field of trial bundles, Mr Justice Latham and James Badenoch QC penned the following in Powers and Harris *Medical Negligence* (2nd edn) p 492, Butterworths:

'Cases difficult enough in themselves are made longer and more complicated when the participants must battle as much with the paperwork as with the opposition. The price paid in needless loss of time, patience and concentration can be a heavy one. Judges are becoming more ready than before to question the entitlement of lawyers to costs which appear to have been wasted as a result of an undisciplined and uncooperative approach to the preparation of bundles. Lawyers may indeed find that they face orders to pay costs considered to have been wasted in this way. This is one area in our process in which cooperation between the parties — and not confrontation — is essential.'

Note (2): Per HHJ Sumner sitting as a Judge of the High Court in *Warner v Jones* (1993) Times, 22 March:

'. . . there were 15 medical reports. More than 50 pages of medical evidence had been put before the court.
It seemed entirely unnecessary to proceed through all that material, much of which was repeating what had been said elsewhere, for the purposes of the judgment.
It would be beneficial if notice could be taken that it would be a great benefit to the parties and a very great benefit to the court if medical evidence could be agreed rather than run in parallel.'

PART 4 AGENDA — FILE REVIEW AFTER EXCHANGE OF EXPERT EVIDENCE — THE PRE-TRIAL CONFERENCE

This conference is critical. It will almost certainly be the last time Counsel gets the papers before the brief for trial.

A Introduction

This conference takes place after disclosure of lay and expert evidence. By now all the material should be collated: the pleadings, further particulars, answers to interrogatories, lay evidence and expert evidence as exchanged with relevant supporting literature and any further discovery.

B Who should attend?

The experts should be in attendance, with the client, assuming the client will be testifying (That will not be the case, for example, in the usual cerebral palsy claim, in which case the parents should be present).

CORE BUNDLE

Do not lose sight of the fact that we are seeking to restrict the core bundle to no more than 100 sides of A4 however large the case.

C Purpose of conference

At this conference, the experts and counsel will probably for the first time see the following from both sides:

- all the lay evidence;

- all the medical expert evidence; and
- the entirety of the schedule and counter-schedule in respect of special loss.

D   Check-list for this conference

Make sure that all witnesses (lay and expert) are prepared for the courtroom — see Chapter 4, Part 2 p 43.

Check-list for conference after exchange of lay and expert evidence — the pre-trial conference

1   **Issues**

- *Circulating a list:* If he has not already done so, counsel should provide a list of *issues* in the case distilled from the pleadings. That list should be circulated to the experts before the conference.
- Lay witness evidence:
  a   Is there anything in the expert evidence now disclosed by the other side which lends support to 'our' *factual case* rather than the other side's on each point in dispute?
  b   Alternatively is there anything in the other side's expert evidence which lends support to their *factual case* rather than 'our' side on each point in dispute?
  c   Which lay witnesses are to attend court in respect of issues on *liability* and *causation*?
  d   Which lay witnesses are to attend court in respect of issues on *quantum*?
  e   If necessary, initiate the service of appropriate Civil Evidence Act notices even though their time for service may strictly have expired (see *RSC Ord 38, rr 21(1), 29(1)*).
  f   *Finally,* check that each of the issues as to fact in the list are covered by the witness statements. ☞ *Check that every fact requiring proof can be established by properly admissible evidence.*

2   **Expert evidence**

a   Have *all* the case notes been disclosed?
b   Is the *chronology* scheduled to the Statement of Claim accurate?
c   Have all discrepancies and inconsistencies between the lay evidence on each side been identified? Can such discrepancies be reconciled? ☞ *How relevant are such discrepancies to the expert opinion?*

Note: Time will be running out. It is very late in the day to be patching up one's case. The letter of instruction to this expert should ideally be drafted there and then and go off in that night's post/fax backed up with a phone call from the conference room to the expert or his secretary. In the absence of consent from the other side, leave will be required to serve.

Experts often disagree when one expert has seen material documents which the other has not seen. Is that the cause for the dispute here?

If there is a claim for past and future nursing care, is it supported by the medical evidence?

In the light of reciprocal disclosure/exchange of information, are there entries in the case notes which now have significance which were previously considered to be unimportant?

d Does 'our' expert evidence cover all the issues relating to negligence and causation? If not, which issue is not covered? Can these experts plug the gap? If not, what expert is required and precisely what is the remit for this new expert? What instructions should be sent to him/her?

e In relation to *issues* of opinion between the respective experts on both sides, where precisely are the areas of agreement and disagreement?

f In relation to the areas of disagreement, why is there this difference of opinion? *Does this demonstrate a 'Bolam' defence?* Check carefully what medical case notes each side has seen. Is it that each side is relying on different medical material/sources. Can 'our' experts stand up in the witness box and justify the proposition (if acting for the plaintiff) that there is no responsible body of medical opinion which would disagree with them or (if acting for the defendant) that they are a responsible body of medical opinion taking a valid stand albeit different from that advanced by the other side.

g After going through the expert evidence in relation to liability and causation, check that every other field of expertise marries up with the pleading and the schedule of loss. Check that every head of claim in the schedule of loss is covered by the medical evidence (or if acting for the defence, go through each head of claim exploring to what extent it is not backed up by expert evidence).

h Have the entries in the medical case notes been reviewed? Is there material in the case notes which was considered to be relevant which now appears irrelevant or vice versa?

i Counsel should for this conference have prepared a first draft of the skeleton argument. He should carefully run through this with the experts.

This is also the opportunity to enquire the extent to which each of the experts has court experience. **Check:**

- which courts;
- in relation to what type of case; and
- whether cross-examined.

Go on to explain to the experts (if necessary) the court process and confirm that they will be present throughout those parts of the trial relevant to the issues upon which they will be testifying. In particular, it is desirable (some would argue, essential) for defence witnesses on liability and causation to see the plaintiff witnesses in the witness box before they themselves give evidence.

Note: This conference should be arranged to allow sufficient opportunity for any amendments to the pleadings and additions to the expert evidence.

☞ *The most experienced of experts may not have been at any time in the witness box, particularly taking into account the tendency of medical negligence claims either to collapse, or settle, before trial.*

3 Timetabling etc

Check with experts if lay witnesses are required at trial. As to those required, on what day(s) need they attend?

PART 5 CONCLUSION

Conditional fee agreements constitute the privatisation of the funding of litigation. Industries when privatised often bear witness to a dramatic shake-out in manpower and that shake-out arises from the industry having to find more cost-effective methods of production or face insolvency. Conditional fee agreements may thus be anticipated to revolutionise case management. The techniques for case management suggested so far focus on the handling of an individual case; there is mileage however in drawing back, and considering office management:

☞ *Long reports may have generated large fees for the expert in the past, with the spin-off of high fees for the solicitor because of the extra work caused in case management.*

A Experts

a On what basis has the solicitor selected the office list of experts?

b How will that square with an environment where the solicitor may bear the disbursements, win or lose?

☞ *Have the experts been told the implications of conditional fee agreements?* **?**

B Choice of counsel

a The name at the end of the pleading carries commercial weight.

b An unknown name is going to carry less weight than a specialist in the field.

c In a no-win no-fee environment, every ounce of weight counts.

d On what basis is the list of counsel selected?

C Use of experts and counsel

a Is not the way through to identify a batch of cases having the same theme, and requiring the same experts.

☞ *A restricted profit margin for the solicitor is virtually guaranteed if counsel and experts are used on a case by case ad hoc basis.*

b Have counsel and the experts in the office at 9.00 am, for the day, screening each of the files.

c Those which are screened out may be capable of being dispatched speedily. Those which pass the screening can go straight to the drafting of the claim on the notebook computer, with a print-out of all pleadings case by case in the course of the day.

d The fees of counsel and experts can then be spread throughout the day, and the cases which pass the screening test will pay (with the 'uplift') for those cases which do not.

In summary: To litigate under restricted funding arrangements by reference to one's case management of the past will be equivalent to trying to fly a plane when one's only comparable experience has been riding a horse. The aim *has* to be to access the correct information from the right person, at the first opportunity.

Chapter 4

Procedural guidance

PART 1   THE FIRST STATEMENT —
HOW TO TAKE IT AND FOR
WHAT PURPOSE

(1)   **The singular characteristic of medical negligence litigation is that the plaintiff probably does not remember:** So very frequently, the treatment complained of occurred during operation. Thus one is deprived of the evidence of one's most immediate witness.

☞ *During the operation the patient is asleep, under anaesthetic.*

(2)   **The purpose of the first statement is primarily three-fold:**

* **Firstly,** to screen the case: '*Do I take this on, even to pursue a preliminary enquiry?*' If the '*screening*' is positive, then
* **Secondly,** to target the right hospital/doctor; and
* **Thirdly,** to provide sufficient information for pre-commencement discovery: see Part 3 below.

(3)   **The first statement generally has no other purpose. Why not?**

* **Firstly,** the client is not a medical expert, and will not know what particular facts are, and are not, relevant.
* **Secondly,** the solicitor equally is not a medical expert.
* **Thirdly,** to invite further information at this stage pre-empts the full enquiry as to relevant information which will be conducted at the first conference with counsel and experts.

(4)   **Does the first statement ever have another purpose?** Sometimes, for example:

* to assess when time began to run, for 'limitation';
* to establish whether there have been any obvious admissions as to liability; or
* to establish a recollection of the client, as early as is reasonably practicable.

Note:
* Covering these points does not necessarily require expensive solicitor/partner time.

- When the client first comes in for an interview, he or she may be expected to be nervous.
- With 'fundholding, capping, competitive tendering' etc, pennies count.

? *Cannot the client be asked to draw up the statement in his or her own time, with the opportunity to think quietly and reflect?*

- After establishing with the client the overall nature of his or her complaint is there any reason why the interviewer has there and then to take a statement? Why cannot the client be given a 'Model Template' in the terms set out in Chapter 2, Part 5, p 23?

(5)   **Pre-commencement discovery:** Assuming the case has been screened as provisionally *'positive'* the next step is pre-commencement discovery. Once the medical case notes are disclosed, the litigator for the proposed plaintiff will collate them in logical order, paginate and index, and seek to achieve an understanding.

- Why? To target the *key expert* first time ie the field of expertise which will unlock/unravel the case. Henceforth, targetting the wrong expert initially will be at the account of the litigator rather than the Legal Aid Board. Thus in brain damage at birth, the first key expert will more likely be a paediatric neurologist to focus on causation rather than an obstetrician.
- What is *not* the purpose of collating case notes, etc:
  a The purpose is *not* to afford to the litigator an opportunity of developing medical skills sufficient to instruct the medical expert with voluminous medical theory. Litigators are lawyers, not doctors.
  b Such medical theorising is so very frequently irrelevant. If the medical expert is sound, he does not need a lawyer to guide him through the medical aspects of the case. If he is not sound or not of the relevant experience, he should not be instructed in the first place. The role of the litigator is to provide the expert with the *legal* framework, not the medical framework.

Note:
- Hitherto, the Legal Aid Board or the Health Authority has paid the bill for such medical discussion. That is set to change.
- Further problems arise from such medical discussion. It may be that the litigator has not in fact addressed the correct medical *issues*. The result so readily arises that the doctor answers the *issues* raised but the case is not in fact advanced. Further, a doctor may be seduced by what is in fact the wrong focus given to him by the litigator. The result then frequently arises that at conference so many hours are spent unstitching experts from opinions which legally were not relevant in the first place.

Lay evidence required prior to service of the claim

(1) **What facts are required for the drafting of the Claim?** The lay evidence is not a trawl though every possible fact in a case. The lay evidence is that which is sufficient and necessary to prove the issue or issues of fact.

(2) **How does one access the 'issues of fact'?** Jessel MR said in *Thorp v Holdsworth* (1976) 3 ChD 637 at 639:

> 'The whole object of pleadings is to bring the parties to an issue .... In fact, the whole meaning of the system (of pleadings) is to narrow the parties to definite issues, and thereby to diminish expense and delay, especially as regards the amount of testimony required on either side at the hearing.'

In this context, Scrutton LJ said at 634 of *Blay v Pollard and Morris* [1930] 1 KB 628:

> 'Cases must be decided on the issues on the record ....'

Thus: One looks to the pleadings to find out what facts are in issue. It is in relation *only* to those facts that the lay witness statements should be focused.

(3) **What facts are pleaded?** The Claim must plead those facts material to the cause of action. A fact is *'material'* if it is necessary for the purpose of formulating a complete cause of action (*Bruce v Odhams Press Ltd* [1936] 1 All ER 287 at 294).

(4) **What is a cause of action?** Lord Esher MR defined this in *Coburn v Colledge* [1897] 1 QB 702:

> '... every fact which it would be necessary for the plaintiff to prove, if traversed, in order to support his right to the judgment of the Court. It does not comprise every piece of evidence which is necessary to prove each fact, but every fact which is necessary to be proved.'

Diplock LJ summarised the position in *Letang v Cooper* [1965] 1 QB 232 at 242:

> '... simply a factual situation the existence of which entitles one person to obtain from the court a remedy against another person.'

(5) **Summary thus far: What lay evidence does one need to draft the Claim?** Answer:

a every fact which is necessary to be proved; but

b *not* every piece of evidence which is necessary to prove each fact.

From where does one elicit those facts which are necessary to be proved? *Answer:* the first conference with the expert(s) and counsel.

PART 2   GUIDANCE TO LAY AND EXPERT WITNESSES ON COURTROOM TECHNIQUE

Accustoming one's lay and expert witnesses for cross-examination

Check-list:

- Understand the question;
- Think before answering;
- Don't accept points made by the other side unless you truly agree with them;
- Do not 'play lawyer' (ie don't try and anticipate where the advocate is going);
- Direct all attention to each question; avoid casual or throwaway remarks;
- Be prepared to say — if it be the fact — 'I don't know';
- When questioned on a document, analyse it scrupulously before answering questions about it. If a letter, check the following before going further:
  a   letterhead;
  b   date;
  c   person to whom it was sent;
  d   the recipient's full address;
  e   the name of the author of the letter;
  f   persons to whom copies are noted.
- Do not argue, it looks unreasonable. Just testify;
- Do not volunteer an answer, wait to be asked;
- Do not allow yourself to be harassed;
- Ignore disparaging cross-examination technique;
- Concentrate;
- Be co-operative — not resentful;
- Do not rush;
- Take care with giving estimates — if you cannot, do not guess;
- Do not be beguiled by diagrams and photographs;
- Do not take pills before you give evidence, unless you must pursuant to prescription;

- Check prior to going into the witness box:

  a every document witness has made including
     letters   and   statements   and   answers   to
     interrogatories;

  b every line of argument/issue in the case;

  c witness statements which contradict his or her's;
     and

  d documents which contradict his evidence.

- Check what the witness might say about any aspect
  of the case upon which he or she can be legitimately
  questioned, but with which they have not dealt in
  their statement(s).

☞ *In short — anticipate the
cross-examination.*

PART 3   MEDICAL NEGLIGENCE CLAIMS — A PROTOCOL FOR OBTAINING HOSPITAL MEDICAL RECORDS

Civil Litigation Committee of the Law Society: August 1995 No 6

Application on behalf of a patient for hospital medical records for use when court proceedings are contemplated

(This Protocol is set out here with the kind permission of The Law Society.)

This application form and response forms have been prepared by a working party of the Law Society's Civil Litigation Committee and approved by the Department of Health for use in NHS and Trust hospitals.

The purpose of the forms is to standardise and streamline the disclosure of medical records to a patient's solicitors, who are investigating or already pursuing a personal injury claim against a third party, or a medical negligence claim against the hospital to which the application is addressed and/or other hospitals or general practitioners.

Use of the forms is entirely voluntarily and does not prejudice any party's right under the Access to Health Records Act 1990, the Data Protection Act 1984, or ss 33 and 34 of the Supreme Court Act 1981. The aim is to save time and costs for all concerned for the benefit of the patient and the hospital and in the interests of justice. Use of the forms should make it unnecessary in most cases for there to be exchanges of letters or other enquiries. If there is any unusual matter not covered by the form, the patient's solicitor may write a separate letter at the outset.

Any enquiries about the forms should be made to the solicitors making the request. Comments on the use and content of the forms should be made to Suzanne Burn, Secretary, Civil Litigation Committee, The Law Society, 50 Chancery Lane, London WC2A 1SX, telephone 0171 320 5739, or to David Towns, NHS Management Executive, Quarry House, Quarry Hill, Leeds LS2 7UE, telephone 0113 254 5537.

Application on behalf of a patient for hospital medical records for use when court proceedings are contemplated

This should be completed as fully as possible

Insert Hospital Name and Address	*TO: Medical Records Officer*
	Hospital

1 (a)	Full name of patient (including previous surnames)	
(b)	Address now	
(c)	Address at start of treatment	
(d)	Date of birth	
(e)	Hospital ref no if available	
(f)	NI number, if available	
2	This application is made because I am considering	
(a)	a claim against your hospital in para 7 overleaf	YES/NO
(b)	pursuing an action against someone else	YES/NO
3	Department(s) where treatment was received	
4	Name(s) of Consultant(s) at your hospital in charge of the treatment	
5	Whether treatment at your hospital was private or NHS, wholly or in part	

6	A description of the treatment received, with approximate dates	
7	If the answer to Q2(A) is 'Yes', details of the likely nature, and grounds for, such a claim, and approximate dates of the events involved	
8	If the answer to Q2(B) is 'Yes' insert: (i) the names of the proposed defendants	
	(ii) whether action yet begun	YES/NO
	(iii) if appropriate, details of Court and action number	
9	We confirm we will pay (i) reasonable copying charges	YES/NO
	(ii) a reasonable administration fee	YES/NO
10	We request prior details of: (i) photocopying and administration charges for medical records	YES/NO
	(ii) number of, and cost of copying, X-ray and scan films	YES/NO
11	Any other relevant information, particular requirements, or any particular documents *not* required (eg copies of computerised records)	
	Signature of Solicitor	
	Name	

	Address	
	Ref	
	Telephone number	
	Fax number	
	Signature of patient: Signature of parent or next friend if appropriate:	***Please print name beneath each signature. Signature by child over 12 but under 18 years also requires signature by parent***
	Signature of personal representative where patient has died:	

First response to application for hospital records

Insert Name and Address of Hospital here		

	NAME OF PATIENT Our ref: Your ref:	
1	Date of receipt of patient's application	
2	We intend that copy medical records will be despatched within 6 weeks of that date	YES/NO
3	We require pre-payment of photocopying charges	YES/NO
4	If estimate of photocopying charges requested or pre-payment required, the amount will be	£ /notified by you
5	The cost of X-ray and scan films will be	£ /notified by you
6	If there is a problem, we shall write to you within those 6 weeks	YES/NO
7	Any other information	
	Please address further correspondence to:	
	Signed	
	Direct telephone number:	
	Direct fax number:	
	Dated:	

Second response enclosing patient's hospital medical records

Address: **Our ref:**
                                          Your ref:

	Name of patient	
1	We confirm that the enclosed copy medical records are all those within the control of this hospital, relevant to the application which you have made to the best of our knowledge and belief, subject to paras 2–5 below	YES/NO
2	Details of any other documents which have not yet been located	
3	Date by when it is expected that these will be supplied	
4	Details of any records which we are not producing	
5	The reasons for not doing so	
6	An invoice for copying and administration charges is attached	YES/NO
	Signed	
	Date	

PART 4   MODEL ORDER FOR DIRECTIONS IN A HIGH COURT MEDICAL NEGLIGENCE ACTION

Plaintiff; list.

☞ **1**   That the Plaintiff within 14 days do serve on the Defendant a list of documents stating what documents are or have been in his/her/its/their possession custody or power relevant to issues arising or likely to arise in this action.

Defendant; list.

☞ **2**   The Defendant do within 14 days serve on the Plaintiff a list of documents stating what documents are or have been in his/her/its/their possession custody or power relevant to issues arising or likely to arise in this action.

Inspection.

☞ **3**   There be inspection of the documents within 14 days of the service of the list.

Note:

Two bites at the discovery cherry.

☞ ● **First**   In relation to clauses 1, 2 and 3 provision is made for discovery. This demonstrates that there are two stages in medical negligence litigation when one seeks discovery — pre-action and during the action. The plaintiff has, as it were, two bites at the discovery cherry. This covers the position, as frequently arises in medical negligence litigation, where medical notes come to light which had previously been thought to be missing or which have been thought not to be in existence. *For example there may be documents referred to in the case notes which are picked up by the legal and medical experts and which were not originally volunteered by the health authority.*

● **Second**   Check Sch 1 of Pt 2 of the defendant's Schedule. There may be listed as privileged from production an *accident report*. Such an accident report, the preparation of which is required by a National Health Service Circular, is not subject to

Accident Reports/Enquiries.   ☞

legal professional privilege where the 'dominant purpose' of its preparation is not submission to solicitors in anticipation of litigation, even though one of the purposes of such reports mentioned in the circular is use by solicitors if litigation, should be commenced in respect of the accident: *Lask v Gloucester Health Authority* (1985) Times, 13 December, CA. Thus where the dominant purpose in the preparation of an accident report is the avoidance of similar accidents in the future the report will not be privileged even though a subsidiary purpose in its preparation is its use in the conduct of anticipated litigation. If such a report is subject to a claim for privilege, an application should be made to the court for disclosure.

4   Pursuant to RSC Ord 38, r 38A as amended the parties do mutually disclose by way of simultaneous mutual exchange the substance of the evidence of all witnesses as to fact on liability issues of negligence and causation of injury and disability that they intend to rely upon at trial (but excluding witnesses and evidence simply as to quantum of damages) in the form of written statements within 3 months of the order herein. For the *Exchange of evidence as to* avoidance of doubt the witness statements to be *fact.* disclosed include the statements of investigating and treating doctors and ancillary hospital staff dealing with matters of primary fact and recollection by excluding any expert opinion of that witness that it is proposed to rely upon. Such statements to be agreed if possible. Unless such statements are agreed the parties be at liberty to call such factual evidence at trial limited to those witnesses whose evidence has been disclosed.

Note:

- Exchange of lay evidence before experts' reports affords to the medical experts and the legal team the opportunity to *check the factual basis* of the other side's case before advancing their case.
- At the conference after exchange of lay evidence but before exchange of experts' reports, it is critical to *explore whether the lay evidence on each side is contradicted by the medical case notes*. If there is any contradiction, this should in turn be explored and if possible reconciled or explained.
- The exchange of lay evidence before expert evidence reflects how the High Court can control its own jurisdiction to like effect. Current guidelines to Commercial Court practice stated that, unless there were reasons to the contrary, expert evidence should wait until after the conclusion of all factual evidence. In *Bayer v Clarkson Puckle Overseas* [1989] NLJR 256 it was held that such was the current practice for commercial actions and was one way in which the High Court regulated its own proceedings, something which it had the power to do under its inherent jurisdiction. *Application to use this procedure should be made to the trial judge on the first day of the trial.*
- Exchange can be effected either by a meeting at which the documents are physically exchanged or by agreeing to put the documents in the post or the Document Exchange at the same time.

Exchange of expert evidence. 🖂

5 **(1)** The parties do mutually disclose by way of simultaneous mutual exchange the substance of all medical expert evidence that they intend to rely upon at trial on liability issues of negligence and causation (including that of investigating and treating doctors and ancillary hospital staff) and on condition and prognosis in the form of written reports within 3 calendar months after the date of exchange of factual witness statements subject to sub-paras (2) and (3). Such reports to be agreed if possible. Unless such reports are agreed, the parties be at liberty to call expert evidence limited to those witnesses the substance of whose expert evidence has been so disclosed and to [**] witnesses for each party.

Note:

These provisions recognise that there are 3 separate *issues* in most medical negligence cases: *Liability*, *causation* and *damage*. Reports as to all 3 *issues* have mutually and reciprocally to be exchanged. The reason why one has exchange of witness statements before exchange of experts' reports is to ensure that each side's experts see the factual basis for the other side's claim. Were it to be otherwise, each expert would be shadow boxing vis-à-vis the factual matrix of the other side.

Updates on condition and prognosis. 🖂

(2) In addition to the simultaneous mutual disclosure by way of exchange provided for above and in respect only of the Plaintiff's present condition and prognosis, each party be at liberty to serve upon the solicitor for the other party the substance of any supplementary written reports from experts whose reports were exchanged pursuant to the preceding sub-paragraph no later than two calendar months before the date fixed for trial. Unless such supplementary reports are agreed the parties be at liberty to call such updating expert evidence on present condition and prognosis, limited to those witnesses the substance of whose expert evidence has been so served.

Note:

This is to ensure that the Court is seized of the up-to-date condition of the plaintiff. Further, this report helps to buttress the Plaintiff's claim (which should be in the schedule of loss) for — if it be the case — future care, loss of earnings, aids and equipment etc.

Non-medical expert evidence exchange. 🖂

(3) The parties do mutually disclose by way of simultaneous mutual exchange the substance of all non-medical expert evidence in the form of written reports no later than 6 calendar months after exchange of factual witness statements (per paragraph 4 above). Such reports be agreed if possible. Unless such reports are agreed the parties be at liberty to call expert evidence on quantum limited to those witnesses whose expert evidence has been so disclosed and to [**] witnesses for each party.

Note:

These provisions cover reports from nursing experts; occupational, speech and physiotherapists; experts in the field of aids and equipment, accountants etc.

(4) If any witness giving expert evidence proposes to rely in her/his evidence at trial on any textbook, article, or other published item or other such unpublished work, a list of such references and copies of the texts shall be disclosed by simultaneous mutual exchange together with the report of that witness.

☞ *Texts and like materials*

6 *Optional extra* The respective parties' medical experts should meet on a date to be fixed but not later than 21 days before trial with a view to isolating the *issues* then in dispute between the parties. Following such meeting an agreed note should be prepared by the parties' solicitors and counsel to be submitted to the trial judge at the commencement of the Trial.

☞ *Without prejudice meeting of experts.*

7 *Limitation* The following issue be tried as a preliminary issue before all other questions or issues in this action, namely: whether the Plaintiff's claim is barred by the provisions of the *Limitation Act 1980*; and the following directions for trial of the preliminary issue be given:

☞ *Limitation.*

- The parties do serve and file an affidavit or affidavits of evidence on the preliminary issue as follows:
  a   the plaintiff within 56 days;
  b   the defendant within 56 days thereafter;
  c   the plaintiff in reply (if so advised) within 28 days thereafter and the affidavits may be read at the trial of the preliminary issue.
- Any deponent do attend the trial of the preliminary issue for cross-examination on his or her affidavit at the request of the other party made not less than 21 days before the trial.

Note:
- This direction enables limitation to be taken as a preliminary issue.
- If the limitation issue goes against the plaintiff, the claim fails and the trial fixture is abandoned.

8 *Special damage and future loss:*
- The plaintiff not later than 6 months before the date fixed for trial deliver to the defendants' solicitors

Schedule of loss. ☜ the then best available schedule of his/her special damages and anticipated future losses and expenses claimed including loss of earnings to date and any continuing loss, such schedule to incorporate full and detailed calculations by reference to supporting documentation;

Counter-schedule of loss. ☜ • The defendant not later than 4 months before the date fixed for trial indicate in writing and whether to what extent each item claimed is agreed and if not agreed the reason why not and any counter proposal.

9 The main action and preliminary issue both be set down for trial within 56 days, the preliminary issue being set down in the Short Cause List.

Note:

• In setting down the action for trial, the rules as to time and lodging documents set out in **RSC Ord 34** must be adhered to.

• In setting down a medical negligence action for trial, the plaintiff's solicitor is looking to fix a date rather than to have the case come on at too short notice for the convenience of his expert witnesses — and he of course should have checked up first the dates of availability of his experts.

• Until exchange of reports has taken place it will not be possible to tell those experts whether they will or will not be needed to give evidence and if they are required to give evidence it will not be possible until perhaps a week before trial (recognising the inconvenience that is bound to cause to them). But on setting down ensure the experts' availability. This is critical to the date of fixture. A subpoena is not an attack on the reliability of the expert, if he is double booked on a trial day, the subpoena takes priority. Debate continues as to the appropriateness of having recourse to the subpoena jurisdiction.

• Remember that setting down sets the clock for the service of notices under the *Civil Evidence Act 1968*, rule 21(1) and 29(1).

10 There be liberty to apply for further directions.

11 The costs of the application be costs in the cause.

Trial Place: ....

Mode: Judge alone

Note:

All medical negligence cases fall in Category B, ie cases of substance or difficulty; conceivably an exceptional case might fall into Category A as a case of 'great substance or great difficulty ...' RSC Ord 25, r 3(7).

12   Estimated length:
- Preliminary issue — X hours.
- Main Action — Y days.

Dated this   day of   1998.

Chapter 5

'*Bolam*' revisited — an approach to the '*Bolam*' test from a tort perspective

PART 1   INTRODUCTION

A   Purpose of this thesis

The *Bolam* test postulates the 'responsible body of medical opinion'. This thesis is aimed at demonstrating how the court can test by reference to legal principle, whether a medical opinion held out by the Defence is in fact 'responsible'. It is submitted that without this tool to help test the validity of a *Bolam* defence, plaintiff lawyers will not be able to make a sufficiently accurate risk analysis of a claim when working to a fixed budget or to a conditional fee agreement.

B   The fundamental approach to liability in the law of tort

It is trite learning, but must be asserted, that when seeking to establish liability for negligence in an accident claim:

- There has to be balanced (broadly speaking) the risk of injury to the proposed plaintiff against precautions to reduce the risk to be taken by the proposed defendant.
- 'General and approved practice', where relevant, can be invoked to help guide the court as to how that balance is to be struck.

C   Is medical negligence different?

Such analysis in the context of medical negligence has been clouded by '*The Bolam Test*', namely that a doctor is to be exonerated if he has acted in accordance with a practice accepted as proper by a responsible body of medical opinion skilled in that particular art. This was, however, nothing more than part of the summing up to a lay jury. Yet 'medical negligence' is an 'action for personal injuries' (RSC Ord 1, r 4).

D   Problem of not treating medical negligence as a genus of an ordinary 'tort' action for personal injuries.

What in fact does *Bolam* achieve? Surely it has two consequences:

Firstly, it merges into one confused and unsatisfactory test, the three entirely separate avenues of analysis otherwise known to the tort lawyer:

a   risk,

b   precautions, and

c   where should the balance be struck.

Secondly, it makes judges subconsciously believe that they exercise judgment on the central issue — *where the balance should be struck?* — as lawyers rather than as laymen.

☞ *This results in each decision involving medical negligence being looked at as a legal precedent rather than for what it is: a decision of fact by reference to basic tort principles.*

E   Justification for the 'tort' approach

The following thesis shows how such tort analysis can be shown to be relevant to medical negligence litigation, with a potential for dramatic savings in:

a   the size of the solicitor's file;

b   the length of the reports of experts;

c   the length of pleadings;

d   the size of the core bundle; and

e   the amount of court time spent on this type of litigation — including the actual length of judgments given.

F   Agenda for this Chapter

The purpose of this chapter is to show that when assessing whether a doctor has been in breach of his or her duty of care to a patient, the court should follow the basic principles for assessing liability in the law of tort, namely:

- Fundamental to any action in the law of tort, the court has to consider the risk of injury and its magnitude on the one hand, and the precautions available to avert that risk on the other.
- The court then has to balance the magnitude of the risk against the available precautions and decide whether such precautions should have been taken.

- The court can consider 'general and approved' practice (if such evidence be relevant). But when considering expert opinion, the court should assess the internal logic of the opinion, rather than taking the reputation of the person volunteering the opinion as a talisman of the quality of the opinion itself.
- The issue 'where should the balance be struck?' between the *magnitude of the risk* on the one hand, and the *precautions* to be taken on the other, is a 'jury' issue and *not* a 'lawyer/judge' issue.
- It is submitted that the failure fully to appreciate that the issue is a *jury* issue has led to results which do not lend themselves to proper risk assessment in medical negligence litigation.

Set out below is the legal analysis to run the argument.

PART 2   THE 'TORT' MATRIX

A   The fons et origo

In *Donoghue v Stevenson* [1932] AC 562, Lord Atkin said at 579–580:

'... You must take reasonable care to avoid acts or omissions which you reasonably foresee would be likely to injure your neighbour. Who, then, in law is my neighbour? The answer seems to be — persons who are so closely and directly affected by my act that I ought reasonably to have them in contemplation as being so affected when I am directing my mind to the acts or omissions which are called in question.'

B   Analysing the components of the 'duty of care'

These dicta of Lord Atkin state only to whom the duty is owed — not the extent of the duty. The extent of the duty is often enough more important than its existence. Like the latter, it depends partly on the nature of the relationship giving rise to the duty and partly on the foreseeability of damage. The extent of a duty of care involves a number of questions:

First: Against what dangers must care be exercised? *Munkman on Employer's Liability* (11th edn) says at p 32:

'The answer to this question varies greatly with the relationship of the parties and the sort of danger likely to arise. The dangers for which a person is responsible are in general those which originate from his activities or are in some way under his control ... While (as the authorities now stand) any real genuine risk of injury to others gives rise to a *duty* of care, the degree of risk is critical in deciding whether the defendant was negligent in failing to take measures against it.'

Second: The standard of care   A priori, one has to remember that the test is by reference to the 'reasonable man':

'The standard of foresight of the reasonable man is in one sense an impersonal test. It eliminates the personal equation and is independent of the idiosyncrasies of the particular person whose conduct is in question. Some persons are unduly timorous and imagine every path beset with lions; others, of more robust temperament, fail to foresee or nonchalantly disregard even the most obvious of dangers. The reasonable man is presumed to be free both from over-apprehension and from over-confidence.' per Lord Macmillan in *Glasgow Corpn v Muir* [1943] AC 448 at 457.

PART 3   JUDICIAL TOOLS FOR GAUGING THE STANDARD OF CARE

A   The three primary 'controls'

To maintain objectivity, the courts have developed the following controls:

- the magnitude of the risk;
- the extent to which it was practicable to take steps to reduce the risk;
- general and approved practice.

B   The magnitude of the risk

Salmond on Torts (10th edn) says at p 438:

'There are two factors in determining the magnitude of the risk — the seriousness of the injury risked, and the likelihood of the injury in fact caused.'

- This statement of the law was approved by the House of Lords in *Paris v Stepney Borough Council* [1951] AC 367. Lord Morton, inter alia, said:

'There are occupations in which the possibility of an accident occurring to a workman is extremely remote, while there are others where there is a constant risk of accident. Similarly, there are occupations in which, if an accident occurs, it is likely to be of a trivial nature, whilst there are other occupations in which ... the result ... may well be fatal ... there is in each case a gradually ascending scale between the two extremes ... the more serious the damage which will happen if an accident occurs, the more thorough are the precautions which an employer must take.'

- Further, the magnitude of the risk has to be weighed against other factors, and particularly against the expense and effort involved in safety measures, and the necessity of carrying out the work in hand. Lord Reid said, for example, in *Morris v West Hartlepool Steam Navigation Co Ltd* [1956] AC 552:

  'It is the duty of an employer, in considering whether some precaution should be taken against a foreseeable risk, to weigh, on the one hand, the magnitude of the risk, the likelihood of an accident happening and the possible seriousness of the consequences if an accident does happen, and on the other hand, the difficulty and expense and any other disadvantage of taking the precaution.'

- Similarly, Lord Reid said in *Overseas Tankship (UK) Ltd v The Miller SS Co Pty* [1967] 1 AC 617 at 642:

  '...it does not follow that, no matter what the circumstances may be, it is justifiable to neglect a risk of such a small magnitude. A reasonable man would only neglect such a risk if he had some valid reason for doing so, eg that it would involve considerable expense to eliminate the risk. He would weigh the risk against the difficulty of eliminating it.'

Such dicta lead to the issue of the 'practicability' of taking steps to reduce the risk.

C   Practicability

Munkman (11th edn) says at p 44:

'To summarise the whole matter, therefore, it is first necessary to decide what safety measures are feasible in the light of current knowledge. Then, to determine what is reasonable, it is necessary to balance the disadvantages of safety measures on the one hand — the effort and expense, the possible frustration of important activities, and the possibility that the precautions will be futile — against the magnitude of the risk on the other hand. If the disadvantages of safety measures altogether outweigh the risk involved, those measures need not be taken.'

'The question what precautions (if any) ought to be taken in a given case is always a question of *fact*, to be answered

by a jury or by a judge acting as a jury: It is not a matter
of law to be governed by decisions in other cases where
the evidence may have been different: *Qualcast
(Wolverhampton) Ltd v Haynes* [1959] AC 743.'

D   General and approved practice

Adopting again the approach of *Munkman* at p 45:

'General practice has always been taken into account in
determining the standard of care, but it is not conclusive,
because "no one can claim to be excused for want of care
because others are as careless as himself": per Cockburn
CJ in *Blenkiron v Great Central Gas Consumers' Co*
(1860) 2 F & F 437. It is easily seen that general practice
may go wrong: motorists quite often go round blind
corners on the wrong side of the road, or take risks in
overtaking, and yet such acts are negligent. Indeed, it is
not so much the uniform *behaviour* of mankind in a
particular field to which the law gives weight, as the
standard of conduct, whether uniformly followed or not,
which is generally accepted as correct: such a recognised
standard of conduct, for example, is contained in the
Highway Code, or in the Regulations for Preventing
Collisions at Sea. The Health and Safety at Work Act 1974,
s 16, authorises the issue of 'codes of practice' for any
matter affecting health and safety at work and these will
have a similar value.'

- In the industrial injury context, Lord Reid said in
  General Cleaning Contractors Ltd v Christmas
  [1953] AC 180 at 192:

  'A plaintiff who seeks to have condemned as unsafe a
  system of work which has been generally used for a
  long time in an important trade undertakes a heavy
  onus; if he is right it means that all, or practically all,
  the numerous employers in the trade have been
  habitually neglecting their duty to their men.'

However, there is a limit to the relevance of general
and approved practice. As Lord Reid explained in
Morris v West Hartlepool Steam Navigation Co Ltd
[1956] AC 552 at 574:

'... an employer seeking to rely on a practice which
is admittedly a bad one must at least prove that it has
been followed without mishap sufficiently widely in
circumstances similar to those in his own case in all
material respects ...'

And as Slesser LJ said in *Carpenters' Co v British
Matual Banking Co Ltd* [1937] 3 All ER 811 at 820:

'... neglect of duty does not cease by repetition to be
neglect of duty ...'

- More importantly perhaps, *Munkman* then goes on to identify why one calls experts to court:

  'Recognised practice has greater force in specialised departments of life, such as medical practice, or the management of engineering works or a coal mine. The reason is that expert knowledge and judgment are required to assess (i) the magnitude of the risks involved, and (ii) what safety measures are practicable — ie what measures are physically possible, how effective they are likely to be, and how much expense, trouble and restraint upon useful activity they will involve. If informed opinion is in agreement, it is almost conclusive, and yet not quite, for the court, after inquiring into the grounds of informed opinion, may find that too little emphasis has been put on safety, and too much on the expense of ensuring it ...'

E   Summary thus far

Drawing back, one perhaps can discern a 'truth' which has perhaps for long been hidden in the welter of litigation since the Second World War.

First   One brings experts to court to advise the judge (sitting as jury) of:

a   the magnitude of the risks involved, and

b   what safety measures are practicable

The experts can properly advise the court as to these matters because they have special knowledge of the field of expertise in question.

Second   It is then a matter for the judge, sitting as the jury to decide whether those safety measures should have been carried out on the facts of the particular case.

That approach can now be examined in the context of medical negligence litigation. The approach is not without precedent, for it was the basis of the decision of the Court of Appeal in *Hucks v Cole* [1993] 4 Med LR 393.

PART 4   *HUCKS v COLE*

A   The facts

See also Appendix 5 at p 259   Although only recently reported this was a case decided in 1968. Doctor Cole was a GP with a diploma in obstetrics. He helped man a local maternity hospital which had no permanent staff of doctors. He failed to treat with penicillin, Mrs Hucks (who had recently given birth) for puerperal fever. Such a condition was by the 1960s very rare and almost unknown, although before the Second World War it had been prevalent and often fatal. The judge at first instance found Dr Cole liable and this was a finding upheld on appeal.

B   Summarising the arguments in 'Hucks'

Sachs LJ, inter alia, said:

'When the evidence shows that a lacuna in professional practice exists by which risks of grave danger are knowingly taken, then, however small the risks, the Courts must anxiously examine that lacuna — particularly if the risks can be easily and inexpensively avoided. If the Court finds, on an analysis of the reasons given for not taking those precautions that, in the light of current professional knowledge, there is no proper basis for the lacuna, and that it is definitely not reasonable that those risks should have been taken, its function is to state that fact and where necessary to state that it constitutes negligence. In such a case the practice will no doubt thereafter be altered to the benefit of patients ...

The Court must be vigilant to see whether the reasons given for putting a patient at risk are valid in the light of any well-known advance in medical knowledge, or whether they stem from a residual adherence to out-of-date ideas ...

The defence medical witnesses, despite the fact that at any rate one of them, Miss Barnes, used on more than one occasion the word 'must' in regard to the need to eliminate such risks, said that many responsible doctors relying on clinical judgment would have taken that particular risk on this particular occasion. To put it in a phrase agreed to by Miss Barnes, the patient was "just unlucky". That is indeed the essence of the defence case. The plaintiff's case is that this bad luck was easily avoidable without any material risk to the patient and should have been avoided.'

C   Balancing the respective arguments

Having summarised the evidence, Sachs LJ went on to weigh the arguments:

'At whose risk then is a mistaken decision made on the basis of potentially deceptive clinical appearances? What should the Court say? If it agrees with the defence, it means that so far as fulminating septicaemia is concerned, it is open to the medical profession to say that where the patient looks well, and there are other useful but inconclusive points tending against the changes of an onset, she can in cases such as the present be properly allowed to bear the avoidable risk of fulminating septicaemia because it is so small. If it agrees with the plaintiff's witnesses, then it is said that an undue burden in relation to minimal risks is being placed on the medical profession, and that thus it is the patient who should be at risk if the decision is wrong, and not the doctor who made it.

Despite the fact that the risk could have been avoided by adopting a course that was easy, efficient, and inexpensive, and would have entailed only minimal chances of disadvantages to the patient, the evidence of the four defence experts to the effect that they and other responsible members of the medical profession would have taken the same risk in the same circumstances has naturally caused me to hesitate considerably on two points. Firstly, whether the failure of the defendant to turn over to penicillin treatment during the relevant period was unreasonable. On this, however, I was in the end fully satisfied that in the light of the admissions made by the defendant himself and by this witnesses — quite apart from Dr May's very cogent evidence — that failure to do this was not merely wrong but clearly unreasonable. The reason given by the four experts do not to my mind stand up to analysis ... The potential irrelevance of the rarity or remoteness of the risk, when the maturing of the risk may be disastrous, is incidentally illustrated in *Chin Keow's case* [1967] 1 WLR 813.

Secondly, as to whether, in the light of such evidence as to what other responsible medical practitioners would have done, it can be said that even if the defendant's error was unreasonable, it was not negligence in relation to the position as regards practice at that particular date. On this second point it is to be noted that this is not apparently a case of 'two schools of thought', (see the speech of Lord Goddard in *Chapman v Rix*, on the 21 December 1960, at page 11): it appears to be more a case of doctors who said in one form or another that they would have acted or might have acted in the same way as the defendant did, for reasons which on examination **do not really stand up to analysis** [authors' emphasis].

Dr Cole knowingly took an easily avoidable risk which elementary teaching had instructed him to avoid; and the fact that others say they would have done the same neither ought nor can in the present case excuse him in an action for negligence however sympathetic one may be to him. However, in so far as the evidence shows the existence of a lacuna of the type to which reference was made earlier in this judgment, that lacuna was, in view of the magnitude of the dangers involved, so unreasonable that as between doctor and patient it cannot be relied upon to excuse the former in an action for negligence.'

D   What is the reference to *Chapman v Rix* to which Sachs LJ referred?

The relevant dicta in *Chapman* read:

'... but I desire to add that if Lord Justice Romer meant that if a doctor charged with negligence could find two other doctors to say they would have acted as he did that of itself entitled him to a verdict, I could not agree with him if there was evidence the other way. But that is not to say that if some doctors think one course should be followed while others prefer another, a judge may not say without actually deciding in favour of one view over the other that he is not prepared to find negligence. An illustration arises in this particular case. Mr Handfield-Jones's opinion was that an exploratory operation should always take place in the case of an abdominal wound, a view to which Sir Hugh Griffith was not prepared to agree. If there are two recognised schools of thought on a subject, to follow one cannot be negligent, and this is what I prefer to think Lord Justice Romer really meant.'

- Similarly, in *Maynard v West Midlands Regional Health Authority* [1984] 1 WLR 634 at 639, Lord Scarman said:

'My Lords, even before considering the reasons given by the majority of the Court of Appeal for reversing the findings of negligence, I have to say that a Judge's 'preference' for one body of distinguished professional opinion to another also professionally distinguished is not sufficient to establish negligence in a practitioner whose actions have received the seal of approval of those whose opinions, truthfully expressed, honestly held, were not preferred. If this was the real reason for the Judge's finding, he erred in law even though elsewhere in his judgment he stated the law correctly. For in the realm of diagnosis and treatment negligence is not established by preferring one respectable body of professional opinion to another. Failure to exercise the ordinary skill of a doctor (in the appropriate speciality, if he be a specialist) is necessary.'

E   What does the phrase mean *'reasons which on examination do not really stand up to analysis?'*

☞ *See also Appendix 4 at p 240*

In *Bolitho v City & Hackney Health Authority* [1993] 4 Med LR 381 Dillon LJ said:

'In my judgment, the Court could only adopt the approach of Sachs LJ and reject medical opinion on the ground that the reasons of one group of doctors do not really stand up to analysis, if the Court, fully conscious of its own lack of medical knowledge and clinical experience, was nonetheless clearly satisfied that the views of that group of doctors were *Wednesbury* unreasonable, ie views such as no reasonable body of doctors could have held. But, in my judgment, that would be an impossibly strong thing to say of the honest views of experts of the distinction of Dr Dinwiddle and Dr Robertson, in the present case.'

There is a question mark, however, of the applicability of the '*Wednesbury*' test. It can be argued that it is too restrictive. In any event, in *Joyce v Merton Sutton & Wandsworth Health Authority* [1996] PIQR P121, Hutchinson LJ said at P153:

'In my judgment (*pace* Dillon LJ at p 392), it does not assist to introduce concepts from administrative law such as the *Wednesbury* test; such tests are directed to very different problems and their use, even by analogy, in negligence cases can, in my judgment, only serve to confuse.'

PART 5   SLOTTING *HUCKS v COLE* INTO THE TORT MATRIX

A   Upon what were the experts in *Hucks* advising?

Their focus was:

- the magnitude of the risk;
- the practicability of prevention.

The approach to these factors in *Hucks* is analysed in turn.

B   The magnitude of the risk

This breaks down into three components:

- **First** the seriousness of the injury risked. This was death. Lord Denning MR said in *Hucks*:

    'In the years before 1935 puerperal fever was a great and fearful danger. If harmful germs reach her, they may give rise to septicaemia. In some cases it may show itself as local sepsis, gradually becoming worse with rising fever. In other cases its onset may be sudden, coming like a thunderbolt, with high fever. Then it is called fulminating septicaemia.'

    Lord Denning continued a little later in his judgment:

    'Dr Cole allowed this young woman to go into this maternity home with a septic finger. He did not tell the

Matron and Sister at the time. They find it out. They move her into another room, separate from other women. He treats it with tetracycline and gets a swab taken. That was quite reasonable. But then he gets this danger signal: a report from a pathologist showing that streptococcus pyogenes was present. His own expert, Miss Barnes, said how serious this was. She was asked: "Does any sort of alarm bell ring in his mind?" She said "Most certainly." "Is it a full turnout to resist attack or do you take it quite calmly and you take a few extra precautions but leave it at that?" She answered: "No, I think you should attack it with all the means in your power. It is a general alarm. Everybody is standing to." Yet Dr Cole did nothing. He never treated her with penicillin, which would have killed the organism ...'

- **Second** The second component in the 'magnitude of the risk' was the **likelihood of death occurring**. In this context, Lord Denning MR said:

    'Before 1935 80 per cent of the women stricken with either kind died. But in 1935 sulphonamide drugs were discovered. With their aid, medical men were able to prevent or treat the infection. The mortality dropped a great deal. Only four per cent of the women got septicaemia, and these were treated in the early stages so that it did not develop. Puerperal fever is now extremely rare — so rare that some of the distinguished medical people who were called had never seen such a case.'

Further Diplock LJ in this context inter alia said:

    '... fulminating septicaemia ... is today very very rare. From the evidence I think there has been no example of it in the area in which Dr Cole practised for 18 years. Even in the wider field in which other witnesses practised only one case had been experienced by two consultants in the course of what Mr Webster described as 40 consultant years. It is a very very rare disease in modern times and it is understandable that Dr Cole forgot about it, and that I think was the cause of the disaster. Some of the witnesses said and there is a great deal of truth in it — that it is only when you experience or get to know of an actual case that it really brings home to you the danger which you have previously only learned about from textbooks and lectures. And so it is understandable, but none the less, it is a danger which general practitioners are taught about in their training, read about in literature, and ought, even in the exigencies of what is no doubt a busy and a heavy practice, to remember, because the danger of that risk is so enormous ...'

- **Third** The third component in the 'magnitude of the risk' was the **extent of the foreseeability of that risk**. Lord Denning MR said:

'... Nevertheless, all (the distinguished medical people called to give evidence) agreed with one accord that any sign of infection in a maternity ward is a danger against which every precaution must be taken. If a nurse or a student had a septic place on a finger, he or she should not be allowed into the ward. If a mother has a septic place, on a finger or anywhere else, she should be isolated lest the infection spread through the ward to other mothers.'

C The practicability of prevention

This involved consideration of the following

- that safety measures (penicillin) were feasible; and
- such safety measures did not generate a prejudice to the health of the patient; and
- there was no realistic effort or expense involved in taking such safety measures.

That being the evidence, it was then a matter of fact for the JURY (albeit the judges were performing that role) to adjudicate whether the defence case really stood up to analysis. The ruling was that Dr Cole ought to have prescribed penicillin.

PART 6 SUMMARY — THE INTERFACE OF EXPERT AND JURY IN THE MEDICAL NEGLIGENCE CONTEXT — THE TRUE ROLE OF THE *'BOLAM'* TEST

A Introduction

The following flows from the analysis set out above.

B For what purpose does one bring experts to court in a medical negligence action?

The role of the experts is to advise the judge (sitting as a jury) of the following:

- As a matter of medical 'mechanics' how the accident happened. In just the same way as one would explain in a factory accident the mechanics of how the machine cut off the plaintiff's arm.

- The magnitude of the risks involved, ie:
  a the foreseeable likelihood of that injury, and
  b the seriousness of the injury which resulted;
- What safety measures are available to avoid such risk of injury.

In a factory accident, the experts advise as engineers on these issues. They are not advising by reference to the *'Bolam'* test but by reference to their special knowledge of the working environment in question. Similarly, in a medical negligence claim, medical men of a speciality relevant to the issues should be called to advise as to the *magnitude* of the *risk* and *precautions* capable of being taken to avert such *risk*.

This approach is implicit in the following dicta of Mitchell J in *Gascoine v Ian Sheridan & Co and Latham* [1994] 5 Med LR 437:

> 'The doctors, by failing to inform themselves upon the current thinking on "risk" in those particular and unusual circumstances (and I am sure that each was not sufficiently informed about it), deprived Mrs Gascoine of the benefit of that current thinking. To proceed to radical treatment in those circumstances, without equipping themselves to perform an informed balancing exercise, was to proceed in a manner which fell short of the standard of reasonable competence which each professed to have and which could reasonably be expected of them.'

C   Where is the balance to be struck between 'risk' and 'precautions'?

Given the precautionary measures available, should they have been taken in the context of the magnitude of the foreseeable risk?

- In a factory setting, the court has recourse (if available) to 'general and approved practice' to help provide a guide as to the balance to be held between risk on the one hand and precautions on the other.
- In a medical setting, the court has recourse to the following guide: What is the stance of responsible bodies of medical opinion?

But in either case, the court is asked to adjudicate in relation to a balance, namely:

> '... the disadvantages of safety measures on the one hand — the effort and expense, the possible frustration of imported activities, and the possibility that the precautions will be futile — against the magnitude of the risk on the

other hand. If the disadvantages of safety measures altogether outweigh the risk involved, those measures need not be taken' per *Munkman* (ibid at p 44).

D Striking the balance between *'risk'* and *'precautions'* — how does the court avoid asserting its own medical judgment?

Judges are not charged with the responsibility of asserting medical standards of conduct. How then is the court to rule in a medical negligence action and yet avoid the trap of setting standards? It is in this context that the following dicta in *Bolitho* fall into perspective:

'In my judgment, the Court could only adopt the approach of Sachs LJ and reject medical opinion on the ground that the reason of one group of doctors do not really stand up to analysis, if the Court, fully conscious of its own lack of medical knowledge and clinical experience, was nonetheless clearly satisfied that the views of that group of doctors were *Wednesbury* unreasonable, ie views such as no reasonable body of doctors could have held.'

In other words, given two conflicting thrusts of expert evidence, a judge can and should choose between them only if one is obviously wrong. This brings us to the third point: From what standpoint does one assess what is obviously wrong — from a legal or lay standpoint?

E The role of the jury

- After considering the expert evidence on **risk** and **precautions**, and the extent to which precautions should have been taken, **then** it is a matter for the judge, sitting as the **jury**, to decide whether those safety measures should have been carried out on the facts of the particular case. To repeat dicta already cited:

  'The question what precautions (if any) *ought* [author's emphasis] to be taken in a given case is always a question of *fact*, to be answered by a jury or by a judge acting as a jury: it is not a matter of law to be governed by decisions in other cases where the evidence may have been different: *Qualcast (Wolverhampton) Ltd v Haynes* [1959] AC 743.'

- That this seems to be accepted by the Court of Appeal is a proposition which it is submitted is justified by the following dicta in the case of *Bolitho v City & Hackney Health Authority* [1993] 4 Med LR 381. Farquharson LJ inter alia said:

'Mr Brennan relies on this authority to support a further attack on Dr Dinwiddie's evidence. He contends that a responsible paediatric doctor should when faced with a patient in the same condition as Patrick was that afternoon have made what Counsel describes a risk/benefit analysis of intubation. If the responsible paediatrician had made such an analysis in this case Counsel argues he would inevitably have concluded that it was right to intubate. The risk to Patrick was slight, even though he would have to have been anaesthetised, whereas the corresponding risk of not intubating bearing in mind the two life threatening episodes during the afternoon was great. Mr Brennan says that in those circumstances the Judge should have rejected the evidence of Dr Dinwiddie as not being representative of responsible medical opinion. He claims that Dr Dinwiddie fails the test referred to by Lord Scarman in *Maynard's* case (supra).

There is of course no inconsistency between the decisions in *Hucks v Coles* and *Maynard's* case. It is not enough for a Defendant to call a number of doctors to say that what he had done or not done was in accord with accepted clinical practice. It is necessary for the Judge to consider that evidence and decide whether that clinical practice puts the patient unnecessarily at risk. For my part I cannot see that that particular issue arises in this case. The findings of the Judge are inconsistent with the suggestions that the approach of Dr Dinwiddie put Patrick unnecessarily at risk. The Judge clearly concluded that Dr Dinwiddie's evidence did constitute "a responsible body of medical opinion" for the reasons already given.'

- That the issue for the judge is one of *fact* is demonstrated clearly by Rougier J in *Flynn v Maidstone Health Authority* (26 October 1992, unreported), QBD. He inter alia said at page 14F of the transcript:

'This brief resume of the experts' evidence shows the daunting task I face in deciding this case. Mr Baker urges me to say that, because he has called three eminent doctors to say that Mrs Wallace's labour was managed in accordance with accepted practice, that is enough. If I find against the hospital, I will have rejected their evidence with consequences not only to their professional reputations, but also to the profession as a whole, since the so-called accepted practice will require radical rethinking.

I do not accept this analysis. In passing I ask rhetorically, what about the reputations of the plaintiff's doctors, if I reject their evidence? However, I do not think that any decision I make will have the consequences of the kind that Mr Baker suggests. I have to decide whether the management of this — that is to say Mrs Wallace's labour — was negligent. Her age, her antenatal history and the progress of her labour are unique to her. None of the experts was there. Their opinions are based on the evidence that they have heard and the documents which they have seen. If I were to conclude that in forming their opinions they have not given sufficient weight to certain features of the case, or have given too much weight to others, that is something that can happen to any of us. It happens to judges daily in the Appeal Courts of this country. That such differences of opinion may occur in the field of obstetrics is well illustrated by the paper put before me, of which Mr Buchan was part author, entitled "Inconsistencies in Clinical Decisions in Obstetrics" ...'

F   Can the dicta of Farquharson LJ in *Bolitho* be reviewed critically?

- The following proposition is tentatively advanced and with humility: In reference to those dicta of Farquharson LJ just quoted, is there not a lacuna? When deciding on where the balance should be struck between risk and precautions, the judge in *Bolitho* was sitting in the capacity of a jury. Thus he had to decide the issue as a matter of fact, as a jury (albeit as a jury directed as to the law). Hutchinson J at first instance volunteered how a jury — ie a layperson — would view this case:

> 'Mr Brennan also advanced a powerful argument — which I have to say, *as a layman* [author's emphasis] appealed to me — to the effect that the views of the defendant's experts simply were not logical or sensible. Given the recent as well as the more remote history of Patrick's illness, culminating in these two episodes, surely it was unreasonable and illogical not to anticipate the recurrence of a life-threatening event and take the step which it was acknowledged would probably have saved Patrick from harm? This was the safe option, whatever was suspected as the cause, or even if the cause was thought to be a mystery. The difficulty of this approach, as in the end I think Mr Brennan acknowledged, was that in effect it invited me to substitute my own views for those of the medical experts.'

- Thus Hutchinson J is surely saying: Were I a layman, I would have agreed with Mr Brennan QC. Is he not a layman for these purposes? The relevant thesis runs thus:

Firstly, the judge is sitting as a lay jury and is exercising a judgment on the facts, not on the law.

There is no law which says without more that a judge cannot substitute his own view for those of the medical experts.

Secondly, it has to be recognised that given experts whose reputations are high, it is no easy matter for a judge to ride roughshod over opinions expressed. Hence the 'control' that a judge should not feel justified in so ruling unless he can demonstrate what Dillon LJ called '*Wednesbury* unreasonableness' in *Bolitho*.

Thirdly, in his dissenting judgment in *Bolitho*, Simon Brown LJ was able to demonstrate why the expert evidence for the defence should be rejected. He said:

> 'When it comes to deciding what inferences here may legitimately be drawn from the established primary facts, prominent among the factors to be borne in mind are surely these. First, the literature in this field of medicine, and not least the generally accepted statements (as found by the judge at pages 32/33) that:
>
>> "... respiratory failure ... is a common complication in many disease processes and should always be readily suspected, especially if there are unexplained signs and symptoms ..."
>
> and
>
>> "... any child who reaches the hospital alive should not ... die from upper airway obstruction."
>
> Second, the very purpose of Sister Sallabank calling for the senior paediatric registrar was to ensure that whatever needed to be done for Patrick was done. The initial assumption must surely be that the doctor's attendance would have been of some use. Third is the indisputable fact that intubation alone would have benefited the child. Given all that, and given fourth the entire history of this case as it would present itself to an attending doctor — ... — I have no difficulty in inferring that whichever doctor had attended would have acted in the one way which would have been effective. In so deciding, I do not overlook Nurse Newbold's evidence or Dr Dinwiddie's school of thought. But it is all very well for the specialists now to theorise over what would or would not have appeared to be indicated by second-hand descriptions of the child's developing condition; the reality is that no one will ever know quite how that condition would have presented itself to a competent doctor, learning the history as he would have done and examining the patient for himself ...
>
> In the final analysis the Judge's conclusion that Dr Dinwiddie's view represented those of a respectable body of medical opinion, so far from being decisive in

the defendant's favour is in my judgment an irrelevance.'

- Simon Brown LJ expressly hung his dicta on the 'causation' peg: Had a doctor in fact responded to the emergency call, he or she would probably have intubated. A reconciliation between the dissenting judgment, and the majority judgment in *Bolitho* is to be found in the dicta of Hutchinson LJ in *Joyce v Merton Sutton & Wandsworth Health Authority* [1966] PIQR P121 at P152–3:

  'Thus a plaintiff can discharge the burden of proof on causation by satisfying the court *either* that the relevant person would in fact have taken the requisite action (although she would not have been at fault if she had not) *or* that the proper discharge of the relevant person's duty towards the plaintiff required that she take that action. The former alternative calls for no explanation *since it is simply the factual proof of the causative effect of the original fault* [Editor's emphasis]. The latter is slightly more sophisticated: it involves the factual situation that the original fault did not itself cause the injury but that this was because there would have been some further fault on the part of the defendants; the plaintiff proves his case by proving that his injuries would have been avoided if proper care had continued to be taken. In the *Bolitho* case the plaintiff had to prove that the continuing exercise of proper care would have resulted in his being intubated. Properly viewed, therefore, this rule is favourable to a plaintiff because it gives him two routes by which he may prove his case — either proof that the exercise of proper care would have necessitated the relevant result, or proof that if proper care had been exercised it would in fact have led to the relevant result.

  In assessing what the exercise of proper care necessitates, no different test is to be applied to that to be applied in any case where professional negligence is alleged, essentially the so-called *Bolam* test. This is because it is the same question as is involved in the initial allegation of fault; the causation question merely extends the ambit of the allegation of fault. The plaintiff's case is still based upon saying what the exercise of proper care required and saying that if proper care had been exercised in all respects and had continued to be exercised, the plaintiff would not have suffered the injury. Nor do any different principles of burden of proof apply; the plaintiff has the same general burden but can rely upon evidential inferences to assist him to discharge that burden ...'

- Support for the approach of Simon Brown LJ in *Bolitho* may be derived from the approach of the judge to weighing evidence in *Smith v Barking, Havering and Brentwood Health Authority* [1994] 5 Med LR 285. In this case, the plaintiff contended that had she been informed of the risk of the operation, she would not have consented to it. Hutchinson LJ inter alia said:

> 'If everything points to the fact that a reasonable plaintiff properly informed, would have assented to the operation, the assertion from the witness box, made after the adverse outcome is known, in a wholly artificial situation and in the knowledge that the outcome of the case depends upon that assertion being maintained does not carry great weight unless there are extraneous or additional factors to substantiate it.'

PART 7   QUALITY CONTROL PROTOCOLS FOR EXPERT EVIDENCE

A   Introduction

In recent times, the courts have developed more precise controls over their handling of expert evidence. In so doing the courts have refined their machinery to retain judicial sovereignty over expert evidence rather than to allow such sovereignty to be delegated to individuals professing to articulate a body of professional opinion.

B   *Loveday v Renton* — the 'Whooping Cough' vaccine case

- Those controls derive inter alia from *Loveday v Renton* [1990] 1 Med LR 117: — Stuart-Smith LJ said:

> 'In reaching my decision a number of processes have to be undertaken. The mere expression of opinion or belief by a witness, however eminent, that the vaccine can or cannot cause brain damage, does not suffice. The court has to evaluate the witness and soundness of his opinion. Most importantly this involves an examination of the reasons given for his opinions and the extent to which they are supported by the evidence. The judge also has to decide what weight to attach to a witness's opinion **by examining the internal consistency and logic of his evidence** [Editor's emphasis]; the care with which he has considered the subject and presented his evidence; his precision and

accuracy of thought as demonstrated by his answers; how he responds to searching and informed cross-examination and in particular the extent to which a witness faces up to and accepts the logic of a proposition put in cross-examination or is prepared to concede points that are seen to be correct; the extent to which a witness has conceived an opinion and is reluctant to re-examine it in the light of later evidence, or demonstrates a flexibility of mind which may involve changing or modifying opinions previously held; whether or not a witness is biased or lacks independence. Criticisms have been made by Counsel of some of the witnesses called on either side and I shall have to consider these in due course ...

There is one further aspect of a witness's evidence that is often important; that is his demeanour in the witness box. As in most cases where the court is evaluating expert evidence, I have placed less weight on this factor in reaching my assessment. But it is not wholly unimportant; and in particular in those instances where criticisms have been made of a witness, on the grounds of bias or lack of independence, which in my view are not justified, the witness's demeanour has been a factor that I have taken into account ...'

- This approach of Stuart-Smith LJ, it is submitted, is not idiosyncratic or reserved for causes of pharmaceutical liability. Indeed, it is reflected in the dicta of Finlay CJ in *Best v Wellcome Foundation Ltd* [1994] 5 Med LR 81 at 98:

'I have carefully considered these conflicting cases and the evidence upon which they are placed, together with the evidence which the various tests and documents show, and I have come to the following conclusions.

1 I am satisfied that it is not possible either for a Judge of trial or for an Appellate Court to take upon it the role of a determining scientific authority resolving disputes between distinguished scientists in any particular line of technical expertise. The function which a Court can and must perform in the trial of a case in order to acquire a just result is to apply commonsense and a careful understanding of the logical and likelihood of events to conflicting opinions and conflicting theories concerning a matter of this kind.'

C Back to *Bolitho*

One asks rhetorically how Hutchinson J would have assessed the evidence of Dr Dinwiddie, had it been expressly subjected to the *Loveday v Renton* quality control criteria.

D   Justification for applying these quality control 'protocols' to experts in medical negligence action

- It is surprising that there has been an inclination to delegate to the medical profession sovereignty over expert opinion in medical negligence litigation, taking into account the jealousy with which the courts have sought to assert their judicial sovereignty in the field of actuarial evidence. For example, in *Auty, Mills, Rogers and Popow v National Coal Board* (1981) Times, 1 July Tudor Evans J said:

  '... If an actuary did make subjective judgments on issues of fact and incorporated them in his calculations, then he was usurping the court's function. A court had no means of testing the weight given to such judgment.'

- Further, the Judicial Committee of the Privy Council concluded in *Edward Wong Finance Co Ltd v Johnson Stokes & Master* [1984] AC 296 that the general practice of solicitors in Hong Kong in respect of mortgage transactions was a negligent practice. The headnote inter alia reads:

  '... that the risk of loss of the appellants by placing the money at the disposition of the vendors' solicitor was a foreseeable risk, namely, the risk of embezzlement by him; that the risk could have been avoided, without undermining the basic features of the Hong Kong style of completion, by taking precautions to ensure that the appellants would have an unanswerable claim against the other side for specific performance of that party's obligations, and in the case of property already subject to a mortgagee which was to be discharged so much of the purchase price as was needed to discharge the prior mortgage could have been paid by cheque in favour of the mortgagee or its duly authorised agent and not by cheque in favour of the vendors' solicitor; that, by following the general practice of completion in Hong Kong without taking precautions when they knew the property was subject to an existing mortgage the respondents had failed to exercise the standard of care which they owed to the appellants and, accordingly, they were negligent and liable to pay the appellants the agreed damages.'

- Lord Brightman agreed with the dissenting judgment in Hong Kong of Li J A, who inter alia said:

'The test for negligence or otherwise in this case means whether a reasonable, diligent and competent solicitor could foresee in January 1976 that damage could result by adopting the Hong Kong practice of completion ... Applying this test to the present case I find Miss Leung, as a solicitor when adopting the Hong Kong practice for completion in January 1976 complied with the general practice which had been practised for years without ill result of the form of damage as in this case flowing from it. That goes a long way to show that she was not negligent. However, that is not conclusive. The further question to be asked is: could she foresee the risk of ill result at the material time as an ordinary, reasonable prudent person? I am afraid the answer must be in the affirmative. As a solicitor, even in January 1976, she should know that her client, the plaintiff, would not obtain what it lent its money for unless and until the vendor had executed the assignment and delivered the title deeds. If she parted with the money without such delivery she did not receive what her client had paid for apart from an undertaking or a promise by a fellow member of her profession. As a reasonable person of ordinary prudence she should or ought to have foreseen the risk of parting with the money before obtaining the property one bought in any ordinary transaction. It was not her skill that was put to the test. It was her common sense. The fact that practically all her fellow solicitors adopted this practice is not conclusive evidence that it is prudent ... acting in accordance with the general practice she took a foreseeable risk for her client while there was no necessity to do so. The fact that other solicitors did the same did not make the risk less apparent or unreal.'

- Warner J adopted a similar approach (rejecting defence submissions based on *Bolam* in the unreported case of *Taylor and Harmans v Warners* (21 July 1987). Similarly in *Neilson v Basildon and Thurrock Health Authority* (15 February 1992, unreported) Garland J (basing his approach inter alia on *Sidaway v Bethlem Hospital*) inter alia said:

'Are these circumstances in which a judge can substitute his own assessment of risk and consequently of the requisite duty of care for that of a responsible body of opinion within the profession? This may be so in an extreme case or where it can be demonstrated that the profession as a whole or a supposedly responsible body of opinion within it have failed to take into account some relevant factor or that some underlying principle of public policy requires them to change their standards.'

- These dicta are consistent with the approach of Lord Bridge in *Sidaway v Board of Governors of Bethlem Royal Hospital* [1985] AC 871 at 900 D-G:

  '... It would follow from this that the issue whether non-disclosure in a particular case should be condemned as a breach of the doctor's duty of care is an issue to be decided primarily on the basis of expert medical evidence, applying the *Bolam* test. But I do not see that this approach involves the necessity "to hand over to the medical profession the entire question of the scope of the duty of disclosure, including the question whether there has been a breach of that duty". Of course, if there is a conflict of evidence as to whether a responsible body of medical opinion approves of non-disclosure in a particular case, the judge will have to resolve that conflict. But even in a case where, as here, no expert witness in the relevant medical field condemns the non-disclosure as being in conflict with accepted and responsible medical practice, I am of opinion that the judge might in certain circumstances come to the conclusion that disclosure of a particular risk was so obviously necessary to an informed choice on the part of the patient that no reasonably prudent medical man would fail to take it. The kind of case I have in mind would be an operation involving a substantial risk of grave adverse consequences, as, for example, the ten per cent. risk of a stroke from the operation which was the subject of the Canadian case of *Reibl v Hughes* (1980) 114 DLR (3d) 1. In such a case, in the absence of some cogent clinical reason why the patient should not be informed, a doctor recognising and respecting his patient's right of decision, could hardly fail to appreciate the necessity for an appropriate warning.'

PART 8   SUMMARY

A   The key to the *'Bolam'* test — a *'responsible'* body of medical opinion

The thesis set out above seeks to demonstrate that whether a body of opinion is *'responsible'* can be tested by reference to the balance struck between *'risk'* and *'precautions'*. In other words, by adopting the *'Bolam'* test and seeking to examine its internal logic in the instant case, the thesis seeks to fulfil the *'Bolam'* test, not to replace it. And when assessing the parameters within which the balance is struck, the following dicta of McNair J in *Bolam v Friern Hospital Management Committee* [1957] 1 WLR 582 at 586 still apply:

'...The test is the standard of the ordinary skilled man exercising and professing to have that special skill. A man need not possess the highest expert skill; it is well established law that it is sufficient if he exercises the ordinary skill of an ordinary competent man exercising that particular art.'

B Two stages to the analysis

When testing a *'Bolam'* defence, there are in fact two stages:

- the court has to be satisfied that it has jurisdiction to explore the internal logic of an opinion advanced before it, and
- assuming it is so satisfied, it must then assess whether the opinion held up as being *'responsible'* is worthy of the adjective.

These two stages are examined in turn, below.

C Stage 1 — jurisdiction to analyse

It is submitted that there is ample authority to justify the court in undertaking this exercise:

a   *McAllister v Lewisham and North Southwark Health Authority* [1994] 5 Med LR 343. In this 'informed consent' case, Rougier J assessed all the evidence with a view to ascertaining the reasonableness of the decision, the risks of operating, the benefits of operating and the risks of not operating.

b   *Gascoine v Ian Sheridan & Co and Latham* [1994] 5 Med LR 437 Mitchell J said at 444:

'I was referred by counsel for the plaintiff to four further authorities namely — *Hucks v Cole* [1993] 4 Med LR 393, CA; *Sidaway v Board of Governors of the Bethlem Royal Hospital and the Maudsley Hospital* [1985] AC 871, HL; *Knight v Home Office* [1990] 3 All ER 237 (Pill J) and *Bolitho v City and Hackney Health Authority* [1993] 4 Med LR 381, CA.

I find it unnecessary to consider these authorities in detail. The general point which counsel sought to make in the context of these authorities was that I was entitled to look critically at the body of medical opinion which is relied upon by the defendant — I need not (as it were) stand idly by and accept uncritically a body of expert evidence called in support of a course of conduct complained of. Lord Diplock made the point during the course of his speech in *Sidaway* (*ante* p 895):

"... *In matters of diagnosis and the carrying out of treatment the court is not tempted to put itself in the surgeon's shoes; it has to rely upon and evaluate expert evidence, remembering that it is no part of its task of evaluation to give effect to any preference it may have for one responsible body of professional opinion over another, provided it is satisfied by the expert evidence that both qualify as responsible bodies of medical opinion.*"

It follows as a matter of common sense that, simply because a number of doctors gave evidence to the same effect, that does not automatically constitute an established and alternative "school of thought" if, for example, the reasons given to substantiate the views expressed do not stand up to sensible analysis: see *Hucks v Cole ante* (Sachs LJ).'

c   *Defreitas v O'Brien* [1995] 6 Med LR 108 where the Court of Appeal dissected the reasoning of HHJ Byrt QC sitting at first instance, rather than just accept at face value the assertion that the body of opinion held up by the defence was '*responsible*'.

D   Stage 2 — Is the *'body'* truly *'responsible'*?

It is here, it is submitted, that one brings in the balance between 'risk' and 'precautions'. The willingness of the judiciary to recognise that their jurisdiction is not to be usurped by the medical profession is reflected in the following dicta of Lord Diplock in *Sidaway v Board of Governors of Bethlem Royal Hospital* [1985] AC 871 at 895; (ibid)

It is in that context, it is submitted, that one should interpret the following dicta of Morland J in *Smith v Tunbridge Wells Health Authority* [1994] 5 Med LR 334 at 339:

'In my judgment by 1988, although some surgeons may still not have been warning patients similar in situation to the plaintiff of the risk of impotence, that omission was neither reasonable nor responsible.'

In other words, the issue whether a body of medical opinion is *responsible* is an issue for the judge. If he concludes that it is *responsible* and properly held in the context of the facts of the individual case, then it is not for him to choose between that body of opinion and another which can also be justified as *responsible*.

E   The enlargement of the judicial 'tool kit'

The submission, that when the court is assessing whether an opinion is 'responsible', it should look at the balance between '*risk*' and '*precautions*', does not mean that the other '*tools*' developed by the judiciary are to be abandoned. Rather, the 'risk/precautions' point goes to expand the tool kit. Case law demonstrates the existence of additional tools which are set out below in Part 9.

PART 9   THE *'BOLAM'* REPERTOIRE

A   To what does *'Bolam'* apply?

Bolam applies to:

- Treatment: *Whitehouse v Jordan* [1981] 1 WLR 246.
- Diagnosis: *Maynard v West Midlands Regional Health Authority* [1984] 1 WLR 634.
- Disclosure of information and consent: *Sidaway v Board of Governors of Bethlem Royal Hospital* [1985] AC 871 at 895.
- In determining the best medical interests of the patient where a person is mentally incompetent to consent: *F v West Berkshire Health Authority* [1989] 2 All ER 545, HL.

B   Burden of proof

On the plaintiff: *Defreitas v O'Brien* [1995] 6 Med LR 108 per Otton LJ at 114:

'My first observation is that the *Bolam* test does not impose any burden of proof upon the defendant to establish that his diagnosis or treatment would be acceptable to a responsible body of medical opinion. The burden of proof is upon the plaintiff.'

C   Sources of evidence

To assess whether the body of medical opinion is responsible:

- *Literature* — this includes textbooks, articles and scientific publications.

Note: the following guide by McPherson J as to the weight to be attached to literature, given in the case of *Cavanagh v Bristol and Weston Health Authority* [1992] 3 Med LR 49 at 55:

> 'In any event, while text books and articles of this kind can justifiably be used in cross-examination and indeed as support for opinions given in evidence, it is important to note that the context or thrust of an article may not be entirely clear. Furthermore, such articles are no substitute for evidence. Dr Marak did not give evidence in our case and thus was not available for elucidation or for cross-examination. I must bear in mind the several references made, but primarily I must decide this case on the evidence that I have heard.'

- *Case notes*, including results of tests, observations and actual treatment. There is no law directly on the issue: *What status do the case notes have?* It is submitted, however, that they have the following status:

  a *As to the facts related*   They constitute in part a discharge of the duty of the hospital to inform a patient as to what care has been provided: *Lee v South West Thames Regional Health Authority* [1985] 2 All ER 385, [1985] 1 WLR 845; and *Naylor v Preston Area Health Authority* [1987] 2 All ER 353, [1987] 1 WLR 958, CA. See also *Stamos v Davies* (1985) 21 DLR (4th) 507 (Ontario High Court) where Krever J held that there is a duty on a doctor to explain if something has gone wrong, which is consistent with *Gerber v Pines* (1934) 79 Sol Jo 13 where a doctor was held to be in breach of duty by not informing the patient that a needle had been left in her body during an operation.

  b *As to admissions against interest*   They constitute evidence against the defendant in relation to the issue the subject matter of the admission. Such admission can only be withdrawn if the defendant can provide a valid explanation as to how the admission came to be made and why it was wrongly made: *Hollis v Burton* [1892] 3 Ch 226.

  c Note the inferences which may be drawn from the absence of case records, as set out in the judgment of Curtis J in *Parry v North West Surrey Health Authority* [1994] 5 Med LR 259.

- *Expert opinion evidence*   See the techniques for evaluation set out in *Loveday v Renton* [1990] 1 Med LR 117 and in the *Ikarian Reefer* [1993] 2 Lloyd's Rep 68.

D The relevance of the size of the body of opinion

This point was discussed in *Defreitas v O'Brien* [1995] 6 Med LR 108, CA. Otton LJ said at p 115:

> '... There was evidence before the learned judge which he clearly accepted to justify his conclusion that a small number of tertiary specialists could constitute a responsible body of medical opinion. It was a matter for the learned judge to assess whether or not he accepted the evidence as to what that opinion was. He clearly did. The issue whether or not to operate could not be determined by counting heads. It was open to him to find as a fact that a small number of specialists constituted a responsible body and that the body would have considered the first defendant's decision justified, or more succinctly, as the learned judge put it, that the plaintiff had failed to discharge the burden of proof that the first defendant was negligent in operating on the second occasion.'

E State of knowledge

The standard of skill and care is determined by reference to the current state of knowledge. Advances in medical science or medical knowledge between the date of the alleged negligence and the date of trial should be ignored when determining whether the defendant exercised reasonable skill and care: *Roe v Minister of Health* [1954] 2 QB 66. Per Denning LJ at 84: 'We must not look at the 1947 accident with 1954 spectacles'.

F Standard of care by reference to position held

The standard is objective and is to be construed in the light of the status of the position held and not the personality holding it: *Junor v McNicol* (1959) Times, 26 March, HL. Thus:

- A specialist is to be judged by the standards of that specialty: *Maynard v West Midlands Regional Health Authority* [1984] 1 WLR 634; *Sidaway v Board of Governors of Bethlem Royal Hospital* [1985] AC 871 at 895. It is therefore not relevant that because of lack of experience, ability or knowledge the standard could not in fact have been reached by any particular practitioner: *Jones v Manchester Corpn* [1952] 2 QB 852, [1952] 2 All ER 125. A novice must recognise his limitations and seek instructions or refuse to undertake work he is not competent to do. In certain cases it may well be negligent not to obtain a second opinion: *Payne v St Helier Group Hospital Management Committee* [1952] CLY 2442, and *Bova v Spring* [1994] 5 Med LR 120.

- The more skilled a position that a person holds, the more that will be demanded of him: *Ashcroft v Mersey Regional Health Authority* [1983] 2 All ER 245 247c–e per Kilner-Brown J:

  'The question for consideration is whether on a balance of probabilities it has been established that a professional man has failed to exercise the care required of a man possessing and professing special skill in circumstances which require the exercise of that special skill. If there is an added burden, such burden does not rest on the person alleging negligence; on the contrary, it could be said that the more skilled a person is, the more the care that is expected of him. It is preferable in my judgment to concentrate on and to apply the test which has long been established in the law and to avoid all commentary and gloss.'

- A hospital specialising in tropical diseases will be judged by the standards expected in tropical medicine generally and not necessarily in specific modes of infection; *Redmayne v Bloomsbury Health Authority* (31 January 1992, unreported), QBD per Garland J.

G   Standard of care and hospital organisation

- The hospital authority must properly supervise its own staff: *Wilsher v Essex Area Health Authority* [1988] AC 1074;
- the hospital authority must provide a proper system of organisation and co-ordination of skilled staff and a proper system of medical care: *Wilsher* [1988] 1 All ER 871;
- such a system includes a duty to take reasonable care not to injure the treating doctor's health by requiring him to work so many hours that his health is undermined: *Johnstone v Bloomsbury Health Authority* [1992] QB 333. Per Stuart-Smith LJ:

  'Mr Beloff's suggested solution was that if a potential house officer thought that he could not perform the hours required, he should not take the job. Although the principle that if you cannot stand the heat in the kitchen you should get out, or not go in, may often be a sound one, it would have serious implications if applied in these circumstances. Any doctor who wishes to practice has to serve at least one year as a house officer in a hospital; the NHS are effectively a monopoly employer. Is the aspiring doctor who has spent many years in training to this point to abandon his chosen profession because the employer may exercise its power to call upon him to work so many hours that his health is undermined? I fail to see why he should not approach the matter on the basis that the employer will only exercise that power consistently with its duty to have proper regard to his health and safety. The fact that one doctor may have less stamina and physical strength than another does not mean that he is any less competent at his profession.'

- Patients are to be protected from the risk of infection while in hospital: *Heafield v Crane* (1937) Times, 31 July.

PART 10   SYNTHESIS

A   How should one instruct a medical expert on liability/causation?

When advising, should not medical experts be asked to address the following issues in the context of the medical treatment and/or diagnosis which is criticised?

- risk;
- precautions;
- where the balance should be struck.

A model letter of instruction to demonstrate this synthesis is set out at p 16. Further, the '*risk*' versus '*precautions*' approach affords one the means logically to articulate a claim and to analyse a *Bolam* defence.

B   The relevance of this approach to the regime of 'conditional fees'

Given the regime of conditional fee agreements, such an approach generates the potential to a plaintiff to continue with the action, despite the appearance of there being ranged against him or her, a responsible body of medical opinion.

C   A new approach to medical reporting

The reports of the expert as to liability should set out
the issues with sufficient succinctness and clarity that
the investigating lawyer should be able to assess
whether a stance taken by the defendant doctor is
realistically tenable. Further, such an analysis allows
the court to take into account developments being
made in medicine because such developments
constitute *precautions* capable of being taken: they
constitute a factor to be cast into the balance as against
risk, thereby enabling the judge to make a common
sense decision as to the merits of how the balance
between *risk* and *precautions* was in fact struck.

PART 11   MODEL SKELETON ARGUMENT

Note:

1 It is an 'Athetoid Cerebral Palsy' claim.

2 The case is fictitious.

3 The names of witnesses and experts are referred to as letters of the alphabet, to avoid any accidental reference to an existing medic.

4 The 'Skeleton' demonstrates how to articulate forensically the argument of '*risk*' versus '*precautions*'.

5 The 'Skeleton' also seeks to demonstrate how to use *Joyce v Wandsworth Health* with particular reference to the interface between *Bolam* and '*Causation*'.

1997 D No 123
IN THE HIGH COURT OF JUSTICE
QUEEN'S BENCH DIVISION

BETWEEN:

<table>
<tr><td></td><td>JOHN DOE</td><td>Plaintiff</td></tr>
<tr><td></td><td>[A minor suing by her father and
Next Friend, Richard Roe]</td><td></td></tr>
<tr><td></td><td>and</td><td></td></tr>
<tr><td></td><td>BARCHESTER HEALTH TRUST</td><td>Defendant</td></tr>
</table>

PLAINTIFF'S SKELETON ARGUMENT

INTRODUCTION:

This is a split trial. Liability and causation.

There is listed immediately following [if relevant] an application for an interim payment.

Colour Code for the trial bundles:

- **Red:** Pleadings.
- **Blue:** Witness statements.
- **Green:** Medical records.
- **Yellow:** Plaintiff medical expert evidence [names of experts and their speciality recited on front of file].
- **Orange:** Defence medical expert evidence [names of experts and their speciality recited on front of file].

THE SKELETON ARGUMENT:

The Plaintiff was born at **12.05pm** on 1 June 1994.

There is no dispute that he suffers from Athetoid Cerebral Palsy, ie damage to the basal ganglia — the deep grey matter of the brain.

Equally, there is no dispute that this was caused by his brain being deprived of oxygen.

The primary issues are:

a   **First:** Up to what time would/should the mother have been delivered?

b   **Second:** Up to that time would John have avoided permanent brain damage?

I take these in turn:

FIRST PRIMARY ISSUE — UP TO WHAT TIME WOULD/SHOULD THE MOTHER HAVE BEEN DELIVERED?

There would appear to be no dispute in relation to the following:

a   The time frame for the Court to consider is from **11.00am** to **12.10pm** on 1 June, a period of about 70 minutes.

b   Throughout that period, the labour up to and including delivery was handled exclusively by a midwife, *Miss MMM*, whose statement is at file divider 6 in the blue file.

c   At no stage until after delivery were the following called:

    i   An obstetrician, or

    ii   A paediatrician.

d   The partogram — the chart which sets out a graphic presentation of the progress in labour — shows the foetal heart rate seriously dipping at and shortly after **11.00am** [See Divider marked '6–8' in the green file].

e   A Cardio-Tocograph Trace (CTG) was applied at **11.09am**. That trace shows (as it is intended to do):

    i   **Cardio:** The foetal heart beat;

    ii   **Toco:** The maternal uterine contractions.

    The purpose of the CTG machinery is to apprise the midwife of the state of the foetal heart and to alert her to any abnormality in its rate and rhythm. [The relevant trace is in Divider 2, green file.]

f   After the trace was applied, there were two 'dips' before about **11.19am**. They are what is sometimes called 'Type II' dips and are more recently referred to medically as 'late decelerations'. This is explained in more detail in the 'Appendix' to this skeleton.

g   Full dilation of the maternal cervix was diagnosed at **11.30am** (although full dilation may have been achieved earlier). The significance of full dilation is:

    i   Full dilation marks the beginning of what is called the 'second stage of labour'.

    ii   The cervix is no longer providing any resistance to the passage of the baby.

h   From **11.38am** to the end of the trace the foetal heart is demonstrating a persistent bradycardia [see Appendix] between pushes. This is an indication of persistent interruption of oxygen delivery to the placenta and foetus. Such interruption seriously increases the likelihood that the foetal brain is being deprived of oxygen. [**Note:** The trace finishes at about noon, ie about 5 minutes before delivery].

i   The Plaintiff was delivered at **12.05pm** with an **Apgar Score** of 2 at 1 and 4 at 5. [This system of scoring was developed by *Virginia Apgar*, to provide a ready means of assessing the condition of the baby at birth, with particular reference to whether there is a need to resuscitate.]

On the question of *liability* the issues appear to be:

a   **First:** *As to midwifery care:*
   i   Should the midwife have called the obstetrician?
   ii   If yes, when?
b   **Second:** *Had the obstetrician been called:*
   i   What in fact would have happened: See *Newell v Goldenberg* (16 March 1995, unreported) per Mantell J, and *Joyce v Merton Sutton & Wandsworth Health Authority* [1996] PIQR P121.
   ii   What would have been '*Bolam*' negligent not to happen? See *Joyce* (ibid) and *Bolitho v City and Hackney Health Authority*.

On the first primary issue, the respective arguments for the parties are:

1   For the Plaintiff:

a   The obstetrician should have been called by **11.19am**.
b   As a matter of fact, that obstetrician would have been the Consultant Obstetrician on duty, *Ms NNN*. She was present in the hospital.
c   Upon her arrival (which would have been within a few minutes of **11.19am**) she would have checked the foetal heart rate and examined the cervix to establish whether or not the mother had reached the second stage of labour.
d   Had she been so called, she would have been particularly concerned about the foetal state in view of the abnormal foetal heart rate pattern.
e   Having by **11.30am** established full dilation, she would then have made ready to do an urgent forceps delivery if required at any time after that.
f   Given the CTG trace at and after **11.38am** had she not already delivered the mother, she would have delivered her by **11.45am**.

2   For the Defence:

a   There is a dispute within their own expert evidence:
   i   Their midwife expert (**AG** — Divider 3 in the orange file) contends that the obstetrician should have been called only at **1145am** and by then it would have been too late to deliver much before noon.
   ii   The Defence Obstetricians (**Messrs XX and YY**, in dividers 1 and 2 of the orange file) accept that the obstetrician should have been called and would have been in attendance by **11.30am**.
b   The defence obstetric experts go on to contend:
   i   The obstetrician would have undertaken a vaginal examination and found full dilation.
   ii   Given full dilation, the obstetrician would have waited to see if the mother would deliver spontaneously.
   iii   That obstetrician would not have opted for a delivery by forceps until **11.43/11.45am**.
   iv   Having made that decision to deliver by forceps that doctor would then have had to prepare for a forceps delivery and anaesthetise the mother.
   v   Given the period during which that obstetrician would have waited for a spontaneous delivery coupled with the additional time to prepare for a forceps delivery, the baby would not have been born until **11.55am**.

vi   Had she been born at **11.55am**, then the Defence expert on 'causation' [Dr Z — Divider 4 in the orange file] contends that it cannot be proved that the baby would have escaped permanent brain damage.

The Plaintiff invites the court to reject the Defence case on this primary issue, on 2 separate bases:

1   First ground for rejecting the defence case — on the facts: As a matter of fact the Court is entitled to assess what would have happened had the doctor been called before **11.30am** [See *Joyce* (ibid)]

a   The doctor who would have been called was *Ms KKK*, a Consultant Obstetrician. [Her statement is Divider 7 in the blue file.]

b   She was highly qualified, being both a physician and an obstetrician. Her entry in the Medical Directory CD Rom for 1997 is set out on the page following the Appendix to this Skeleton.

c   Given her qualifications the court can draw the inference that had she been in attendance there was no way she would have failed to deliver the mother by **11.45am**.

d   Equally the court can draw the inference that if at **11.30am** she had adopted a 'wait-see' policy, she would have at the same time ensured that all was ready for an urgent forceps delivery if required. This point is expressly made in the report of *Professor ZZZ* at paragraph 38.6 [see Divider 1 of the yellow file]. This point is also expressly made in the short supplemental reports of Plaintiff obstetric experts *Mr AA* and *Mr BB*. The point is implicit in the primary reports of *Mr AA* and *Mr BB* which are at Dividers 2 and 3 of the yellow file. See *Mr AA* at page 7: '. . . the baby would have been born by about **11.45am**, thus avoiding a further 20 minutes of hypoxia'. Also see *Mr BB* at P13: 'Had *Ms KKK* seen the CTG at **11.41am** . . . there can be no doubt that she would have proceeded with an operative vaginal delivery . . . *Ms KKK* would have delivered the baby within a minute or two, and certainly by **11.45am** at the latest.'

e   In her statement *Ms KKK* does not cover the issue what she would have done had she been in attendance at between **11.25/11.30am** and **11.45**. This is significant for 2 reasons:

i   **First:** The issue is directly raised in the pleadings. See paragraph 4(b) of the Amended Statement of Claim:

> *'Steps which should have been taken by the midwife: Urgently securing an obstetric opinion [Had such a doctor been called, he or she would have come with expedition, undertaken a vaginal examination and delivered the plaintiff by forceps prior to her sustaining irreversible brain damage.]'*

ii   **Second:** By reference to the following dicta of Hobhouse LJ in *Joyce* at page P152 this is a legitimate argument for the Plaintiff to run:

> *'Thus a plaintiff can discharge the burden of proof on causation by satisfying the court either that the relevant person would in fact have taken the requisite action (although she would not have been at fault if she had not) or that the proper discharge of the relevant person's duty towards the plaintiff required that she take that action. The former alternative calls for no explanation since it is simply the factual proof of the causative effect of the original fault.'*

That **Ms KKK** would have been in attendance from **11.30am** is however conceded by the Defence obstetric expert, **Mr PPP** who inter alia says on page 4 of his report [yellow divider 2 in orange bundle]:

> '. . . Had she called the resident Consultant obstetrician, that doctor would have been present by **11.30am**. It is likely that she, the Consultant, would then have carried out a vaginal examination and that she would have confirmed full dilation at **11.35am** and then waited in the room to assess events as they unfolded.'

2   Second ground for rejecting the Defence case on liability — 'Bolam' negligence:

a   There was an increasing risk of catastrophic brain damage. That was apparent from:

   i   the foetal heart rate at and shortly after **11.00am** dipping to 100 bpm as shown on the partogram;

   ii   the late decelerations shown on the CTG between **11.09am** and **11.19am**;

   iii   the further late decelerations up to **11.37am**;

   iv   the persistent bradycardia commencing at about **11.37/11.38am** and thereafter.

b   Brain damage of the athetoid variety in the term infant is a well known consequence of severe oxygen deprivation of the foetal brain prior to delivery.

c   The precautions capable of being taken to avoid that catastrophe were simple: A forceps delivery at or shortly after full dilatation.

d   Once there is full dilatation, there is no obstruction or resistance to a delivery by forceps. Thus:

   i   delivery could have been readily achieved at **11.30am**;

   ii   but if the obstetrician chose to wait for a spontaneous delivery, the time spent waiting erodes the buffer of safety. The more that such buffer of safety erodes, the more ready one must be to deliver as a matter of urgency. Hence, it is submitted, the ease with which the Court can draw the inference that had the decision been made not immediately to deliver at **11.30am**, the contingency plan would have been immediate preparation for a forceps delivery if that proved immediately to be necessary as a matter of urgency (and the trace at **11.38am** indeed showed a forceps delivery immediately to be necessary as a matter of urgency).

e   The Plaintiff's experts on clinical causation [**Drs RRR, SSS** and **TTT** — Dividers 5, 6 and 7 of the yellow file] were originally of the view that the baby would have escaped permanent brain damage if delivered by **11.50am**. They have on further consideration come to the view on the balance of probabilities that this time can properly be pitched at **11.55am**. **Dr ZZZ** for the Defence argues that by **11.55am**, the prospect of some damage is such that the Plaintiff cannot prove her case on this issue on the balance of probabilities. **Submitted:** If the margin of damage/no damage is so fine (a matter of moments, rather than minutes) then there is an overwhelming duty on the hospital to deliver well before that margin of catastrophe arises.

Putting this another way: balancing the obvious risk of catastrophe against the means capable of being taken to avoid it, the plaintiff contends that any opinion which supports delay beyond delivery at **11.45am** is not an opinion which stands up to rational analysis: see for example Roch LJ in *Joyce* at P140:

'. . . In the present case, the question was not whether Dr Stewart had omitted to re-explore the artery but whether his decision not to re-explore because there was a palpable pulse, albeit of small volume, was in accordance with accepted clinical practice and *whether that clinical practice stood up to analysis*.' [My emphasis].

SECOND PRIMARY ISSUE — UP TO THAT TIME WOULD JOHN HAVE AVOIDED PERMANENT BRAIN DAMAGE?

1   **Preliminary point:**

a   On this issue, the Defence rely on one expert, the paediatric neurologist, *Dr ZZZ*.

b   **Submitted:** His opinion is based on the premise that delivery would not have taken place until **11.55am**. He says on page 32 of his report [Divider 4 — orange file]:

> '. . . *the expert obstetrician and midwifery reports and the relevant witness statements make it clear . . . that appropriate medical management could only have enabled John to have been delivered some ten minutes sooner than she was.*'

c   **Thus further submitted:** If that medical opinion is not accepted by the court, *Dr ZZZ's* opinion ceases to have relevance. His opinion is dependent upon the defence obstetric evidence.

The following matters are advanced without prejudice to that submission.

2   **The respective cases:**

a   **Plaintiff:**

   i   In their initial reports, the Plaintiff's experts on this issue expressed the opinion that had the Plaintiff been delivered by **11.50am** she would have escaped permanent brain damage [Dividers 5, 6 and 7, yellow file].

   ii   After exchange of expert evidence, and after further review of the case, they have served supplemental evidence which volunteers the following opinion: That on the balance of probabilities, the Plaintiff would have escaped permanent brain damage had she been delivered by **11.55am**.

b   **Defence:** Given the Defence obstetric case that the Plaintiff would not in any event have been delivered until **11.55am** even if proper care had been provided, it cannot be proved that at that time she would have escaped permanent brain damage.

The grounds for the Plaintiff expert opinion that the Plaintiff would certainly have escaped permanent brain damage by **11.50am** and would probably have escaped it by **11.55am** are:

a   The Plaintiff suffers only from mild athetosis. This is clear from a video film which is available to be shown to the Court. Drs *RRR*, *SSS* and *TTT* will contend that it is difficult to understand clinically how the Plaintiff could have any less damage than she has, and still be damaged.

b   There is preserved cortical function (ie intellect).

c   No meconium was passed at birth.

d   The foetus suffered from no more than moderate acidosis easily capable of correction [this suggests that oxygen starvation had not been going on for more than a short period].

e   There is no evidence of multi-organ involvement [this goes to the issue of how long the foetus was actually suffering from hypoxia. The absence of multi-organ involvement is evidence of a short lived episode of oxygen starvation].

f   The Plaintiff resuscitated reasonably quickly which is corroborated by the Apgar scores.

g   The Plaintiff was a term baby and was well developed at birth. She would have been expected to have reasonable reserves, to compensate for oxygen starvation.

h   Had the Plaintiff been delivered earlier at 11.50am or 11.55am, she would not have suffered the depression [or that degree of depression] at birth which she did suffer at 12.05pm, which generated the risk of further brain damage before resuscitation.

i   Adequate resuscitation was not started until about 5 minutes after the delivery. Thus a further period of 5 minutes would have been added to the period of asphyxia. Thus had there been delivery at 11.55am, about *15 minutes* of asphyxia would have been avoided [ie between 11.55am and 00.10pm], *not* 10 minutes

APPENDIX 1

1   Late deceleration/Type II dip:

a   *Definition:* A transient fall in the foetal heart rate shown on the 'cardio' trace where the lowest point reached is at least 15 seconds after the peak of the contraction, shown on the 'toco' trace.

b   *Explanation:* Interference of oxygen delivery to the placenta and consequently to the foetus.

c   *Implication:* This constitutes an abnormal appearance of the foetal heart rate and is an indication of potential risk of the brain of the foetus being deprived of oxygen.

2   Medical terms:

- *Bradycardia:* Slowing of the heart rate.
- *Cephalic:* Of the head.
- *Hypotonic:* Floppy
- *Uterine cervix:* Exit gate of the womb.

Chapter 6

The clinical negligence scheme for trusts

PART 1   THE CONTEXT

In his foreword to the first edition of a major textbook on medical negligence, Lord Bridge of Harwich said:

> 'Litigation in the field of medical negligence continues regrettably to grow in volume. The growth is probably attributable to two principal causes; first, the greater awareness of patients of their legal rights and a greater willingness to enforce them; secondly, the ever increasing sophistication of medical procedures. It is ironic but perhaps inevitable that the further advances medical science makes in being able to offer potential cures for conditions previously incurable or fatal the more the medical profession lays itself open to attack in respect of the mistakes which can occur in the highly complex and delicate procedures necessary to make the cures effective.'

This was written in 1990 and it is probably even more true today as medicine becomes ever more sophisticated and as patients' expectations continue to grow.

The cost of such claims in 1995/96 was £150m, compared to £53m in 1990/91.

The result of this changing trend is that there has been a rising cost of clinical negligence claims. Even if the incidence of claims remained at today's rate there would be rising expenditure on litigation because of the lengthy time-lag involved in settling claims already being processed. Projections indicate that the figure could be as high as £600m by the turn of the century.

About 5,000 claims are settled or adjudicated each year, but it is thought that the number of settlements is matched by the number of new claims entering the system.

Given this number of claims and the level of expenditure it is clearly in the interests of the NHS and the public that clinical negligence claims are handled as effectively as possible. To this end the NHS Executive have put in place a number of key changes in the organisation and management of clinical negligence claims.

In terms of the numbers of clinical negligence claims, it is estimated that there are currently about 20,000 claims outstanding against the NHS, of which about 2,500 are thought to have a value in excess of £100,000.

PART 2   THE NATIONAL HEALTH SERVICE LITIGATION AUTHORITY (NHSLA)

The National Health Service Litigation Authority (NHSLA) came into existence in November 1995 and is constituted as a Special Health Authority under the National Health Service Litigation Authority (Establishment and Constitution) Order 1995 and pursuant to s 21 of the National Health Service and Community Care Act 1990.

Under s 21 (1) of the National Health Service and Community Care Act 1990 the Secretary of State has power to establish a scheme whereby NHS Trusts may make provision to meet 'liabilities to third parties for loss, damage or injury arising out of the carrying out of the functions of the bodies concerned'. The Act further provides under s 21(4) that 'where a scheme provides for it to be administered by the Secretary of State, a health authority or NHS Trust shall carry out such functions in connection with the administration of the scheme by the Secretary of State as he may direct'. Accordingly the NHSLA was established to administer on behalf of the Secretary of State the following:

- Existing Liabilities Scheme (ELS)
- Clinical Negligence Scheme for Trusts (CNST)
- Former Regional Health Authority liabilities.

A   The Clinical Negligence Scheme for Trusts (CNST)

Introduction

The NHSLA administers the voluntary scheme known as the Clinical Negligence Scheme for Trusts (CNST). Its membership comprises 385 NHS Trusts, 90% of the Trusts in England. The CNST provides cover for incidents which occurred after 1 April 1995. Membership of the scheme is determined by the National Health Service (Clinical Negligence Scheme) Regulations 1996 (SI No 251).

Why was the CNST established?

The creation of NHS Trusts in 1991 resulted in their being responsible for the settlement of clinical negligence claims. For all Trusts the highest claims form the majority of the costs and are the most infrequent and least predictable; for example, an acute Trust may face more than one claim in excess of £1m in any one year. Similarly, several claims over £50,000 would be just as damaging for smaller Community or Ambulance Trusts. At that time a Trust could either settle a claim from its annual income or borrow against its External Financing Limit. There was concern that in time the effect of having to meet the costs of settlements may have limited an individual Trust's ability to provide for planned improvements in patient care and ultimately may have threatened its financial viability.

As a result of the real concerns of Trusts, the CNST was created to protect Trusts specifically against the adverse effects of the larger and relatively infrequent clinical negligence claims and to provide a mechanism for smoothing the financial risk based on the principles of mutuality. Equally the CNST is not centrally funded and Trusts must expect, over a period of years, to meet the full costs of their clinical negligence liabilities. The scheme will, however, allow for greater certainty in budgeting and planning by protecting against the impact of an extremely large settlement, or a cluster of settlements in any year.

> *It is not designed to protect against small claims for which self insurance is the recommended means of funding.*

Aims and objectives of the Scheme

The aims and objectives of the scheme are as follows;

- *Improved budgeting and planning*   By joining and remaining a member of the scheme, Trusts are exchanging an unknown, random and extremely variable liability, clinical negligence, into a less variable and reasonably predictable liability, their contribution.
- *Protection against larger claims*   Under the Scheme members are protected from a large run of claims which might put severe pressure on the Trust's financial position.
- *Mutuality*   Since the Scheme embraces the mutual concept, public money is kept in the public sector. In addition it is non-profit making and the contributions are used to meet the needs of its members and to cover overheads.
- *Claims management*   It is the intention to improve the quality of claims management within the NHS.

- *Risk management*   For the first time there are a set of co-ordinated specific and achievable risk management standards in place. The standards ensure that risk management is conducted in a focused, planned and effective manner which is beneficial for patient care.
- *National database and educational role*   In due course, the Scheme will build a clinical negligence database which will be of considerable educational value to members and to the NHS.
- *Pay As You Go Funding*   The Scheme has been set up on the basis of 'Pay As You Go Funding' with an immediate advantage that liabilities are not pre-funded.

> *Large amounts of public money are not, therefore, tied up in anticipation of liabilities that may mature in future years which leaves maximum funds available for patient care.*

How will the Scheme meet its objectives?

The way in which the Scheme will meet its aims and objectives is summarised in figure 1:

Figure 1:

Objectives	How Scheme will meet its objectives
Improve quality of care	• Contributions linked to risk management • Proposals for development of clinical practice protocols and guidelines
	• Improvements in communication with patients through education • Improved financial planning
Minimise the risk that patient care in a particular community is jeopardised by a large settlement against its Trust	• Limits the financial exposure of Trusts to adverse awards and settlements • In-built aggregate protection for serial claims (excess of 2% of total income)
Minimise the cost of clinical negligence by reducing incidents of negligence and reduce the costs of litigation	• Development of best practice in claims and risk management • Concentration of expertise in the handling of high claims • Far-ranging educational and risk management programme
Maximise the incentive for Trusts to improve cost of effective clinical risk and claims management	• Achievable objectives for risk and claims management leading to reduction in contributions

Objectives	How Scheme will meet its objectives
Minimise incentives for defensive medicine	• Development of good practice guidelines and protocols • Dissemination of information and educational programme
Spread costs of individual Scheme members more evenly over time	• Financially sound, equitable design

How does the Scheme operate?

The Scheme operates by pooling contributions from members. The Scheme only collects enough money each year, by way of contributions, to pay the actual costs, damages and defence costs which will fall due to be paid in that year (ie Pay As You Go Funding). Contributions are set based on actuarial advice and reflect the type of NHS Trust involved and its range of services. Later it will be possible to determine contributions based on claims history.

Figure 2 shows the circumstances in which clinical negligence claims would be covered.

Figure 2:

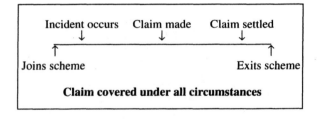

Thus if an incident occurs, and a claim is made and settled during the membership period, then the claim is covered. Alternatively, if a Trust leaves the Scheme before settlement, then the Trust would not be entitled to any benefits from the Scheme.

A basic principle of the Scheme is that members should always contribute towards each claim settlement. By retaining a portion of the liability for each claim (the excess) the Trust's contributions to the scheme will be reduced to take account of the excess chosen. There is also an ultimate threshold that is linked to the excess chosen. For claims that are settled below the excess, the Trust will meet all expenses. For those above this level the Trust pays 20% thereafter up to the ultimate threshold, ie the Scheme contributes 80% of the claim between the excess and the ultimate threshold. Above the ultimate threshzold the scheme contributes 100% of the balance of any claim. The way these benefits are structured is shown in figure 3.

Figure 3:

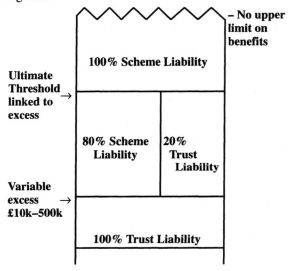

What are the arrangements for claims management?

In order to strike a balance between the autonomy of individual Trusts and equity among members, it is necessary to demonstrate that members' contributions are not going towards the settlement of claims which result from poor claims management. The same requirements exist for the reporting of CNST claims as for ELS claims, namely:

● Trusts will keep the NHSLA informed of progress of claims and will take account of the views of the NHSLA in the handling of claims.

● Trusts will not make any offer to settle except with the approval of the NHSLA.

There is a specific requirement upon Trusts to report claims by category to the Scheme Managers as follows:

Category A claims: these are claims below a Trust's chosen excess and details of these claims are to be reported once a claim is closed.

Category B claims: where a total settlement falls above a chosen excess but below £500k. These claims are to be reported during their life.

Category C claims: where a total settlement is in excess of £500k. These claims are also to be reported during their life.

The Trusts are required to provide key details on each of the claims together with supporting documentation which enables the Scheme Managers to form an early view on the management of a claim and enables them to advise on its subsequent management.

Risk management standards

To promote the operation of satisfactory risk management procedures within Trusts, the scheme has developed a set of risk management standards against which Trusts are assessed. There are ten 'core' standards, together with an additional 'standard 11', dealing with obstetric care. The standards are aimed at ensuring that Risk Management is conducted in a focused and effective fashion which is intended to have a positive contribution towards the improvement of patient care.

The basic standards are as follows:

Standard 1: The Board has a written risk management strategy that makes its commitment to managing clinical risk explicit.

Standard 2: An Executive Director of the Board is charged with responsibility for clinical risk management throughout the Trust.

Standard 3: The responsibility for management and co-ordination of clinical risk is clear.

Standard 4: A Clinical Incident Reporting System is operated in all medical specialities and clinical support departments

Standard 5: There is a policy for rapid follow-up of major clinical incidents.

Standard 6: An agreed system of managing complaints is in place.

Standard 7: Appropriate information is provided to patients on the risks and benefits of the proposed treatment or investigation, and the alternatives available, before a signature on a Consent Form is sought.

Standard 8: A comprehensive system for the completion, use, storage and retrieval of medical records is in place. Record-keeping standards are monitored through the clinical audit process.

Standard 9: There is an induction/orientation programme for all new clinical staff.

Standard 10: A clinical risk management system is in place.

Standard 11: There is a clear documented system for management and communication throughout the key stages of maternity care.

The standards have been designed to:

- be measurable
- be achievable
- increase Clinical Risk Management awareness
- improve standards and procedures
- reduce the level of claims
- ensure that Members' contributions equitably reflect their standards of Clinical Risk Management
- reflect risk exposure
- be capable of progressive development.

B   Conclusion

The creation of the National Health Service Litigation Authority clearly signals a period of change in the handling of claims within the NHS and the priority that is now being given to this issue. The NHSLA has said that it will start by acquiring a solid base of fact and that its decisions as to how to control, manage or audit claims will depend on what it finds to be the facts, particularly as the management of the Scheme unfolds.

Chapter 7

Helpful cases on clinical issues

GUIDE TO THE USE OF THESE TABLES

(1) These tables contain details of all major cases involving judicial pronouncement on clinical medical issues contained in the All England Reports from 1957 to 1988, and thereafter all cases involving clinical issues reported in the Medical Law Reports since their inception up to date to August 1996, Volume 7 Part 8.

(2) The tables do not include

- decisions of jurisdictions other than England and Wales;
- decisions as to quantum only where these turn on the particular facts of the case rather than on matters of principle;
- decisions concerning limitation of actions only.

(3) Cases have been ordered according to the major medical topic involved, and within topics in ascending date order to enable the reader to gain an appreciation of the development of judicial approach to the subject over a period of time;

(4) The forum of the hearing and the medical specialty of the experts used by plaintiff and defendant have been extracted in reliance on the case reports themselves and no representation is made as to their accuracy;

(5) Care must be taken in selecting medical experts on the basis of this table; the expert may now be retired or have since incurred judicial disapproval; in particular reference should be made to the case report itself which in some cases has contained criticism of the expert by the judge which may influence the reader's decision;

(6) The tables should be used as a rough guide only for the practitioner's use in preparing for the client interview, drafting instructions to experts and considering expert reports — it is recommended that the full case report is read before relying on the case, either in advices to clients or in preparing instructions to counsel.

MEDICAL TOPIC	ISSUES	HOW ISSUES DECIDED	EXPERTS USED	QUANTUM (general damages only unless otherwise stated)	CASE NAME AND REFERENCE
ACOUSTIC NEUROMA - Failure to diagnose by General Practitioner - 18 month delay in diagnosis - surgery following diagnosis resulting in death of patient	(1) Whether General Practitioner was negligent in failing to refer the patient presenting with deafness to an ENT Specialist; (2) Whether the surgery ultimately carried out would have failed had it had taken place one to two years earlier.	**NOT NEGLIGENT** (1) No reason at earlier date for doctor to have instituted searching enquiries in view of symptoms then; these were far worse at later date so by then he could not be suffering from middle ear disease; (2) Neuroma was 5 cm by diagnosis; assuming average growth rate of 4mm per annum, was 4.45 cm at time diagnosis could have been made; (3) Plaintiff failed to prove as matter of probability that the operation conditions or prospects would have been significantly different or more favourable in the event of the earlier diagnosis.	Plaintiff:- Dr. Walter Scott, expert GP; Mr. Whatmore, consultant neurosurgeon; Defendant:- Dr. Halle, expert GP; Mr. King, consultant neurosurgeon; Mr. Morris, ENT consultant.	No award made but had been agreed at total of £210,000 without breakdown.	**Richardson v Kitching** [1995] 6 Med LR 257 QBD; Mance J

MEDICAL TOPIC	ISSUES	HOW ISSUES DECIDED	EXPERTS USED	QUANTUM (general damages only unless otherwise stated)	CASE NAME AND REFERENCE
ANAESTHESIA - **Cardiac arrest following surgery under general anaesthetic - irreversible brain damage - plaintiff only intermittently sentient with little appreciation of what had occurred - quantum**	Quantum of damages for pain suffering and loss of amenity in view of plaintiff being incapable of feeling the loss.	**Defendant's appeal to the House of Lords dismissed:-** Damages for loss of amenities were awarded for the fact of deprivation whether the plaintiff was aware of it or not, and in the absence of legislation it would be wrong to reverse this by judicial decision - there is a clear distinction between damages for pain and suffering and damages for loss of amenities - the former depend on the plaintiff's personal awareness of pain, her capacity for suffering; the latter are awarded for the fact of deprivation, whether the plaintiff is aware of it or not.	Not stated.	£20,000 general damages.	**Lim Poh Choo v Camden Health Authority** QBD; Bristow J at frist instance; [1979] 1 All ER 332 Court of Appeal; Lord Denning MR, LJs Lawton and Browne; [1979] 2 All ER 910 House of Lords; Lords Diplock, Simon of Glaisdale and Scarman, Viscount Dilhorne.

ANAESTHESIA - Cardiac and respiratory arrest following surgery - severe anoxic brain damage - tetraplegia - quantum only	Damages for pain, suffering and loss of amenity where plaintiff aware of her condition.	When considering the measure of damages for tetraplegia, one starts with the figure of £90,000 (for 1989) then applies the factors referred to by LJ O'Connor in *Housecroft v Burnett* (1986) 1 All ER 332 at 338, namely on the increasing side, physical pain and any diminution in the powers of speech, sight or hearing, and on the decreasing side, lack of awareness of the condition and a reduction in expectation of life. These figures can cancel each other out, especially where there is severe brain damage.	Not stated.	General damages for pain, suffering and loss of amenity:- £90,000.	**Kralj v McGrath** [1986] 1 All ER 54 QBD; Woolf J

MEDICAL TOPIC	ISSUES	HOW ISSUES DECIDED	EXPERTS USED	QUANTUM (general damages only unless otherwise stated)	CASE NAME AND REFERENCE
ANAESTHESIA - **Brain damage and tetraplegia - cardiac and respiratory arrest following routine surgery - 39 year old woman - quantum only**	(1) what was the applicable multiplier; (2) damages for pain, suffering and loss of amenity in circumstances where the plaintiff was a brain-damaged tetraplegic.	(1) on the facts, where the life expectancy was 15 years, the appropriate multiplier was 10 years; (2) the proper approach is to start with the figure properly awarded for tetraplegia and then apply factors including lack of awareness of condition; where there is a total or substantial degree of lack of awareness on the part of the patient of her condition the damages will be scaled down accordingly.	Plaintiff:- Dr Eases; Dr Jenkins, consultant in rheumatology and rehabilitation; Defendant:- Dr CJ Earl and Dr Anthony Roberts, consultant neurologists.	£90,000 for pain, suffering and loss of amenity.	**Cunningham v Camberwell Health Authority** [1990] 2 Med LR 49 Court of Appeal; LJs Mustill and Farquharson and Sir Michael Kerr

| ANAESTHESIA - Brain damage - hypoxia during recovery following routine operation and general anaesthetic | (1) Whether doctrine of res ipsa loquitur applied; (2) Whether caused by silent regurgitation of gastric content. | CAUSATION ESTABLISHED (1) The defendant health authority accepted that res ipsa loquitur applied but contended that the hypoxia had occurred because of silent regurgitation of gastric content; (2) The defendant's explanation of silent aspiration of gastric content is implausible and there is no instance recorded of silent aspiration leading to brain damage, and only one such case referred to in evidence. Accepted Professor Paynes' evidence that silent regurgitation could not have occurred without laryngeal or broncho spasm being readily apparent. (3) Note that the defendants' experts had (*continued over*) | Plaintiff:- Dr Liddell, consultant anaesthetist; Professors Robinson and Payne, professors of anaesthesia; Defendant:- Dr Taylor, Dr Greig, consultant anaesthetists. | £150,000 agreed - no breakdown. | **Coyne v Wigan Health Authority** [1991] 2 Med LR 301 QBD; Rose J |

MEDICAL TOPIC	ISSUES	HOW ISSUES DECIDED	EXPERTS USED	QUANTUM (general damages only unless otherwise stated)	CASE NAME AND REFERENCE
		failed to make mention in their reports of a cardex entry concerning cyanosis, and neither had addressed their minds as to when hypoxia occurred. Judge found their approach unsatisfactory.			
ANAESTHESIA - Cardiac Arrest - **four year old child suffering cardiac arrest at conclusion of Colonna's capsular arthroplasty for congenital dislocated hip**	(1) Whether doctrine of res ipsa loquitur applied; (2) Whether arrest was caused by paradoxical embolism; (3) Whether decision to reverse anaesthetic and not to continue ventilating with oxygen was wrong.	**NEGLIGENT** (1) A fit child does not arrest under anaesthesia if proper care is taken in the anaesthetic and surgical processes - the doctrine of res ipsa loquitur applied; (2) on the balance of probabilities, the hypothesis of paradoxical embolism as an explanation for the arrest was nowhere near established; (3) there was no clear evidence that in 1978 any alternative procedure would have been adopted in a case such as this.	Plaintiff:- Dr David Hatch and Dr Michael Rosen, consultant anaesthetists; Dr Gerald Graham, consultant cardiac physiologist; Mr J Watson-Farrar, consultant orthopaedic surgeon; Defendant:- Dr Gordon Jackson Rees, consultant anaesthetist; Dr Susan Jones, consultant paediatric anaesthetist.	Liability trial only	**Saunders v Leeds Western Health Authority; Robinson;** [1993] 4 Med LR 355 QBD; Mann J

ANAESTHESIA - General anaesthesia - further administration of caudal block causing 2 days' paralysis - consent form - informed consent	NOT NEGLIGENT		No award made.	Davis v Barking, Havering and Brentwood Health Authority [1993] 4 Med LR 85 QBD:- McCullough J
(1) Whether the plaintiff was entitled to recover damages for assault in the absence of having signed a consent form; (2) Whether the plaintiff's condition was caused by the block, or by underlying condition of multiple sclerosis.	(1) the combination of caudal block with general anaesthetic was in accordance with proper medical practice, its chief advantage being that the plaintiff can recover from the general anaesthetic without feeling any pain, and it is not then necessary to administer strong analgesia such as morphine of pethidine; (2) The analgesic effect being greater than intended or longer to regress than usual, up to a period of 60 hours, or even causing permanent neurological damage, can all happen without negligence by the anaesthetist; (3) caudal blocks are not contra-indicated in patients with multiple sclerosis; *(continued over)*	Plaintiff:- Professors Payne and Robinson, professors of anaesthesia; Dr Paul Lewis, consultant neurologist and neuropathologist and Professor W B Matthews, professor of clinical neurology; Defendant:- Professors Aitkenhead and Rosen, professors of anaesthesia; Dr Michael Swash, consultant neurologist.		

MEDICAL TOPIC	ISSUES	HOW ISSUES DECIDED	EXPERTS USED	QUANTUM (general damages only unless otherwise stated)	CASE NAME AND REFERENCE
		(4) while by trial (1992) it was the normal practice to inform the patient of the intention to administer a caudal block and that they may experience after effects, this was not the usual practice in 1987 and it was not negligent practice then not to have done so; (5) there is no obligation on the surgeon to inform the patient of every step that is proposed; the extent of particularity required must be left to the clinical judgment of the doctor; here there was no realistic distinction between omitting to tell a patient that while she was under a general anaesthetic a caudal block would be administered, and telling the patient that a tube would be placed in her trachea, which would not require informed consent.			

| ANAESTHESIA - Epidural paralysis during labour - causing total permanent paralysis in the saddle area, double incontinence and loss of vaginal sensation - causation only | (1) Whether injury was caused by mistaken injection of toxic substance (plaintiff's case) or by ischaemia, caused either by an embolus which occluded the anterior spinal artery and blocked the blood supply to the conus medullaris, or a sudden and spontaneous interruption of the blood supply to the lower end of the spinal cord or the cauda equina (defendant's case);

 (2) Whether penetration of dura had been established | **CAUSATION ESTABLISHED**

 (1) on the evidence the lesion was in the cauda equina and not the conus or above; as the embolus would have to be in the conus or above the cause could not be embolus;

 (2) spontaneous infarction was ruled out as literature shows that the conus is particularly well vascularised and if it was the cause it would have shown up on the MRI scans;

 (3) on the evidence the doctor had been prepared to cut corners - poor quality of note-taking, depth of epidural not recorded, failure to record top-up of epidural, ignoring protocols;

 (continued over) | Plaintiff:- Professors Aitkenhead and Rosen, professors of anaesthesia; Dr Ivan Moseley, consultant radiologist; Dr Pallis, consultant neurologist - evidence preferred; Dr Paul Lewis, consultant neurologist and neuropathologist;

 Defendant:- Professor Felicity Reynolds, professor of anaesthesia, Dr DB Scott, consultant anaesthetist; Dr Alan Valentine, consultant neuroradiologist; Dr Peter Harvey, consultant neurologist. | Liability only. | **Ritchie v Chichester Health Authority** [1994] 5 Med LR 187

 QBD; HH Judge Anthony Thompson QC |

MEDICAL TOPIC	ISSUES	HOW ISSUES DECIDED	EXPERTS USED	QUANTUM (general damages only unless otherwise stated)	CASE NAME AND REFERENCE
		(4) there was evidence that lists of drugs in drug cabinet beside the theatre were not 100% accurate; judge found that there was same potential for wrong drug to find its way onto the trolley as there was for the wrong drug to be picked up in the operating theatre; (5) raised protein level and presence of xanthochromia in the CSF following myelogram 4 days later were evidence that the dura had been penetrated; (6) in the absence of direct evidence of a neurotoxic injection, judge was prepared to find inferentially that the deficit was a cauda equina lesion caused by inadvertent intrathecal infection of a neurotoxic substance.			

		NOT NEGLIGENT			Early v Newham Health Authority
ANAESTHESIA - Unsuccessful intubation - plaintiff coming to whilst body still partly paralysed resulting in panic and distress	(1) Whether SHO Anaesthetist was negligent in failing to successfully intubate; (2) Whether the procedure laid down by the health authority for dealing with unsuccessful intubation was such that no competent health authority would have adopted it.	(1) There are occasions where even experienced anaesthetists have had unexpected difficulties in intubating patients even though there have been no obvious anatomical abnormalities to be seen in pre-anaesthetic examination - in this case the anaesthetist had not been negligent; (2) Unless a medical procedure is patently unsafe or goes against common practice or usage, a court should not attempt to substitute its views for those of the profession - here the procedure had been put before the division of anaesthesia in the hospital ie 7 or 8 of whom are consultants, who decided it was a proper procedure to follow and minutes of the discussion were kept - the procedure was competent and reasonable.	Plaintiff:- Professor Robinson, professor of anaesthesia; Defendant:- Dr Challands, Dr McAteer and Dr Hargrove, consultant anaesthetists.	Agreed at £6,500 total in the event the plaintiff succeeded - no breakdown provided.	[1994] 5 Med LR 214 QBD; Mr Bennett QC sitting as Deputy Judge of the High Court

MEDICAL TOPIC	ISSUES	HOW ISSUES DECIDED	EXPERTS USED	QUANTUM (general damages only unless otherwise stated)	CASE NAME AND REFERENCE
ANAESTHESIA - Hypoxia followed by cardiac arrest	(1) Whether Anaesthetist was negligent in switching off pulse oximeter which had alarmed on the basis that it was a false alarm; (2) Whether cardiac arrest was caused not by hypoxia but by gas embolism resulting from use of hydrogen peroxide.	**NEGLIGENT** (1) Doctrine of res ipsa loquitur was applicable; (2) The doctor was negligent to switch off the oximeter without establishing why it had gone off; (3) The defendants failed to rebut the inference in that they failed to establish that hydrogen peroxide gas embolism caused during cleaning of wound track was responsible.	Plaintiff:- Professors Payne and Robinson, professors of anaesthesia; Dr. E.M. Grundy; Defendant:- Professors Aitkenhead and Spector, professors of anaesthesia.	Judgment on liability only.	**Glass v Cambridge Health Authority** [1995] 6 Med LR 91 QBD; Rix J

ANAESTHESIA - Hypotensive anaesthesia resulting in development of anterior spinal artery syndrome (ASAS)	NEGLIGENT		£925,000 agreed total - no breakdown provided.	Hepworth v Kerr [1995] 6 Med LR 129 QBD; McKinnon J
(1) Whether anaesthetist was negligent in reducing patient's blood pressure to provide surgeon with blood free operating field; (2) Whether risk of ASAS ought to have been reasonably foreseeable in 1979.	(1) Defendant had by the time of plaintiff's operation used technique on 1500 patients but never attempted to embark on any proper scientific validation of his technique; for such a fundamental departure from traditional wisdom the minimal investigations he carried out after each procedure were inadequate; he had exposed the plaintiff to an unnecessary degree of risk; preponderance of the literature was all one way against the procedure; overwhelming probability was that the technique was unsafe; (2) Although on the expert evidence the specific risk of ASAS as result of technique could not have been reasonably foreseen, the known source of danger i.e. risk of major organ under perfusion, was reasonably foreseeable in 1979 - what happened was but a variant of the foreseeable.	Plaintiff:- Anaesthetics - Professors Hull and Robinson, Dr P Simpson; Dr Paul Lewis, consultant neurologist and neuropathologist; Mr R. McClelland, consultant in spinal injuries; Defendant:- Anaesthetics - Professor Rosen, Dr WR MacRae, Dr Hale Enderby; Mr Ironside, consultant otolaryngologist; Dr Venables, consultant neurologist.		

MEDICAL TOPIC	ISSUES	HOW ISSUES DECIDED	EXPERTS USED	QUANTUM (general damages only unless otherwise stated)	CASE NAME AND REFERENCE
ANAESTHESIA - **Spinal anaesthetic - piercing of dura by guide needle resulting in escape of cerebro-spinal fluid causing severe spinal headaches**	(1) Whether penetration of the dura was caused by negligence; (2) Whether the post-operative care was negligent.	**NOT NEGLIGENT** (1) Found that the doctor had inserted the needle carefully and in inserting the needle some further slight penetration took place despite all reasonable care which penetrated the dura; (2) It was reasonable to persist with conservative treatment; decision not to administer blood patch which would have eased her headaches was within that reasonable band of decisions that were open to competent anaesthetists.	Plaintiff:- Professor Aitkenhead, professor of anaesthesia; Defendant:- Professor Reynolds, professor of anaesthesia.	No award made.	**Muzio v Northwest Herts Health Authority** [1995] 6 Med LR 184 QBD; Deputy Judge Douglas Day QC

ANAESTHESIA - Cholecystectomy under general anaesthetic - left arm used for administration of anaesthetic - lesion of the brachial plexus					Delaney v Southmead Health Authority [1995] 6 Med LR 355 Court of Appeal; LJs Dillon, Butler-Sloss and Stuart-Smith
	(1) Whether the anaesthetist was negligent in placement of patient's arm during surgery lasting 45 minutes where the plaintiff argued that having fractured her clavicle ten years earlier, there had been callous formation which had reduced her thoracic outlet in the left arm; further, that the arm had been hyper-abducted and externally rotated, imposing excessive strain and stretch on the nerve; (2) Whether the anaesthetist was negligent in placement of the arm during surgery lasting 45 minutes.	**At first instance:-** (1) there was no significant narrowing of the thoracic outlet therefore no negligence in using the left arm for the administration of the anaesthetic; (2) the anaesthetist had carried out his usual practice and had not rotated the arm externally; **On appeal - appeal dismissed:-** (1) the judge's findings accorded with the probabilities; (2) even if res ipsa loquitur applied, it was open to the defendant to rebut this either by giving an explanation of what happened which was inconsistent with negligence , or by showing that the defendants had exercised all reasonable care, and the judge was entitled to come to the conclusion that he did as to (*continued over*)	Plaintiff:- Dr Pallis, consultant neurologist; Defendant:- Dr Earl, consultant neurologist.	No award made.	

MEDICAL TOPIC	ISSUES	HOW ISSUES DECIDED	EXPERTS USED	QUANTUM (general damages only unless otherwise stated)	CASE NAME AND REFERENCE
		the position of the arm during the operation, therefore no lack of care. Could not accept that medical science is such a precise science that there cannot in any particular field be any room for the wholly unexpected result occurring in the body from the carrying out of a well-recognised procedure.			
ANAESTHETIC - **Epidural - 1975 - administration of epidural anaesthetic and cortico-steroid by in-dwelling epidural catheter - later development of epidural abscess, followed by meningitis then arachnoiditis then syringomyelia due to infection by staphylococcus aureus, causing severe disablement**	(1) Whether the epidural procedure had caused the infection; (2) Whether the orthopaedic surgeon was negligent in failing to diagnose that abscess was located in the epidural space thus allowing the infection to become established in the epidural space leading to the successive infections; (3) Whether the department of neurology which saw the plaintiff in 1977 was negligent in	NO CAUSATION (1) Staphylococcus aureus is a commensal organism that is normally present on the body; it develops with rapidity and there is a rapid increase in signs and symptoms after the infection has taken root; the absence of such signs in the plaintiff when she was seen 8 days after the procedure in casualty and for a number of days thereafter point strongly against the period of catheterisation as the cause;	Plaintiff:- Dr Hannington-Kiff, consultant anaesthetist; Mr Williams, surgeon; Defendants:- Mr Garfield, neurosurgeon (now retired); Dr Illis, consultant neurologist; Professor Weller, Professor of neuropathology.	No award made.	**El-Morssy v Bristol and District Health Authority** [1996] 7 Med LR 232 QBD COL; Turner J

failing to diagnose syringomyelia, leading to delay in diagnosis till 1989, and whether had it been diagnosed then it would have been susceptible to more effective treatment.	(2) Preferred the defendant's expert evidence that as a matter of high probability there had been no infection in the epidural space and that the abscess had been located paraspinally; (3) The plaintiff had failed to establish that she had meningitis at the time alleged; (4) The plaintiffs' experts' statistical base was insufficient to displace the defendants' experts' evidence that arachnoiditis is often encountered for which there is no ascertainable cause.	

MEDICAL TOPIC	ISSUES	HOW ISSUES DECIDED	EXPERTS USED	QUANTUM (general damages only unless otherwise stated)	CASE NAME AND REFERENCE
ANAESTHETIC AWARENESS - During caesarean section - 1981	Quantum only Appropriate quantum of damages for pain, suffering and loss of amenity where subsequent psychiatric illness.	Where psychiatric illness affected sexual relations with husband; where plaintiff refused to undergo further necessary surgery under general anaesthetic, had problems in bonding with child, proximal insomnia and depression - appropriate award was £12,000 plus cost of psychiatric treatment, taking into account plaintiff's pre-accident psychiatric vulnerability.	Plaintiff:- Professor Robinson, professor of anaesthesia; Dr Downham, consultant psychiatrist; Defendant:- Professor Goldberg, consultant psychiatrist.	£12,000 general damages for pain, suffering and loss of amenity.	**Ackers v Wigan Health Authority** [1991] 2 Med LR 232 QBD; Russell J.

| ANAESTHETIC AWARENESS - During caesarean section - 1985 | Whether the consultant anaesthetist failed to use the proper procedure, failed to exercise skill and judgment in the selection of drugs and failed to monitor levels of anaesthetic agent. | NOT NEGLIGENT (1) Accepted that the anaesthetic technique was generally accepted as suitable for a caesarian section in 1985 and was carried out by the doctor in a careful and competent manner ; rejected plaintiff's experts' evidence on basis that they were long- retired from active practice; (2) On balance of probabilities, the plaintiff's episode of awareness did not occur during the operation but afterwards, in the reversal stage:- (i) her description of events was consistent with events taking place at the reversal (ii) nothing in plaintiff's description exclusively referable to a time at or about the time of birth; *(continued over)* | Plaintiff:- Dr DB Scott, consultant anaesthetist retired 1986; Professor Payne, professor of anaesthesia retired 1987; Dr Walter Braude, consultant psychiatrist; Defendant:- Dr IJ Davies, consultant anaesthetist; Dr Bradley, consultant psychiatrist; Professor Aitkenhead, professor of anaesthesia, Dr BR Wilkie, consultant obstetric anaesthetist. | Not discussed. | **Taylor v Worcester & District Health Authority** [1991] 2 Med LR 215 QBD; McKinnon J. |

MEDICAL TOPIC	ISSUES	HOW ISSUES DECIDED	EXPERTS USED	QUANTUM (general damages only unless otherwise stated)	CASE NAME AND REFERENCE
		(iii) no reference to her hearing her baby cry nor any reference to the sensation of touch or of where people were in the operating theatre; (iv) no clinical signs whatever of pain or distress during the operation - accepted evidence that some clinical signs are to be expected if awareness associated with pain or distress; (v) on technique used, there would have been sufficient anaesthetic cover throughout the operation. Helpful description of normal caesarian section as carried out in 1985 ie operative procedure and anaesthetic substances used. Lengthy discussion of drug concentrations and timing including historical context.			

ANAESTHETIC AWARENESS - **During leg surgery involving deep cutting and drilling to bone**	Quantum only.	Conventional figures for anaesthetic awareness do not apply - there is a difference between incision to the skin and being stitched and deep cutting and drilling to the bone. For the experience on the operating table alone, £5,000 awarded.	Not stated.	£10,000 pain, suffering and loss of amenity.	**Phelan v East Cumbria Health Authority** [1991] 2 Med LR 419 QBD:- Schiemann J
ANAESTHETIC AWARENESS - **Of pre-operative procedures causing mental injury**	(1) Whether Judge entitled on medical evidence to conclude that Plaintiff's memory after she had come round from anaesthetic was likely to be unreliable; (2) Whether Plaintiff would have become unconscious after she received Nitrous Oxide; (3) Whether Plaintiff's memory could only be explained in terms of pre-operative memory.	**APPEAL DISMISSED** (1) Ample evidence that a person's memory, after having received a large number of various types of drugs, would become unreliable; (2) Although sequence pointed on balance of probability towards pre-operative memory, the judge had to weigh up all the other evidence on the case before coming to his decision; (*continued over*)	Not stated.	No award made.	**Jacobs v Great Yarmouth and Waveney Health Authority** [1995] 6 Med LR 192 Court of Appeal LJs Stephenson, O'Connor and Griffiths

MEDICAL TOPIC	ISSUES	HOW ISSUES DECIDED	EXPERTS USED	QUANTUM (general damages only unless otherwise stated)	CASE NAME AND REFERENCE
		(3) A prima facie case had been raised by proving plaintiff had pre-operative awareness, but this had been fully answered by all the evidence in the case. Plaintiff likely to be one of those unfortunate people who do experience some degree of awareness, although there are no signs from which the anaesthetist can recognise what is going on.			
BIRTH INJURY - 1970 - trial of forceps delivery - Kielland's Forceps - severe brain damage due to asphyxia	Whether during the course of delivery the doctor pulled too long and too hard on the child's head, thereby causing the brain damage.	At first instance:- NEGLIGENT - (1) the plaintiff's evidence that she was lifted off the bed could be interpreted as meaning that she was pulled toward the bottom of the bed in a manner inconsistent with a properly carried out trial of forceps; (2) the defendant doctor's evidence that after 5 pulls	Plaintiff:- Professor McLaren and Sir John Stallworthy, professors of obstetrics; Defendant:- Sir John Dewhurst, professor of obstetrics and Dame Josephine Barnes, consultant obstetrician. Also Sir John Peel.	At first instance, £100,000 total - no breakdown.	**Whitehouse v Jordan and another** QBD; Bush J; [1980] 1 All ER 650 Court of Appeal; Lord Denning MR, LJs Lawton and Donaldson [1981] 1 All ER 267 House of Lords; Lords Wilberforce, Edmund-Davies, Fraser of Tullybelton, Russell of Killowen and Bridge of Harwich

there was no further progress meant that he had pulled too long and too hard, causing the head to become wedged or stuck, and this caused the asphyxia;

Court of appeal:- appeal allowed:- if the judge's finding that the doctor pulled too long and too hard was correct, this amounted merely to an error of clinical judgment, and as such was not negligence in law; in any event this was an unjustifiable interpretation of the evidence;

House of Lords:- upheld decision of the Court of Appeal.

MEDICAL TOPIC	ISSUES	HOW ISSUES DECIDED	EXPERTS USED	QUANTUM (general damages only unless otherwise stated)	CASE NAME AND REFERENCE
BIRTH INJURY - **Asphyxia - second twin - delay in delivery of maternity services - 1970**	Whether the health authority was negligent in its organisation and delivery of maternity services, in that they were divided between two sites, one mile from each other, resulting in 68 minute delay in the delivery of the second twin (which had been in a breech position), due to delay in securing the attendance of a suitably qualified medical practitioner.	**NEGLIGENT** Excellent discussion of principles of delivery of a second twin - both sides' experts accepted that:- (i) second twins ought to be delivered as soon as possible after the first and in any event within 20 minutes; (ii) delay in delivery place the unborn twin at risk of oxygen deprivation; (iii) the pulling of the umbilical cord which is normal in the case of single delivery to deliver the afterbirth, is likely to cause damage in the case of uniovular twins because its removal damages the placenta and puts the unborn twin at risk of hypoxia; (iv) uniovular twins share the same placenta and one twin may draw more than its fair share of nutrients at	Plaintiff:- Mr Evan Arthur Williams, consultant obstetrician and gynaecologist; Sir John Stallworthy, professor of obstetrics and gynaecology; Dr Charles Brook, consultant paediatrician; Dr Mary Lindsay, consultant in mental handicap and child psychiatry; Defendant:- Professor Hull and Professor Harris, consultant neonatologists; Professor Symonds and Sir Jack Dewhurst, professors of obstetrics and gynaecology.	Not stated.	**Bull and Another v Devon Health Authority** Judgment handed down on 2/2/1989; not reported till:- [1993] 4 Med LR 117 Court of Appeal:- LJs Slade, Dillon and Mustill.

the expense of the other twin, thus causing oxygen deprivation, known as chronic foeto-foetal transfusion;

HELD:-

(1) In this case the delay in summoning and securing the attendance of the doctor were so substantial as to place upon the defendant the evidential burden of justifying them ie res ipsa loquitur applied;

(2) In cases where a multiple birth was involved, the system in operation had to be operated with a maximum of efficiency or mother and child were at obvious risk; in this case, all the most likely explanations of the failure point strongly either to inefficiency in the system for summoning the assistance of the doctor or to negligence by some individual or individuals in the working of that system - res ipsa applied, and the defendant had failed to to negligence by some

(continued over)

MEDICAL TOPIC	ISSUES	HOW ISSUES DECIDED	EXPERTS USED	QUANTUM (general damages only unless otherwise stated)	CASE NAME AND REFERENCE
		individual or individuals in the working of that system - res ipsa applied, and the defendant had failed to discharge its onus of explaining the delay satisfactorily; (3) any hospital which provides a maternity service for expectant mothers ought to be able to cope with the not particularly out of the way case of a healthy young mother with premature labour with twins.			
BIRTH INJURY - Asphyxia - causing cerebral palsy - tetraplegia - quantum only - where Plaintiff had a life expectancy of 61 years of age and condition had resulted in tetraplegia as well as loss of power of speech	What was the correct level of award:- *(only matters of interest in principle set out here)* (1) where as well as tetraplegia the plaintiff was suffering from loss of power of speech; (2) value of parental care; (3) future parental care given that the father was leaving the home to remarry.	(1) correct level for pain and suffering for tetraplegia was £97,500; loss of speech made this worse and where little improvement expected, award should be increased to £105,000; (2) cost of equivalent care by professional resident carers should be halved, then attendance, mobility and invalid care allowance deducted;	Plaintiff:- Dr Gwilym Hosking, consultant paediatric neurologist; Mrs Rosemary Statham, nursing expert; Touche Ross, forensic accountants; Defendant:- Dr Lewis Rosenbloom, consultant paediatric neurologist; Mrs Tessa Gough, nursing expert.	General damages for pain, suffering and loss of amenity:- £105,000.	**Almond and Almond v Leeds Western Health Authority** [1990] 1 Med LR 370 QBD; Fennell J

(3) on the basis that the plaintiff would live at home until he was 22, the mother should receive £10,000 to compensate her, but the father would not be awarded a sum under this heading.			General damages for pain, suffering and loss of amenity:- £115,000.	**Janardan v East Berkshire Health Authority** [1990] 2 Med LR 1 QBD; McCullough J
BIRTH INJURY - **Asphyxia - causing choreic and athetotic cerebral palsy - mental faculties unimpaired - life expectancy of 55 years - quantum only**	The plaintiff is more fortunate than the typical tetraplegic in that he has some purposeful movement, will acquire bladder and bowel control, and is less prone to infection. He is less well off in that he has no speech, has to contend with the involuntary movements of head, trunk and limbs, has difficulty chewing and swallowing, and a tendency to vomit, and might develop deformities which could require orthopaedic surgery later in life. Also has been deprived of normal childhood and adolescence. Long life expectation will mean he has to experience his *(continued over)*	Dr Nicholas Cavanagh, consultant paediatric neurologist; Professor Roger Robinson, professor of paediatrics; Dr M J Brueton, paediatric gastroenterologist; Mrs Mary Lobascher, clinical psychologist; Mrs Lesley Carroll, paediatric speech therapist; Mrs Joanne Biddle, paediatric occupational therapist; Mrs Isabel Chilton, paediatric physiotherapist; Miss J Harrison, occupational therapist; Mrs Vanessa Wynn-Griffiths, nursing expert; Miss Tessa Gough, nursing expert; Mr WJ Hibbert, rehabilitation specialist; Mr Keith Carter, employment specialist. *(continued over)*		
	Comparison with tetraplegic cases where assessing damages for pain and suffering.			

MEDICAL TOPIC	ISSUES	HOW ISSUES DECIDED	EXPERTS USED	QUANTUM (general damages only unless otherwise stated)	CASE NAME AND REFERENCE
		Therefore given the range of £100,000 and £120,000 disabilities for longer than almost all tetraplegics between plaintiff and defendant valuations, awarded £115,000.	(no indication in judgment as to which were plaintiff and which were defendant experts).		
BIRTH INJURY - Asphyxia - stillbirth - following abortive forceps delivery - quantum only	Quantum where plaintiff of vulnerable personality, following prolonged labour and psychological damage.	(1) It is common ground that any stillbirth will be damaging to the mother who suffers the experience; in this case the stillbirth was particularly damaging to the plaintiff for two reasons:- (i) the variety of inconsistent explanations she was given as to the cause of death; (ii) the fundamental cause of death was mismanagement of labour; (2) she is entitled to compensation for loss of the child and of the satisfaction of bringing the pregnancy to a successful conclusion, and in	Plaintiff:- Dr Bourne, consultant psychiatrist; Defendant:- Dr Hay, consultant psychiatrist.	£12,500 general damages plus £1,250 for layette.	**Grieve v Salford Health Authority** [1991] 2 Med LR 295 QBD; Rose J

				Marsden v Bateman & Others [1993] 4 Med LR 181 QBD; Rose J
		£750 damages for scleroederma and associated neonatal illness.		
	addition, the psychological damage she suffered and its prognosis; (3) in this case due to her vulnerable personality - including prebirth obsession with having a baby - any future pregnancy would be more worrying to the plaintiff; her damage was likely to last four years after the birth; (4) therefore compensation awarded £12,500 general damages.	**CAUSATION NOT PROVEN** (1) serious neonatal neurological damage solely due to hypoglycaemia is a very rare condition indeed, particularly in a full-term infant; (2) coma, apnoea and fits are to be expected if the CNS has been affected - in this case, there was no such evidence; (*continued over*)	Plaintiff:- Dr Barrie, consultant neonatal paediatrician; Professor Corbett, professor of developmental psychiatry and epidemiologist; Dr Kendall, consultant neuroradiologist; Defendant:- Dr Roberton, consultant paediatrician; Dr Rosenbloom, consultant paediatric neurologist.	
IRTH INJURY - Alleged hypoglycaemia - resulting in brain damage - home delivery by general practitioner and midwives	Causation - whether the defendant's admitted negligence in failing to arrange for the child to be admitted to hospital was the cause of her substantial mental disabilities.			

MEDICAL TOPIC	ISSUES	HOW ISSUES DECIDED	EXPERTS USED	QUANTUM (general damages only unless otherwise stated)	CASE NAME AND REFERENCE
		(3) accepted Dr Rosenbloom's evidence that the probability is that the child had a genetic disorder at gene level, even though she had no chromosome deficiency and no family history of genetic disorder. This damage probably occurred during brain development stage of cell migration during the 3rd to 5th month of gestation; (4) but allowed very small claim for scleroedema skin condition and associated neonatal illness caused by failure to refer child earlier to hospital.			

| BIRTH INJURY - Asphyxia - causing cerebral palsy - breech presentation in 1975 | Whether the obstetrics team was negligent in not arranging caesarean section and alternative method of delivery. | NOT NEGLIGENT

Helpful discussion of principles of breech presentation - caesarian section has been the policy choice for many years in America and Scotland. In England, and more particularly in 1975, vaginal delivery was the widespread policy choice in the absence of specific contraindications. CS was then regarded as increasing the risk of maternal fatality and as a potential adverse influence in subsequent pregnancies.

Contraindications in 1975 were signs at the antenatal stage suggesting potential disproportion, typically a large baby, and a small or asymmetric pelvis. At the labour stage, suggested or actual disproportion, lack of progress, particularly arrested labour, significant foetal distress as manifested by foetal heart rate and rhythm and the passage of meconium. Further, deliverer should be sufficiently skilled through acquisition of supervised experience.

(continued over) | Plaintiff:- Mr John Megarry, Mr Donald Menzies, consultant obstetricians and gynaecologists and Professor R W Taylor, professor of obstetrics and gynaecology; Dr Lewis Rosenbloom, consultant paediatric neurologist.

Defendant:- Mr Michael Brudenell and Mr Paul Vinell, consultant obstetricians and gynaecologists and Professor Max Elstein, professor of obstetrics and gynaecology; Professor N B O'Donoghue, professor in paediatrics. | No award made. | **Hinfey v Salford Health Authority**

[1993] 4 Med LR 143 QBD DJ Holland QC |

MEDICAL TOPIC	ISSUES	HOW ISSUES DECIDED	EXPERTS USED	QUANTUM (general damages only unless otherwise stated)	CASE NAME AND REFERENCE
		In this case, was not prepared to find from the records and the circumstances that there was a negligent omission to take heed of the baby's size, or that the doctor delivering the child had breached the relevant standard of care and skill.			
BIRTH INJURY - Asphyxia causing death within 2 days of birth - parental psychiatric injury including nervous breakdown and breakdown of the marriage - causation	Whether causative factor of parental psychiatric condition was shock or grief.	CAUSATION ESTABLISHED (1) the parents clearly passed the first hurdle of proximity of relationship to the defendant ie they were deeply emotionally tied into the birth of their child and the mother was also being physically handled by the defendants; (2) it is plain they have suffered more than grief, distress or sorrow following the death of the child. Each has a form of psychiatric illness ie pathological grief reaction which is not just a slight	Dr Bourne, consultant psychiatrist.	General damages - £32,500 payable to the father - (florid and very severe pathological mourning - nervous breakdown and a full time psychiatric patient ever since) and £17,500 to the mother (serious and persistent pathological mourning).	Tredget and Tredget v Bexley Health Authority [1994] 5 Med LR 178 London County Court; White J

exaggeration of the average mourning process but in each case a serious condition, that of the father being the more severe;

(3) the injuries were caused by "shock" - there was an "event" being the actual birth, with its chaos, or pandemonium, the difficulties of the mother in delivery, the arrival of the child in a distressed condition requiring immediate resuscitation, the short period of the chid's life in intensive care leading to his death. It would be wrong to separate these out and isolate the delivery as the event;

(4) the mother was not to be distinguished from the father, who had watched the delivery, just because she did not see the child at birth and was in pain, sedated and suffering from exhaustion and therefore not fully conscious of what was happening about her.

MEDICAL TOPIC	ISSUES	HOW ISSUES DECIDED	EXPERTS USED	QUANTUM (general damages only unless otherwise stated)	CASE NAME AND REFERENCE
BIRTH INJURY - **Prolonged severe foetal bradycardia during labour involving trial of scar - 69 minute delay between onset of foetal bradycardia and delivery by caesarian section - cerebral palsy**	Whether the Defendant was negligent in conduct of trial of scar and in failing to observe prolonged severe foetal bradycardia.	**NOT NEGLIGENT** (1) the critical time during which fault could be alleged against the defendant was at a time by which the bradycardia had been in progress for 9 minutes; during this period the midwife was absent from the room; (2) from the point of view of forestalling any risk that might arise from trial of scar, her continuous presence was not medically essential - the plaintiffs' criticism has the hallmarks of wisdom in the event; (3) Even if it had been a breach of the standard of care, the plaintiff was unable to prove that a reduction of at most 10 minutes would have materially lessened the disability.	Plaintiff:- Dr Huntingford, and Mr Patel, consultant obstetricians; Dr Hamilton, consultant paediatric neurologist. Defendant:- Dr Michael and Mr Woolfson, consultant obstetricians; Dr Lewis Rosenbloom, consultant paediatric neurologist.	No award made.	**James v Camberwell Health Authority** [1994] 5 Med LR 253 QBD; HH Judge Fawcus

| BIRTH INJURY - Attempted forceps delivery of high head baby - leading to episode of bradycardia causing acute hypoxic ischaemia | (1) Whether Registrar was negligent in leaving case to be managed by midwives;

(2) or in attempting to deliver foetus by forceps delivery;

(3) Whether midwife was negligent in conduct of delivery. | NEGLIGENT

(1) The high head had been a warning sign;

(2) It had been reported to the Registrar but the registrar did not examine the patient and gave the junior doctor instructions to leave the patient for a few hours until the head descended a little, then to give her syntocinon - it would have been appropriate for him to have seen her at some stage, and his failure to do so effectively deprived him of any first-hand knowledge of the patient; he left the whole case to be managed by the midwives with serious consequences;

(3) the risk of an arrested descent existed and would have been present to the mind of the reasonably competent doctor;

(4) the midwife was not entitled to discount the pushing that had occurred before her return, having

(continued over) | Plaintiff:- Mr Sharp and Mr Roger Clements, consultant obstetrician and gynaecologists;

Defendant:- Mr Pearson, consultant obstetrician;

Also Drs Dear and Wyatt, consultant paediatricians. | Liability trial only. | **Parry v Northwest Surrey Health Authority**

[1994] 5 Med LR 259 QBD; HH Judge Curtis |

MEDICAL TOPIC	ISSUES	HOW ISSUES DECIDED	EXPERTS USED	QUANTUM (general damages only unless otherwise stated)	CASE NAME AND REFERENCE
		regard to the trace and the patient's distress; further her assessment of the baby's position was unacceptable - she did not abdominally palpate but relied purely on vaginal examinations and this was unacceptable; the accepted practice is to do an abdominal palpation first and then a vaginal examination; (5) the attempt by the registrar to deliver the child by Kielland's forceps was done at an unacceptably high level and materially contributed to the episode of bradycardia which caused the acute hypoxia-ischaemia.			

BIRTH INJURY - Dyskinetic athetoid cerebral palsy - quantum only	Quantum in a boy of 17 years of age where counsel for the plaintiff argued that £100,000 was appropriate as the plaintiff in the round should be viewed as a tetraplegic; and the defendant argued that the plaintiff was better off in that he could dress and undress, feed himself, attend to bodily functions; bathe, shave and walk a few steps at a time, and his intellectual ability was not severely impaired, and contended for £80,000.	Held:- in such a case the judge could do worse than split the difference; in any event the case Krishnamurthy v East Anglia Regional Health Authority (1985) CLY 959 - a comparable if rather worse case arising from cerebral hypoxia during prolonged labour - would reflect today in a similar award :- £ 90,000. **Judgment includes useful and detailed assessment of general, special and future damages in a CP case.**	Professor Holt, Professor of paediatric development; Dr Barrie, consultant paediatrician.	£674,500 total damages, including £90,000 general damages.	**Nash v Southmead Health Authority** [1994] 5 Med LR 74 QBD; Alliott J
BIRTH INJURY - Hypoxia - suffered by second twin causing brain damage	Whether surgeon was negligent in treating the birth on the basis of longitudinal lie when in fact it was a transverse lie.	**NEGLIGENT** The surgeon ought to have realised the lie was transverse and not longitudinal - preferred the evidence of the plaintiff's experts that the doctor was not acting in accordance with acceptable practice on the Bolam test ie taking it into account.	Plaintiff:- Mr Roger Clements, consultant obstetrician and gynaecologist; Professor Taylor, chair of obstetrics and gynaecology; Defendants:- Mr MacKenzie and Miss Henson, consultant obstetricians and gynaecologists.	Generals to the Estate £52,000; not including £7500 bereavement damages included in specials.	**Bowers v Harrow Health Authority** [1995] 6 Med LR 16 QBD; Sir Michael Davies sitting as a deputy judge of the High Court

MEDICAL TOPIC	ISSUES	HOW ISSUES DECIDED	EXPERTS USED	QUANTUM (general damages only unless otherwise stated)	CASE NAME AND REFERENCE
BIRTH INJURY - Asphyxia caused by tightening of cord around neck leading to cerebral palsy - doctor's failure to attend mother and thereafter to proceed to caesarian section	(1) Whether the doctor had been negligent in failing to attend when informed of tachycardia on the CTG trace by the midwife; (2) Whether had the doctor attended he would have concluded that it was necessary to rupture the membranes and thereafter proceed to a caesarean section.	**NEGLIGENT** (1) The doctor was negligent in failing to attend because he should not have relied on the judgment of the midwife, there was no supervening emergency that prevented him from attending and no responsible medical practitioner would have supported his decision not to attend; (2) It could be inferred from the doctor's failure to attend trial that had he so attended, he would have concluded it was necessary to rupture the membranes, and thereafter to proceed to caesarian section; (3) Excellent assessment of the risks and benefits of carrying out an artificial rupture of the membranes at that time followed by caesarian section; conclusion that on the balance of probabilities, no	Plaintiff:- Mr Anthony Johnson and Mr G J Jarvis, consultant gynaecologists and obstetricians; Defendant:- Mr R R Macdonald and Professor E J Thomas, consultant obstetricians and gynaecologists.	Damages agreed but not stated.	**Wiszniewski v Central Manchester Health Authority** [1996] 7 Med LR 248 QBD Liverpool; Thomas J

					Murphy v Wirral Health Authority [1996] 7 Med LR 99 QBD; Kay J
				Not stated.	
			Plaintiff:- Dr Gibb, consultant gynaecologist; Mr Roger Clements and Mr Johnson consultant obstetricians and gynaecologists; Defendant:- Mr McDonald, consultant gynaecologist; Professor Symonds, professor of obstetrics and gynaecology.		
responsible body of opinion would have decided other than to rupture at that time and proceed to caesarian section; (4) Had caesarian section been performed at that time the cord would not have tightened round the neck during birth and the cerebral palsy would have been avoided.	NEGLIGENT - (1) CTG trace - as at 1984, a reasonably competent midwife or doctor was entitled to conclude that (i) an early deceleration was not in itself of adverse clinical significance but required observation; (ii) a late deceleration was not an adverse sign unless other features were present; and (iii) the loss of beat to beat variation was of significance if it fell below five beats per minute:- in *(continued over)*				
BIRTH INJURY - **1984 - placental abruption - secondary arrest of labour - failure by midwife to summon doctor**	Whether failure to recognise secondary arrest of labour and summon doctor was negligent				

MEDICAL TOPIC	ISSUES	HOW ISSUES DECIDED	EXPERTS USED	QUANTUM (general damages only unless otherwise stated)	CASE NAME AND REFERENCE
		this case, in all but one instance the decelerations were late and there was no loss of variability within the 5 beats per minute variation before 4.10pm, therefore not reasonably necessary for competent midwife to summon a doctor in reliance simply on the foetal heart rate trace before 4.15pm; (2) But there were other factors which suggested that the doctor should be summoned:- it is clear from the literature and the evidence that the first examination should be plotted and that any variation by more than two hours from the expected line has to be viewed as significant - ie a vaginal examination ought to have been carried out at least every two hours so that any such significant variation could be detected:- in this case the next examination was			

delayed for a further fifteen minutes, and this fell below reasonable standards of competence and skill of midwives; (3) on the facts, had a doctor been called at the appropriate time Syntocinon would have been administered in time and the injury would not have occurred. (4) on the basis that the plaintiff would live at home until he was 22, the mother should receive £10,000 to compensate her, but the father would not be awarded a sum under this heading.			**Kerby v Redbridge Health Authority** [1993] 4 Med LR 178 QBD; Ognall J
		Total of £16,607 including £11,500 general damages to mother plus £3,500 statutory bereavement, plus funeral expenses plus £750 general damages to estate of deceased.	
BIRTH INJURY - **Maternal injury -** **Hypoxia of second twin leading to death - maternal depression of moderate severity - quantum of general damages for mother and child**	(1) Measure of general damages to the estate of the deceased baby; (2) Measure of general damages for the mother's pain and suffering; (3) Whether the mother was entitled to recover for dashed hopes.	(1) the baby only lived for 3 days, sedated and on a life support system, with no insight into his condition, therefore could award no more than £750; (2) The mother was entitled to recover damages for *(continued over)*	Not stated.

MEDICAL TOPIC	ISSUES	HOW ISSUES DECIDED	EXPERTS USED	QUANTUM (general damages only unless otherwise stated)	CASE NAME AND REFERENCE
		(i) the rigours of an additional pregnancy to make up for the lost child, discounted for the fact that she may not fall pregnant or it may not reach a successful conclusion - £1,500 under this head; (ii) her awareness that things were not right after delivery of first twin and feeling she ought to have said more; surgical intervention and ensuing scar; immediate trauma on news of child's condition and of decision to turn off life-support; all as the immediate background to her moderately severe depressive illness for 6 month period; and in addition the constant reminder of the child when looking at the surviving twin - £10,000 under this head; (3) Disapproved decision of Simon Brown J in Bagley's Case 24/10/86 New Law Journal - dashed			

		hopes are no more than the normal facets of a mothers' emotions when bereaved of a child in these circumstances, and to award damages would be to award damages for bereavement twice over, or to award damages for a head of claim not recognized by English law.			
BIRTH INJURY - Maternal injury - **Post traumatic stress caused by erroneous advice that baby had died at birth**	(1) Whether on balance of probabilities the plaintiff was told her baby was dead when in fact it was not; (2) Whether the period of misinformation was a material and substantial cause of the PTSD; (3) Whether the hospital was negligent in failing to arrange appropriate counselling where management of the mother's care had been shared by hospital and GP.	**NEGLIGENT** (1) Found for the plaintiff on the facts on this issue; it was not disputed that the defendants were under a duty of care in respect of statements of this sort and it was an extraordinarily negligent thing to do; (2) found that the period of misinformation was a material and substantial cause of the PTSD and therefore the whole of the injury fell to the defendant's liability; (3) it was putting the duty of care of the defendants too high to say they were wrong in failing to arrange *(continued over)*	Plaintiff:- Mr Buchan, consultant gynaecologist and obstetrician; Dr Bennett, consultant psychiatrist; Defendant:- Dr Bradley, consultant psychiatrist.	£20,501 total, including £10,000 general damages for PTSD.	**Allin v City and Hackney Health Authority** [1996] 7 Med LR 167 Mayor's and City of London Court; HH Judge McMullan

MEDICAL TOPIC	ISSUES	HOW ISSUES DECIDED	EXPERTS USED	QUANTUM (general damages only unless otherwise stated)	CASE NAME AND REFERENCE
		counselling in circumstances where the plaintiff had a good GP, well-known to the hospital, who had been very involved with the whole matter and into whose hands the plaintiff had been discharged.			
BRACHIAL CARDIAC CATHETERISATION - **Suturing error causing vascular complications**	(1) Whether Registrar should have appreciated that vascular complications were occurring; (2) Whether he should have called for assistance of Vascular Surgeons.	**At first instance:- NOT NEGLIGENT** (1) It was probable the missuturing was not apparent to the doctor at the time as had it been visible it was highly likely that he would have seen it and done something about it; (2) allowing the patient to proceed to day ward without re-exploring the closure or calling for assistance of others including a vascular surgeon was in accordance with proper and accepted practice. The risks associated with both interventionist and	Plaintiff: Dr Wainwright, Prof Oakley, consultant cardiologists; Mr Scurr, vascular surgeon; Prof Steiner, consultant radiologist; Dr Paul Lewis, consultant neuropathologist; Defendants:- Dr Dawkins, Dr Hall, consultant cardiologists; Prof Ruckley, vascular surgeon.	No award made.	**Joyce v Wandsworth Health Authority** [1995] 6 Med LR 60 QBD; Overend J; On appeal:- [1996] 7 Med LR 1 Court of Appeal LJs Nourse, Roch and Hobhouse

Subject	Issues	Decision	Parties	Damages	Citation
		conservative approach to the management of weak pulses are evenly balanced. **ON APPEAL:- appeal dismissed** (1) NEGLIGENT - proper procedures were not followed which culminated in a decision to discharge the plaintiff and to do so without a warning or advice that was appropriate to his case, preceded by inadequate observations of his condition and an inadequate recognition of the risk category into which he fell but (2) this did not on the facts have a causative effect.			**Ratty v Haringey Health Authority and Payne** [1994] 5 Med LR 413 Court of Appeal LJs Balcombe, Kennedy and Evans
CANCER - BOWEL - Abdomino - perineal resection (APR) - during colo-rectal surgery for suspected cancer of bowel - Marnham's Rule	(1) Whether the Surgeon was negligent in proceeding to abdomino- perineal resection in the absence of histological proof of presence of cancer; (2) Whether Surgeon was negligent in inadequate repair of torn bladder and failure to discover damage to ureters during surgery.	**In the first instance:- NEGLIGENT -** (1) As a general rule (Marnham's Rule), an APR should not be performed in the absence of clinical evidence of cancer; the defendant had been precipitate in going *(continued over)*	Plaintiff:- Mr Gazet and Mr Jackson, consultant surgeons; Defendant:- Mr Mann and Mr Addison, consultant surgeons.	At first instance, total of £127,932 (no breakdown provided); Following appeal:- £5,000 general damages for pain, suffering and loss of amenity for damage to bladder and ureters.	

MEDICAL TOPIC	ISSUES	HOW ISSUES DECIDED	EXPERTS USED	QUANTUM (general damages only unless otherwise stated)	CASE NAME AND REFERENCE
		to an APR without careful analysis of every conflicting aspect of the evidence before him; (2) repair of the bladder had been inadequate; **ON APPEAL:- allowed in part:-** (1) Accepted the defendants' experts' argument that Marnham's Rule was a useful guide but not one which had to be followed in every case; in this case there was evidence at surgery supporting a diagnosis of an extensive cancer; even if at some stage in the operation the defendant had paused and thought, he would not if exercising reasonable skill and care, have necessarily been led to the conclusion that he ought not to proceed as he did;			

		(2) but agreed that the balance of the evidence favoured the conclusion that the repair of the bladder was inadequate, and that the failure to discover the damage to the ureters was negligent.			
CANCER - OVARIAN - Total pelvic clearance for lump believed to be malignant - later histology showed mass was endometriosis	(1) Whether defendant had obtained informed consent before the procedure; (2) Whether decision to carry out the radical surgery was negligent	**NOT NEGLIGENT** (1) On the facts, informed consent had been obtained; (2) the decision to proceed to pelvic clearance was not negligent as the defendant had been reasonably misled by the pathology reports obtained previously in Pakistan.	Plaintiff:- Mr John Megarry, consultant obstetrician and gynaecologist; Professor Fox, consultant pathologist; Mr J Carron Brown, consultant obstetrician and gynaecologist (retired); Dr Graham Read, consultant clinical oncologist; Defendant:- Mr John Shepherd, consultant gynaecological surgeon and oncologist; Professor Stephen Smith, professor of obstetrics and gynaecology.	No award made.	**Abbas v Kenney** [1996] 7 Med LR 47 QBD; Mr Justice Gage

MEDICAL TOPIC	ISSUES	HOW ISSUES DECIDED	EXPERTS USED	QUANTUM (general damages only unless otherwise stated)	CASE NAME AND REFERENCE
CARDIAC SURGERY - Operation to correct patent ductus arteriosis - child suffered cardiac arrest resulting in brain damage	(1) Whether the Paediatric Registrar was negligent in failing to attend child with respiratory difficulties; (2) Whether Registrar would have intubated if she had attended.	PLAINTIFF'S APPEAL DISMISSED (1) It had been agreed by both parties that it was negligent on the part of the doctor not to have attended the child when summoned by the sister; (2) But (per LJs Farquharson and Dillon, Simon Brown LJ dissenting) where the judge was dealing with a breach of duty which consisted of an omission, it was necessary for him to decide what course of events would have followed had the duty been discharged; even though he was dealing with causation, he was bound to rely on the evidence of the experts available to him, and it was for the plaintiff to prove (i) that had the doctor attended, she probably would have intubated;	Plaintiff:- Dr Newman, ; Dr Stimmler, Mr Roberts, and Professor Holt, consultant paediatricians ; Dr Heaf, consultant paediatrician; Defendant:- Dr Dinwiddie, consultant paediatrician; Professor Hull, consultant neonatologist; Dr Robertson.	No award made.	**Bolitho & Others v City & Hackney Health Authority** [1993] 4 Med LR 381 Court of Appeal; LJs Dillon, Farquharson and Simon Brown

Procedure / Condition	Issues	Decision	Experts	Award	Case
	(ii) that if she did not do so, the failure would have been contrary to accepted medical practice; (3) In this case, Dr Dinwiddie's opinion that he would not have intubated in this case was representative of a responsible body of opinion and the judge was entitled to rely on this evidence in dealing with causation.			No award made.	**Hughes v Waltham Forest Health Authority** [1991] 2 Med LR 155 Court of Appeal; LJs Fox, Butler-Sloss and Beldam
CHOLECYSTECTOMY - **Followed by fistula and blockage of common bile duct causing death from acute necrotising pancreatitis**	(1) Whether the consultant surgeons were negligent in failing to send the Plaintiff for endoscopic retrograde cholangio-pancreatocogram (ERCP); (2) Whether surgeons were negligent in discharging the Plaintiff from hospital too soon.	**NOT NEGLIGENT -** (1) the decision not to proceed to ERCP was in accordance with a practice accepted as proper within the profession by an eminent surgeon practising in the same field, and the specialist unit which would have conducted the ERCP examination also considered the decision a proper one. The fact that two other distinguished surgeons were critical of the decision, or that the decision ultimately turned (*continued over*)	Plaintiff:- Professor Robin Williamson; Mr D R Reid; Defendant:- Mr Russell.		

MEDICAL TOPIC	ISSUES	HOW ISSUES DECIDED	EXPERTS USED	QUANTUM (general damages only unless otherwise stated)	CASE NAME AND REFERENCE
		out to be mistaken, did not prove that the doctors fell short of the standard of care to be expected of competent surgeons; (2) the interpretation of the results of tests was only one factor in the complex clinical picture which the competent surgeon would take into account as a whole. The figures had to be judged against the background of the physical signs and any symptoms of which the patient complained. These were all matters leading to a clinical judgment and which was not shown to be negligent merely because looking back with hindsight the position could be seen plainly.			

COSMETIC SURGERY- 11 to 13 operations to correct port wine birthmark on eyelids, nose, cheek and upper lip of young girl, taking place between 1962 and 1974 - mark had been capable of being hidden by cosmetics - significant worsening of condition by scarring from surgery	Whether the surgeon was negligent in 1962 in deciding to operate at all.	**NEGLIGENT** Accepted the plaintiffs' expert's evidence that in 1962 there was realistically no sufficient chance that plastic surgery would improve the cosmetic appearance of the untreated port wine stain, even though competently done over a long series of operations. Even if there were any such chance, it must be outweighed by all the indications against surgery, the predictable end result, the predictable number of operations, the predictable effect of these operations on the child and on the child's childhood.	Plaintiff:-Professor Yule, chartered clinical psychologist; Mr Golden, consultant plastic surgeon; Defendant:- Mr Sandon, Mr Robinson, consultant plastic surgeons.	£30,000 general damages for 11 to 13 operations during childhood and disastrous overall psychological effect.	**Doughty v North Staffordshire Health Authority** [1992] 3 Med LR 81 QBD; Henry J

MEDICAL TOPIC	ISSUES	HOW ISSUES DECIDED	EXPERTS USED	QUANTUM (general damages only unless otherwise stated)	CASE NAME AND REFERENCE
DEHYDRATION - **Hypernatraemic dehydration in an infant following gastroenteritis resulting in brain damage**	(1) Whether GP was negligent in circumstances where he had told the mother, who was an intelligent and caring mother, living in a good home atmosphere, to ring him the next morning if there was no improvement in the child's condition, in not having checked the following morning even when there was no contact from the mother; (3) Causation - whether it was failure to make second visit or feeding by mother that caused brain damage.	**NOT NEGLIGENT** (1) the defendant was under no such additional duty and gave the mother adequate instructions; (2) it was the mother's concern that the baby was not eating which was the cause of the problem, because had she carried out the doctor's instructions, and merely given the child a little fluid, rather than feeding the child cereal, she would not have unwittingly masked the development of the condition of hypernatraemic dehydration, and would have got in touch with the doctor.	Plaintiff:- Dr Carne and Dr Goodhart, general practitioners; Dr Rosenbloom, consultant paediatric neurologist; Defendant:- Dr Kershaw, general practitioner; Dr Burman, retired consultant paediatrician.	No award made although in event of successful result parties had agreed damages for pain and suffering and loss of amenity at £31,000 inclusive of interest.	**Durrant v Burke** [1993] 4 Med LR 258 QBD; HH Judge Fallon

	NEGLIGENT		£6,000 general damages.	**Bovenzi v Kettering Health Authority**
DILATATION AND CURETTAGE - **Perforation of uterus and damage to small bowel**	(1) Whether perforation of the uterus is negligent during D&C; (2) Whether perforation and small bowel damage is negligent during D&C.	(1) Perforation is relatively common - most if not all surgeons have done it - statistical evidence to support that one in fifty evacuations result in perforation - but perforation and small bowel damage is so rare as to be outside the range of normal practice; judge was influenced by the rarity of the occurrence - this supports evidence that the injury was caused negligently; (2) In this case, the clot passed by the plaintiff indicated an incomplete and careless evacuation and the damage to the myometrium denoted use of excess force; while these did not in themselves prove negligence, the evidence of the plaintiffs' experts was compelling and it is accepted that the doctor must have felt some resistance during the procedure.	Plaintiff:- Mr Flood, Mr Ellis, consultant urologists; Defendant:- Mr Fyfe, consultant urologist.	[1991] 2 Med LR 293 QBD; Nolan J

MEDICAL TOPIC	ISSUES	HOW ISSUES DECIDED	EXPERTS USED	QUANTUM (general damages only unless otherwise stated)	CASE NAME AND REFERENCE
EPIGLOTTITIS - Delay in diagnosis by Senior Houseman in Accident & Emergency - resulting in brain damage	(1) Whether senior houseman was negligent in failing to notice the patient's inability to swallow, failing to obtain a proper history and subsequently failing to obtain information which would have induced him to refer the patient for further investigation; (2) Standard of skill to be applied in Accident & Emergency diagnosis.	**NEGLIGENT** (1) Doctor was negligent in failing to elicit nature and extent of condition and probing for more information in view of presenting condition; (2) Standard of care to be applied was that of reasonably competent senior houseman acting as a casualty officer without reference to length of experience.	Plaintiff:- Mr. Harris and Mr. Frampton, consultant ENT surgeons; Dr. Hughes, consultant physician; Mr Sach, consultant in accident and emergency; Defendants:- Dr. Evans, consultant physician; Mr. Millington, orthopaedic surgeon.	Damages to be assessed.	**Djemal v Bexley Health Authority** [1995] 6 Med LR 269 QBD; The Hon Sir Haydn Tudor Evans.
GENTAMICIN ADMINISTRATION - Failure to monitor leading to ototoxicity causing irreversible and bilateral loss of vestibular function	(1) Whether dosage which was in excess of the manufacturer's guidelines was proper; (2) Whether duration of the treatment was negligent; (3) Whether monitoring of treatment was negligent ie monitoring of troughs and peaks.	**NOT NEGLIGENT** (1) The dose was a proper one - there was no sufficient consensus of opinion to say that the dose was so high as to be beyond what a reasonably competent practitioner would prescribe; further, the guidelines laid down by the manufacturers and MIMMS are too conservative and err on the side of caution;	Plaintiff:- Dr. Eykyn - consultant clinical biologist; Dr Jordan and Dr. Oakley - consultant cardiologists; Dr. Pallis - consultant neurologist; Defendant:- Dr Cooke, professor of clinical microbiology; Dr Reeves, consultant microbiologist ; Dr Sowton, consultant cardiologist.	Had the plaintiff succeeded, £17,500 general damages.	**Vernon v Bloomsbury Health Authority** [1995] 6 Med LR 297 QBD; Tucker J

(2) there was no sufficient consensus of expert opinion concerning the length of the course; found that the doctors were acting in the best interests of the plaintiff in continuing the course of therapy for 3 weeks - they were treating a life-threatening condition in difficult circumstances, without knowing the type of organism they were dealing with; they were not dealing with a patient with known renal failure; therefore they acted competently;

(3) the level of monitoring was acceptable in 1982; the defendant's experts represent a considerable body of responsible and distinguished medical opinion - the doctors had conformed with the standards of reasonable competent medical men at the time; in any event even had they been negligent it would not have made any difference to the outcome - the plaintiff was one of the unfortunate few who were

(continued over)

MEDICAL TOPIC	ISSUES	HOW ISSUES DECIDED	EXPERTS USED	QUANTUM (general damages only unless otherwise stated)	CASE NAME AND REFERENCE
		more vulnerable than most to the toxic effects of the drug - found on the evidence that ototoxicity can occur despite normal trough levels.			
HANDWRITING - Illegibility of doctors' handwriting resulting in prescription of Daonil rather than Amoxil to a non-diabetic resulting in hypoglycaemia and irrevocable brain damage	(1) Whether GP was liable for injury where his bad handwriting on a prescription was read incorrectly by the pharmacist; (2) Whether the chain of causation between the GP's handwriting and the injury was broken by the fact that the prescription should have put the pharmacist on enquiry.	**NEGLIGENT** (1) Liability:- A doctor who writes out a prescription for a patient owes a duty to the patient to write the prescription legibly; in this case the doctor fell below the standard of legibility required in the exercise of this duty; (2) Causation:- It was not beyond reasonable foreseeability that Daonil would be prescribed, and looking at the case as a whole, the chain of causation from the bad handwriting was not broken;	Not stated.	£137,647 in total - no breakdown provided.	**Prendergast v Sam and Dee Limited, Kozary & Miller** [1989] 1 Med LR 36, Court of Appeal: LJs Dillon, Ralph Gibson and Woolf

HIP INJURY - **1977 - delay in diagnosis of acute traumatic fracture separation of the left femoral epiphysis - avascular necrosis of the hip - quantum**	Quantum where there was an underlying 75% risk of the disability developing in any event, but the medical staff's failure had turned that risk into an inevitability.	(3) Apportionment of liability - 25 per cent was not too high. **At first instance:-** the plaintiff would be awarded £11,500 representing 25% of the full value of the damages awardable for the disability, since the defendant's negligence had denied the plaintiff of a 25% chance of a good recovery; **On appeal to the Court of Appeal:-** upheld the trial judge's reasoning; **On appeal to the House of Lords:- appeal allowed:-**	Not stated.	£46,000 adjudged to be the full value of the disability.	**Hotson v East Berkshire Area Health Authority** [1985] 3 All ER 167 QBD; Simon Brown J; [1987] 1 All ER 210 Court of Appeal: Sir John Donaldson MR, LJs Dillon and Croom-Johnson;

MEDICAL TOPIC	ISSUES	HOW ISSUES DECIDED	EXPERTS USED	QUANTUM (general damages only unless otherwise stated)	CASE NAME AND REFERENCE
HYDROCEPHALUS - **Surgery to implant bilateral shunt following unsuccessful right frontal craniotomy for removal of cyst - right sided hemiplegia and aphasia resulting from technique**	(1) Whether the neurosurgeon's technique of not moving head of patient during bilateral shunt operation was acceptable to a respected body of neuro-surgeons; (2) whether the fact that the catheter ended up in a Sylvan fissure raised presumption of negligence.	**NOT NEGLIGENT** (1) The technique of not moving the head was acceptable to a widely respected body of neurosurgeons; (2) the plaintiff's injury resulted, on balance ,from spasm of the middle cerebral artery located in the Sylvan fissure when the advancing catheter made contact with it: this was not due to any relevant fault on the part of the treating doctor.	Plaintiff:- Mr C Adams, consultant neurosurgeon; Defendant:- Mr Till, Mr Kalbag, and Professor Miller, consultant neurosurgeons; Dr McPherson, consultant neuro-radiologist.	No award made.	**Burgess v Newcastle Health Authority** [1992] 3 Med LR 224 QBD; Turner J
HYDROCEPHALUS - **Blockage of intracranial shunt - failure to diagnose raised intracranial pressure causing severe headaches, organic brain damage and psychological harm**	(1) Whether the GP was negligent in diagnosing stress and failing to recognise the true nature of the plaintiff's symptoms in view of the presence of her intracranial shunt; and in failing to refer the plaintiff to a neurologist and informing the neurologist that the plaintiff had had a shunt fitted;	**NEGLIGENT** (1) The GP's notes of the plaintiff's attendances did not form a reliable evidential base - they were scanty in the extreme, rarely recorded her complaints or symptoms or his observations, and were sometimes accompanied by a cryptic or derogatory remark; the failure to take	Plaintiff:- Mr Jonathan Punt, consultant neurosurgeon; Dr Shenderey, expert general practitioner; Dr Harris, consultant psychiatrist; Mr Jamie, clinical psychologist; Defendant:- Dr CJ Earl and Dr Sumner, consultant neurologists; Dr Halle, expert general practitioner.	£17,500 general damages for pain, suffering and loss of amenity.	**Rhodes v Spokes and Farbridge** [1996] 7 Med LR 135 QBD; Mrs Justice Smith

(2) Whether the neurosurgeon was negligent in not referring plaintiff for a CT scan at her first consultation; (3) Whether delay as result of (1) and/or (2) had resulted in damage.	proper notes is not evidence of negligence or inadequate treatment but lays the doctor open to a finding that his recollection is faulty and the patient's is correct; (2) on the facts the GP was negligent as alleged; while he reasonably considered the plaintiff to be of a nervous and anxious disposition, he also knew of her childhood illness and the presence of her shunt; (3) the neurosurgeon was negligent in that he did not ask his usual series of questions but directed his main thrust to psychiatric questions and failed to explore possibilities of organic reasons for the symptoms; had he done so he would have found out about her shunt and suspected intracranial pressure and referred her for a CT scan; (4) had the GP not been negligent, the plaintiff would have made a good recovery. She would have (*continued over*)	Dr Ghadiali, clinical psychologist.

MEDICAL TOPIC	ISSUES	HOW ISSUES DECIDED	EXPERTS USED	QUANTUM (general damages only unless otherwise stated)	CASE NAME AND REFERENCE
		avoided the unnecessary prolongation of her unpleasant illness including tiredness, unsteadiness, intermittent double vision, slight loss of heating and an overwhelming sense of general malaise during the summer with concomitant anxiety; on balance she would also have avoided some mild cognitive impairment which has been enough to prevent her return to work, some slight change of personality.			
HYDROMYELIA - Surgery for drainage resulting in permanent tetraplegia - causation only	(1) Whether surgeon was negligent in failing to warn of tetraplegia when the patient would have suffered tetraplegia nine months later in any event; (2) Whether had the plaintiff received proper warning of tetraplegia she would have proceeded with the surgery.	CAUSATION NOT PROVEN (1) there is no doubt that the plaintiff should have had a full and careful explanation of the risks and benefits inherent in the operation, in general terms her prognosis without the surgery, and a clear indication of the surgeon's recommendation;	Plaintiff:- Mr Galbraith, consultant neurosurgeon; Defendant:- Professor Hankinson, Mr Garfield, consultant neurosurgeons.	£3,000 for shock and depression caused by immediate onset of tetraplegia of which she had not been warned.	**Smith v Barking, Havering & Brentwood Health Authority** [1994] 5 Med LR 285 QBD; Hutchison J

INFECTION - rubella - Failure to diagnose and treat mother during pregnancy SEE PREGNANCY (below)	(2) but had she been properly warned, the strong probability is that she would have had the surgery.	**McKay and another v Essex Area Health Authority and another** [1982] 2 All ER 771 Court of Appeal; LJs Stephenson, Ackner and Griffiths
INFECTION - of shunt In hydrocephalic infant SEE SHUNT INFECTION (below)		**Robinson v Jacklin and Others** [1996] 7 Med LR 83 QBD; Mr G Hamilton QC sitting as deputy judge of the High Court
INFECTION - during administration of epidural anaesthetic SEE ANAESTHESIA (above)		**El-Morssy v Bristol and District Health Authority** [1996] 7 Med LR 232 QBD COL; Turner J

MEDICAL TOPIC	ISSUES	HOW ISSUES DECIDED	EXPERTS USED	QUANTUM (general damages only unless otherwise stated)	CASE NAME AND REFERENCE
KNEE INJURY - 19 day delay in diagnosis of rupture of lateral ligaments and cruciate mechanism, and damage to lateral popliteal nerve - discharge from casualty on day 1 with diagnosis of bruising - fall on day 2 - 3 to 4 month delay in repair surgery - permanent foot drop	Causation only - whether the ultimate injury was due to negligent diagnosis.	CAUSATION PROVEN - Preferred plaintiffs' experts' evidence that had a primary repair been carried out within the first 48 hours, the end result would have been much better and on the balance of probabilities, there would have been a return of function to 90% ie more or less complete recovery; the fall on day 2 did not on the evidence damage the nerve any further or materially contribute to the damage already suffered.	Plaintiff:- Mr Anderson and Mr Tom Wadsworth, consultant orthopaedic surgeons; Defendant:- Mr Roger Vickers, and Mr Mathewson, consultant orthopaedic surgeons.	£6,000 general damages.	**Walker v Huntingdon Health Authority** [1994] 5 Med LR 356 QBD; Otton J
LAPAROTOMY - Unnecessary surgery following incorrect diagnosis of ovarian cyst - subsequent death of foetus	(1) Whether it was negligent to proceed to laparotomy without ultrasound scan to exclude or confirm pregnancy; (2) Whether it was negligent to advise patient after scan that she was pregnant with a live baby when the baby may have been dead; (3) Quantum of general damages.	(1) NEGLIGENT - At the time she saw the consultant there were signs of pregnancy including missed period, abdominal distension and enlarged breasts; the defendants' expert was unable to fully support the defendants' actions under cross examination and judge preferred evidence of plaintiff's expert;	Plaintiff:- Mr Buchan, consultant gynaecologist; Defendants:- Mr McDonald, consultant gynaecologist.	Generals £7500 including £3500 for laparotomy alone.	**Tucker v Tees Health Authority** [1995] 6 Med LR 54 QBD; May J

			Howard v Wessex Regional Health Authority [1994] 5 Med LR 57 QBD Morland J
		No award made.	
	(2) NOT NEGLIGENT - accepted defendants' evidence that baby was alive at time of scan. Further, no evidence that baby died as result of laparotomy; **(3)** While she was not entitled to damages for distress caused by fact that she was pregnant with live child which then died, she was entitled to damages for greater part of her grief and distress caused by addition of unnecessary surgery close in time to induced still birth.	Plaintiff:- Professor Rood, Mr Posposil, maxillo-facial professor and consultant respectively; Dr Pallis, consultant neurologist; Dr Moseley, consultant neuro-radiologist; Dr Paul Lewis, consultant neuropathologist; Professors Healy and Payne, professors of anaesthesia; (*continued over*)	
		NOT NEGLIGENT (1) The crucial decision is whether the plaintiff had satisfied the court on the balance of probabilities that her tetraplegia was the result of traumatic injury negligently inflicted upon her cervical spine during surgery - if it was equally likely that the injury was caused by emboli, her case would fail. Throughout, (*continued over*)	
	MAXILLO-FACIAL SURGERY - **Tetraplegia following sagittal split osteotomy to correct overjutting of upper over lower jaw - paralysis from C6 downwards**	(1) Whether res ipsa loquitur appropriate where tetraplegia following a sagittal split osteotomy is unknown as a complication; (2) Causation.	

MEDICAL TOPIC	ISSUES	HOW ISSUES DECIDED	EXPERTS USED	QUANTUM (general damages only unless otherwise stated)	CASE NAME AND REFERENCE
		the onus of proving negligent cause was squarely on the plaintiff - res ipsa loquitur was inappropriate; (2) Defendant's non-negligent explanation that emboli located themselves in the arteries and/or veins supplying the cervical cord, causing ischaemia to the cord and a "fat cord" at the level of C6, causing tetraplegia, which occurred without trauma (fibro-cartilaginous embolism- FCE) was accepted as the probable and likely cause.	Defendant:- Dr Sumner, lecturer in neurology; Dr CJ Earl, consultant neurologist; Professor Hankinson, professor of neurosurgery; Professor Poswillo, professor of maxillo-facial surgery; Mr Cook, consultant oral surgeon; Dr Hargrove, consultant anaesthetist; Dr Burrows, consultant neuro-radiologist; Dr Hughes, consultant neuropathologist.		
MENINGITIS - Baby presenting with temperature, inflammation of conjunctiva and redness of the eye - causing profound deafness, inability to speak and other neurological problems	Whether GP had negligently rejected the possibilities of peri-orbital cellulitis and failed to properly assess nature and degree of the illness and refer the plaintiff to hospital.	NOT NEGLIGENT (1) It was accepted that this was not a case of failure by the GP to diagnose meningitis; (2) Plaintiffs' experts' diagnosis of periorbital cellulitis rejected; on the balance of probabilities,	Plaintiff:- Dr Isaac and Dr D'Ambrumenil, general practitioners, Dr Snodgrass and Dr Rosenbloom, consultant paediatricians; Defendant:- Dr Halle and Dr Kershaw, expert GPs; Dr Holmes Sellars, ophthalmic surgeon, Dr Hall, consultant paediatrician.	No award made.	**Thornton & Others v Nicol** [1992] 3 Med LR 41 QBD; MacPherson J

		the defendant was justified in his diagnosis of conjunctivitis - evidence of Dr Hall and Dr Sellars preferred; (3) On the evidence, the GP cannot be judged to gave been guilty of such failure as no other doctor of ordinary skill would be guilty of if acting with ordinary care - evidence of Drs Halle and Kershaw preferred.			**Bolam v Friern Hospital Management Committee** [1957] 2 All ER 118 QBD; McNair J
MENTAL ILLNESS - **Electro-convulsive therapy -** **Dislocation of both hip joints with fractures of pelvis**	Whether the hospital was negligent in delivering the ECT without relaxant drugs or manual control which would have avoided the injuries.	**JURY TRIAL - judge's directions to jury:-** A doctor is not negligent if he is acting in accordance with a practice accepted as proper by a responsible body of medical men skilled in that particular art, merely because there is a body of such opinion that takes a contrary view; In this case, there were two bodies of opinion, one of which favoured the use of relaxant drugs or manual control as a general practice, and the *(continued over)*	Plaintiff:- Dr Randall, consultant psychiatrist, St Thomas' and Charing Cross Hospital; Defendant:- Drs Baker and Marshall, consultant psychiatrists.	No award made.	

MEDICAL TOPIC	ISSUES	HOW ISSUES DECIDED	EXPERTS USED	QUANTUM (general damages only unless otherwise stated)	CASE NAME AND REFERENCE
		other of which, thinking that the use of the drugs had a mortality risk, confined the use of relaxant drugs to cases where their use was specifically indicated; the same applied to the use of manual constraints; **Jury found NOT NEGLIGENT**			
MENTAL ILLNESS - manic depression - State of relapse - GP did not admit to hospital - plaintiff subsequently jumping from balcony causing severe injury	(1) Whether GP negligent in failing to carry out sufficient examination of patient and then referring to local mental health team for assessment, treatment, observation and supervision; (2) Whether plaintiff succeeded on issue of causation.	**NEGLIGENT** (1) The defendant appreciated that the plaintiff was probably in a state of relapse, and had he asked the appropriate questions it was more likely than not that the extent of the plaintiff's anxiety would have been appreciated. He should have made it clear that assessment and follow-up were needed as a matter of urgency;	Plaintiff:- Dr Lipsedge, consultant psychiatrist; Dr Cole, expert GP; Defendant:- Dr Reveley, consultant psychiatrist; Dr Le Frenais, expert GP.	£190,000 in total - no breakdown supplied.	**Mahmood v Siggins** [1996] 7 Med LR 76; QBD; HH Judge Butter QC

Facts	Issue	Decision	Award	Citation
		(2) Preferred plaintiff's expert psychiatric evidence that had the appropriate referral been made, the risk of the accident occurring would have been reduced to less than 50 per cent.	Not stated.	
NERVE INJURY - Mediastinoscopy - exploratory surgery to determine whether suffering from Hodgkin's disease - damage to left laryngeal recurrent nerve - paralysis of vocal chord causing speech defect - plaintiff in fact suffering from tuberculosis	Whether the doctors were negligent in proceeding to mediastinoscopy before receiving results of test for tuberculosis, where tuberculosis was the most likely diagnosis.	**At first instance:- NEGLIGENT:-** Trial judge preferred the plaintiff's experts' evidence that the doctors were negligent in so doing; **Court of Appeal:- reversed the decision; House of Lords:-** It was not sufficient for the plaintiff to show that there was a body of opinion that considered the doctors wrong, if there also existed a body of opinion, equally competent, that considered the decision reasonable in the circumstances; just because the Court might prefer one body of opinion to another does not make the defendant doctor negligent.	Award at first instance not stated.	**Maynard v West Midlands Regional Health Authority** QBD: Comyn J; Court of Appeal; LJ Cumming-Bruce and Sir Stanley Rees, LJ Dunn dissenting; [1985] 1 All ER 635 House of Lords: Lords Fraser of Tullybelton, Elwyn-Jones, Scarman, Roskill and Templeman

MEDICAL TOPIC	ISSUES	HOW ISSUES DECIDED	EXPERTS USED	QUANTUM (general damages only unless otherwise stated)	CASE NAME AND REFERENCE
NERVE INJURY - **Sciatic nerve paralysis (SNP) - during hip replacement surgery**	Whether the paralysis was due to inherent risk in dislocation procedure or whether caused by (i) pressure on the nerve (proposed by Mr Strachan); (ii) stretching of nerve; (iii) ischaemic lesion of the nerve due to occlusion of the precarious blood supply to the nerve (proposed by Dr Earl).	**NEGLIGENT** (1) The balance of the medical evidence is firmly against pressure on the nerve; (2) there was no evidence that the plaintiff had a precarious blood supply and there were no cases in the literature showing ischaemic lesion as the cause of SNP; or that there was any connection between the plaintiff's polycythemia and the sciatic nerve damage; (3) the strong probability is that the injury was caused by the stretching or traction of the sciatic nerve at a rapid speed during the process of dislocation; (4) even if this analysis is incorrect, the doctrine of res ipsa loquitur is applicable and the defendants have failed to rebut the inference of negligence by pointing to any tenable explanation of the plaintiff's injury.	Plaintiff:- Professor O'Connor, and Mr Strachan, consultant orthopaedic surgeons; Dr Geoffrey Rushworth, consultant neurophysiologist; Professor Samuel Machin, consultant haematologist; Defendant:- Dr CJ Earl, consultant neurologist; Mr Robin Ling, and Professor Jack Stevens, consultant orthopaedic surgeons.	£80,000 agreed - no breakdown	**Bentley v Bristol and Weston Health Authority (No. 2)** [1991] 3 Med LR 1 QBD; Waterhouse J

NERVE INJURY - **Left mastoidectomy - peri-operative bilateral ulnar nerve palsy**	(1) Whether pressure on the ulnar nerves necessarily connotes negligence; (2) Whether res ipsa loquitur applied.	**NOT NEGLIGENT** (1) It is well known that there is a risk of damage to ulnar nerve if lower part of back of upper arm is allowed to rest on a hard object in same position for a long time; (2) There was a duty on surgeon to protect ulnar nerve by wrapping it, or otherwise protecting it by material which would serve to absorb and disperse pressure from weight of arm and to protect arm from other pressure; (3) In this case no evidence of negligence in use of arm pads which had been designed for the very purpose; (4) Accepted defendants' expert evidence that plaintiff had a polyneuropathy; treated with reservation Mr Scurr's evidence that ulnar nerve lesions should not occur even in patients with a generalized polyneuropathy; *(continued over)*	Plaintiff:- Mr John Scurr, general surgeon; Dr Capildeo, consultant neurologist; Defendant:- Professor Thomas; Dr CJ Earl, consultant neurologist; Dr Greenwood, consultant neurologist (performed the EMG studies).	Judge stated that he would have awarded £14,000 general damages	**Moore v Worthing District Health Authority** [1992] 3 Med LR 431 QBD; Owen J

MEDICAL TOPIC	ISSUES	HOW ISSUES DECIDED	EXPERTS USED	QUANTUM (general damages only unless otherwise stated)	CASE NAME AND REFERENCE
		(5) While res ipsa loquitur prima facie applied, the defendant had shown a way in which injury could have occurred without negligence ie by reason of plaintiff's unusual susceptibility to nerve lesions because of his underlying polyneuropathy.			
NERVE INJURY - lingual nerve - **following removal of wisdom teeth**	Whether injury was caused by negligence (drill burr coming into contact with nerve, or crushing or nipping of nerve by elevator/retractor), or by necessary stretching of nerve which was not negligent.	**CAUSATION ESTABLISHED** (1) Negligent causes of nerve injury would include the drill burr coming into contact with the nerve, the crushing or nipping of the nerve by the retractor/elevator or severe or violent stretching of the nerve; (2) the defendant's theory that the nerve was injured by necessary stretching, undertaken carefully, gently and properly, had no basis for a positive conclusion on the evidence;	Plaintiff:- Mr Pospisil, consultant maxillofacial surgeon; Mr McAndrew, consultant oral and maxillofacial surgeon; Defendant:- Professor Poswillo, professor of oral and maxillofacial surgery.	£14,000 agreed damages; no breakdown provided.	**Christie v Somerset Health Authority** [1992] 3 Med LR 75 QBD: Sir Michael Ogden QC sitting as Deputy High Court Judge.

	(3) accepted the plaintiff's experts' evidence that this injury could not have been caused by non-negligent stretching; (4) the fact that no neuroma was seen does not mean that one was not present; the presence of a neuroma would indicate the severing of a fascicle in the nerve; (5) on balance of probabilities the injury was caused by the retractor or burr.	Plaintiff:- Professor Rood, professor of anaesthesia; Mr Walker; Defendant:- Professor Robinson, professor of anaesthesia.	£12,000 general damages for pain, suffering and loss of amenity.	**Heath v West Berkshire Health Authority** [1992] 3 Med LR 57 QBD; Mantle J
NERVE INJURY - lingual nerve - During extraction of wisdom teeth	(1) Whether the injury occurred through a want of care or was unavoidable; (2) whether the defendant's failure to warn that wisdom tooth extraction carries a small percentage risk of unavoidable injury to the lingual nerve, which can result in the temporary alteration of sensations in the mouth, was negligent; (3) Quantum where the injury resulted in permanent injury, including partial loss of taste, *(continued over)*	**NEGLIGENT** (1) Some damage can be caused to the lingual nerve quite unavoidably - eg in placing a retractor between periosteum and bones surrounding tooth to be removed, a stretching or crushing injury, producing temporary symptoms, may occur and this would not be negligent; (2) But were it the case that the lingual nerve became divided, severed or sectioned by drill used *(continued over)*		

MEDICAL TOPIC	ISSUES	HOW ISSUES DECIDED	EXPERTS USED	QUANTUM (general damages only unless otherwise stated)	CASE NAME AND REFERENCE
	unpleasant sensations of pins and needles and occasional shooting pains of moderate severity in her mouth, and tongue.	to remove bone surrounding the wisdom tooth, then it may be that this could only be explained in terms of negligence on the part of the operator; (3) in this case plaintiff had established on balance of probabilities that injury occurred as a result of retractor being incorrectly positioned in front of nerve or incorrectly adjusted to the drill in front of nerve or through some inadvertent misapplication of drill itself - therefore bound to find that injury occurred through a want of due care; (4) in 1986 there was a respectable and responsible body of professional opinion which would not have warned ; even if the plaintiff had been warned, she would probably have consented to the procedure anyway.			

NERVE INJURY - lingual nerve - During extraction of wisdom tooth - causing permanent pain and numbness of tongue	Whether orthodontist negligent when drill penetrated lingual plate of mandible and severed lingual nerve.	**NEGLIGENT** (1) Current practice in 1985 was not to warn of permanent damage to the lingual nerve, nor is it a universal practice now (ie 1993); it was the practice to mention the risk of some damage to the aviolan nerve and thus altered lip sensation; (2) It is plain that the risk of lingual tissue damage was appreciated in 1985, and that the lingual nerve could be damaged when wisdom teeth were being removed; (3) The wisdom in the literature is that if the lingual split method is not successful, the operator will go on to use a drill with a burr end to vertically section the tooth and remove the relevant parts of the tooth; (4) The procedures for sectioning a tooth properly carried out by an experienced and careful operator should not *(continued over)*	Plaintiff:- Mr McAndrew, consultant and maxillo-facial surgeon; Defendant:- Mr Christopher Blackburn, consultant and maxillo-facial surgeon.	£28,000 agreed damages inclusive of interest - no breakdown provided.	**Tomkins v Bexley Health Authority** [1993] 4 Med LR 235 QBD; HH Judge Wilcox

MEDICAL TOPIC	ISSUES	HOW ISSUES DECIDED	EXPERTS USED	QUANTUM (general damages only unless otherwise stated)	CASE NAME AND REFERENCE
		involve penetration of the lingual plate and the lingual tissues and severance of the lingual nerve. The fact that all these structures were penetrated by the burr indicates a want of care by the operator.			
NEUROSURGERY - **To correct arteriovascular malformation (AVM) which was causing difficulties in gait in leg, resulting in hemiplegia**	(1) Whether the decision that the AVM was operable was negligent; (2) Whether surgeon was negligent in failing to warn of 10% risk of hemiplegia; surgeon had warned that there was a 20% chance that the surgery would make the leg worse but that if she did not have the surgery she would require a calliper in the not too distant future; (3) Whether, had the warning been given, the plaintiff would not have proceeded to surgery.	**NEGLIGENT** (1) Operative resection of AVM presented a risk of damage to upper limb which was more than negligible; but fact that risk was comparatively high does not mean that doctor acted contrary to any reasonable body of thought; on the literature, risk of leaving an AVM untreated was 2% per annum cumulative ie over 30 years, 60%. The spectre of death hanging over plaintiff makes it almost impossible to say that defendant was negligent in deciding to operate; on	Plaintiff:- Mr Christopher Adams, consultant neurosurgeon; Professor Chadwick, professor of neurology; Dr Brian Kendall, consultant neuro-radiologist; Defendant:- Mr Strong, consultant neurosurgeon; Professor Mendelow, consultant neurosurgeon; Dr Cox, consultant radiographer.	Quantum left to be decided.	**McAllister v Lewisham & North Southwark Health Authority, the Bethlem Royal Hospital, the Maudsley Hospital Special Health Authority** [1994] 5 Med LR 343 QBD; Rougier J

literature there was a school of thought which condoned his decision although it was in minority;

(2) but there is no doubt surgeon seriously underestimated risks of procedure in his own mind - not only risks to arm and leg, but also risk of further sensory deficit of 100%. Despite this being the hardest case he had encountered he did not seek farther afield in literature or among colleagues, to try to discover more about benefit/risk ratio; fact that operation took 3 times longer than expected also points to this conclusion. From here it is a short and inevitable step to conclude that his description of risk given to plaintiff fell far short of reality and constituted an actionable breach of duty.

MEDICAL TOPIC	ISSUES	HOW ISSUES DECIDED	EXPERTS USED	QUANTUM (general damages only unless otherwise stated)	CASE NAME AND REFERENCE
ORAL CONTRACEPTIVE - Depo-Provera injection - unpleasant side effects of contraceptive drug - December 1978	Whether hospital was negligent in failing to provide proper counselling, warning and advice on after-effects of drug where hospital consultant (not the prescribing doctor) had been collating a file of information about the drug including its side effects.	NOT NEGLIGENT (1) there was no obligation to pass on to the plaintiff all the information available to the hospital; the question as to what the plaintiff should be told in answer to a general enquiry cannot be divorced from the Bolam test and must depend on the nature of the enquiry, the nature of the information which is available, its reliability, relevance, the condition of the patient etc.; (2) there is no rule of law , where questions or doubt are raised by a patient, requiring a doctor to hand over all the information on the subject which may be available in the files of a consultant who may have made a special study of the subject.	Plaintiff:- Professor Huntingford, consultant gynaecologist; Defendant:- Dame Josephine Barnes, consultant gynaecologist.	Judge in first instance awarded £3500 general damages for 2 years' irregular bleeding and menstrual irregularity.	**Blyth v Bloomsbury Health Authority** [1993] 4 Med LR 151 Court of Appeal LJs Kerr, Neill and Balcombe

| ORAL CONTRACEPTIVE - Trinordial prescribed by GP to patient with high blood pressure - death due to cerebral thrombosis caused by pill | (1) Whether GPs had sufficiently warned of contraindications to the oral contraceptive;

(2) Whether they had sufficiently heeded plaintiff's complaints of headaches and visual disturbances;

(3) Whether they were negligent in permitting plaintiff to continue taking the pill. | **NOT NEGLIGENT**

(1) Sufficient warning had been given - accepted defendants' account of the consultation;

(2) Contemporaneous records of defendants' preferred to statement evidence of deceased's (by trial) dead father - allegations of repeated visits and complaints rejected;

(3) Two out of three of the plaintiff's own experts did not consider the prescription unreasonable; Bolam test applied and defendants not negligent. | Plaintiff:- Dr Walter Scott, expert GP; Dr Bickerstaff, consultant neurologist; Mr John Megarry, consultant obstetrician and gynaecologist;

Defendants:- did not call any expert evidence but relied on evidence of medical witnesses as to fact. | No award made. | **Coker v Richmond, Twickenham and Roehampton Area Health Authority and Others**

[1996] 7 Med LR 58; QBD; Mr R Jackson QC (sitting as Deputy Judge of the QBD) |

MEDICAL TOPIC	ISSUES	HOW ISSUES DECIDED	EXPERTS USED	QUANTUM (general damages only unless otherwise stated)	CASE NAME AND REFERENCE
PNEUMONIA - **Failure to diagnose by trainee General Practitioner - wrong diagnosis of muscle strain - death from acute pneumococcal pneumonia**	Whether a competent trainee GP should have spotted the signs and symptoms of pneumonia.	**NEGLIGENT** (1) Where the patient is visibly sick or not well perfused, a strip thermometer which can only measure skin temperature, rather than a mercury or electronic thermometer which will measure core temperature, may be inadequate; (2) the history obtained by the doctor from the patient of muscle strain was contrary to the natural history of such strains; patient tend to rationalise their problem, which is a further reason for the doctor to be more circumspect when eliminating possible causes of the symptoms. The doctor erred in proceeding from the absence of confirmatory signs of pneumonia to an unequivocal diagnosis of muscle strain to the chest; he was negligent in failing to recognize the	Plaintiff:- Dr Berresford, consultant histopathologist; Dr D'Ambrumenil, general practitioner; Dr Lancaster, consultant physician; Defendant:- Dr Al Haboubi, consultant pathologist; Dr Robertson, consultant physician.	Liability only	**Bova v Spring** [1994] 5 Med LR 120 QBD; Sedley J

	uncertainties attending his diagnosis. Had he done so he would have had in mind the real possibility that the patient's chest pain might be pleural and a sign of pneumonia; (3) had he done so, he would have arranged a follow-up visit or told the patient to call for a further visit if not better and in either event, the further examination would have elicited the classic signs of pneumonia, followed by prompt admission to hospital, and life saving medical treatment.			
PREGNANCY - **wrongful birth -** **Failed vasectomy -** **failure to warn of risk of** **failure of procedure -** **1975**	(1) Whether advice that the operation would result in irreversible sterility amounted to a warranty; (2) Whether failure to warn was negligent; (3) Whether plaintiff entitled to an award of damages for discomfort and distress of an unwanted pregnancy, confinement and delivery.	**NEGLIGENT:-** (1) As medicine is not an exact science, the results of operations were to some extent unpredictable, so that a doctor could not objectively be regarded as guaranteeing the success of any operation or treatment unless he expressly said as much in clear an unequivocal terms; in this case, the contract was to carry out *(continued over)*	Not stated.	**Thake v Maurice** [1984] 2 All ER 513 QBD; Peter Pain J; [1986] 1 All ER 497 Court of Appeal; LJs Kerr, Neill and Nourse Dealing with treatment in 1975.
			£1500 for discomfort and pain of pregnancy and delivery.	

MEDICAL TOPIC	ISSUES	HOW ISSUES DECIDED	EXPERTS USED	QUANTUM (general damages only unless otherwise stated)	CASE NAME AND REFERENCE
		the vasectomy with reasonable care and skill, not to sterilise the plaintiff - the plaintiff was not entitled to a 100% guarantee of success; (2) But the failure of the defendant to give his usual warning amounted to a breach of care, because the warning was necessary to alert the wife to the risk that she might again become pregnant and so enable her to seek an abortion at an early stage; (3) the plaintiffs were entitled to damages for distress, pain and suffering, since the prenatal distress of both plaintiffs, and the pain and suffering of the birth was a separate head of claim which was not cancelled out by the relief and joy felt after the birth of a healthy baby.			

PREGNANCY - wrongful birth - Failed sterilisation - 1976 - refusal by plaintiff to undergo abortion - child born with congenital abnormality	At first instance -	Not stated.	£3,000 for pain and suffering up to trial and £10,000 for future pain, suffering and loss of amenity likely to occur during the life of the child.	**Emeh v Kensington and Chelsea and Westminster Area Health Authority** [1984] 3 All ER 1044 Court of Appeal; LJs Waller, Slade and Purchas Dealing with treatment in 1976.
(1) Effect on causation and damages of the plaintiff's refusal to undergo an abortion;	(1) Plaintiff's refusal to abort was so unreasonable as to amount to a novus actus interveniens or failure to mitigate damage and eclipsed negligence for which defendant was responsible;			
(2) On the assumption that it was contrary to public policy for damages to be recoverable if the child was born normal and healthy, whether the cost of bringing up a normal child should be deducted from the cost of bringing up an abnormal child.	(2) damages were therefore limited to compensation for plaintiff's pain and suffering up to time she discovered pregnancy and pain and inconvenience of undergoing second sterilisation operation;			
	On appeal:- appeal allowed:- CAUSATION ESTABLISHED			
	(1) avoidance of further pregnancy and birth was object of sterilisation procedure; by its negligence, defendant had confronted plaintiff with the very dilemma of an abortion which she had sought to avoid by having herself sterilised; defendant had no right to expect that, (*continued over*)			

MEDICAL TOPIC	ISSUES	HOW ISSUES DECIDED	EXPERTS USED	QUANTUM (general damages only unless otherwise stated)	CASE NAME AND REFERENCE
		under such circumstances, plaintiff would undergo an abortion with its attendant risks, pain and discomfort; it was instead reasonably foreseeable that plaintiff would decide to keep child; (2) there was no rule of public policy which prevented plaintiff from recovering in full the financial damage sustained by her as a result.			
PREGNANCY - wrongful birth - 1977 - failed sterilisation - normal healthy baby - liability admitted	Extent to which plaintiff entitled to damages for cost of carrying out necessary extensions to the home and of bringing up the child.	(1) It is contrary to public policy to award such damages to a mother because (i) it was undesirable that the child should know there was a court decision that his life or birth had been a mistake and that he was unwanted or rejected; (ii) in order to assess damages, the court would have to deduct an amount	Not stated.	£8,000 for pain, suffering, inconvenience and anxiety.	**Udale v Bloomsbury Area Health Authority** [1983] 2 All ER 522 QBD; Jupp J Dealing with treatment in 1977.

		for the value of the child's life as perceived by the mother, so that an uncaring mother would recover more than a caring one; (iii) doctors would be placed iunder pressure to carry out abortions; (iv) the birth of a normal healthy child was a beneficial, not detrimental, event; But these principles did not prevent the mother from recovering damages for lost income and for the pain, suffering, inconvenience, anxiety and disruption to the family's finances caused by the unexpected pregnancy.		
PREGNANCY - rubella infection - **Mother contracting rubella during pregnancy - failure to diagnose and treat infection - child born severely disabled - child claiming damages for wrongful entry into life**	Whether the doctor owed a legal duty to the foetus to terminate the pregnancy in order to prevent its existence in a disabled state.	**CLAIM STRUCK OUT:-** (1) The duty to an unborn child is not to injure it. On the facts, the child had not been injured by the defendant but by the infection contracted by the mother without the fault of the defendant; (2) Although the doctor *(continued over)*	Not stated.	No award made.	**McKay and another v Essex Area Health Authority and another** [1982] 2 All ER 771 Court of Appeal; LJs Stephenson, Ackner and Griffiths

MEDICAL TOPIC	ISSUES	HOW ISSUES DECIDED	EXPERTS USED	QUANTUM (general damages only unless otherwise stated)	CASE NAME AND REFERENCE
		owed a duty to the mother to advise her of the infection and its potential and serious effects and the desirability of an abortion, it did not follow that the doctor was under a legal obligation to the foetus to terminate its life, or that a foetus had a legal right to die; such a claim for wrongful life would be contrary to public policy as a violation of the sanctity of human life; (3) It would be impossible for the court to evaluate damages by comparing the value of non-existence and the value of existence in a disabled state. Therefore no reasonable cause of action.			

| PREGNANCY - wrongful birth - Failed vasectomy - failure to warn of 1 in 2000 risk of recanalisation - 1985 | (1) Whether vasectomist negligent in failing to warn of risk of late recanalisation in 1985, where defendant accepted that he had failed to adopt usual practice of giving the plaintiffs an information leaflet in which the risk was identified and warning orally in consultation, but asserted that in not warning he adopted a practice of a responsible body of medical opinion; (2) Whether husband and wife would have agreed to sterilisation in any event. | NEGLIGENT:- At the date of operation the risk of late recanalisation was well known to the profession; given this knowledge, a patient was entitled to be told of the operation's effectiveness, not only so as to enable him to judge whether to have it or to pursue other methods of contraception, but also so as not to excite suspicion against the wife if the operation failed; therefore ever since the risk was appreciated, the better practice has been to warn; the judge appreciated that in 1985 there were some doctors who would not have warned, but in doing so such doctors could not be considered to be acting reasonably or responsibly. In any event the defendant admitted that it was his practice to warn - the judge could not understand how he then sought to rely on a body of medical opinion which did otherwise; *(continued over)* | Plaintiff:- Mr Patrick Smith; Mr Harrison, Mr Peter Thompson, consultant urologists; Defendant:- Mr William Stahl; Mr Peter Sykes, general surgeon; Mr KF Parsons, Royal Liverpool University Hospital. | £500 for the anxiety and distress caused to the plaintiffs on finding the wife was pregnant (on the evidence the pregnancy had excited the husband's suspicion, causing marital disharmony). | **Newell & Newell v Goldenberg** [1995] 6 Med LR 371 QBD; Mantell J Dealing with treatment in 1985. |

PREGNANCY - wrongful birth - Failed vasectomy - 1986 Failure to warn in 1986	(1) Whether the Surgeon was negligent in giving no clear warning of risk of late reversal in 1986; (2) Measure of general damages.	**NEGLIGENT** (1) Literature and expert evidence shows that by 1986 vasectomists knew or ought to have known that there was a small but identifiable risk of a spontaneous late reversal of vasectomy; (2) The doctors' own practice since 1984 had been to warn; (3) Accepted the plaintiff's evidence that no warning had been given in this case; (4) Had the warning been given, judge drew the inference that the plaintiff would have taken the contraceptive pill - she conceived easily and was desperate not to have more children.	Plaintiff:- Mr Patrick Smith, consultant urologist.	£ 2500 general damages as contended by the plaintiff - relatively easy pregnancy and birth, but shock and distress on knowing she was pregnant and "the cloud over her" when only possible explanation appeared to be that she had had an affair - **NB** the judge considered this to be below what he would have expected.	**Gowton & Another v Wolverhampton Health Authority** [1994] 5 Med LR 432 QBD; Gage J Dealing with treatment in 1986.

CAUSATION - NOT ESTABLISHED:- Had the couple been properly advised, they would have been content to take the risk.

PREGNANCY - wrongful birth - Resulting from undiagnosed pregnancy	NEGLIGENT	Plaintiff:- Mr Michael House, consultant gynaecologist and obstetrician; Defendant:- Professor Bonner, consultant gynaecologist and obstetrician.	General damages:- £1250 for the few weeks she knew she was pregnant and the pain and suffering of a normal delivery.	**Gardiner v Mounfield & Lincolnshire Health Authority** [1989] 1 Med LR 205 QBD; Scott Baker J.
(1) Whether a consultant obstetrician and gynaecologist was negligent in failing to diagnose a pregnancy in an excessively overweight woman referred by her GP for possible endocrinal disorder; (2) Measure of general damages.	(1) Liability:- Accepted plaintiff's evidence that she thought she might be pregnant and did not wish to have a child; that she complained of tenderness of breasts and felt movements in her abdomen; in view of the fact that plaintiff had stopped taking pill two months earlier but continued to have regular sexual intercourse with partner using a sheath, defendant was negligent in dismissing possibility that plaintiff might be pregnant because she was overweight and he could see no clinical signs of pregnancy; (2) Causation:- plaintiff was pregnant when she first saw defendant; defendant had advised plaintiff in very strong terms that she was not pregnant; had she been told she was at the time he would have had a termination; at that time *(continued over)*			

MEDICAL TOPIC	ISSUES	HOW ISSUES DECIDED	EXPERTS USED	QUANTUM (general damages only unless otherwise stated)	CASE NAME AND REFERENCE
		the relevant criteria under the Abortion Act 1967 would have been met; (3) Damages:- general damages for the few weeks of her pregnancy when she knew she was pregnant and for pain and discomfort of a normal delivery: specials including lost earnings, benefits and leaves, clothing and maintenance of child to trial, and futures for future cost of maintaining the child and her own future losses.			
PREGNANCY - wrongful birth - spina bifida baby	Whether radiologist was negligent in failing to seek second opinion on a scan at 25 weeks because he believed that a termination after 19 weeks would have been unlawful.	**NOT NEGLIGENT** (1) There would have been obstetricians available who would have been willing to perform a termination at 28 weeks in bona fide belief that such termination would be lawful under Infant Life (Preservation) Act 1929 and Abortion Act 1967;	Plaintiff:- Dr Levick and Dr Margaret Buck, consultant radiologists; Mr Huntingford, Dr Brudenell and Professor Campbell, consultant obstetricians; Dr Pearse, consultant neo-natologist; Defendant:- Mr Mackenzie, consultant obstetrician; Dr Robertson, consultant neo-natologist.	No award made.	**Rance v Mid Downs Health Authority and Storr** [1990] 2 Med LR 27 QBD; Brooke J

(2) It was probable that child was 26 weeks at time of relevant scan and would have been 27 weeks by time of referral;

(3) On the literature and statistical evidence, had child been born at 27 weeks, he would have been born alive and would have survived first 28 days of life; he would have been capable of being born alive under 1929 Act and therefore any termination at time would have been unlawful;

(4) doctors view that 24 weeks was upper limit of time for performing abortions was an approach which was accepted as proper by a responsible body of medical men skilled in radiology and obstetrics.

Excellent summary of the law in this area.

MEDICAL TOPIC	ISSUES	HOW ISSUES DECIDED	EXPERTS USED	QUANTUM (general damages only unless otherwise stated)	CASE NAME AND REFERENCE
PREGNANCY - wrongful birth handicapped child - quantum only	Whether the plaintiffs were entitled to cost of maintenance of child where they had intended to have more children - defendants argued they were not entitled to basic maintenance costs but only to the additional costs attributable to the child's condition.	**In the first instance:-** Had the defendants not been negligent, the plaintiffs would have willingly incurred the cost of maintaining a normal child; due to the negligence, they are now incurring the cost of bringing up a severely handicapped child and they never wanted, and did not want, a handicapped child. The cost of maintaining him is, therefore, something they never wanted. Therefore they are entitled to the normal basic cost of maintaining the child. **On appeal:- APPEAL ALLOWED:-** the general principle is to place the injured party, as far as possible in financial terms, in the same position as he would have been had the negligent act not occurred; accordingly, the decision of the parents not to have	Not stated.	General damages £5000 for pain and suffering of the mother, including her continuing deep emotional feelings.	**Salih v Enfield Health Authority** [1990] 1 Med LR 333, QBD; Drake J **On appeal:-** [1991] 2 Med LR 235 Court of Appeal; LJs Butler-Sloss, Mann and Sir Christopher Slade

PREGNANCY - wrongful birth - Failed sterilisation - premature baby with speech and behavioural problems - quantum only.	(1) Quantum of general damages where baby born prematurely, and with residual speech and behavioural problems; (2) Quantum of special damages for loss of mother's earnings in those circumstances.	(1) £10,000 general damages for pain and discomfort and problems associated with pregnancy and delivery, pain and discomfort from operation to remove fallopian tubes, consequent residual problems of scarring and discomfort and additional anxiety, stress and burden involved in bringing up a premature baby which is to some extent handicapped; (2) It was entirely reasonable for the mother not to return to part time work until the child went to school in circumstances where the child had significant handicaps and medical problems during infancy. another child and the resultant saving of future expenditure was a relevant consideration and damages in respect of the basic cost of maintaining the child should be disallowed.	Not stated.	£ 10,000 general damages. Robinson v Salford Health Authority [1992] 3 Med LR 270 QBD; Moorland J

MEDICAL TOPIC	ISSUES	HOW ISSUES DECIDED	EXPERTS USED	QUANTUM (general damages only unless otherwise stated)	CASE NAME AND REFERENCE
PREGNANCY - wrongful birth - **Failed salpingectomy - no hystero-salpingogram performed**	Whether surgeon negligent in failing to offer hystero-salpingogram to check that clips were properly applied, following surgery where operation note indicated that the surgeon had initial difficulty with the clips.	**NOT NEGLIGENT** (1) The surgeon was satisfied that she had applied the clip to both tubes, since if not she could have proceeded to laparotomy as covered by the consent form; (2) HSGs were not performed routinely, were uncomfortable with a chance of infection, radiation and the possibility of re-opening the occluded tube - the defendant was not negligent in not offering it, nor in letting the plaintiff leave hospital with the impression she had undergone a successful sterilization.	Plaintiff:- Mr Vincent Argent, consultant gynaecologist; Defendant:- Mr David Millar, consultant gynaecologist.	No award made.	**McLennan v Newcastle Health Authority** [1992] 3 Med LR 215 QBD; Alliott J

| PREGNANCY - wrongful birth -

failure to diagnose pregnancy which then survived sterilization procedure | Quantum only - principles applicable to measurement of financial cost of bringing up child. | (1) Where doctor is in breach of duty resulting in birth of a child whose life would have otherwise been lawfully terminated, mother is entitled to recover damages for foreseeable loss and damage suffered in consequence;

(2) She is entitled to general damages and any associated financial special damage for discomfort and pain associated with pregnancy and delivery of child, although offset against this must be a sum in respect of avoidance of pain and suffering and associated financial loss which would have resulted from termination of pregnancy under general anaesthetic;

(3) she is also entitled to damages for economic loss for (i) financial loss she suffers to maintain a growing child; (ii) financial loss suffered because she has lost or may lose earnings because

(*continued over*) | Not stated. | £ 62,217 general damages including the mother's future loss of earnings (£29,715), child-minding costs (£2,850), maintenance of the child to 18 years of age (£27,152), mother's pain and suffering and loss of amenity (£2,500). | **Allen v Bloomsbury Health Authority**

[1992] 3 Med LR 257 QBD; Brooke J |

MEDICAL TOPIC	ISSUES	HOW ISSUES DECIDED	EXPERTS USED	QUANTUM (general damages only unless otherwise stated)	CASE NAME AND REFERENCE
		of her obligation toward child; (4) the law will not allow damages for wear and tear and tiredness in bringing up a healthy child, since this is set off against benefit of bringing a healthy child up to maturity; but the law will recognize a claim for foreseeable extra stress and anxiety involved in bringing up a handicapped child.			
PREGNANCY - wrongful birth - Spina bifida baby - nursing services - mother with multiple sclerosis - quantum only	Whether, in addition to an award for nursing services provided by the mother herself for the child, the mother was entitled to an award for loss of earnings, or whether such would amount to double recovery.	(1) The essence of the case is that the plaintiff is not entitled to make a profit out of the situation; it would have been wrong for the judge to have awarded her full loss of earnings on top of the value of her services in caring for the child; (2) Had she given up work which gave her a great	Agreed expert:- Dr Cawdery.	£9,000 general damages for pain and suffering and loss of amenity awarded to the mother.	**Fish v Wilcox** [1994] 5 Med LR 230 Court of Appeal LJs Nourse, Stuart-Smith and Mann

					Lybert v Warrington Health Authority [1996] 7 Med LR 71 Court of Appeal; LJs Otton, Nourse and Millett
				Not stated.	
	deal of pleasure, that deprivation might have formed part of her general damages; had she given up highly paid work for her daughter, then she would have recovered that figure by way of loss or earnings rather than the figure which the judge assessed for the cost of providing professional care; (3) In this case the judge properly awarded an additional element for the additional burden of looking after the child as opposed to the work which the plaintiff had previously done.	Not stated.		
		NEGLIGENT (1) Warning to be given prior to sterilisation procedure must cover that it is irreversible; that there is a risk of failure; that it is imperative to seek immediate medical advice in the event of signs of (*continued over*)			
PREGNANCY - wrongful birth - **Failed sterilisation - tubal ligation at time of caesarian section - subsequent pregnancy - healthy infant**	(1) Whether there was failure to warn of risk of failure of procedure and of necessity to seek medical advice forthwith in the event of any signs of further pregnancy after the procedure; (2) Whether in addition to giving appropriate warning there was a duty to ensure (*continued over*)				

MEDICAL TOPIC	ISSUES	HOW ISSUES DECIDED	EXPERTS USED	QUANTUM (general damages only unless otherwise stated)	CASE NAME AND REFERENCE
	it was properly understood; (3) Whether the trial judge's finding that in addition to sterilization the plaintiff would have used contraception had she been warned was intrinsically improbable; (4) Whether had the plaintiff been properly warned she would have terminated the resulting pregnancy.	pregnancy after the procedure; (2) On the evidence she had never been given reasonable warning; previous history of 3 caesarian sections, earlier agreement to a hysterectomy and failure of sheath contraception during earlier wait for hysterectomy supported her genuine concern over any risk of conception and inherent likelihood she would have heeded any warning had it been given, and that if so advised would have agreed to use conventional contraception in the interim period; (3) Duty on defendants was to give clear and comprehensible warning that was reasonable in the circumstances; but no duty to ensure that it was understood; (4) See (1) above - in normal circumstances it was intrinsically			

		improbable that a plaintiff would use contraception in addition to sterilisation - these were not normal circumstances. (5) Found for the plaintiff on the facts.		
PREGNANCY - wrongful birth - **Failed vasectomy - claim brought by patient's sexual partner - patient not warned he needed to use any additional form of contraception after his vasectomy**	Whether the defendant was in a sufficient or any special relationship with the patient's existing or future sexual partners such as gave rise to a duty of care.	**NOT NEGLIGENT** (1) there was no duty of the defendant to the plaintiff - the reality is that the doctor advised the patient; the plaintiff is no nearer the doctor adviser than someone who 3 and a half years after the surgery commenced sexual relations with the patient; equally the class to which the plaintiff belongs is potentially excessive in size and uncertain in character; (2) the doctor knows he is advising the patient and (if married) his wife; he does not know or ought to know that he also advises any future sexual partners of his patient who chance to receive his advice at second hand; *(continued over)*	Not relevant. No award made.	**Goodwill v British Pregnancy Advisory Service** [1996] 7 Med LR 129 Court of Appeal; LJs Peter Gibson and Thorpe

MEDICAL TOPIC	ISSUES	HOW ISSUES DECIDED	EXPERTS USED	QUANTUM (general damages only unless otherwise stated)	CASE NAME AND REFERENCE
		(3) a woman exploring the development of a sexual relationship with a new partner takes much on trust before experience corroborates or exposes his assurances - her responsibility is to protect herself against unwanted conception and to take independent advice on whatever facts he presents.			
PREMATURE BABY - **Catheter inserted in vein rather than artery and delivered excess oxygen -** **retrolental fibroplasia (RLF) casing total blindness in one eye and severe impairment of vision in the other**	(1) Whether the plaintiff's condition was caused by the excess oxygen or by five other conditions common in premature babies, from all of which the plaintiff had suffered; (2) Whether the burden of proof was reversed.	**First instance -** **NEGLIGENT -** Hospital had failed to take precautions against allowing excess oxygen to be delivered, and since plaintiff then suffered the very thing that such precautions were designed to prevent, burden lay on defendant to show that there was no breach of duty and that damage did not result from breach; here defendant had failed to discharge that burden;	Not stated.	£116,119 total damages at first instance - no breakdown provided.	**Wilsher v Essex Area Health Authority** QBD; Peter Pain J [1986] 3 All ER 801 Court of Appeal; LJs Mustill and Glidewell, Sir Nicholas Browne-Wilkinson dissenting. [1988] 1 All ER 871 House of Lords; Lords Bridge of Harwich, Fraser of Tullybelton, Lowry, Griffiths and Ackner

Court of Appeal:-
affirmed decision at first instance.

House of Lords:-
reversed decision:-

Where plaintiff's injury is attributable to one of a number of possible causes, one of which is defendant's negligence, combination of injury and defendant's breach do not give rise to presumption that defendant caused injury; burden remains on plaintiff to prove the causative link; here, condition could have been caused by any one of a number of different agents, and it had not been proved that it was caused by defendant's failure to prevent excess oxygen to plaintiff.

MEDICAL TOPIC	ISSUES	HOW ISSUES DECIDED	EXPERTS USED	QUANTUM (general damages only unless otherwise stated)	CASE NAME AND REFERENCE
RADIATION INJURY - (Professional negligence claim against legal advisers) - external pelvic irradiation following hysterectomy for carcinoma - Stage 1a micro-invasive case where risk of lymphatic involvement very small - radiation injury necessitating ileostomy.	Whether decision to treat by external beam radiotherapy was negligent in 1978; whether decision to treat by external beam radiotherapy was negligent in 1978.	**NEGLIGENT** - ie the plaintiff would have had 60 per cent chance of establishing negligence against the doctors:- (1) The gynaecologist:- faced by the unexpected finding of invasive cancer following performance of simple hysterectomy, the gynaecologist had an obligation to seek advice - he should have consulted others with a greater knowledge than he patently had of gynaecological cancer and applied his mind to the possibility of over-treating if irradiation was prescribed; in 1978 there was medical literature which would have cautioned him against radiotherapy in a Stage 1a case; as the referring gynaecologist it was as much his responsibility to familiarize himself with current thinking on the	Plaintiff:- Professor Wells, consultant pathologist; Dr Keith Halnan, consultant radiotherapist; Dr Michael House and Dr Peter Huntingford, consultant gynaecologists; Defendant:- Dr Krausz, consultant pathologist; Professor Dische, consultant radiotherapist; Professor Hudson and Dr William Souter, consultant gynaecologists.	Not stated.	**Gascoigne v Ian Sheridan & Co (A Firm) and Latham** [1994] 5 Med LR 437 QBD; Mitchell J

topic of risk as it was of the radiotherapy consultant;

(2) The radiotherapist:- her insight into the nature of the plaintiff's cancer was likewise totally inadequate; she also therefore had a duty to consult;

(3) Had they so consulted, there was some prospect in 1978 of them being advised that the mainstream of current thinking was against proceeding to treat by radical irradiation.

Case	Facts	Issue	Findings	Experts	Damages
Smith v Tunbridge Wells Health Authority [1994] 5 Med LR 334 QBD; Morland J	**RECTAL SURGERY -** Wells operation in 1988 for full thickness rectal prolapse on straining - nerve damage resulting in impotency and bladder malfunction in young, sexually active married man - informed consent only	Whether Surgeon was under a duty to warn the patient of the possibility of impotence and incontinence.	**NEGLIGENT** (1) having regard to evidence of the experts, and the literature between 1959 and 1988 showing frequency of complication of between 0 - 30 %, although some surgeons may still not have been warning patients similar in situation to the plaintiff of the risk of impotence, that (*continued over*)	Plaintiff:- Mr Northover, colorectal surgeon; Mr John Scurr, consultant general surgeon; Mr Carroll, consultant urologist; Defendant:- Mr Kirkham, consultant general surgeon; Professor Golligher.	£130,000 agreed damages - no breakdown provided.

MEDICAL TOPIC	ISSUES	HOW ISSUES DECIDED	EXPERTS USED	QUANTUM (general damages only unless otherwise stated)	CASE NAME AND REFERENCE
		omission was neither reasonable nor responsible; (2) on the balance of probabilities, the doctor had failed to explain with sufficient clarity to be expected in 1988 of a consultant general surgeon with his interest in colorectal surgery the risk of impotence and was negligent; (3) on the evidence the plaintiff would have refused the surgery had the risk of impotence been explained to him.			

SEPTICAEMIA - Puerperal fever following childbirth - fulminating septicaemia developing from septic spot - 1963	NEGLIGENT	Plaintiff:- Dr May; Mr Bourne; Professor Camps;	£4000 general damages.	Hucks v Cole
		Defendant:- Miss Barnes; Dr Hickman; Miss June Smith.		[1993] 4 Med LR 393 Court of Appeal Lord Denning MR, LJs Diplock and Sachs (8th May 1968)
(1) Whether GP's failure to prescribe penicillin for septic spot was negligent, following unsuccessful tetracycline course, when the hospital pathologist's report on the septic spot swab stated that the plaintiff had streptococcus pyogenes which was a virulent organism capable of killing and in addition that penicillin would kill the germs, but was silent concerning tetracyclines;	Per Denning LJ:- (1) The pathologist's report would ring an alarm bell for every practitioner; (2) on the evidence, by the end of the course of tetracycline, the lesions had not fully healed; (3) the judge was wholly justified in holding that the doctor ought to have given the plaintiff treatment with penicillin, and the doctor's conduct in failing to prescribe penicillin was inexcusable;			
(2) Quantum where the plaintiff suffered a grave illness from which she nearly died, her mental state was affected for a long time, suffers from depression, is very clumsy with her hands, has pseudo-bulbar speech, cannot join social life or help her husband - whether £2500 general damages for pain and suffering was sufficient.	(4) £2500 is far too low and should be increased to £4000. Per Sachs LJ - in this case the doctor knew that penicillin could easily and inexpensively be administered before the onset of fulminating septicaemia occurred; thus *(continued over)*			

MEDICAL TOPIC	ISSUES	HOW ISSUES DECIDED	EXPERTS USED	QUANTUM (general damages only unless otherwise stated)	CASE NAME AND REFERENCE
		the onset was due to a lacuna between what could easily have been done and what was in fact done; when the evidence shows that a lacuna exists by which risks of grave danger are knowingly taken, then, however small the risks are, the courts must anxiously examine that lacuna - particularly if the risks can be easily and inexpensively be avoided.			

| SEPTICAEMIA - Delay in diagnosis - in infant resulting in severe brain damage | (1) Whether GP was negligent in failing to attend patient; (2) Whether GP was negligent in failing to send patient to hospital after initial diagnosis; (3) Causation. | NOT NEGLIGENT (1) Accepted defendant GP expert's opinion that it was in accord with good medical practice to send an experienced practice nurse in response to the first call; (2) considering the conduct of the GP against standards to be expected of reasonably competent GPs, the failure to admit after midnight was not negligent - the standard set by Professor Holt was too high and the evidence of the expert GP was more compelling; (3) on the balance of probabilities, admission 3 hours earlier would not have made any difference; the observations would have been the same and the diagnosis made no earlier. | Plaintiff:- Professor Holt, consultant paediatrician; Mr Gamsu, consultant neonatologist; Defendant:- Professor Malcolm Levene, consultant paediatrician; Dr Peter Williams, expert GP. | No award made. | **Stockdale v Nicholls** [1993] 4 Med LR 191 QBD; Otton J |

MEDICAL TOPIC	ISSUES	HOW ISSUES DECIDED	EXPERTS USED	QUANTUM (general damages only unless otherwise stated)	CASE NAME AND REFERENCE
SHUNT INFECTION - **Ventricular peritoneal shunt in hydrocephalic infant - failure to diagnose shunt problem resulting in catastrophic brain damage**	(1) Whether more senior doctor than a senior house officer in casualty should have been delegated to contact neurosurgical team to discuss the patient; (2) Whether the neurosurgical registrar consulted by phone by the SHO was wrong in not advising the SHO that the patient should be sent to a hospital with a neurological unit when there were symptoms of neurological difficulty; (3) Whether the paediatric team were negligent in paying insufficient attention to signs and symptoms which might indicate a neurological problem and failing to refer the infant admitted with VP shunt infection to a hospital with a neurological unit.	(1) SHO in casualty NOT NEGLIGENT - He had taken detailed history and examination and was therefore obvious person to contact neurosurgical registrar at London Hospital - there was no doubt that he was competent to do so and did so efficiently; (2) Neurosurgical registrar NOT NEGLIGENT - While wrong in not telling the SHO that child should be sent to neurological department at London Hospital, this was a long way from saying that he was negligent for failing to do so; (i) it is easy to be wise in hindsight; (ii) the plaintiff had not established that the failure to advise transfer was an action which no neurosurgical registrar of ordinary skill would follow (applying Maynard);	Plaintiff:- Dr Newton, consultant paediatric neurologist; Dr Wallis, consultant paediatrician; Mr Briggs and Mr Wilson, consultant neurosurgeons; Mr Forrest, consultant paediatric surgeon retired in 1987; Defendants:- Mr Hockley, consultant neurosurgeon, Dr Tarlow, consultant paediatrician.	£1,250,000 agreed damages - no breakdown provided.	**Robinson v Jacklin and Others** [1996] 7 Med LR 83 QBD: Mr G Hamilton QC sitting as deputy judge of the High Court

(3) Paediatric team
NEGLIGENT -

Team knew that plaintiff had a shunt in place; they knew there was a danger of intracranial infection that might spread rapidly; that such infection could only be treated by a neurosurgical team which was available at the London Hospital; further, the patient did in fact suffer from raised intracranial pressure caused by intracranial infection; yet they did not transfer the patient till he had been fitting for about 6 hours. This fell below the standards of professional people in their position.

MEDICAL TOPIC	ISSUES	HOW ISSUES DECIDED	EXPERTS USED	QUANTUM (general damages only unless otherwise stated)	CASE NAME AND REFERENCE
SPINAL INJURY - **Avascular fibrosis in spinal cord, insulation of sub- arachnoid space and angulation of spine 20 years following serious spinal injury, causing incontinence, and foot drop, sciatica and weakness in the right leg**	(1) Whether it was negligent of the GP to have failed to seek further expert advice from a neurologist or neurosurgeon when neither the urologist nor the orthopaedic consultant to whom he had been referred with incontinence and foot-drop respectively had done so; (2) Whether it was negligent of the urological team to have failed to refer the plaintiff to a neurologist or neurosurgeon; (3) Whether it was negligent for the two orthopaedic teams involved to have failed to order a myelogram and spinal surgery.	**NOT NEGLIGENT** (1) single foundation for the plaintiff's case was the evidence of Mr Radley-Smith that cause of his problems was growth of new bone at the original fracture site or possible disc protrusion there; there was no evidence supporting this, and symptoms were familiar long-term consequences of spinal injury, caused by arachnoid adhesions; (2) GP:- no breach - he had made the appropriate referrals and his own belief that the plaintiff was suffering typical ischaemic spinal cord deterioration with age had been reassured by two major teaching hospitals; Orthopaedic consultant:- while he could have taken a fuller history, even had he done so this would not nor should have made any difference to the treatment offered;	Plaintiff:- Mr Radley-Smith, neuro-surgeon (retired); Mr Wilkinson, consultant urologist; Dr Hempling, GP; Defendant:- Mr Garfield, consultant neurosurgeon, Dr Kocen, consultant neurologist; Mr Riddle, consultant urologist; Mr Vickers, consultant orthopaedic surgeon; Dr Pollock, GP.	No award made.	**Scott v Bloomsbury Health Authority & Others** [1990] 1 Med LR 214, QBD; Brooke J

		Decision	Parties	Damages	Citation
		Urological team:- while there were many urologists who would have referred for neurological opinion, it would depend on the experience of the urologist; the treating urologist was very experienced and distinguished and understood well what was happening to the plaintiff's bladder and this understanding was correct.			**Sidaway v Bethlem Royal Hospital Governors and others** QBD; Skinner J; [1984] 1 All ER 1018 Court of Appeal; Sir John Donaldson MR, LJs Dunn and Browne-Wilkinson [1985] 1 All ER 643 House of Lords; Lords Scarman, Diplock, Deith of Kinkel, Bridge of Harwich and Templeman
SPINAL SURGERY - 1974 - for persistent pain in neck and shoulders - warning of possibility of disturbing a nerve root but not of damage to the spinal cord - injury to spinal cord causing severe disablement	Whether the failure to warn of risk of damage to spinal cord was negligent.	**At first instance:- NOT NEGLIGENT:-** **Court of Appeal - appeal dismissed;** **House of Lords:- appeal dismissed:-** (1) The test of liability in respect of failure to warn is the same as that applicable to diagnosis and treatment, namely that the doctor should act in accordance with a practice accepted at that time as proper by a responsible body of medical opinion; however although a *(continued over)*	Plaintiff:- Mr Uttley, consultant neurosurgeon; Defendant:- not stated.	£67,500 agreed total damages, subject to liability - no breakdown provided.	

MEDICAL TOPIC	ISSUES	HOW ISSUES DECIDED	EXPERTS USED	QUANTUM (general damages only unless otherwise stated)	CASE NAME AND REFERENCE
		decision on which risks should be disclosed was primarily a matter of clinical judgment, the disclosure of a particular risk of serious adverse consequences might be so obviously necessary for the patient to make an informed choice that no reasonably prudent doctor would fail to disclose that risk; this includes a requirement to warn the patient of any dangers which were special in kind or magnitude or special to the patient; (2) When questioned specifically by a patient of apparently sound mind about the risks involved in a particular treatment proposed, the doctor's duty is to answer both truthfully and as fully as the questioner requires; (3) In this case, the failure to warn was in accordance with responsible opinion at the time and was therefore not negligent.			

SPINAL SURGERY - **Congenital abnormality C1-C2 - occipital/cervical fusion - application of Ransford loop - plaintiff rendered tetraplegic**	(1) Whether Surgeon failed in properly informing the Plaintiff of benefits of both surgical and non-surgical management; (2) Whether CT scan should have been taken before surgery; (3) Whether surgery was carried out negligently; As to quantum:- (4) Extent to which diagnosis of ankylosing spondylitis after trial of liability issues affected claim for damages, including loss of earnings as a window-cleaner.	**NEGLIGENT** (1) It was widely known in 1988 that in patients with atlanto-axial occipital fusion, death or paralysis could occur as result of trauma causing further degree of subluxation; therefore plaintiff was prime candidate for this surgery; although no consideration had been given to possibility that pain may have simply emanated from C3/4 where degenerative changes were present, nor to case for conservative treatment, no reason to think that had doctor taken proper steps in his assessment, he would have reached any different conclusion, nor would such conclusion have been negligent; (2) on facts, risks of paralysis or death from surgery were never made clear to plaintiff - they should have been xplained, defendant was negligent in that regard; but had warning been given, plaintiff would have proceeded with surgery; *(continued over)*	Plaintiff:- Mr Adams, consultant neurosurgeon; Dr Pallis, consultant neurologist; Dr Butler, consultant rheumatologist; Defendant:- Mr Finlay and Mr Johnston, consultant neurosurgeons; Dr David Sumner, consultant neurologist; Dr Holt, consultant rheumatologist.	£60,000 general damages for pain, suffering and loss of amenity.	**Smith v Salford Health Authority** [1994] 5 Med LR 321 QBD; Potter J **As to quantum:-** [1995] 6 Med LR 311 QBD; Potter J

MEDICAL TOPIC	ISSUES	HOW ISSUES DECIDED	EXPERTS USED	QUANTUM (general damages only unless otherwise stated)	CASE NAME AND REFERENCE
		(3) on unanimous views of experts, a CT scan should have been taken before the surgery, but this was not directly causative of injury; (4) but doctor was negligent in use of aneurism needle, which was inherently likely to intrude too far into spinal canal.			
SPINAL SURGERY - **Exploratory surgery for suspected nerve root compression - breach of dural sac wall - resulting in chronic arachnoiditis**	Whether decision to operate was negligent in the absence of clear and unequivocal clinical or radiological evidence supporting surgery.	**At first instance:- NOT NEGLIGENT** (1) On the evidence there is a separate specialism of spinal surgeons comprising both orthopaedic and neurosurgeons who specialise wholly or mainly in spinal surgery; (2) Not unreasonable for spinal specialist to carry out exploratory surgery in and around the spine provided adequate safeguards in place.	Plaintiff:- not stated; Defendant:- Mr Findlay, consultant neurosurgeon ; Mr Webb, consultant orthopaedic surgeon, both specialising in spinal surgery.	No award made.	**De Freitas v O'Brien & Connolly** [1993] 4 Med LR 281 Mayor's and City Court; HH Judge Byrt QC; **On appeal -** [1995] 6 Med LR 108 Court of Appeal LJs Leggatt, Otton and Swinton-Thomas.

ON APPEAL:- appeal dismissed

(1) It was not unreasonable for a doctor to draw the inference that there might be nerve root compression even in absence of unequivocal evidence to that effect, therefore there was evidence to support decision to operate in absence of radicular pain;

(2) A small number of tertiary specialists (in this case, eleven throughout the UK out of a total of well over 1,000 orthopaedic surgeons and neuro-surgeons) may constitute a responsible body of medical opinion.

MEDICAL TOPIC	ISSUES	HOW ISSUES DECIDED	EXPERTS USED	QUANTUM (general damages only unless otherwise stated)	CASE NAME AND REFERENCE
SPINAL SURGERY - **Decompression of spine to correct prolapsed thoracic disk (laminectomy and transpedicular approach following a costotransversectomy) - resulting in paraplegia**	Whether method of surgery was negligent given that it was unique in its combination of procedures, in circumstances where the plaintiff had been warned of risk of paraplegia.	**NOT NEGLIGENT** (1) Applying Maynard, that merely because the approach was novel did not make it negligent; there was a body of competent professional opinion which supported the decision made by the surgeon; (2) further, judge was not satisfied that there was anything done which was contrary to reasonable, professional opinion; (3) in any event the plaintiff would not have been able to prove causation ie that the injury was not caused by aspects of the surgery that were conceded not to be negligent.	Plaintiff:- (The late) Mr Bernard Williams, consultant neuro-surgeon; Defendant:- Professor BA Bell, professor of neurosurgery; Mr Robert Bradford, consultant neurosurgeon.	No award made.	**Waters v West Sussex Health Authority** [1995] 6 Med LR 362 QBD; Buxton J

| STAB WOUND -

Butcher's knife - failure by General Practitioner to appreciate seriousness of perforation leading to fulminating peritonitis followed by death | (1) Whether the GP was negligent in failing to communicate with the deceased's own doctor;

(2) Whether doctor was negligent in failing to appreciate seriousness of wound. | **In the first instance - NEGLIGENT**

The doctor's diagnosis of superficial wound was not negligent although too optimistic. However, the doctor was negligent in failing to communicate with the plaintiff's own doctor and telling him of the exact nature of his findings when he examined the wound;

On appeal - REVERSED;

On appeal to the House of Lords:- appeal dismissed -

But reasoning of dissenting judges more helpful - a doctor who is expected to look after a patient with an abdominal wound, which has already been diagnosed and treated by another doctor, should be put in possession of information on what has been observed and done by the first doctor; the first doctor should have foreseen that by failing to

(*continued over*) | Not stated. | No award made. | **Chapman v Rix**

Date of judgment 21/12/60

[1994] 5 Med LR 239
House of Lords:
Lords Keith, Goddard, Morton, Denning and Hodson |

MEDICAL TOPIC	ISSUES	HOW ISSUES DECIDED	EXPERTS USED	QUANTUM (general damages only unless otherwise stated)	CASE NAME AND REFERENCE
		pass on material information in his possession he was probably depriving the patient's own doctor of the fore-knowledge that he should have had to deal properly with the patient's case; that non-communication amounted to negligence in law.			
SYMPATHETIC OPTHALMITIS - **Delay in enucleation i.e. surgical removal of right eye, leading to development of posterior sympathetic opthalmitis in left eye and blindness in both eyes**	(1) Whether the ophthalmic surgeon was negligent in failing to follow up the plaintiff after receiving a second opinion and keeping the plaintiff under regular review; (2) Whether had he done so, late enucleation would have had a reasonable chance of success in preventing the onset of the disease.	**NEGLIGENT** (1) in the circumstances the plaintiff should have been followed up - the second opinion letter indicated that the steroid drops should be continued and that there was still inflammation and warned that the plaintiff should be told to report development of further troubles; (2) had the plaintiff been followed up, the deterioration of the right eye would have been noted and it would have been enucleated by October	Plaintiff:- Mr MJ Roper Hall, Mr Nicholas Phelps Brown; Defendant:- Mr Leaver, Mr Grey, Mr John Scott.	Assessment of damages postponed.	**Cavanagh v Bristol & Weston Health Authority** [1992] 3 Med LR 49 QBD; MacPherson J

	1985 on a balance of probability; (3) the plaintiff's expert's evidence that this would have prevented the development of sympathetic opthalmitis in the other eye may not be the majority's view, but even if this is so, the question of causation is not to be decided against a plaintiff upon the basis of a reasonable body of medical opinion - that would be to import the Bolam test into causation where it has no proper place. [cf *Bolitho* (p 152, above)].				Sa'd v Robinson, Dunlop, Sa'd, Ransley and Mid Surrey Health Authority [1989] 1 Med LR 41 QBD; Leggatt J.
THERMAL INJURY - Thermal injury to child's throat caused by inhalation of steam from teapot spout resulting in irreversible brain damage	(1) Whether GP was negligent in failing to visit the child promptly, promptly to refer to hospital, show parents the way to the hospital and thereafter to arrange appropriate reception committee in casualty department at hospital; (*continued over*)	(1) GP - NEGLIGENT - in failing to recognize the essential difference between ingesting tea from a spout and drinking from a cup; this difference was crucial as the former may involve the inhalation of steam and that the liquid will be close to boiling-point; and in failing in any event to ask more questions which would (*continued over*)	Plaintiff:- Professor Rosen, professor of anaesthesia; Defendant:- Dr Dinwiddie, consultant respiratory paediatrician; (*continued over*)	£535,000 in total - no breakdown - although normal in appearance, she is so severely brain-damaged that she can neither speak nor recognize her mother, but is unaware of her plight.	

MEDICAL TOPIC	ISSUES	HOW ISSUES DECIDED	EXPERTS USED	QUANTUM (general damages only unless otherwise stated)	CASE NAME AND REFERENCE
	(2) Whether the consultant paediatrician was negligent in failing to arrange for intubation of the child by an anaesthetist.	have clarified any misapprehension; and in failing to refer child to the hospital; later in failing to realise urgency of need for admission to hospital and in the circumstances, failing to show the parents the way the hospital himself, ensuring the parents went to casualty and explaining seriousness of condition to the hospital over the phone thereby ensuring appropriate reception committee; (2) Consultant Paediatrician - **NOT NEGLIGENT** - this was an almost unique case; the doctor had been overtaken by a number of events within a short time; whether to summon a consultant anaesthetist was within the scope of the doctor's discretion, and in not doing so there was no failure on her part to exercise the ordinary skill of a consultant paediatrician; by the time	Other experts:- Dr Livingstone; Dr Bush; Dr Armstrong; Dr Hargrove, consultant anaesthetist; Dr Walter Scott, expert GP.		

URETERIC INJURY - **During hysterectomy - right ureter unintentionally ligated - incontinence and necessity for remedial surgery**	(1) Whether this was a case of non-culpable ureteric damage in abdominal hysterectomy; (2) Causation.	**NEGLIGENT** (1) On the literature and expert evidence, found that the incidence of non-culpable ureteric damage in normal cases is exceedingly rare, and unlikely to be greater than 1 in several thousand - so remote that a court would be justified in disregarding that as a possible explanation in the absence of evidence supporting it. Most of the cases of damage to the ureters in normal anatomy are due to poor technique; (2) Expressly found that pre-existing adhesions had no causative relevance; (3) In this case found that the ureters were damaged by encircling of ureter by a suture when the uterine pedicle was being ligated, and that this was negligent.	Plaintiff:- Dr Huntingford, consultant gynaecologist; Mr Smith, consultant urologist; Defendant:- Mr Brudenell and Dame Josephine Barnes, consultant gynaecologists; Mr Fyfe, consultant urologist.	Not stated.	**Hendy v Milton Keynes Health Authority (No.2)** [1992] 3 Med LR 119 QBD; Jowitt J

she could have arranged for the anaesthetic equipment, it would have made no difference.

MEDICAL TOPIC	ISSUES	HOW ISSUES DECIDED	EXPERTS USED	QUANTUM (general damages only unless otherwise stated)	CASE NAME AND REFERENCE
URETERIC INJURY - During hysterectomy - extent of fibroids requiring removal of uterus in two sections - damage causing blockage of right ureter causing kidney damage	(1) Whether damage caused during the procedure rather than as result of post-operative infection; (2) Whether the damage was caused by a lack of care; (3) Quantum where 45 year old female plaintiff - gave up work due to presence of permanent pain; pain varied, was always present and caused loss of sleep; affected mood and sexual relations; recurrent urinary infections six times per annum treated with antibiotics; elevated blood pressure; unable to lead a normal life.	**NEGLIGENT -** (1) Accepted the plaintiff's evidence that she had suffered back pain soon after the operation and this indicated that damage was done during course of the operation; (2) Such is the known danger of damage to a ureter that, if a surgeon misjudges their position and damages it, then in the absence of sufficient explanation, the misjudgment amounts to negligence; in this case, damage arose either because there was insufficient deflection of the bladder or due to placement of a clamp; the presence of oozing was insufficient explanation or abnormality to justify the injury; (3) Appropriate level of damages was £25,000.	Plaintiff:- Mr Worth, consultant urologist; Mr Harris, consultant gynaecologist; Dr Bell, consultant nephrologist; Defendant:- Mr Harrison, consultant urologist; Mr Brudenell, consultant gynaecologist.	General damages: £25,000.	**Bouchta v Swindon Health Authority** [1996] 7 Med LR 62 Wandsworth County Court; HH Judge Sumner

Appendices

APPENDIX 1

Practice Direction (Civil Litigation: Case Management) (Lord Taylor CJ)

24 January 1995, [1995] 1 All ER 385, [1995] 1 WLR 508

Practice — High Court — Case management — Judges' control over preparation for and conduct of hearings — Practitioners' failure to conduct cases economically to be penalised in costs — Pre-trial review and skeleton arguments — RSC Ord 18, r 7; Ord 34, r 10(2)

1   The paramount importance of reducing the cost and delay of delay of civil litigation makes it necessary for judges sitting at first instance to assert greater control over the preparation for and conduct of hearings than has hitherto been customary. Failure by practitioners to conduct cases economically will be visited by appropriate orders for costs, including wasted costs orders.

2   The court will accordingly exercise its discretion to limit (*a*) discovery; (*b*) the length of oral submissions; (*c*) the time allowed for the examination and cross-examination of witnesses; (*d*) the issues on which it wishes to be addressed; (*e*) reading aloud from documents and authorities.

3   Unless otherwise ordered, every witness statement shall stand as the evidence in chief of the witness concerned.

4   RSC Ord 18, r 7 (facts, not evidence, to be pleaded) will be strictly enforced. In advance of trial parties should use their best endeavours to agree which are the issues or the main issues, and it is their duty so far as possible to reduce or eliminate the expert issues.

5   RSC Ord 34, r 10(2)(a) or (c) (the court bundle) will also be strictly enforced. Documents for use in court should be in A4 format where possible, contained in suitably secured bundles, and lodged with the court at least two clear days before the hearing of an application or a trial. Each bundle should be paginated, indexed, wholly legible, and arranged chronologically and contained in a ring binder or a lever-arch file. Where documents are copied unnecessarily or bundled incompetently the cost will be disallowed.

6   In cases estimated to last for more than ten days a pre-trial review should be applied for or in default may be appointed by the court. It should when practicable be conducted by the trial judge between eight and four weeks before the date of trial and should be attended by the advocates who are to represent the parties at trial.

7   Unless the court otherwise orders, there must be lodged with the listing officer (or equivalent) on behalf of each party no later than two months before the date of trial a completed pre-trial check-list in the form annexed to this practice direction.

8   Not less than three clear days before the hearing of an action or application each party should lodge with the court (with copies to other parties) a skeleton argument concisely summarising that party's submissions in relation to each of the issues, and citing the main authorities relied upon which may be attached. Skeleton arguments should be as brief as the nature of the issues allows, and should not without leave of the court exceed 20 pages of double-spaced A4 paper.

9   The opening speech should be succinct. At its conclusion other parties may be invited briefly to amplify their skeleton arguments. In a heavy case the court may in conjunction with final speeches require written submissions, including the findings of fact for which each party contends.

10   This direction applies to all lists in the Queen's Bench and Chancery Divisions, except where other directions specifically apply.

Pre-trial check-list
[Short title of action]
[Folio number]
[Trial date]
[Party lodging check-list]
[Name of solicitor]
[Name(s) of counsel for trial (if known)]

Setting Down
1   Has the action been set down?

Pleadings
2   (a) Do you intend to make any amendment to your pleading? (b) if so, when?

Interrogatories
3   (a) Are any interrogatories outstanding? (b) If so, when served and upon whom?

Evidence
4   (a) Have all orders in relation to expert, factual and hearsay evidence been complied with? If not, specify what remains outstanding. (b) Do you intend to serve/seek leave to serve any further report or statement? If so, when and what report or statement? (c) Have all other orders in relation to oral evidence been complied with? (d) Do you require any further leave or orders in relation to evidence? If so, please specify and say when you will apply.
5   (a) What witnesses of fact do you intend to call? [names] (b) What expert witnesses do you intend to call? [names] (c) Will any witness require an interpreter? If so which?

Documents
6   (a) Have all orders in relation to discovery been complied with? (b) If not, what orders are outstanding? (c) Do you intend to apply for any further orders relating to discovery? (d) If so, what and when?
7   Will you not later than seven days before trial have prepared agreed paginated bundles of fully legible documents for the use of counsel and the court.

Pre-trial review
8   (a) Has a pre-trial review been ordered? (b) If so, when is it to take place? (c) If not, would it be useful to have one?

Length of trial

9 What are counsel's estimates of the minimum and maximum lengths of the trial? [The answer to question 9 should ordinarily be supported by an estimate of length signed by the counsel to be instructed.]

Alternative dispute resolution (**see** *Practice Statement (Commercial Court: Alternative dispute resolution)* (*The Times* December 17, 1993; [1993] TLR 659, [1994] 1 WLR 14).

10 Have you or counsel discussed with your client(s) the possibility of attempting to resolve this dispute (or particular issues) by alternative dispute resolution?

11 Might some form of alternative dispute resolution procedure to resolve or narrow the issues in this case?

12 Have you or your client(s) explored with the other parties the possibility of resolving this dispute (or particular issues) by alternative dispute resolution?

[Signature of solicitor, date]

Note: This check-list must be lodged not later than two months before the date of hearing with copies to the other parties.

APPENDIX 2

'Tayloring' Case Management to *Woolf's* Litigation Highway

Introduction

Lord Taylor's Practice Direction of 24 January 1995, is entitled: *'Civil litigation: Case management'*. It contains the following fundamental points:

- **Cost and delay:** 'The paramount importance of reducing the cost and delay of civil litigation.'
- **Abridgment of time in court:** 'The court will accordingly exercise its jurisdiction to limit.
  a 'Discovery';
  b 'The length of oral submissions';
  c 'The time allowed for the examination and cross-examination of witnesses';
  d 'The issues on which it wishes to be addressed'; and
  e 'Reading aloud from documents and authorities'
- **Narrowing of expert evidence:** Issues of expert evidence are to be reduced to a minimum or eliminated entirely.
- **Wasted costs:** Sanction for misbehaviour:

  'Failure by practitioners to conduct cases economically will be visited by appropriate orders for costs, including wasted costs orders.'

The procedural underpinning of the practice direction

Procedurally, the practice direction has the following characteristics:

- First, the word **'issues'** is repeated seven times:
  a The court will state on which **ISSUES** it wishes to be addressed.
  b In advance of trial the parties should use their best endeavours to agree which are the **'SSUES** or the main **ISSUES**.
  c No less than three clear days before the hearing of any action or application each party should lodge with the court (with copies to other parties) a skeleton argument concisely summarising that

party's submissions in relation to each of the **ISSUES**

d   Skeleton arguments should be as brief as the nature of the **ISSUES** allows, and should not without leave of the court exceed 20 pages of double-spaced A4 paper.

e   ADR

(i)   Have you or counsel discussed with your client(s) the possibility of attempting to resolve this dispute (or particular **ISSUES**) by alternative dispute resolution?

(ii)   'Might some form of alternative dispute resolution procedure to resolve or narrow the **ISSUES** in this case?'

- Secondly, the duty to achieve case management IS A DUTY OF RESULT:

a   Lord Taylor does not state whether barristers or solicitors should be responsible for the various stages of litigation;

b   nor does he require that the legal profession use best endeavours.

The requirements is that the result IS TO BE ACHIEVED, irrespective of who achieves it, with the sanction of wasted costs orders.

Issues—the bedrock of the system of dispute resolution

The concept of the **'issues'** is central to the United Kingdom dispute resolution process: *Thorp v Holdsworth* [1876] 3 ChD 637 at 639 per Sir George lessel:

'The whole object of pleading is to bring the parties to an issue, and the meaning of the rules of [Order 18] was to prevent the issue being enlarged, which would prevent either party from knowing when the cause came on for trial, what the real point to be discussed and decided was. In fact, the whole meaning of the system is to narrow the parties to definite issues, and thereby to diminish expense and delay, especially as regards the amount of testimony required on either side at the hearing.'

A reason why dispute resolution is now so slow, and so costly, is that the traditional processes have changed to the extent that they have broken down.

The traditional (oral) system of United Kingdom dispute resolution by reference to *issues* had the potential to be highly cost-effective. It involved:

- **Judicial authority:** The authority of the judge of almost absolute power.

- **The Bar/Bench relationship:** The spontaneity of the courtroom, between a closely associated Bar and Bench.
- **Paucity of documents:** All documents had to be prepared with personal signatures, which had to be delivered by hand to the court, and could only be altered by court order.
- **Cheap overheads:**
  a barristers working with ridiculously small overheads; and
  b firms of solicitors who ran litigation through poorly paid, but highly experienced, managing clerks;
  c no damage could be caused to a case in writing before the hearing in the courtroom, because orality was everything, so everything could be left to be 'sorted out in court'.

What has gone wrong with 'issue' driven litigation?

The potential of this system of dispute resolution was speed and cost-effectiveness. What has changed may be interpreted as including;

- **Breakdown of traditional society structures:** The traditional systems of dispute resolution in our society have broken down: the village policeman, the priest, the vicar, the terraced street, the local busybody. Now disputes, which would have been resolved without more than the neighbourhood knowing, are pumped into the court system. *The pump is cranked by both the extensive advertising of legal services, and demand-led legal aid.*
- **Breakdown in professional traditions:** The 'old boy network' is tainted as a concept. That said, the traditional network, whatever its inadequacies, performed a role not very different from those dispute resolution processes which kept traditional society together, namely the terraced street, etc.
- **Experts:** The increasing role of the expert with the reciprocal exchange of expert evidence.
- **Solicitors:** The much greater involvement of solicitors (as opposed to unqualified clerks) in the litigation process, triggered by a number of factors including:
  a the decline in the profitability of traditional fields of practice such as domestic conveyancing;

   b a perception of access to justice as co-extensive with increased funding;

   c funding which has been demand-led and paid at an hourly rate;

- **Proactivity:** As new avenues of legal enquiry have opened up (environmental, professional negligence and so forth) the market-makers have been the solicitors. This has resulted in the following:

   a Barristers, traditionally 'reactive,' have been called upon to operate pursuant to their own traditions — doing what they were instructed to do — in the context of solicitor file management which, over the last decade, has become 'proactive'.

   b Case management increasingly involves the drafting of documents which cover ground which was once the oral preserve of counsel in the courtroom.

   c Those documents, required as they are for the courtroom, should be focused on the **issues** as clearly and succinctly distilled from the pleadings.

   d However, the result is that litigation has born witness to the profileration of paper without a corresponding application of forensic discipline to control the generation of **issues**.

   e The barrister's advice on evidence used to be the tool to harmonise case management with the courtroom. But that stems from an era where how the case was managed could not damage the interests of the client in the courtroom (because the courtroom was the 'orality' forum for the finding of fact).

> *Such documents, however, are increasingly brought into existence by solicitors who have until very recently had little or no formal training in pleading, evidence, advocacy or courtroom procedures.*

Rationale of Lord Taylor's practice direction — 'back to basics'

Thus we can see Lord Taylor's Practice Direction in context:

- The aim is not to change, but to restore. It is to restore the traditional United Kingdom system of dispute resolution. That system is:

   a speedy focus on **issues**;

   b distilled out of the facts;

   c by practical litigators with a real grip of the law as a working tool.

- Thus, Lord Taylor's practice direction seeks to:
  a embrace the new generation of litigators (be they 'barristers' or 'solicitors'), and
  b accommodate within the traditional system of United Kingdom dispute resolution, the presentation of a case at least partly in writing, rather than exclusively orally.

Previously, of course, the *issues* were distilled orally in court. Now, however, before the court hearing;

- the *issues* have to be distilled; and
- the law has to be explored;
- the evidence (lay and expert) has to be marshalled, weighed and focused on the *issues;*
- the expert evidence has to be tested before the court hearing, rather than await examination at court.

> *In summary, as litigation is conducted increasingly on paper and away from the force-field of the courtroom itself, so the traditional courtroom controls (the discipline of the courtroom and the management of the judge) have proved unequal to the task of controlling the distillation of issues (and the proliferation of paper).*

Lord Taylor's Practice Direction — consequences for case management

Litigators will find themselves with eroding profits if the following is not assimilated:

- **Firstly — quality control:** Litigators can no longer rely on the immunity from action in a claim for professional negligence in respect of anything said or done in the courtroom: quality control protocols attach to the written word. Both barrister and solicitor carry responsibility for negligence in the context of the written word. **Submitted:**
  a Solicitors cannot be negligent in case management and hide behind the barristers' immunity in the courtroom if the dispute resolution process falters through litigator fault.
  b Barristers cannot hide behind their immunity in the courtroom, if their acts or ommissions at an interlocutory stage generate a result in the courtroom which wrongly works to the prejudice of the client.
- **Secondly — value for money:** Once file management is reduced entirely to writing, the client can see at a glance for what he has paid. So if there are 100 lever arch files, he or she is entitled to ask:
  a *What* are the **issues**?
  b *Why* so much paper?
  c Please explain to what **issues** each lever arch file goes.

The answers to these questions can have a bearing on the result of a taxation. The taxing master is now in a much stronger position to investigate whether the case management has been cost-effective. The pressure for succinctness becomes overwhelming in the context of the conditional fee agreement and fixed/budgeted fee remuneration.

- **Thirdly — a new relationship with the client:** The client wants to put something in his statement: that something is put in. He wants the other side to see a document (relevant or otherwise) — the other side has been shown the document. He wants a question asked in court: that question is asked. That has to to stop. Wasted costs orders are the sanction. The relationship with the client — however dressed up for purposes of good client relations — has to be based on the following premise: the client has to be told (and warned) of the tight discipline now asserted in all matters relating to the resolution of disputes through the court process. However it is dressed up, he or she has to appreciate the following:

  Once orality is abrogated, and documentary presentation of evidence and argument is asserted, the principle in Rondal v Worsley *and* Saif Ali *is irrelevant.*

  In recent times particularly, litigation has been client driven. The concept of consumer rights has been given a novel interpretation in the forensic environment.

  a As a litigant, he is part of the litigation process. As such he is subject to the discipline of the court.

  b If he does not co-operate efficiently with requests made of him by his lawyers, the lawyers will not be able to comply with the strict procedural requirements set down by the court.

  c Thus the client must be told of the need for *full and frank* disclosure at the beginning of the retainer of the lawyer. He must give not only the 'upside' of his case, but also the 'downside'.

  d The client must be told that it is the litigator who decides what is to go into the final statement for exchange. That is a legal, not a lay document. Its contents are subject to strict legal rules.

  e As to discovery, the client has got to understand that if he holds back on relevant documents, the solicitor must end his retainer (*Myers v Elman*).

- **Fourthly — a new relationship with experts:** Now (but perhaps not before Lord Taylor's practice direction) the litigator can courteously but firmly get hold of his experts and ensure that they work cost-effectively within the strict framework of the court process. The following language addresses the issues:

  'In the past, you drafted your reports your way, and win lose or draw, we all got paid out. So it was not very important whether you were in the witness box for a day or a month. Indeed, the longer you were in the witness box, the more the case took on a life of its own.

The longer the case, the more money the litigators earned and the greater the opportunity to say to any client who lost: "We are awfully sorry. The problem is that there are always risks in litigation. The action was so terribly complicated: As you know, the evidence took so very long to unravel and after a 4 week hearing the judge approached the case entirely differently from what was envisaged when it started. But there we are. It is all a matter of judicial discretion. There are no grounds for appeal."

Now, we are living in a very different forensic environment. Fees are no longer payable on a demand-led basis. Further, the evidence which an expert can give is now subject to very robust guidance from the court. We must warn you that if your expert evidence does not address the right issues succinctly and cost-effectively, then we litigators can be ordered to be fined by way of a wasted costs order. Please make sure that your approach is confident, well-researched and clear. Only in that way can we distil the issues between you and the expert called against you by the other side.'

- **Fifthly — the time for the advice on evidence:** Traditionally, the issues in the case were identified, and the evidence marshalled, through the medium of the barristers' Advice on Evidence.

  a That document was prepared shortly before irrevocable steps were taken in the proceedings — ie shortly before the case came into the courtroom.

  b But now, irrevocable steps in proceedings can be taken as soon as file is opened.

  c Thus it is submitted that the time for the primary Advice on Evidence is *at the moment the file is opened*.

- **Sixthly — what should be in the Advice on Evidence?** It is submitted that there should be adopted a new approach to case management, namely, 'template' litigation. The template (subject of course to flexibility) must set out the cause of action, the evidence both lay and expert required to prove it, the documents and the issues to be covered.

- **Seventhly — aims of case management:** The aim of case management should be:
  a to bring into existence only those words on papers which are essential to the proof of the **issues** in the case, and not a word more;
  b that the paper so brought into existence should be the bare minimum to achieve that result, and not a sheet more;
  c thus when the file grows, it grows only down preordained channels, where the paper created has a direct relevance to the **issue** to be resolved.

Summary thus far

The following is submitted: Lord Taylor's practice direction does NOT (and CANNOT) generate the following responses:

- **First:** there is now yet another level of cost and administration to be addressed.
- **Secondly:** the Practice Direction does not do anything new. Good litigators have been doing this for years.

Law-making in the twenty-first century

Certainly into the 1970s (and one suspects, way beyond), from the moment the aspiring lawyer enters law school, the emphasis has been on matching oneself to the unique brilliance of the professions (which were of course, the best in the world).

The primary focus of legal training has traditionally been by reference to (voluminous) precedent. This inevitably draws on what the judges have ruled over the previous century, and implicitly treats their dicta as equivalent to a holy text, to be relied upon or distinguished (but not assessed as 'wrong in law').

> *Because of the vast quantities of paper produced courtesy of the present approach to case management, the Advice on Evidence now involves screening out equally vast quantities of irrelevant fact and expert evidence.*

We are thus potentially deprived, at the most formative period in our lives, of an objective view of our decision and lawmaking process.

Thus, we are not orientated to look at our system of dispute resolution in the following light:

- Whether such law as is to be made turns on total random events such as, for example: whether there is funding; whether (for example) a litigant client has a commercial motive for running an action collateral to the need to have the dispute resolved;

whether it is reported (and if it is, where, and how much is set out in the report).

> *A close examination of the model conditional fees agreement, produced by the Law Society, demonstrates the importance, in that context, of lawyer and client jointly agreeing on their aims and objectives, establishing lead roles and working together with total transparency.*

- In an era of consumer demand for an increasingly better product, our lawmaking machinery could be perceived as being erratic and haphazard.
- Is there not an increased role for the Law Commission? There has been so much case law in the post-war era, that principles cannot readily be distilled from the volumes of dicta.
- Law school teachers equally would have less recourse to the recitation of cases as an agenda for a lecture, and devote a greater focus to the explanation of principle, and how in practice (eg by court forms, letters, questionnaires, check-lists and so forth) such principles are to be worked through to resolve a dispute in the real world.

> *In other words, the court — through court management — controls file management.*

Identifying the super-highway

There are, in fact, two highways:

- **Firstly:** The electronic means to access the law and practice in a particular field (CD Rom — networking — low overheads).
- **Secondly:** The litigation highway:

> *Once one has identifiable highways, with recognised staging posts, one can budget.*

  a Once we are travelling down Lord Taylor's motorway, there are no long breaks at the 'services'. They are brief interlocutory stops.

  b And to those who say, 'The other side will throw every obstruction in our way to impede progress', they may be reassured: Lord Woolf's reforms will remove the obstacles from the tarmac. Litigators who want to make a margin, will not only acquiesce in Lord Woolf's reforms; they will be anxiously demanding them, and earlier rather than later. Boulders on the highway which obstruct passage erode a margin in a fixed fee or conditional fee environment.

> *Thus, before getting on to that motorway, one has to be fully equipped for the journey: the journey has to be mapped out; there has to be enough fuel in the tank; the vehicle has to be well serviced and running efficiently; the driver has to be properly qualified; and any breakdowns have to be fixed with the commitment to speed of a Grand Prix pit-stop.*

- **Thirdly:** There is more than one highway. Just as with computer games, one may expect to be able to elect one's level of play in the new world of computer-driven litigation. The level of play may be:

  a   up to £5,000

  b   £5,000 to £15,000

  c   £15,000 — £50,000

  d   £50,000 — £250,000

  e   £250,000+

Each 'programme' can be adjusted to the level of play. You do not need full discovery, extensive medical evidence and lengthy pleadings for a claim of £2,000. Each programme will be court-driven. Documents will be lodged with the court by electronic mail. Once the clock is set, the 'game' starts — and one is locked into the court-driven dispute resolution process which continues until trial, or settlement or discontinuance. And one is locked into a pre-set speed.

- **Fourthly:** A litigator will be able to cost out before an action starts how much it will cost, and how much will be involved from staging-post to staging-post. Management accounting in the office is facilitated therefore in a *conditional fee* environment and, if the consumer (eg an insurance company) wants a block of work done for a fixed fee, then this can also be properly budgeted for. We are going to live in a very different world, where the quality of one's product and the price at which it is charged is paramount. The contemporary approach to litigation will look strangely quaint to the new generation of litigator pumped out of law school into the system, after (say) the year 2000.

Conclusion

Perhaps at the time of the Lord Chancellor's Green Paper in 1988, the professions had not grasped the extent of the urgency of the need for reform, or the reasons for it. Indeed, a positive reaction from the legal profession would have run counter to culture. Writing in 1889, David Dudley Field said:

'Whenever any considerable amelioration has been obtained, either in the form or in the substance of the law, in procedure or in doctrine, it has come from a minority of lawyers supported by the voice of laymen. I do not complain of this. It is in the nature of the profession. The lawyer becomes wedded to old things by the course of his daily avocations. He reposes trust upon the past. He is concerned with what is, not with what should be. The rights he defends are old rights, grounded, it may be, in the ages that have gone before him. Nor is this conservative tendency altogether to be regretted. Rooted in the past, and covered with the branches of many generations, the legal profession may be said to stand like the oak as a barrier and shelter in many an angry storm, though it may at the same time dwarf the growth. With its innumerable traditions and its sentiments of honour, it is one of the strong counteracting forces of civilisation, and we should hold fast to it, with all its good and in spite of its evil, though we may have occasions to combat and overcome its resistance as often as new wants and altered circumstances make them necessary.'

Indeed, taking that as a backdrop, we can see our own procedural reforms in the context of an American experience over a century ago: in 1848, against resistance similar to that encountered by the 1988 Green Paper, the New York Legislation Code was enacted. 391 sections were passed within weeks. Opposition to the measure was bitter and intense among both lawyers and laymen. Given time for organisation, the 'Sons of Zeruiah', it was feared, might again, as in Cromwell's day, have been too strong for the spirit of law reform. But being once clothed with authority of actual, operating law, the new movement was better able to make headway against that 'antipathy to reformation' which lawyers feel, and perhaps are bound to feel.

Fifty years later, reform of that Code fell for consideration. And the conservative forces of the United States Bar, so long and so bitterly opposed to the Code, were arrayed in its support.

One can readily anticipate legal historians of the latter end of the twenty-first century assessing the necessity for such reform as being obvious, and the result of such reform as being:

> *Lords Mackay, Taylor and Woolf usher into a new era our contemporary system of dispute resolution. It is an era characterised by electronic communication, the rights of the consumer, and a multi-racial society which is increasingly perceived as entitled to genuinely equal rights.*

- genuine dispute resolution for genuine disputes;
- a much more cost-effective product;
- a dramatic increase in efficiency;
- a level procedural playing field;
- a court hearing being a process of dispute resolution of last resort;
- opportunity for all trained litigators, irrespective of race, sex, colour or creed, to play on that playing field.

APPENDIX 3

Part 1

Practice Direction No 49 (6 November 1996, Law Society Gazette) Medical Negligence

1   From 1 November 1996, Master Foster has been assigned to hear all interlocutory applications in actions involving claims arising out of allegations of medical/clinical negligence.

2   The following arrangements will apply to all such actions to which a master has not been assigned prior to 1 November 1996.

3   a   The plaintiff in such actions must issue a summons for directions within 28 days of the close of pleadings and shall mark the summons in the bottom right hand corner 'medical negligence'. On seeking a hearing for the summons, the counter staff in room E214 are to be told that the case involves allegations of medical negligence.

   b   The plaintiff shall serve with a copy of the summons:
   (i)   a summary description of the action limited to 250 words; and
   (ii)   a chronology of material events in the form of a schedule.

   c   The defendant shall, within 14 days of receipt of a copy of the summons:
   (i)   produce an initial list of outstanding issues limited to 250 words;
   (ii)   comment on the plaintiff's chronology.

4   Such applications will be listed before Master Foster on Tuesdays or Fridays within 28 days of issue. In the vacation, the summons will be listed within 28 days of the start of the next term or will be taken by one of the vacation masters.

5   At the first hearing of the summons for directions:

a   Each party shall produce an initial list of their potential witnesses as to fact.

b   Each party shall specify the number and discipline of the experts it currently intends to rely on, when their reports will be available and the issues to which they will be directed.

c   Each party must state whether alternative dispute resolution has been considered and if not why not, and if alternative dispute resolution has been rejected why this is so.

d   Paras 1 to 12 and 19 of practice form 50 will be dealt with and a date fixed for dealing with the remaining directions including updating the list of issues and the listing of admissions. This date will be shortly after the latest date for exchange of experts' reports and witness statements.

6   The documents referred to in para 3(b) and 3(c) should be lodged with Master Foster at least 48 hours before the time fixed for hearing the summons for directions.

7   All time summonses in medical negligence cases after 1 November 1996 will be heard:

a   in term, by Master Foster at 10am on Tuesdays and Fridays;

b   in vacation, in accordance with the current practice.

8   In all medical negligence actions the plaintiff should serve each intended defendant with a letter before action, at least three months before issue of the writ. Such a letter should set out the fullest available information as to the basis of the claim. If the plaintiff does not serve such a letter then the court may grant an appropriate extension of time to the defendant for serving a defence.

9   The hearing of all summonses (other than time summonses) in medical negligence actions must be attended by the solicitor in charge of the case or counsel instructed therein. If, for good reason, this is not possible, a fully briefed deputy may attend. However, if the summons cannot be dealt with properly because of the deputy's lack of familiarity with the case, a wasted costs order may be made.

This practice direction was issued by Senior Master Robert Turner of the Queen's Bench Division.

Part 2

IMPLICATIONS OF THIS PRACTICE DIRECTION

The implications can be summarised in a phrase: ***Front-End Loading***.

Thus before the launch of proceedings, the Plaintiff litigator must have made sufficient investigation to be ready to provide the Master with the following information after the Defence is served:

a   A summary description of the action limited to 250 words: Is not this the essence of the Statement of Claim? If not, what is the purpose in pleading it? This puts a premium on focus and succinctness on the part of the pleader. See agenda at p 24.

b   A chronology of relevant dates and times: Should this not be sorted out at the first conference with experts? See agenda at p 24.

c   The initial list of the names of witnesses as to fact. Is not the optimum time to draft this, at the first conference with the experts, prior to Service of the Claim?

d   The number of experts to be called, and their disciplines: Again, the framework of the case has to be established clearly, before service of the Claim.

Warning: In the light of this Practice Direction, governing as it does the Central Registry, litigation can no longer be conducted on the premise of 'Serve now, think later'.

Hitherto, office management has focussed perhaps too much on physically serving documents to a time table. The priority now is not only having those documents to meet the time-table, but making sure that from the beginning, they record the correct information, in the correct place, at the correct time, and focussing on the correct issues.

APPENDIX 4

Bolitho v City and Hackney Health Authority **(CA)**

The following cases were referred to in the judgments:

Bolam v Friern Hospital Management Committee [1957] 1 WLR 582
Bonnington Castings Ltd v Wardlaw [1956] AC 613
Corn v Weir's Glass (Hanley) Ltd [1960] 2 All ER 300
Hotson v East Berkshire Area Health Authority [1987] AC 750
Hucks v Cole [1993] 4 Med LR 393
Hunter v Hanley 1955 SLT 213
Maynard v West Midlands Regional Health Authority [1984] 1 WLR 634
McGhee v National Coal Board [1973] 1 WLR 1
McWilliams v Sir William Arrol & Co Ltd [1962] 1 WLR 295
Wilsher v Essex Area Health Authority [1988] AC 1074

LORD JUSTICE FARQUHARSON: This is an appeal against a judgment of Hutchison J given on February 15, 1991 when he dismissed a claim for damages for injuries suffered by the first plaintiff (hereinafter referred to as 'Patrick') allegedly caused by the negligence of a doctor employed by the defendant.

At the time of the events upon which his claim is based Patrick was but two years old. The story starts in May 1983 when his parents took him on holiday to Spain. At the conclusion of the holiday while waiting at Barcelona airport Patrick had a fit, as his mother described it. His body went cold and he became blue in the face. He was seen by a doctor who diagnosed a minor heart condition. The parents decided to wait in Barcelona until Patrick's condition stabilised, but he then had a number of what his mother called 'white fits' during which he became cold and white and had difficulty in breathing.

On his return to England he was taken to Brompton Hospital where his condition known as patent ductus arteriosis was diagnosed. This involved a minor gap in two arteries leaving the heart which normally closes at birth. The condition was cured by an operation carried out at the hospital in December 1983.

On January 11, 1984 Patrick was admitted to St Bartholomew's hospital suffering from croup. His clinical record of course revealed the fact of the recent operation. He was treated in a humidifying tent and rapidly improved. Dr Horn and Dr Rodgers who examined him observed a defect in his breathing on the left side. He was described as suffering from acute croup.

The following morning his condition appeared to have deteriorated and he was having difficulty in his breathing. A careful account of his condition and treatment while at the hospital during this period is given in Hutchison J's judgment and there is no need to repeat it here.

A significant feature was that on January 13 he appeared to be cyanosed though he recovered quickly. On January 15, Patrick had sufficiently recovered to be discharged and sent home. That night Patrick did not sleep well and was restless. His parents, concerned about his increased difficulty in breathing and his 'wheezing', took him back to the hospital where he was readmitted. Dr Rodgers examined him and found that his respiration rate was high and there was some evidence of recession in his breathing. This increased during the course of the evening and the doctor decided that he should be 'specialed' that is to say he was looked after that night by a nurse on a one-to-one basis.

The following morning, according to the medical notes Patrick was very much better though he still had reduced air entry on one side. During the course of the morning the consultant examined him while on his ward round but in the absence of any note there was not apparently any feature of Patrick's condition that excited his attention. Dr Horn was present. Mrs Bolitho, Patrick's mother, spent much of the morning with him but at 12 noon his condition so worried her that she called for the ward sister, Sister Sallabank. The latter was highly qualified in the nursing of children and regarded by law as highly competent. She plays an important role in the events of January 17, and the judge records that 'she made an extremely good impression in the witness box, giving her evidence clearly and impartially'. She made a statement on October 10, 1990 which in evidence she said was correct and the following account is taken from that document.

When she came on duty Sister Sallabank discovered that Patrick had been nursed in a 'croupette' overnight but she observed that during the morning he was up and running about. He was well at the time the consultant made his round, and later ate a large lunch. Sister Sallabank recalls that she was summoned to look at Patrick at around 12.40 pm. She described his respiratory sounds as 'awful' but to her surprise he was still talking. Patrick was very white in colour. She was sufficiently concerned about his condition to 'bleep' the senior paediatric registrar, Dr Horn, rather than to go through the usual chain of command by contacting the senior houseman Dr Rodgers. This was her practice when she felt something was acutely wrong. When Dr Horn answered her call Sister Sallabank asked her to come and see Patrick straight away as he was having difficulty in breathing and was very very white. Dr Horn seemed alarmed that Patrick was in such distress when he had appeared perfectly well a short time before during the consultant's round. Sister Sallabank added that Patrick sounded as though something was stuck in his throat. The doctor said she would attend as soon as possible. When Sister Sallabank returned to Patrick who was extremely surprised to see him walking about again with a decidedly pink colour.

She left a nurse to stay with Patrick after his mother had left. The second episode occurred at about 2 pm when the same nurse called her back to Patrick once again. Sister Sallabank saw that he was in the same difficulty as at 12.40 pm and being worried went off to telephone Dr Horn who had not yet arrived. Dr Horn said she was on afternoon clinic and had asked Dr Rodgers to come in her place. Whilst talking to Dr Horn the nurse told the sister that Patrick was now pink again, and so she told Dr Horn about the two episodes.

Unfortunately Dr Rodgers did not attend Patrick at this point either. Her 'bleep' was not working because of flat batteries so that she never got the message. Sister Sallabank then left State Enrolled Nurse Newbold to sit with Patrick. As a matter of chronology it will be useful to interpolate Nurse Newbold's account of the next half hour. Her evidence also is of great importance in the context of the issues in this case. The learned judge found her a careful and reliable witness. She also made a statement which she identified as being correct: She remembers Patrick as a bright little boy. On January 17, she was asked by Sister Sallabank to sit with Patrick and was told that the doctors were coming to see him at any time because he had been unwell earlier. Nurse Newbold tried to take Patrick's pulse and rate of respiration but this proved very difficult as he appeared quite well and was jumping about and playing in his cot. She describes Patrick as being very chatty and interested in reading the letters on a dish. However at about 2.30 pm there was a change in his condition. Although he retained his colour he became a little agitated and began to cry. Being worried she left a colleague with Patrick and reported to Sister Sallabank who told her to 'bleep' the doctors again. While on the telephone the emergency buzzer sounded having been set off by the nurse left with Patrick. She immediately returned to Patrick. Sister Sallabank also heard the buzzer and sent out a call for the cardiac arrest team.

Patrick had collapsed because he was unable to breathe. As a result he suffered a cardiac arrest. Strenuous efforts were made to revive him but there was an overall period of nine or ten minutes before the restoration of respiratory and cardiac functions. The consequence was that Patrick sustained severe brain damage.

There were a number of allegations of negligence made against the defendants arising out of the medical treatment of Patrick but it is not now contended that there is any basis for criticism of the hospital staff for their actions after Patrick's collapse. The negligence relied upon to establish the plaintiff's claim lay in the failure of Dr Horn or another doctor on her behalf to attend Patrick on either of the occasions that Sister Sallabank telephoned her asking her to come, that is to say after the two episodes at 12.40 pm and 2 pm respectively. There was some conflict between Sister Sallabank and Dr Horn as to what was said by the one to the other at the material time, Dr Horn's recollection being that she had not been asked to attend Patrick on those occasions. However the judge preferred the sister's account. In those circumstances it was agreed by both parties that it was negligent on the part of Dr Horn not to have attended Patrick when summoned in the terms used by the sister.

No less than eight doctors gave evidence at the trial as to what treatment should have been given to Patrick had Dr Horn attended. It was the case for the plaintiffs supported by the opinion of the five doctors called on their behalf that after the first episode suffered by Patrick and certainly after the second he should have been intubated. This would have provided a supply of oxygen to him in the event of his respiratory tubes being entirely blocked. The defendant's experts rejected that suggestion. Intubation of a child of Patrick's age would involve anaesthetising him and on the evidence of his condition in this case such a course was not necessary or desirable.

In approaching this issue the defendant conceded that if Patrick had been intubated at any time prior to the cardiac arrest at 2.35 pm this would as a matter of probability, have averted his collapse and/or any serious consequence arising from it. The issue between the parties which had to be resolved was what Dr Horn would have done had she attended in response to either of Sister Sallabank's calls. The judge put it this way (p 27):

'As it seems to me if Dr Horn would have intubated, then the plaintiff succeeds, whether or not that is a course which all reasonably competent practitioners would have followed. If however Dr Horn would not have intubated then the plaintiff can only succeed if such failure was contrary to accepted medical practice....'

Towards the end of his judgment the judge put the question more precisely (p 62):

'... has it been proved that following the second episode at latest, no Senior Registrar of ordinary skill would have failed to have Patrick intubated? This question can be framed in various ways, but all involve recognising that the matter is to be tested by applying the standard of the ordinary skilled man exercising and professing to have the special medical skill in question.'

I do not understand that there was any criticism at the trial of the judge putting the issue in this way.

Besides the difference between the considerable number of experts on the question whether Patrick should have been intubated there was by no means any unanimity on what was precisely wrong with him. The clinical picture of his behaviour on January 17 was confusing. On the one hand he had during the bulk of the morning been active, playful and hungry while at the time of the two episodes prior to 2.30 pm he was in a very serious condition. The judge posed this question:

> 'Was Patrick over the last two hours or even over the last half hour in a state of respiratory distress progressing inexorably to hypoxia and respiratory failure, or was he in general quite well but subject to two sudden acute episodes?'

One of the plaintiffs' medical experts, Dr Newman, was of the opinion that Patrick was suffering from persisting thick secretions in the upper airway causing progressive respiratory failure leading to hypoxia. The explanation of the two attacks was that on each occasion a gobbet of mucus obstructed his airway and impaired his ability to breathe until removed by coughing. This description of a 'mucus plug' obstructing the bronchial air passages was accepted by one of the defence witnesses, Dr Dinwiddie. This theory was accepted by the judge as being the probable explanation.

The thrust of evidence given by the plaintiffs' doctors was of course that Dr Horn should have intubated Patrick if she had attended him at the material time.

Dr Newman says that she should have arranged for intubation certainly after the second incident, and that would involve little risk. Dr Stimmler said that Patrick was on a knife edge during the attacks; and there was always a risk, as turned out to be the case, of further attacks. He also took the view that any competent doctor would have intubated after the second episode. Mr Roberts and Professor Holt expressed similar opinions.

While all these gentlemen were distinguished paediatricians none of them specialised in the field of paediatric respiratory illness. Neither had two of the witnesses called by the defendant, Professor Hull and Dr Robertson. The two specialists in that field were Dr Heaf called for the plaintiffs and Dr Dinwiddie for the defendant.

Dr Heaf's evidence in summary form was to the effect that a patient with Patrick's case history should have been first closely watched for signs of airflow obstruction, and that there should be a thorough examination of the chest. Following that examination if the assessment was that the obstruction was very severe he should have been intubated immediately. If the child's condition was not so severe but there was a significant obstruction, he should have been moved into a unit for special observation. In the case of Patrick Dr Heaf said:

> 'The only safe thing really to do when the child has done this twice is to intubate him ... these were clear warning signs.'

The final witness called was Dr Dinwiddie for the defendant. He said that he would certainly have expected a doctor receiving Sister Sallabank's first report to come and carefully examine Patrick even though by then there was apparent recovery. Even if there was no evidence of airway obstruction she would be mindful of the nurse's observations. Dr Dinwiddie would have himself kept Patrick under observation but would not have moved him into an intensive treatment unit and would certainly not have intubated. After the second episode a further examination by the doctor would be called for. The doctor would be dealing with an acute short-lived episode and while the fact that it happened twice would be a serious cause for concern it would not lead to thoughts of intubation. The picture was not one of relentless decline leading to respiratory arrest and given Patrick's recovery from the earlier episodes, he would not intubate. He was of the opinion that if Patrick had been suffering from progressive respiratory distress after 2 pm Nurse Newbold would have noticed it.

Dr Horn herself gave evidence and said that had she attended Patrick at the time of the two episodes she would not have intubated him, but as she was giving an opinion on a scenario which to her mind had never taken place her evidence may be discounted to some degree.

Faced with this division of expert opinion the learned judge 'felt compelled to hold' that it had not been proved that any competent doctor, in the position of Dr Horn, would have intubated Patrick before his collapse. He went on to say:

> 'It is not for me to make a choice between Dr Heaf and Dr Dinwiddie one of whom is convinced that any competent doctor would, that other that she would not, have undertaken that procedure. Plainly in my view this is one of those areas in which there is a difference of opinion between two distinguished and convincing medical witnesses as to what as a matter of clinical judgment proper treatment requires.'

This approach is in accord with the speech of Lord Scarman in *Maynard v West Midlands Regional Health Authority* [1984] 1 WLR 634 at p 639:

> 'My Lords, even before considering the reasons given by the majority of the Court of Appeal for reversing the findings of negligence, I have to say that a judge's "preference" for one body of distinguished professional opinion to another also professionally distinguished is not sufficient to establish negligence in a practitioner whose actions have received the seal of approval of those whose opinions, truthfully expressed, honestly held, were not preferred. If this was the real reason for the judge's finding, he erred in law even though elsewhere in his judgment he stated the law correctly. For in the realm of diagnosis and treatment negligence is not established by preferring one respectable body of professional opinion to another. Failure to exercise the ordinary skill of a doctor (in the appropriate speciality, if he be a specialist) is necessary.'

The only ground put forward in the plaintiffs' first notice of appeal was that the judge should not have found Dr Dinwiddie to be a reliable witness and to be representative of a responsible body of medical opinion when he was not. Mr Brennan has called this submission 'The nature of the evidence issue.'

The first complaint under this head was that Dr Dinwiddie had submitted a report expressing his opinion on the issues in the case before he had seen the statement of Sister Sallabank. The doctor's report was dated November 9, 1990 while, as already pointed out, Sister Sallabank's statement was dated the following day. This may not have been significant if he had seen a copy as was suggested at the trial. However the judge pointed out that there are a number of passages in the doctor's report which he found irreconcilable with that suggestion. He believed Dr Dinwiddie to be mistaken, and had not read the draft till later. Mr Brennan criticises the doctor sharply at this point: if the doctor's report had been prepared without seeing the important evidence of Sister Sallabank's — as all acknowledge it to be — how could he sustain precisely the same opinion after he had read that statement?

This is no doubt a strong point of criticism but the judge in that context said that the fact the doctor only saw the statement at a later stage did not lead him to doubt the objectivity of his evidence or to believe that at the hearing he did not give full weight to what she observed and described. Later he said:

'Dr Dinwiddie did undoubtedly, in my view, in his evidence, fully appreciate both the substance and the effect of Sister Sallabank's account of these two episodes.'

Mr Brennan boldly calls the judge's comments 'unsustainable', but the view he expressed could only be made by somebody who saw and heard the witness. Once it is shown that the judge took the criticism into account there is no basis upon which this court could interfere.

Mr Brennan next criticises Dr Dinwiddie's evidence for failing to attach sufficient weight to the fact that Patrick had suffered two attacks of respiratory difficulty, and failed to recognise that these episodes were life threatening. These criticisms seem to be a re-statement of the issue between the parties. If the plaintiffs' experts are correct in their assessment that Patrick's condition showed a deteriorating condition during the course of the day with two life-threatening episodes at 12.40 pm and 2 pm then no doubt Dr Dinwiddie has underrated the significance of those episodes; but if Dr Dinwiddie be right that the two episodes were instances of temporary blocking of Patrick's breathing system during a day when he was otherwise active and well then the criticism cannot be sustained. The complaint is merely another way of saying that the judge should not have given weight to his evidence.

Another complaint was that Dr Dinwiddie's evidence was based on the evidence of Nurse Newbold who was a far less experienced nurse than Sister Sallabank. In the first place the experienced judge found that the doctor did give full weight to Sister Sallabank's evidence, but I have not understood the basis of the criticism of Nurse Newbold's evidence. As already observed the judge found her a careful and reliable witness, but in fact her evidence in no way conflicts with that of the sister. It was concerned only with the period of 2–2.30 pm when Patrick quickly recovered from the second episode and became very lively. This was consistent with Sister Sallabank's account of his recovery from the first episode. While the diagnosis of this condition would require a greater expertise than Nurse Newbold possessed, she was quite capable of giving an objective account of Patrick's behaviour while she was with him.

The remainder of the criticism of Dr Dinwiddie's evidence is in very much the same vein and I do not propose to go through them individually. What they amount to in effect is a contention that Dr Dinwiddie's evidence should not have been accepted by the judge and that the evidence of the plaintiffs' experts should be preferred. In the light of the judge's findings about the doctor this contention cannot be sustained. Apart from Dr Heaf he was the only expert in paediatric respiratory medicine. At different points in the summing up the judge referred to Dr Dinwiddie as one of the most distinguished and experienced experts called in the case (he is in fact a consultant in this speciality at Great Ormond Street); that his views were clearly and moderately expressed; and that Dr Heaf and Dr Dinwiddie were by experience and qualification the two witnesses best equipped to give opinions in the matter, and

'I found them immensely impressive witnesses whose opinions are entitled to the greatest respect, and that he (Dr Dinwiddie) displayed what seemed to me to be a profound knowledge of paediatric respiratory medicine, coupled with impartiality and there is no doubt in my view of the genuineness of his opinion that intubation was not indicated.'

It must be rare for a witness to be commended in such glowing terms.

There is no dispute that when considering whether there is breach of duty by a doctor the test prescribed by McNair J in *Bolam v Friern Hospital Management Committee* [1957] 1 WLR 582 at p 586 is the correct one to apply namely:

'The test is the standard of the ordinary skilled man exercising and professing to have that special skill. A man need not possess the highest expert skill; it is well established law that it is sufficient if he exercise the ordinary skill of an ordinary competent man exercising that particular art.'

Mr Brennan however points out that measuring up to the standard of the competent practitioner does not excuse the courtroom examining the question whether the patient is still at risk. It relies on an unreported case *Hucks v Cole* where Sachs LJ said (at p 11 of the transcript):

'On such occasions the fact that other practitioners would have done the same thing as the defendant practitioner is a very weighty matter to put on to the scales on his behalf; but it is not conclusive. The court must, be vigilant to see whether the reasons given for putting a patient at risk are valid in the light of any well known advance in medical knowledge or whether they stem from a residual adherence to out-of-date ideas.'

Mr Brennan relies on this authority to support a further attack on Dr Dinwiddie's evidence. He contends that a responsible paediatric doctor should, when faced with a patient in the same condition as Patrick was that afternoon, have made what counsel describes as a risk/benefit analysis of intubation. If the responsible paediatrician had made such an analysis in this case counsel argues he would inevitably have concluded that it was right to intubate. The risk to Patrick was slight, even though he would have to have been anaesthetised, whereas the corresponding risk of not intubating bearing in mind the two life-threatening episodes during the afternoon was great. Mr Brennan says that in those circumstances the judge should have rejected the evidence of Dr Dinwiddie as not being representative of responsible medical opinion. He claims that Dr Dinwiddie fails the test referred to by Lord Scarman in *Maynard's* case supra.

There is of course no inconsistency between the decisions in *Hucks v Cole* and *Maynard's* case. It is not enough for a defendant to call a number of doctors to say that what he had done or not done was in accord with accepted clinical practice. It is necessary for the judge to consider that evidence and decide whether that clinical practice puts the patient unnecessarily at risk. For my part I cannot see that that particular issue arises in this case. The findings by the judge are inconsistent with the suggestion that the approach of Dr Dinwiddie put Patrick unnecessarily at risk. The judge clearly concluded that Dr Dinwiddie's evidence did constitute 'a responsible body of medical opinion' for the reasons already given.

By an amended notice of appeal the plaintiffs raise two further points. The first relates to the issue of causation. In *Maynard's* case Lord Scarman when advancing the test of 'responsible medical opinion' was dealing with breach of duty. He was not dealing with causation. Accordingly it is argued that causation was a matter for the judge to decide in the normal way under ordinary common-law principles as set out in such cases as *Wilsher v Essex Area Health Authority* [1988] AC 1074, namely had the admitted negligence on the part of Dr Horn caused or materially contributed to the injury suffered by Patrick? Counsel submits that the test of responsible medical opinion is not relevant to this issue of causation. Applying those principles he argues that there is a formidable case for saying that the failure of Dr Horn to attend in answer to the two calls made to her was the probable cause of the cardiac arrest. The factual position was that all the staff concerned with Patrick knew that he was seriously ill. Dr Horn had been in charge of his treatment during the first stay in hospital when he was found to be suffering from acute croup. Although he had been discharged his parents had to bring him back to hospital within a matter of hours. During January 17, there had been the two life-threatening incidents. In all these circumstances and knowing that intubation caused no risk or at worst, only a slight risk, a judge should be bound to hold, that if she had attended when required to do so Dr Horn would probably have given instructions that Patrick should be intubated. While the judge may be guided by expert evidence he is not on this issue to be directed by it.

While these are powerful arguments I cannot accede to them. In this case the judge was dealing with a breach of duty which consisted of an omission, and it was necessary for him to decide what course of events would have followed had the duty been discharged. Even though he was dealing with causation the learned judge was in these circumstances bound to rely on the evidence of the experts available to him. Whether Dr Horn's failure to appear would have made any difference in the event depended upon what she would have done had she been present. It was for the plaintiffs to prove that she would probably have intubated, and further, that if she did not do so her 'failure was contrary to accepted medical practice'. In my judgment the learned judge was not equipped to resolve those issues without the assistance of the expert evidence.

The final point taken by Mr Brennan is a variant of the other two. It is submitted that there was no clinical analysis of Patrick's condition because of Dr Horn's failure to attend, and Dr Dinwiddie's evidence was to the effect that proper medical practice required that such an examination should have taken place. As in the circumstances no examination did take place, the failure to attend must have contributed materially to Patrick's injury.

The answer to that submission is that it begs the question of what action Dr Horn would have taken had she examined the child.

For these reasons I would dismiss the appeal.

LORD JUSTICE SIMON BROWN: The facts of this case are most cogently related in the judgment of Farquharson LJ and need not be repeated here. But since I have the misfortune to disagree with My Lords upon the outcome of this appeal it may be helpful to indicate briefly what I understand to have been the essential basis of the learned judge's approach and findings. These may, I believe, be summarised as follows:

1 'At both 12.40 pm and 2 pm Patrick did not receive the care and attention he should have received.' [69B] Indeed, once Sister Sallabank's account of her conversation with Dr Horn was accepted, negligence in the action was admitted.

'It is not disputed on behalf of the defendants that, receiving communications such as Sister Sallabank made, Dr Horn should on each occasion have attended herself or secured the attendance of some other competent doctor. That she did not do so is accepted to be a breach of the duty of care that was owed to Patrick.' [23C]

2 There remained the issue of causation. It was formulated in two separate passages in the judgment, strikingly different from the other:

a   'The whole case depends upon whether the plaintiffs have established that, had Dr Horn or a suitable substitute attended on one or both occasions, some step would have been taken, some treatment initiated, some precaution put in place, which would as a matter of probability have averted the catastrophe that occurred at 2.35 pm.' [23D]

Hereafter 'the probability test'.

b   'The outcome of this case depends entirely on the answer to this question: has it been proved that, following the second episode at latest, no Senior Registrar of ordinary skill would have failed to have Patrick intubated?' [62G]

Hereafter 'the *Maynard* test'.

Clearly the issue was finally resolved according to the *Maynard* test. Whether or not it should have been is a critical question arising upon this appeal and I shall return to it shortly.

c   Two competing theories were advanced as to Patrick's condition before his final collapse and thus as to its immediacy. In broad terms the plaintiffs' experts suggested that he was in a state of respiratory distress progressing inexorably to hypoxia and respiratory failure, whereas the defendant's experts suggested that he was in general quite well but subject to two sudden acute episodes respectively at 12.40 pm and at 2 pm.

d   Given the judge's preference for the latter view and his finding that the most probable explanation of the two earlier episodes and of the final collapse at about 2.35 pm was that Patrick's airway had become blocked by a plug of mucus, the most crucial witnesses were Dr Heaf for the plaintiff, Dr Dinwiddie for the defendants. Both had addressed that particular scenario. Both of them the judge found to be 'immensely impressive'. Mr Owen QC for the defendants unsuccessfully argued that, given the judge's findings as to the case of collapse, Dr Heaf's evidence should be interpreted as supporting the defendant's case that intubation was not indicated. [64F] Mr Brennan QC for the plaintiffs equally unsuccessfully sought to attack Dr Dinwiddie's evidence on the footing that he had underestimated or trivialised Sister Sallabank's evidence. [65F]

e   The many other experts were found less compelling witnesses: the plaintiffs' because for the most part their approach to the critical question 'Should Patrick have been intubated?' postulated the rejected theory of progressive decline. The defendant's — Professor Hull and Dr Robertson — because, unlike Dr Dinwiddie, they had indeed tended to underestimate or trivialise Sister Sallabank's evidence.

f   I have described the judge's approach to causation as that of the *Maynard* test since it was explicitly founded upon the well-known passage from Lord Scarman's speech in *Maynard v West Midlands Regional Health Authority* [1984] 1 WLR 634:

'In the realm of diagnosis and treatment negligence is not established by preferring one respectable body of professional opinion to another. Failure to exercise the ordinary skill of a doctor (in, the appropriate specialty, if he be a specialist) is necessary.'

That approach clearly coloured the judge's response to Mr Brennan's main criticism of the defendants' experts:

'Mr Brennan also advanced a powerful argument — which I have to say, as a layman, appealed to me — to the effect that the views of the defendant's experts simply were not logical or sensible. Given the recent as well the more remote history of Patrick's illness, culminating in these two episodes, surely it was unreasonable and illogical not to anticipate the recurrence of a life-threatening event and take the step which it was acknowledged would probably have saved Patrick from harm? This was the safe option, whatever was suspected as the cause, or even if the cause was thought to be a mystery. The difficulty of this approach, as in the end I think Mr Brennan acknowledged, was that in effect it invited me to substitute my own views for those of the medical experts. [66D–G]

The judge reiterated that approach two pages later:

> 'It is not for me to make a choice between Dr Heaf and Dr Dinwiddie, one of whom is convinced that any competent doctor would, the other that she would not, have undertaken that procedure. Plainly, in my view this is one of those areas in which there is a difference of opinion between two distinguished and convincing medical witnesses, as to what as a matter of clinical judgment proper treatment requires.' [68G]

g   In the result, applying the *Maynard* test, the judge found against the plaintiff:

> 'I feel compelled to hold that it has not been proved that any competent doctor, in the position of Dr Horn, would have intubated Patrick before his collapse.' [68F]

The phrase 'any competent doctor' was there clearly used in the sense of 'every competent doctor' or 'all competent doctors'.

Turning to the argument advanced upon the appeal, I share My Lords' view that it would be quite wrong for this court to disturb the learned judge's conclusion that Dr Dinwiddie's approach to the question when a patient should be intubated was one representative of a responsible body of medical opinion. I would certainly not feel entitled to reject it, as Mr Brennan urged us to do, on the footing suggested by this court's decision in *Hucks v Cole* (transcript May 8, 1968), ie as unreasonable and unable to stand up to analysis.

I proceed, therefore, to Mr Brennan's second argument, that the judge should have applied the probability test rather than the *Maynard* test to the issue of causation.

Although this argument lies at the heart of the appeal, I do not propose to spend long on it. Frankly it seems obviously right. The *Maynard* test recognised jurisprudential Path marked out by such decisions as *Hunter v Hanley* 1955 SLT 213 and *Bolam v Friern Hospital Management Committee* [1957] 1 WLR 582, was forged specifically in the context of liability, of negligence, not of causation. And one can readily detect and accept the underlying principle: that differences of medical opinion do exist and, where each is shown to be respectable, it would be quite wrong to brand as negligent those who choose to adhere to one rather than another such body of opinion.

But, as it seems to me, quite different considerations come into play when the issue is one of causation, arising in the particular way that issue arises in the present case. This case does not involve a doctor adhering to one body of responsible medical opinion rather than another. No doctor in this case ever took a decision whether or not to intubate. The plain fact here is that no doctor ever arrived at Patrick's bedside. It is that want of attention that constitutes the undoubted negligence in the case.

I have no doubt that the resultant issue, the issue of causation, was correctly formulated by the judge in the first of the two passages I have quoted from his judgment — applying the test of probability. More particularly, in the light of his subsequent medical findings, it could have been formulated thus: had Dr Horn or a suitable substitute attended when called, would Patrick on the balance of probabilities have been intubated?

That clearly was not a question which in the event the judge addressed. Must the case therefore be retried? — always an unsatisfactory result, and not least in this type of action. Or, as I understand both parties to contend, can this court now determine the question — as the plaintiff contends, in his favour, or, as the defendants submit, in theirs having regard to the burden of proof?

Before turning to the rival contentions I must deal first with a sub-issue which was raised before the learned judge, and which, as it occurs to me, may well have led him into what I regard as the error of ultimately applying the wrong test.

Having earlier formulated the probability test the judge (at 27E) said this:

> '... the issue was what would Dr Horn or another competent doctor sent in her place have done had they attended ... If Dr Horn would have intubated, then the plaintiff succeeds, whether or not that is a course which all reasonable competent practitioners would have followed. If, however, Dr Horn would not have intubated, then the plaintiff can only succeed if such failure was contrary to accepted medical practice (I am not purporting to consider the legal tests in detail, and merely using shorthand at this stage).'

Having then considered Dr Horn's evidence as to what she would have done had she attended, the judge found that she would probably not have intubated.

That involved, I believe, a wrong approach. In the first place, it is far from clear that it was Dr Horn, the senior paediatric registrar, who would have attended. On the evidence, it might well have been Dr Rodgers, the senior house officer, but for the regrettable fact that her bleeper batteries were flat. But that aside, it would seem to me unsatisfactory to place much reliance upon any doctor's evidence in these circumstances as to what he or she would have done had they complied with their duty to attend (or arranged for someone else to attend) a patient. Inevitably, if unconsciously, any doctor would in that situation tend to believe and suggest that their attendance could and would have made no difference.

I see no reason why the position here should be any different to that arising if a nurse's call is not responded to and no evidence exists as to which of several doctors might have attended. The question surely is: what would an attending doctor probably have done? And given that the doctor would probably do that which she or he should do, the question becomes: what should a doctor do in such circumstances?

How then should that question be approached?

It is convenient to start with the burden of proof. This, there can be no doubt, rests upon the plaintiff. It is for the plaintiff to prove that the defendant's negligence caused or materially contributed to his injury. It is not discharged merely by the plaintiff pointing to the combination of the defendant's admitted breach of duty and his own subsequent catastrophe. That is to confuse exposure to the risk of injury with the causing of it — not necessarily the same thing — see the decision of the House of Lords in *Wilsher v Essex Area Health Authority* [1988] AC 1074. Nor will the burden be discharged merely by the plaintiff demonstrating some prospect that whichever doctor arrived would have decided to intubate, not even by proof that 50 per cent of doctors would have intubated. That much too is plain — see the decision of the House of Lords in *Hotson v East Berkshire Area Health Authority* [1987] AC 750. And these are the decisions upon which the defendants now primarily rely. Given, they argue, that doctors could properly take either one of the two views espoused respectively by Dr Heaf and Dr Dinwiddie, how can it be said that whoever had attended would more probably have belonged to Dr Heaf's school of thought than to Dr Dinwiddie's? Superficially the argument is appealing; on analysis however, it seems to me ill-founded.

Let me deal first with *Hotson*. That, clearly, was a decision on very different facts, raising a very different principle. The negligence there consisted of the defendants' failure to diagnose correctly and treat promptly the plaintiff's already sustained injury. In light of the finding of fact that there was a 75 per cent chance that the plaintiff's injury was such that prompt treatment would not in any event have benefited him, the question of law raised was: should the patient recover 25 per cent of the claim's full value for loss of a chance, or nothing for having failed to prove on the balance of probabilities that the admitted negligence caused him loss. The House of Lords held the latter. But this plaintiff is not suing on the footing that he lost a 50 per cent chance that whichever doctor attended would have intubated him. His case is that probably he would have been intubated.

I turn next to *Wilsher*, clearly somewhat closer in point. The facts there were that the infant plaintiff suffered a serious retinal condition (RLF) which could have been caused by the defendants' negligence in exposing him to excess oxygen but could instead have resulted from any one of four other possible causes. The trial judge held that, since the hospital had failed to take proper precautions to prevent excess oxygen being administered, and since the plaintiff had suffered the injury against which the precautions were designed to protect, the burden lay on the health authority to show that the damage did not result from the breach. The Court of Appeal supported the decision on the ground that the breach of duty and the plaintiff's injury were such that the hospital was to be taken as having caused the injury notwithstanding that the existence and extent of the contribution made by the hospital's breach of duty could not be ascertained. The House of Lords allowed the defendants' appeal, holding that, where a plaintiff's injury was attributable to a number of possible causes, the combination of the defendants' breach of duty and the plaintiff's injury did not give rise to a presumption that the defendant had caused the injury; instead the burden remained on the plaintiff to prove the causative link.

The question here, of course, is not 'Which of two or more possible causes resulted in this plaintiff's catastrophe?', but rather 'Would the doctor who should have attended Patrick have intubated him?' But *Wilsher* is nevertheless in my judgment illuminating in the present context for the light it throws upon the court's proper approach to such a question.

Much of Lord Bridge's speech in *Wilsher* was devoted to explaining the earlier misunderstanding and misapplication of *McGhee v National Coal Board* [1973] 1 WLR 1. McGhee had not, as had been thought, introduced a fiction into the law, the fiction that when negligence increases the risk of injury and injury then occurs, the negligence is assumed without more to have caused it. McGhee was rather an illustration, as was *Bonnington Castings Ltd v Wardlaw* [1956] AC 613 before it, of the courts

'adopting a robust and pragmatic approach to the undisputed primary facts of the case ... (and concluding) that it was a legitimate inference of fact that the defenders' negligence had materially contributed to the pursuer's injury.' [per Lord Bridge in *Wilsher* at 1090D]

Both Bonnington Castings and McGhee were, it may be noted, cases where the proved breach of duty materially contributed to, rather than solely caused, the plaintiff's injury. Both involved exposure to a mixture of 'guilty' and 'innocent' contamination. Bonnington was a pneumoconiosis case where the plaintiff inhaled damaging dust particles for some only of whom the defendants were liable; McGhee, a dermatitis case where the plaintiff's condition arose from exposure to brick dust, the defendants' liability consisting of exposing him to contamination for longer than was necessary by their failure to provide proper washing facilities. As Lord Bridge said in *Wilsher* at page 1088A:

'... the consecutive periods when "innocent" and "guilty" brick dust was present on the pursuer's body may both have contributed to the cause of the disease or, theoretically at least, one or other may have been the sole cause. But where the lay man is told by the doctors that the longer the brick dust remains on the body, the greater the risk of dermatitis, although the doctors cannot identify the process of causation scientifically, there seems to be nothing irrational in drawing the inference, as a matter of common sense, that the consecutive periods when brick dust remained on the body probably contributed cumulatively to the causation of the dermatitis. I believe that a process of inferential reasoning on these general lines underlines the decision of the majority in McGhee's case.'

Lord Bridge then cited with apparent approval passages from a number of speeches in McGhee, including this from Lord Reid:

'Nor can I accept the distinction drawn by the Lord Ordinary between materially increasing the risk that the disease will occur and making a material contribution to its occurrence. There may be some logical ground for such a distinction where our knowledge of the material factors is complete. But it has often been said that the legal concept of causation is not based on logical philosophy.'

In short, I understand *Wilsher* to recognise that, when the court's knowledge of all the material factors is not complete, on occasion it will be legitimate to adopt a robust and pragmatic approach and infer from those facts which are established that the defendants' proven negligence did indeed cause or contribute to the plaintiff's injury. That was not, however, an approach which on the facts of *Wilsher* itself the House of Lords felt able to adopt. Rather they approved the contrary view expressed by Sir Nicholas Browne-Wilkinson, V-C in his dissenting judgment in the Court of Appeal:

'To my mind, the occurrence of RLF following a failure to take a necessary precaution to prevent excess oxygen causing RLF provides no evidence and raises no presumption that it was excess oxygen rather than one or more of the four other possible agents which caused or contributed to RLF in this case ... a failure to take preventive measures against one out of five possible causes is no evidence as to which of those five caused the injury.'

The trial judge as well as the majority of the Court of Appeal in *Wilsher* having applied McGhee as it had earlier been misunderstood, there had been no resolution of the primary conflict of opinion between the experts whether the negligent exposure to excessive oxygen had in fact caused or materially contributed to the plaintiff's condition. In the result, the House of Lords felt constrained to order a re-trial.

Is the present case, then, one which must similarly be re-tried or is the material before us sufficient to enable this court to decide the matter finally one way or the other? Before addressing that question, I would first refer to two other authorities.

Corn v Weir's Glass (Hanley) Ltd [1960] 2 All ER 300 concerned a plaintiff who was injured when he fell from unguarded stairs. The defendants were in breach of their duty under the building regulations to have provided a handrail. The plaintiff nevertheless failed because he failed to prove that a handrail would have protected him from injury. In the Court of Appeal, Wilmer LJ (with whose judgment Hodson LJ agreed), expressed himself satisfied

'that the breach of duty of which (the defendants) were admittedly guilty in failing to fit a handrail, was in no sense a cause of the plaintiff's injuries.'

Devlin LJ, having referred to *Bonnington Castings Ltd v Wardlaw*, said this (ibid at p 306):

'the plaintiff must show that on balance of probabilities the breach of duty caused or materially contributed to his injury. This does not in my judgment leave it open to the defendant when the nature of the accident is known to think out as many ways as he can in which the regulation could conceivably be complied with and then demand that the court tests the question of causation by reference to the way which is of least use to the plaintiff in the circumstances of his accident. The rule requires the plaintiff to show that if before the accident the regulation had been complied with, his injury — probably would not have occurred; and this test of probability means, I think, that the court should consider independently of the accident how the employer would probably have complied with the regulation if he had done as he ought. If there are two or more ways in which he might have done so and one would, on the facts of the accident, have protected the plaintiff and the others would not have protected him and if no one can say that any one way is more likely to have been chosen than the others, then the plaintiff as a matter of probability fails. In my judgment the defendant cannot rely on a method that he is unlikely to have used simply because it is within the letter of the regulation.'

That passage, it seems to me, helps to this limited extent: it shows that a defendant cannot escape liability merely by establishing that he could have complied with his duty in such a way that the plaintiff would still have been injured. So here it is insufficient for the defendants' purposes to establish that a doctor of Dr Dinwiddie's persuasion might well have attended in response to Sister Sallabank's calls and so (without negligence) not have intubated. The court must instead consider what probably would have occurred.

The other decision which to my mind provides some assistance is one not referred to in argument, *McWilliams v Sir William Arrol & Co Ltd* [1962] 1 WLR 295. The appellant there was the widow of an experienced steel erector who had fallen 70 feet to his death whilst working without a safety belt. His employers were in breach of their duty to provide such a belt. The claim nevertheless failed on the issue of causation. As Viscount Kilmuir, LC stated in the House of Lords:

'The evidence demonstrates to a high degree of probability that if safety belts had been available the deceased would, in any event, not have worn one.'

The speeches, however, to my mind cast some light upon the approach which the court should properly adopt to the drawing of inferences in this sort of situation.

Viscount Simonds said this:

'It may ... be said that, where the employer is in breach of his duty, there is in that fact some prima facie evidence of a causal connection between the breach and the subsequent damage. So far in this case I would go with the appellant.'

Lord Reid, disapproving an earlier decision in which it had been held that an employer in breach of duty to provide items of safety equipment could not be heard to say 'Even if I had done so they would not have been worn', said this:

'I know of no ... ground on which a defender can be prevented from proving a fact vital for his defence. If I prove that my breach of duty in no way caused or contributed to the accident I cannot be liable in damages. And if the accident would have happened in just the same way whether or not I had fulfilled my duty, it is obvious that my failure to fulfil my duty cannot have caused or contributed to it. No reason has ever been suggested why a defender should be barred from proving that his fault, whether common law negligence or breach of statutory duty, had nothing to do with the accident.'

Lord Reid appears to have regarded the evidential if not the legal burden as being upon the defendant.

Lord Hodson said this:

> 'a pursuer ... must prove that the fault of the defendant caused, or contributed to, the danger which he has suffered. But proof need not be by direct evidence. If general practice or a regulation requires that some safety appliance shall be provided, one would assume that it is of some use, and that a reasonable man would use it. And one would assume that the injured man was a reasonable man. So the initial onus on the pursuer to connect the failure to provide the appliance with the accident would normally be discharged merely by proving the circumstances which led to the accident, and it is only where the evidence throws doubt on either of these assumptions that any difficulty would arise. Normally it would be left to the defender to adduce evidence, if he could, to displace these assumptions. So in practice it would be realistic, even if not theoretically accurate, to say that the onus is generally on the defender to show that the man would not have used the appliance even if it had been available. But in the end, when all the evidence has been brought out, it rarely matters where the onus originally lay, the question is which way the balance of probability has come to rest.'

With all those authorities in mind I return to the present appeal. Is there sufficient material before us to reach a final conclusion in favour of one or other party, or must this case, like *Wilsher*, now be retried?

In my judgment there is, indeed, sufficient material to conclude the case and, as I believe, to conclude it in favour of the plaintiff. Not merely do I feel entitled to infer that the necessary causative link is here established; the evidence as it seems to me compels that conclusion.

As stated, the ultimate question for decision here is not: Would it have been unreasonable and thus negligent for an attending doctor not to intubate Patrick? (to which the answer is clearly 'no'). It is rather: Should and therefore would an attending doctor probably have intubated Patrick? The answer to that question to my mind is an equally clear 'yes'. It was, of course, the defendants' case that it would have been positively wrong for an attending doctor to intubate. But that is surely an impossible contention having regard not least to the agreed fact that intubation alone would have averted this catastrophe.

When it comes to deciding what inferences here may, legitimately be drawn from the established primary facts, prominent amongst the factors to be borne in mind are surely these. First, the literature in this field of medicine, and not least the generally accepted statements (as found by the judge at pp 32/33) that:

> 'respiratory failure ... is a common complication in many disease processes and should always be readily suspected, especially if there are unexplained signs and symptoms...'

and

> '... any child who reaches the hospital alive should not ... die from upper airway obstruction.'

Second, that the very purpose of Sister Sallabank calling for the senior paediatric registrar was to ensure that whatever needed to be done for Patrick was done. The initial assumption must surely be that the doctor's attendance would have been of some use. Third is the indisputable fact that intubation alone would have benefited the child. Given all that, and given fourth the entire history of this case as it would present itself to an attending doctor — the background to Patrick's re-admission on January 16, his being 'specialed' that day, Sister Sallabank's view at the time of the first episode that something was so acutely wrong that she wanted Patrick seen by the senior paediatric registrar and not merely the senior houseman, her decision that a nurse should then remain permanently with him, and, when the second episode occurred, her renewed worry and decision again to call the senior paediatric registrar — I have no difficulty in inferring that whichever doctor had attended would have acted in the one way which would have been effective. In so deciding, I do not overlook Nurse Newbold's evidence nor Dr Dinwiddie's school of thought. But it is all very well for the specialists now to theorise over what would or would not have appeared to be indicated by second-hand descriptions of the child's developing condition; the reality is that no one will ever know quite how that condition would have presented itself to a competent doctor, learning the history as he would have done and examining the patient for himself. In my judgments therefore, the case called for the 'robust and pragmatic approach' endorsed by *Wilsher*, and the assumption of causation suggested by the speeches in *McWilliam* so at least it strikes me, although not, as I recognise, My Lords.

In the final analysis the judge's conclusion that Dr Dinwiddie's views represented those of a respectable body of medical opinion, so far from being decisive in the defendant's favour, is in my judgment an irrelevance. Unless only it suffices to rebut the assumptions otherwise arising in Patrick's favour and to defeat the inferences otherwise to be drawn that a doctor's attendance was not merely required but would probably have benefited the child, it serves no purpose. And that to my mind it cannot do: it certainly fails to persuade me that attendance in response to Sister Sallabank's calls would have been useless.

I add only this. I believe that that would have been the trial judge's conclusion too had he ultimately come to apply the probability test rather than the *Maynard* test and had he felt entitled to choose for himself between Dr Heaf and Dr Dinwiddie, more particularly as to which of their approaches should properly have been followed and inferentially therefore was likely to have been followed had a doctor attended. That I deduce from the earlier quoted passage in his judgment dealing with Mr Brennan's main argument which appealed to him as a layman. But whether or not I am right in that surmise is really immaterial.

In the result I would have allowed this appeal and entered judgment for the plaintiff for damages to be assessed.

LORD JUSTICE DILLON: In *Maynard v West Midland Regional Health Authority* [1984] 1 WLR 634 Lord Scarman stated very clearly at p 638E–F what is now trite law viz:

> 'A case which is based on an allegation that a fully considered decision of two consultants in the field of their special skill was negligent clearly presents certain difficulties of proof. It is not enough to show that there is a body of competent professional opinion which considers that theirs was a wrong decision, if there also exists a body of professional opinion which considers that theirs was a wrong decision, if there also exists a body of professional opinion, equally competent, which supports the decision as reasonable in the circumstances.'

The present case is not directly such a case because there was no considered decision by the medical staff at St Bartholomew's as to Patrick's treatment at the relevant time. Instead there was admitted negligence in that the senior registrar, Dr Horn, failed to come to examine Patrick despite the urgent appeals to her to do so by Sister Sallabank at 12.50 pm and again at 14.00 pm on January 12, 1983 and failed to get the senior house officer, Dr Rodgers, to attend in her place because Dr Rodgers had failed to appreciate that the batteries in her bleeper were flat and so did not receive the message Dr Horn tried to send her.

The question for us is therefore essentially one of causation, viz was the admitted negligence causative of the damage which Patrick undoubtedly suffered? As to this it is not in doubt that the onus remained on Patrick to prove causation ie to prove that the fault of Dr Horn and Dr Rodgers caused, or materially contributed to, his injury. See *Bonnington Castings Ltd v Wardlaw* [1956] AC 613 and *Wilsher v Essex Area Health Authority* [1988] AC 1074. What that means, in a case where the fault of the defendant has been a failure to act, is explained by Devlin J in *Corn v Weir's Glass (Hanley) Ltd* [1960] 2 All ER 300 at p 306E–F; after referring to *Bonnington Castings Ltd v Wardlaw* he said:

> 'The rule requires the plaintiff to show that if before the accident the regulation had been complied with, his injury probably would not have occurred; and this test of probability means, I think, that the Court should consider independently of the accident how the employer would probably have complied with the regulation if he had done as he ought. If there are two or more ways in which he might have done and one would, on the facts of the accident, have protected the plaintiff and the others would not have protected him, and if no one can say that any one way is more likely to have been chosen than the others, then the plaintiff as a matter of probability fails.'

As to this, we have on the one side a most impressive body of cogent medical evidence called on behalf of Patrick to the effect that the proper course for any doctor attending on Patrick after Sister Sallabank's second urgent call to Dr Horn at 14.00 would have been to intubate Patrick. There would have been time for that to have been done before 14.35 and it is common ground that, if it had been done, he would not have suffered the disastrous collapse, respiratory arrest and consequent cardiac arrest at 14.35.

As against that, Dr Horn says that if she had attended after the 14.00 call she would not have intubated Patrick. She would merely have had him kept under close observation to see what happened next. Dr Dinwiddie, a paediatrician specialising in respiratory disease and a consultant at Great Ormond Street Hospital, agreed with Dr Horn and said that in the circumstances he too would not have intubated Patrick, despite the risk, which he appreciated that course involved, of a sudden respiratory arrest. Dr Robertson, a consultant paediatrician at Addenbrookes Hospital, would also not have intubated Patrick.

In view of the judge's acceptance of Nurse Newbold, who was watching Patrick from 14.00 until she went for help immediately before the collapse at 14.35, as a careful and reliable witness it must follow that if Patrick had not been intubated by whoever answered the 14.00 call, the final collapse would inevitably have happened as it did; it came so swiftly at 14.35 that it would not have been possible to avoid it by last-moment intubation. It is not suggested, nor could it be, that this court should interfere with the judge's assessment of Nurse Newbold.

Thus the case comes indirectly to raise the same issue as is referred to by Lord Scarman in *Maynard* in the passage above cited. This can be reached by either of two routes. In the first place if the starting place is the evidence of Dr Horn, as the doctor who ought to have attended, as to what she would have done, that could only be displaced by showing that if she had done that she would have been negligent; but her evidence is supported by a body of medical opinion, Dr Dinwiddie and Dr Robertson. Alternatively, if Dr Horn's evidence is ignored, the position is that, as against the evidence in favour of intubation after the 14.00 call, there is another body of medical opinion, Dr Dinwiddie and Dr Robertson, against it.

The judge was clearly, and in my judgment, rightly, satisfied that Dr Dinwiddie had correctly appreciated the evidence of Sister Sallabank and Nurse Newbold. He was therefore addressing his mind to the correct scenario. The same, so far as I can see, goes for Dr Robertson.

There, therefore, remains the final question whether the court is entitled to disregard the evidence of Dr Dinwiddie and Dr Robertson on some such ground as that on which Sachs LJ acted in the unreported case of *Hucks v Cole* decided on May 8, 1968.

In that case an onset of puerperal septicaemia had occurred because penicillin had not been administered to the patient. Sachs LJ said in his judgment at p 11B–F:

'It was not administered and the onset occurred; if it had been administered the onset would not have occurred. Thus (unless there was some good cause for not administering it) the onset was due to a lacuna between what could easily have been done and what was in fact done. According to the defence, that lacuna was consistent with and indeed accorded with the reasonable practice of other responsible doctors with obstetric experience.

When the evidence shows that a lacuna in professional practice exists by which risks of grave danger are knowingly taken, then, however small the risks, the Courts must anxiously examine that lacuna — particularly if the risks can be easily and inexpensively avoided. If the Court finds on an analysis of the reasons given for not taking those precautions that, in the light of current professional knowledge, there is no proper basis for the lacuna, and that it is definitely not reasonable that those risks should have been taken, its function is to state that fact and where necessary to state that it constitutes negligence. In such a case the practice will no doubt thereafter be altered to the benefit of patients.

On such occasions the fact that other practitioners would have done the same thing as the defendant practitioner is a very weighty matter to be put in the scales on his behalf; but it is not ... conclusive. The Court must be vigilant to see whether the reasons given for putting a patient at risk are valid ...'

Sachs LJ continued at 14F–15B:

'Despite the fact that the risk could have been avoided by adopting a course that was easy, efficient and inexpensive and which would have entailed only minimal chances of disadvantages to the patient, the evidence of the four defence experts to the effect that they and other responsible members of the medical profession would have taken the same risk in the same circumstances has naturally caused me to hesitate considerably.'

He concluded, however, that the course taken by the defendant was clearly unreasonable, and the reasons given by the four experts did not stand up to analysis. He said finally at 15F–16B:

'this is not apparently the case of "two schools of thought"; it appears more to be a case of doctors who said in one form or another that they would have acted or might have acted in the same way as the defendant did, for reasons which on examination do not really stand up to analysis.'

As against that, however, it is clearly stated by Lord Scarman in *Maynard* at 639G–H that:

'a judge's "preference" for one body of distinguished professional opinion to another also professionally distinguished is not sufficient to establish negligence in a practitioner whose actions have received the seal of approval of those whose opinions, truthfully expressed, honestly held, were not preferred.'

In my judgment, the court could only adopt the approach of Sachs LJ and reject medical opinion on the ground that the reasons of one group of doctors do not really stand up to analysis, if the Court, fully conscious of its own lack of medical knowledge and clinical experience, was none the less clearly satisfied that the views of that group of doctors were *Wednesbury* unreasonable, ie views such as no reasonable body of doctors could have held. But, in my judgment, that would be an impossibly strong thing to say of the honest views of experts of the distinction of Dr Dinwiddie and Dr Robertson, in the present case.

The difficulty is that after each of the two episodes of respiratory distress which caused Sister Sallabank to telephone Dr Horn at 12.50 and 14.00 Patrick apparently recovered very speedily and presented as an active, healthy little boy with a good colour. Even over the last half-hour before 14.35, Patrick was not in a state of respiratory distress progressing inexorably to hypoxia and respiratory failure; he was in general quite well but subject to two sudden acute episodes. The defendant's experts therefore regarded the two sudden acute episodes as chance episodes, unconnected to each other, from which Patrick had recovered. They therefore considered the risk of a third chance episode as slight. As against that, Dr Dinwiddie shrank from intubating an active and apparently healthy little boy since to intubate him would involve sedating him for quite a time, while Dr Robertson thought that intubation carried a danger of leading to a sense of false security as to the true reason for Patrick's sudden crises.

The matter is one of clinical judgment. I am unable to regard the view of Dr Dinwiddie, and for that matter Dr Robertson, *Wednesbury* unreasonable. Therefore, I cannot disregard their views or prefer the views of the witnesses who would have intubated Patrick. Therefore it must follow, in accordance with the authorities cited above, that causation of damage has not been proved, and Patrick's claim for damages must fail.

I agree, therefore, with the reasoning the conclusions of the learned judge, and also with the reasons given in the judgment of Farquharson LJ; like Farquharson LJ, I would dismiss this appeal. I am greatly indebted to Farquharson LJ for his very clear summary of the facts and of the parties' arguments.

I differ with regret from Simon Brown LJ, but I do not believe that, on the state of the medical evidence, there is any material which entitles us to say that on the balance of probabilities Patrick would have been intubated if a doctor had come promptly in response to Sister Sallabank's 14.00 call.

APPENDIX 5

Hucks v Cole

Court of Appeal
Before Lord Denning MR, Lord Justice Diplock and Lord Justice Sachs
Date of judgment: May 8, 1968

The following cases are referred to in the judgments:

Chapman v Rix, December 21, 1960
Chin Keow's case, [1967] 1 WLR 813
Hornal v Neuberger Products Ltd [1957] 1 QB 247
Roe v Minister of Health [1954] 2 QB 66

JUDGMENTS

LORD DENNING MR: Mrs Hucks is a young married woman who was living at Wellington in Somerset. In 1963 she was expecting her third child. She was under the care of Dr Cole, a general practitioner. She went into the Wellington Maternity Hospital to have a baby. She was there 10 days. After she got home she was stricken with puerperal fever, from which she nearly died. She was rushed to the Taunton Hospital. Her life was saved but her health has been considerably impaired. Now she brings this action against Dr Cole for negligence.

In the years before 1935 puerperal fever was a great and fearful danger. A woman after childbirth is for a time very liable to infection. If harmful germs reach her, they may give rise to septicaemia. In some cases it may show itself as a local sepsis, gradually becoming worse with rising fever. In other cases its onset may be sudden, coming like a thunderbolt, with high fever. Then it is called fulminating septicaemia. Before 1935, 80 per cent of women stricken with either kind died. But in 1935 sulphonamide drugs were discovered. With their aid, medical men were able to prevent or to treat the infection. The mortality dropped a great deal. Only four per cent of the women got septicaemia, and these were treated in the early stages so that it did not develop.

Puerperal fever is now extremely rare — so rare that some of distinguished medical people who were called had never seen a case. Nevertheless, all agreed with one accord that any sign of infection in a maternity ward is a danger against which every precaution must be taken. If a nurse or a student has a septic place on a finger, he or she should not be allowed into the ward. If a mother has a septic place, on a finger or anywhere else, she should be isolated lest the infection spread through the ward to other mothers.

Now let me come back to Mrs Hucks herself. She was expecting her child in the early days of October 1963. On October 4, while at home, her ring finger was swollen and painful. She had the wedding ring off. Underneath there was a little sore septic spot about half-an-inch in diameter with three little yellow spots inside it. She treated it herself with a Kaolin poultice. On October 7, Dr Cole visited her at home. She showed him the septic spot. Dr Cole told her, she says, that there was no need to worry about it. He gave her no treatment for it. He took a swab to find out the bacteria. He did not warn the maternity hospital about it. Three days later, on October 10, the baby was imminent. She went to the hospital. About mid-day she had her child. It was a baby girl. On the next day, October 11, the nurse washing her noticed a reddened area on her ring finger. It was the septic spot. The nurse looked for other places over her body and found another spot on her toe. She told the sister. The sister told the matron. They were alarmed. They moved Mrs Hucks from the ward (where there were other mothers) into a room by herself. They telephoned the doctor and made a special note to say that they had telephoned him about it.

Mrs Hucks says that the matron and the sister were annoyed — annoyed because they had not been told. I think we should accept her evidence: because, surprisingly enough, the matron and sister were not called at the trial. They were present in court but not called. They were doubtless annoyed because the doctor had allowed Mrs Hucks to come into the ward with a septic place on her finger and told them nothing about it. The next day, October 12, Dr Cole came. He looked at the spot. He then did what was quite right in the circumstances. He gave orders that a swab should be taken and sent to the pathologist so as to see what were the bacteria which were causing the sepsis. He told them to administer an antibiotic, called tetracycline, given by tablets over five days. Tetracycline is a broad spectrum antibiotic which served to prevent many harmful bacteria from developing, thus it does not kill them. It is bacterio-static, but not bacteriocidal.

During the next few days the septic places did heal somewhat. On October 14, the pathologist's report was received. It was shown to Dr Cole on October 15. The report is of crucial importance. It gave on the first page this result:

'Much pus and a fair number of organisms. Culture (1) staphylococci aureus. (2) Streptococci pyogenes.'

It then gave on the second page some information as to the effect of drugs on those cultures. The report said that penicillin would kill the streptococci pyogenes, but did not say what tetracycline would do to the streptococci pyogenes. It said that tetracycline would have no effect on the staphlococci aureus.

That report was a danger signal. The organism streptococcus pyogenes was a virulent organism capable of killing. It would ring an alarm bell for every practitioner. The plaintiff says that, on seeing it was present, Dr Cole ought at once to have stopped the tetracycline and put the patient on to penicillin, because the report said that penicillin would kill this organism. Or, at any rate, he ought to have telephoned the laboratory for further details. But Dr Cole did not do so. He kept on with the tetracycline to the end of the five-day course. The judge found, however, that he was not negligent in so doing. Many medical men think that these antibiotics ought to go the full five-day course; otherwise there might be a resistance set up. In addition, the tetracycline might have been doing some good in containing the streptococcus pyogenes, although not killing it. At all events, Dr Cole's decision (to let the tetracycline course be finished) was not negligence on his part.

On the evening of October 16 the five days were up. The tetracycline course was completed. The plaintiff says that Dr Cole ought then, on October 17, to have put her on to penicillin and killed this virulent germ. But he did nothing. He knew that the septic place was not fully healed. He should have known there was still danger from it. Yet he allowed her to go home on October 19. She was stricken seriously ill soon afterwards with fulminating septicaemia.

On this point much depends on the condition of the finger and the toe on and after October 16. Were the septic places healed or not? If they were not healed, the evidence shows beyond doubt that, as long as there is an open place of sepsis on the mother's body, she may with her hand transmit this infection to other parts of her body. It may pass on to the sheets, or when the nurse is washing her, and such like. As long as there is the open place unhealed there is a risk — a real and grave risk — of the mother infecting herself. The septic place itself may be healing but, until it is completely healed, the dangerous germs may still be there. She is not safe until the womb gets back into its ordinary position. Now upon this point of healing, the evidence was incomplete. The matron and the sister could have given evidence on it. They were present in court. But Dr Cole did not call them. The records, however, show that the septic places were far from being completely healed. On October 16 there is a note:

'Toe still moist and one core from finger.'

And the judge held — I think quite justifiably — that on this October 17, when the tetracycline course was finished, these lesions had not healed, at any rate not fully healed. They were still open, and there was serious danger to the mother unless something was done. In these circumstances there was considerable evidence to show that Dr Cole ought to have treated Mrs Hucks with penicillin. Such evidence was given particularly by a distinguished expert from the London Hospital, Dr May. He said that on October 17, Dr Cole ought, as a responsible practitioner, to have administered penicillin so as to get rid of this virulent organism. There might be a side effect of penicillin, but that could hardly be weighed in the scale. Dr May summed it up in one sentence: 'No responsible practitioner would stop treatment under those conditions.' But Dr Cole did stop treatment. He gave no further treatment with any antibiotics. His explanation was that he looked at the clinical picture. The finger and the toe were both healing well. The mother herself was in good condition. It was not desirable to add yet another antibiotic.

Distinguished experts were called an each side. On behalf of Mrs Hucks there were called Mr Bourne, Professor Camps and Dr May. On behalf of Dr Cole there was Dr Cole himself. In addition Miss Bames, a distinguished consultant at the Charing Cross Hospital, Dr Hickman and Miss June Smith from Chippenham. These said that they would have done the same if they had been faced with the problem with which Dr Cole was faced. On balancing the rival contentions, the judge accepted Dr May's evidence. He held that Dr Cole was negligent on October 17, because he did not prescribe an antibiotic on that day to get rid of this very virulent organism. Was this finding justified?

A charge of negligence against a medical man, a solicitor or any other professional man, stands on a very different footing to a charge of negligence against a motorist or an employer. The reason is because the consequences for the professional man are far more grave. A finding of negligence affects his standing and reputation. It impairs the confidence which his clients have in him. The burden of proof is correspondingly greater. The principle applies that: 'In proportion as the charge is grave, so ought the proof to be clear': see *Hornal v Neuberger Products Ltd* [1957] 1 QB 247. Another difference lies in the fact that, with the best will in the world, things do sometimes go amiss in surgical operation or medical treatment. A striking illustration was *Roe v Minister of Health* [1954] 2 QB 66. So a doctor is not to be held negligent simply because something goes wrong. It is not negligent to invoke against him the maxim res ipsa loquitur save in extreme cases. He is not liable for mischance or misadventure. Nor is he liable for an error of judgment. He is not to be liable for choosing one course out of two which may be open to him or for following one school of thought rather than another. He is only liable if he falls below the standard of a reasonable competent practitioner in his field — so much so that his conduct may fairly be held to be — I will not say deserving of censure but, at any rate, inexcusable.

Applying those principles, here is Dr Cole. He qualified in 1959. He gained a Diploma in Obstetrics in 1961. He is to be judged as a general practitioner with a Diploma in Obstetrics. And here is this Wellington Maternity Hospital, a hospital in the National Health Service. It has no permanent staff of doctors. The local practitioners run it themselves. Dr Cole allowed this young woman to go into this maternity home with a septic finger. He did not tell the matron and sister at the time. They find it out. They move her into another room, separate from the other women. He treats it with tetracycline and gets a swab taken. That was quite reasonable. But then he gets this danger signal: a report of the pathologist showing that streptococcus pyogenes was present. His own expert, Miss Barnes, said how serious this was. She was asked: 'Does any sort of alarm bell ring in his mind?' She said: 'Most certainly'. She was asked:

> 'Is it a full turnout to resist attack or do you take it quite calmly and you take a few extra precautions but leave it at that?'

She answered:

> 'No ... I think you should attack it with all the means in your power. It is a general alarm. Everybody is standing to.'

Yet Dr Cole did nothing. He never treated her with penicillin, which would have killed this organism. In the light of that evidence, I think that the judge was justified in holding that Dr Cole ought to have given Mrs Hucks treatment with penicillin, at any rate on October 17. It is a very difficult case, and I have considerable sympathy with Dr Cole, but I think he has not measured up to the duty required of him. His conduct, I fear, was inexcusable. I am much influenced by the fact that the matron and sister, although they were in court, were not called to give evidence. In my opinion, this appeal should be dismissed.

LORD JUSTICE DIPLOCK: I agree. During the hearing of this appeal I must confess I have had grave doubts as to whether the learned judge was not requiring a higher standard of prescience and caution than is to be expected of a general practitioner with obstetric qualifications which four out of five general practitioners have; but, for the reasons given by my Lord, I do not feel that I am justified in taking a different view from the learned judge, who, after all, had heard the evidence, although he was deprived of what, from either party's point of view, might have been the vital evidence, namely, that of the matron or the sister as to the state of healing of the wounds upon October 17, on which the whole propriety of the treatment adopted by Dr Cole depended.

Though I feel compelled to dismiss the appeal, I would not like to do so without expressing considerable sympathy for Dr Cole, who, I think was lulled into a fake sense of security, as many other general practitioners might be, by the efficacy of antibiotics in the treatment of septicaemia at the present day. It is well known that septicaemia will normally give warning of its onset by local sepsis which has easily recognisable symptoms, and when those symptoms are recognised, the administration of antibiotics can prevent septicaemia developing and cure the local sepsis; so that in the ordinary way any risk taken by not administering antibiotics before symptoms of septicaemia arise can be cured by a subsequent administration when those symptoms do arise. But there is one exception to this, and that is the case of fulminating septicaemia. It is today very very rare. From the evidence I think there had been no example of it in the area in which Dr Cole practised for 18 years. Even in the wider field in which other witnesses practised only one case was ever experienced by two consultants in the course of what Mr Webster described as 40 consultant years. It is a very very rare disease in modern times and it is understandable that Dr Cole forgot about it, and that I think was the cause of this disaster. Some of the witnesses said and there is a great deal of truth in it that it is only when you experience or get to know of an actual case that it really brings home to you the danger which you have previously only learned about from text books and lectures. And so it is understandable, but none the less, it is a danger which general practitioners are taught about in their training, read about in the literature, and ought, even in the exigencies of what is no doubt a busy and a heavy practice, to remember, because the danger of that risk is so enormous. Sympathetic as I am to Dr Cole, understandable as I find his lapse to be, nevertheless, I feel that I ought not to interfere with the judge's decision in this case.

LORD JUSTICE SACHS: Puerperal septicaemia is and has for long been known to be potentially lethal. Before 1935, according to one very experienced witness, Dr Bourne, 80 per cent of those who suffered from it died, as the Master of the Rolls pointed out. Today, owing to the proper and diligent use of antibiotics, the incidence is so greatly diminished that experienced obstetrical practitioners hardly ever see a case except where there has been an unlawful abortion. If, however, the puerperal patient concerned contracts it and it happens to be of the rare fulminating type, it is almost inevitable that the results will be rapid and extremely serious: if it is of the non-fulminating type, her chances are relatively much better.

Streptococcus pyogenes is a cause of puerperal septicaemia, and was rightly in the course of the trial referred to as a killer. It is an important fact that from a septic spot it can go direct into the blood stream: in addition, it can, of course, be carried by external routes — not least by the hand. When once its presence in a puerperal patient is known, the only way to make reasonably sure that she does not suffer in this way is to use a bacteriocidal as opposed to a bacteriostatic antibiotic. All those facts are common knowledge amongst all ranks of obstetric practitioners and were known in particular to Dr Cole. Actually well-known were the following facts: a septic place of the type under consideration in this case is a source of danger if once it has the streptococcus pyogenes in it, and until it has completely healed (that is to say, the skin fully re-formed and the scab off) the danger has not been eliminated. A septic place on the finger involves special risks, as witness the alarm of the matron when she saw on October 11 what Dr Cole had seen four days earlier. (The fact that neither matron nor sister was called — despite the indications given on behalf of the defendant to the court by counsel that he would probably call one or both — is not without a significance which goes further than the inference to be drawn on the issue of the precise state of the finger and toe at material times.) Moreover, fulminating puerperal septicaemia can, albeit rarely, be caused by this streptococcus passing, as I have indicated, straight from the infected area into the bloodstream. If it does so, the results, as already stated, can be rapid and disastrous.

One additional set of points which emerged as common grounds needs to be noted. In so far as the current well-being of the patient is relied upon as a factor when forming a clinical judgment in cases such as the present — and it was a factor much relied upon by Dr Cole — it is in one important sense a deceptive factor. That point emerged from the evidence of two of the defence witnesses, Dr Hickman (Day 6, page 18) and Dr June Smith (Day 6, page 35-E), and conceded by Mr Webster. The onset of septicaemia may occur despite that well-being. If the onset is fulminating, then, such is its rapidity, that it may well occur without there being any clinical symptoms which can be observed before the onset reaches a disastrous stage. The patient becomes at once in dire peril. On the other hand, if the onset of the septicaemia is not fulminating, there may be a reasonable chance of containing it. Those being facts which it is common ground were well known, it seems to me that once it is also known that a puerperal patient has a septic place that has been infected with streptococcus pyogenes and that this streptococcus in that patient is sensitive to penicillin, then for that patient to die or be brought near to death from puerperal septicaemia comes very close to being prima facie in itself wrong unless, of course, there be some special reason which results in that knowledge being unable to be applied.

In the present case Dr Cole knew, on October 15, that the septic places from which the plaintiff was suffering had been infected by streptococcus pyogenes; that for this streptococcus in this patient penicillin was bacteriocidal whereas tetracycline, which was being administered, was not; and that penicillin could easily and inexpensively be administered before the onset occurred. It was not administered and the onset occurred: if it had been administered the onset would not have occurred. Thus (unless there was some good cause for not administering it) the onset was due to a lacuna between what could have easily been done and what was in fact done. According to the defence, that lacuna was consistent with and indeed accorded with the reasonable practice of other responsible doctors with obstetric experience.

When the evidence shows that a lacuna in professional practice exists by which risks of grave danger are knowingly taken, then, however small the risks, the courts must anxiously examine that lacuna — particularly if the risks can be easily and inexpensively avoided. If the court finds, on an analysis of the reasons given for not taking those precautions that, in the light of current professional knowledge, there is no proper basis for the lacuna, and that it is definitely not reasonable that those risks should have been taken, its function is to state that fact and where necessary to state that it constitutes negligence. In such a case the practice will no doubt thereafter be altered to the benefit of patients. On such occasions the fact that other practitioners would have done the same thing as the defendant practitioner is a very weighty matter to be put in the scales on his behalf; but it is not, as Mr Webster readily conceded, conclusive. The court must be vigilant to see whether the reasons given for putting a patient at risk are valid in the light of any well-known advance in medical knowledge, or whether they stem from a residual adherence to out-of-date ideas — a tendency which in the present case may well have affected the views of at any rate one of the defendant's witnesses, who, at a considerable age, seemed not to have any particular respect for laboratory results.

Having thus stated the general approach that seems applicable to the problems raised by this case, it is convenient to refer as briefly as may be to certain essential facts as they existed on October 15, when Dr Cole had received the bacteriological report which made it clear that the pus submitted for examination had in it streptococcus pyogenes. Those facts have in the main been already referred to by the Master of the Rolls, and it is to be noted that, in so far as they related to the findings of fact by the trial judge, Mr Webster specifically stated that he did not substantially challenge them. The most important finding was that as to which the trial judge said:

'It is important that I should state my findings as to the condition of the plaintiff's two septic lesions when Dr Cole saw her on the 15th October 1963. I adjudge that they had improved but that they were still obviously septic and had not healed.'

In support of this finding he referred to the manuscript report of October 16: 'Toe still moist. One core from finger'. He referred to the fact that in Dr Cole's view whilst the toe was much better than it had been, it was yet not quite so well advanced as the finger; and gave other reasons as well for his finding. The learned judge referred, as did the Master of the Rolls, to the fact that neither the matron or anyone from the nursing staff were called; and it follows to my mind that no unduly favourable inference should be drawn from the wording used by the nursing staff in the reports.

Later in his judgment the trial judge went on to deal with the question of the time at which the infection of fulminating septicaemia could have taken place; there being a distinction between fulminating septicaemia and other septicaemia. He said:

'On the evidence it is impossible to be more certain about the beginning of the infection as the time lag between onset and the appearance of clinical signs can vary between 24 hours and 5 days. Mr Bourne expressed the opinion that the usual time is between 3 and 5 days. As he had had much more clinical experience of puerperal septicaemia than any other medical witness the onset of the infection was probably between the 15th and the 17th October.'

He also referred to the importance of remembering that tetracycline administered orally could not be expected to do more than have bacteriostatic action; it could contain but it could not kill. Dr Cole knew this. Finally it is to be noted that at p 15 the trial judge says:

'I accept Dr May's evidence that during a short period of treatment the development of resistant strains is very unlikely. I have weighed these risks and disadvantages (which I find would have been minimal) against the serious risks of sepsis and septicaemia from streptococcal infection.'

That passage related to the point which stressed in this court that there might have been disadvantages in relation to the administration of penicillin at the relevant stage.

In the result it becomes clear that there was a period of days between October 15 and 19, when the septic places were by no means completely healed — indeed they were open; that the onset of puerperal septicaemia was due to infection occurring during that period; that it would have been prevented by administering penicillin; and that the disadvantages of administering penicillin were minimal.

Before seeking to crystallise the basic problem with which the court is upon the above footing faced, it is as well to clear away one matter that rather bedevilled some of the arguments on this appeal having regard to the cross notice. The court has to consider whether the failure to turn to penicillin at some time during the period between October 15 and 19, and thus to act in a way prima facie contrary to basic principles inculcated into students, was negligent; and not whether the negligence consisted of failure so to act on any particular day during that period.

Looking now at the aggregate of the above facts, against what I have previously referred to as the background, what is the position which has to be so closely examined? Dr Cole deliberately took a risk on the basis of its being so small — he so stated in his evidence, (Day 5, p 20). The defence medical witnesses, despite the fact that at any rate one of them, Miss Barnes, used on more than one occasion the word 'must' in regard to the need to eliminate such risks, said that many responsible doctors relying on clinical judgment would have taken that particular risk on this particular occasion. To put it in a phrase agreed to by Miss Barnes, the patient was 'just unlucky'. That is indeed the essence of the defence case. The plaintiff's case is that this bad luck was easily avoidable without any material risk to the patient and should have been avoided.

At whose risk then is a mistaken decision made on the basis of potentially deceptive clinical appearances? What should the court say? If it agrees with the defence, it means that so far as fulminating septicaemia is concerned, it is open to the medical profession to say that where the patient looks well, and there are other useful but not conclusive points tending against the chances of an onset, she can in cases such as the present be properly allowed to bear the avoidable risk of fulminating septicaemia because it is so small. If it agrees with the plaintiff's witnesses, then it is said that an undue burden in relation to minimal risks is being placed on the medical profession, and that thus it is the patient who should be at risk if the decision is wrong, and not the doctor who made it.

Despite the fact that the risk could have been avoided by adopting a course that was easy, efficient, and inexpensive, and which would have entailed only minimal chances of disadvantages to the patient, the evidence of the four defence experts to the effect that they and other responsible members of the medical profession would have taken the same risk in the same circumstances has naturally caused me to hesitate considerably on two points. Firstly, whether the failure of the defendant to turn over to penicillin treatment during the relevant period was unreasonable. On this, however, I was in the end fully satisfied that in the light of the admissions made by the defendant himself and by his witnesses — quite apart from Dr May's very cogent evidence — that failure to do this was not merely wrong but clearly unreasonable. The reasons given by the four experts do not to my mind stand up to analysis. It is in this connection perhaps as well as at this stage to mention one other point. The fact that great discoveries have been made which by their unremitting use so far eliminate dangers that the modern practitioner is unlikely ever to see the effects of these dangers is no reason for failing to be unremitting in their use even when the risks have become very small. It is not to my mind in point for a practitioner to say, as Dr Cole said (Day 5, p 20) and as Dr June Smith appeared to say (Day 6, p 32) that if he had previously actually seen how dire the effects were of not taking the relevant precaution he would have taken it, but his experience had not up till then led him to see such results. (The potential irrelevance of the rarity or remoteness of the risk, when the maturing of the risk may be disastrous, is incidentally illustrated in *Chin Keow's* case, [1967] 1 WLR 813.) Secondly, as to whether, in the light of such evidence as to what other responsible medical practitioners would have done, it can be said that even if the defendant's error was unreasonable, it was yet negligence in relation to the position as regards practice at that particular date. On this second point it is to be noted that this is not apparently a case of 'two schools of thought', (see the speech of Lord Goddard in *Chapman v Rix*, on December 21, 1960, at p 11): it appears more to be a case of doctors who said in one form or another that they would have acted or might have acted in the same way as the defendant did, for reasons which on examination do not really add up to analysis.

Dr Cole knowingly took an easily avoidable risk which elementary teaching had instructed him to avoid; and the fact as others say they would have done the same neither ought to nor can in the present case excuse him in an action for negligence however sympathetic one may be to him. Moreover, in so far as the evidence shows the existence of a lacuna of the type to which reference was made earlier in this judgment, that lacuna was, in view of the magnitude of the dangers involved, so unreasonable that as between doctor and patient it cannot be relied upon to excuse the former in an action for negligence.

I accordingly agree that the judgement under appeal should not be disturbed.

Lord Denning MR — The appeal is dismissed.

APPENDIX 6

Joyce v Merton, Sutton and Wandsworth Health Authority

Court of Appeal, Civil Division

Date of hearing: 28 July 1995

The following cases were referred to in the judgments:

Associated Provincial Picture Houses Ltd v Wednesbury Corp [1947] 2 All ER 680, [1948] 1 KB 223, CA.
Bolam v Friern Hospital Management Committee (1957) 1 BMLR 1, [1957] 2 All ER 118, [1957] 1 WLR 582.
Bolitho v City and Hackney Health Authority (1992) 13 BMLR 111, [1993] 4 Med LR 381, CA.
Hotson v East Berkshire Health Authority [1987] 2 All ER 909, [1987] AC 750, [1987] 3 WLR 232, HL.
Loveday v Renton [1990] 1 Med LR 117.
Wilsher v Essex Area Health Authority (1988) 3 BMLR 37, [1988] 1 All ER 871, [1988] AC 1074, [1988] 2 WLR 557, HL.

JUDGMENTS

ROCH LJ: The appellant is 57 years of age. He is married and has three daughters. On 22 June 1987 he underwent an arch aortogram at St James's Hospital. A thrombus dislodged in the course of that procedure occluded the appellant's basilar artery thereby causing upper brain stem infarction. Thereafter the appellant's condition rapidly deteriorated to the point where the only voluntary movements of which he was capable and is not capable are a slight rotation of the head to the right and limited lateral movement and vertical movement of his eyes. The appellant's condition is what is called a locked-in syndrome. The appellant can see and hear although he cannot speak. He can understand speech and has insight into his condition.

In February 1990 the appellant commenced proceedings against the respondents for damages for personal injuries. The action came before Overend J sitting as a judge of the Queen's Bench Division. Judgment was given for the respondents on 14 December 1994. This is an appeal from that judgment.

The background to this very tragic case is that the appellant, who worked as a butcher's manager, suffered a mild heart attack in September 1986, which was followed by a period of cardiac pain. The appellant was admitted to Epsom District Hospital, under Dr Gould. The appellant was prescribed medication, a beta blocker Atenolol, and was referred to the cardiac unit at St George's Hospital, Tooting for further investigation. There were two consultant cardiologists at that unit, Dr Pumphrey and Dr Ward. The appellant saw Dr Pumphrey on 21 January 1987 and was advised to undergo a cardiac catheterisation.

Cardiac catheterisation is an investigative procedure designed to identify areas of arterial disease and to assess the functioning of the heart. In early 1987, a normal method of catheterisation employed at the cardiac unit at St George's Hospital was with entry being made into the right brachial artery at the elbow. The patient was admitted on a day basis. The procedure was done in one of a pair of cardiac laboratories, under local anaesthetic. The procedure involved the insertion of a catheter into the arterial system, the introduction of a radioactive dye and the taking of X-ray pictures as well as the use of the catheter to take blood pressure readings in various places and in particular in the aorta and to monitor the function of the ventricles of the heart. Following withdrawal of the catheter, the incision through which entry into the artery was obtained would be sewn up, the artery lowered back into its position in the right ante cubital fossa and, if the right radial pulse were present and there were no significant bleeding from the artery, the wound above the artery would be closed with dissolving sutures.

The patient would be admitted as a day patient and, following the procedure, would return to the day ward where the patient should have been the subject of regular recorded observations of the volume and rate of pulse, the colour and warmth of the right hand, movement in the right hand, blood pressure and the absence of bleeding from the wound for a period of at least four hours.

The brachial cardiac catheterisation (which I shall refer to as BCC) performed on the appellant was carried out between 10.35 and 11.30am on 4 March 1987 by Dr J Stewart, who was at that time one of Dr Pumphrey's registrars. Dr Pumphrey was then abroad on holiday, but Dr Ward, the other consultant cardiologist, who had in fact trained Dr Stewart, was available as was the Senior Registrar, Dr Dawson, who was working in the other laboratory. The catheter was withdrawn at 11.11 am. In stitching the brachial artery, Dr Stewart picked up the lining of the back wall of the artery causing, as is now common ground, a partial occlusion of the artery.

Mr Joyce was the subject of timed and recorded observations in the day ward made by Nurse Eugene at 11.30 am, 12.00 noon and 1.00 pm. The observation at 11.30 recorded the pulse as faint present with a rate of 60 beats per minute, the right hand as being pale and cold but having movement and the blood pressure as being 100 over 76. The observation recorded at noon showed the pulse as being faint with a rate of 64 beats per minute, the hand as being pale, warm with movement and the blood pressure as being 100 over 80. At 1.00pm the observation showed the pulse to be faint with a rate of 56 beats per minute, the hand to be pale and warm with movement and the blood pressure to be 90 over 66. At all three observations there was no oozing from the wound.

Nurse Eugene also made a cardex entry with regard to Mr Joyce.

The appellant arrived at his home having been driven home by his eldest daughter and son-in-law at about 4.30 pm, his home in Sutton being some minutes drive from St George's Hospital. The time of the appellant's release from the day ward was not recorded. The last five lines of the cardex entry read:

'On return very pale looking.
Observations: B/P 100-110/70 Pulse 60 BPM very faint.
No oozing.
Radial pulse present, hand very pale looking.
Seen by Dr Stewart OPD 2 wks with EX test.'

In her statement made on 28 January 1994, Nurse Eugene had attributed the observations recorded in the last five lines of the cardex entry to the appellant's return to the day ward, that is to say to 11.30 am. In her evidence, Nurse Eugene said this part of her statement was incorrect and those observations would have been taken just prior to the appellant's discharge from the day ward at a time after the time he would have been seen in the day ward by Dr Stewart. Neither Dr Stewart nor Nurse Eugene had any memory of the appellant or this particular BCC. Both gave evidence to the judge of what they normally did and the respondents invited the judge to conclude that they had followed their normal procedures in the appellant's case. The evidence of Dr Stewart was that Mr Joyce should and would have been given clear oral instructions to get in touch with the cardiac unit or with his general practitioner, whichever was the more convenient, if he was aware of any problems to do with the arteriotomy site or to do with his hand or if his angina should become more frequent. Dr Stewart said that he would not have warned the appellant of every possible complication; he would have said words to the effect: 'If there are any problems get in touch.' The evidence of Dr Stewart and Nurse Eugene was that a patient would only be discharged from the day ward if they were both agreed that the patient was fit to be discharged. Nurse Eugene's evidence was that Mr Joyce would have been given, on his discharge, a sheet of 'Instructions for Day Case Cardiac Catheter Patients'. Those instructions read:

'1 Your arm will feel a little sore and you will have some bruising for a couple of days. Rest your arm in a comfortable position with as little bending as possible.
2 You may take the bandage and dressing off the next day following your catheter.
3 If you notice any bleeding use a clean hankerchief and apply firm pressure for 5 – 10 minutes. If the bleeding still persists contact your GP or the hospital.
4 There will be a loop stitch where the test was done. the stitch can be trimmed using a clean pair of scissors after 5 days. Cut as near to the skin as possible at both ends. The stitch will dissolve under the skin in a few weeks.
5 Pain relieving tablets such as paracetamol can be taken.
6 Do not attempt to drive home. If you feel unwell on the same day contact your GP or the hospital.'

The appellant's evidence was that he was not given that instruction sheet and the evidence of Mrs Joyce was to the effect that her husband did not bring such an instruction sheet home with him.

The appellant on his return home was suffering from pain in his right arm. That pain was of a level to make the appellant cry, according to the evidence of his middle daughter, Carol. She had not seen her father cry before. It also caused Mrs Joyce to ring her own surgery and speak to a doctor about her husband's pain. The doctor asked whether there was a bandage and advised that the appellant should place his arm in warm water. That was not done because the appellant did not want to get the wound wet. That night the appellant, according to the evidence of himself, his wife and his daughter, did not sleep with his wife but remained downstairs on account of the pain in his arm.

On the Friday, that is to say 48 hours after the procedure, Mrs Joyce rang the day ward at St George's hospital and told them that her husband's pain was unbearable. She was told that her husband should continue to take pain killers and if it remained bad he should return to see them. In her oral evidence, Mrs Joyce added to the evidence in her statement on this point (her statement being dated 21 July 1993), that the hospital had advised that her husband should go back to see them on the following Wednesday, 11 March. Mrs Joyce also said in cross-examination.

'I only know that his arm from there downwards was painful since 4 March.'

Mrs Joyce could not, at the hearing, recall an incident when her husband's hand had become numb with two white fingers for a period of approximately an hour.

On 11 March Mrs Joyce returned to the day ward, being taken there by his middle daughter, Carol, and her fiance. Both Mr Joyce and his daughter gave evidence that there he saw Dr Stewart who treated him in an off-hand manner, saying that Mr Joyce should not be such a baby, that his complaints were caused by a bit of gunge which would clear in time and that Dr Stewart did not examine Mr Joyce's right arm at all. Initially, in the defence, it was denied that the appellant had returned to the hospital and been seen by Dr Stewart on 11 March. There was no record of any such visit. Evidence from another patient who was shown by the hospital's records to have been at the hospital on that Wednesday that he had seen and spoken to the appellant in the day ward of the hospital on that Wednesday lead the respondents into accepting that the appellant had indeed visited the cardiac unit's day ward on that date and that he had probably seen and been seen by Dr Stewart. The evidence of Dr Stewart was that although he had no recollection of seeing the appellant on that day, he would not have spoken to or treated the appellant in the manner described by the appellant and his daughter. He would have established the presence of the radial pulse in the plaintiff's right wrist, which would have involved a brief palpitation of the wrist, and examined the wound because infections in the wound may give rise to pain. Dr Stewart also said in evidence that if the appellant had complained of his arm not feeling right and of two fingers having gone cold and numb for an hour and then recovered he would have examined the arm and if he could not find any reason for the fingers going cold and numb or for disturbed sensation in the arm and if the profusion of the forearm and hand was satisfactory with the radial pulse being present he would have told Mr Joyce that he could not explain the occurrence and would have asked him to come straight back to the unit should it happen again. He would not have spoken to the appellant as the appellant and his daughter stated because it was not his practice to belittle people for expressing anxieties. On the following day, 12 March, the appellant visited his GP, Dr Said. the note made by Dr Said was:

'Pain right arm and feeling weak. Has had catheterisation. Double vessel disease. Atenolol 50 mg daily.'

Dr Said's statement was that if he prescribed pain killers for a patient he always recorded that fact in the patient's notes.

Mr Joyce returned to St George's Hospital on 19 March in order to perform exercise tests prior to his being seen again by Dr Pumphrey on 24 March. The exercise tests were supervised by Dr Cameron who at that time was a House Officer at St George's Hospital. Dr Cameron completed much of the record of those exercise tests. The appellant's heart rate at the outset was recorded as 74 beats per minute and his blood pressure at 100 over 60. The exercise test consisted of moving on a treadmill with the speed of the treadmill being increased in stages. Each stage lasted for three minutes. The tests were stopped two minutes into stage three because of breathlessness and tiredness on the part of Mr Joyce. Dr Cameron recorded that there was no chest pain, no ectopics. There was good recovery after stages one and two of the test. Dr Cameron gave evidence that although he could not remember the tests on the appellant, he could say because of the configuration of the test room and the layout of the equipment that the appellant's blood pressure would have been taken using a cuff around the right upper arm and listening for a pulse in the right arm. If Mr Joyce had made any complaint to him of pain in the right arm then he would have recorded that complaint in his report on the exercise test. No such complaint was recorded by Dr Cameron. Further, Dr Cameron's evidence was to the effect that if he had not been able to find a pulse in the right arm when taking the blood pressure readings prior to the test being carried out and during each stage of the test, he would have investigated the absence of a pulse first with the patient concerned and then with the members of the cardiac unit for whom he was working that day. Dr Cameron told the court that he believed that he would have noticed any clear signs of arterial insufficiency in the appellant's right arm had they existed on 19 March. Observation of such signs would have lead him to consult one of the doctors of the cardiac unit, probably Dr Stewart had he been available. Following the exercise test, Mr Joyce was seen again by Dr Pumphrey on 24 March. Dr Pumphrey in his notes of that consultation recorded:

'Brachial artery occluded. Hand severely ischaemic. Refer Mr Dormandy.'

That day, Dr Pumphrey wrote to Dr Gould at Epsom District Hospital:

'I reviewed Mr Joyce following his recent day case catheterisation. Unfortunately he has developed an occluded brachial artery which is causing quite marked ischaemic symptoms in his right arm. He has had no further angina, so I think the priority is to sort out his hand. I have therefore asked him to see Mr Dormandy in his out-patients for his opinion.'

The appellant was seen by Mr Dormandy's registrar, Mr Llellwyn Williams on 27 March. In the notes recorded by Mr Williams this appears:

'Cardiac catheter 4/3/87 via R brachial approach — sludge — artery apparently. Index/3rd finger went numb/white about one week later — lasted 1 hour and then recovered fully. Now R hand feels cold + week + claudication R wrist.'

Neither the appellant nor Mrs Joyce had any memory of this visit to the hospital.

Mr Dormandy was the consultant vascular surgeon at St George's Hospital. Mr Dormandy saw Mr Joyce on 9 April and advised a reconstruction of the brachial artery and requested a further investigation by way of digital subtraction angiogram which is a technique allowing for a clearer picture of the patient's circulatory system to be obtained. That procedure was carried out on 14 April and showed the blockage of the right brachial artery extending proximally for 5 to 6 cms. On 21 April when the appellant was admitted to hospital, an admission note was written up by a medical student which recorded a history of the right hand experiencing:

'coldness and numbness in 4 to 5 fingers 8 or 9 days after the BCC, and for the last 3 weeks there had been coldness and numbness on slight activity which caused difficulty in shaving. The ring and little fingers were worse than the rest of the hand. There was also an associated dead ache on more strenuous activity.'

On the following day a right brachial artery reconstruction was performed by Mr Pattison who in April 1987 was a senior registrar in vascular surgery under the consultant, Mr Dormandy. Mr Pattison wrote in the history sheet for the operation:

'The brachial artery appeared completely occluded by a suture at the site of the catheterisation. Distally the artery was of small calibre but had good back flow. Proximally there was organised thrombus to the level of the axilla.'

The note goes on to record the steps taken by Mr Pattison to clear the obstruction in the artery, to re-establish a flow of blood through the artery and to repair the artery by means of a graft.

Unhappily, that operation was not successful and a week later, on 29 April, there was a re-exploration of the right brachial artery together with a thrombectomy and replacement of the vein graft. During the operation a large clot and intima were removed. That operation was performed by Mr Dormandy and Mr Pattison. On 5 May a pathologist, Dr Corbishly, reported on the thrombus removed from the appellant's brachial artery:

> 'The specimen consists of organising thrombus showing prominent fibro-vascular and vascular proliferation. The appearances are consistent with brachial artery thrombus of approximately 1 month's duration following catheterisation.'

Again, the operation was not successful. On 22 May the appellant's GP recorded a visit by the appellant with complaints of 'not sleeping, pain plus plus'. On 21 June the appellant was admitted to hospital for further investigation of the causes of the condition of his right arm which by that time he was unable to use. On 22 June the arch aortogram was performed at St James' Hospital with the tragic and catastrophic result for the appellant and his family. A writ was issued on the appellant's behalf against the respondents and the Mid Surrey District Health Authority, they being responsible for the hospital at Epsom to which the appellant had been admitted following his mild heart attack in September 1986. Proceedings against that health authority were not pursued.

The appellant's pleaded case against the respondents was that the artery had been occluded by the stitch. The allegations of negligence relating to 4 March were: the occluding of the artery with the suture, the failure to observe that the artery had been occluded whilst being sewn up; failing on completion of the sewing up of the artery to diagnose that the artery had been occluded; failing to obtain the opinion or assistance of a vascular surgeon; failing to warn and advise the appellant to return to hospital if he were to suffer problems with his right arm; failing to require the appellant to return for review prior to 24 March. With regard to 11 March it was alleged that Dr Stewart had failed to examine the appellant properly or at all, had failed to assess the circulation in the appellant's right arm despite the appellant's complaints of pain and that Dr Stewart had failed to cause a proper investigation to be made into the appellant's complaints on that occasion. The appellant's pleaded case made allegations of negligence with reference to the conduct of Dr Pumphrey on 24 March and to the lapse of time between that date and operative intervention on 22 and 29 April and the further angiogram on 22 June 1987. The thrust of the pleaded case was that the respondent's doctors had not acted swiftly enough, but had allowed time to pass during which the blood clot in the artery had developed and become organised. There was a further allegation that on and after 22 June the respondents' doctors had failed to treat the appellant's evolving brain stem infarction by means of anti-coagulants. These allegations were abandoned at the trial, it being accepted on the appellant's behalf that the handling of his case after 11 March was not open to a sustainable charge of negligence.

The respondents, through their counsel Miss Ritchie QC, made a concession on the issue of causation which was recorded in the judge's judgment in these terms:

> 'There is no issue as to causation, it being accepted by Miss Ritchie QC on behalf of the defendants, subject to proof of negligence and the matters set out below, that the subsequent attempts at vascular repair and the further angiogram on June 22 1987, during which the tragic cerebro-vascular accident occurred, all flowed from the allegedly negligent acts. She made it clear however, that her agreement on causation did not include any concession as to what a vascular surgeon would have done, if Dr Stewart negligently failed to call for the

assistance of a vascular surgeon on either March 4 or March 11: nor did she concede that the result of surgery carried out on or after March 11 would have been any different from that which in fact occurred.'

This concession was explored in this court by Hobhouse LJ and it became clear that the concession did not include any acceptance that the tragic cerebro-vascular accident which befell the appellant was a risk which should have been foreseen and weighed in the balance by those responsible for the appellant's treatment either on 4 or 11 March.

The respondent's case was that the picking up of the posterior wall of the artery or its lining with a stitch was something which could occur unobserved, however careful the operator at the BCC tried to be. The artery had not been completely occluded. The fact that the posterior wall or its lining had been caught by a stitch would not have been observable to the operator. Despite the small volume of the pulse, there was after the procedure an observable and viable flow of blood to the lower part of the appellant's right arm. Dr Stewart's decision not to re-explore the artery was, in the light of the signs and symptoms exhibited by the appellant in the catheter laboratory and later in the day ward on 4 March, reasonable and in accordance with a practice accepted at the time as proper by a responsible body of medical opinion skilled in brachial artery catheterisation. The decision to discharge the appellant on 4 March had been reasonable and the oral advice given to the appellant adequate, albeit it was conceded that the printed notes of guidance were not adequate.

The events of 11 March could not have occurred as described by the appellant and his daughter because Dr Stewart would never have behaved towards a patient in that manner. In any event, the evidence of Dr Camron and the notes of the exercise tests which the appellant underwent on 19 March showed that the brachial artery was still patent at that time and that either the brachial pulse or the radial pulse were detectable and were used for the purposes of taking the appellant's blood pressure.

In short, the appellant's present condition was a tragic accident; a rare and remote risk of the catheterisation procedure which had occurred without negligence by those responsible for the appellant's treatment.

The judge's judgment commenced with a short background to the case, a description of Mr Joyce's then condition, a summary of the allegations of negligence and a statement of the law. Having reviewed the authorities, the judge directed himself in these terms:

'I take the above authorities to hold that, in the field of diagnosis and treatment, a defendant is not guilty of negligence if his acts or omissions were in accordance with acceptable clinical practice, provided that clinical practice stood up to analysis and was not unreasonable, in the light of the state of medical knowledge at that time . . . In dealing with a breach of duty which consists of an omission . . . it is necessary for the court to decide what course of events would have followed had the duty been discharged.'

The judge then gave a detailed description of the procedure for BCC followed at that time at St George's Hospital. The reason for this was that in the reports of two of the expert medical witnesses called on behalf of the appellant, criticism had been made of certain of the details of that procedure. Although, in the event, those criticisms were not maintained, still less was it the evidence of the appellant's experts that the technique employed at St George's Hospital was negligent. For exempt, Dr Wainwright, one of the cardiologists called on behalf of the appellant, reported that he made a lateral incision with a scalpel into the brachial artery rather than a transverse incision with the point of a scissor. Dr Wainwright did not in the witness box suggest that the making of a transverse incision was wrong. Having described the technique of BCC, the judge set out in chronological order the detail of the events from 4 March to 22 June including, where facts were in dispute, the differing versions of events. As the judge performed that exercise, the judge identified seven questions of fact which required resolution as they arose during the setting out of the history of the appellant's case. Those questions were: 1. Was the brachial artery totally occluded at the time of closure of the arteriotomy? 2. Did the suture pick up the intima of the artery or go through the back wall? 3. Did Mr Joyce's artery occlude totally on the evening of 4 March after his return home? 4. What was the nature and extent of pain suffered by Mr Joyce after his return home? 5. What were the signs and symptoms exhibited and experienced by Mr Joyce on 11 March 1987? 6. What were the signs and symptoms exhibited and experienced by Mr Joyce on 19 March 1987? 7. Did the brachial artery become totally occluded after 19 March?

On the completion of the history the judge turned to six medical issues raised by the differences of opinion among the medical experts.

A Can collateral circulation provide a radial pulse after sudden and total occlusion of the brachial artery? The judge found on the balance of probability that in the absence of an abnormal anatomy, the collateral circulation would not allow a radial pulse to be felt after sudden and total occlusion of the brachial artery. On the evidence presented a reasonable cardiologist would accordingly reasonably treat the presence of a radial pulse as an indication of arterial flow at the site of the BCC.

B Is there a difference between critical and severe ischaemia? The judge found that it had been proved on the balance of probability that there are differences between critical and severe ischaemia, namely the intensity of the pain suffered, the circumstances in which the pain is suffered (at rest, not just when used), the timing of the onset of symptoms (within half an hour), the length of time that the symptoms last (they continue unabated) plus the risk to the limb if not operated on within a matter of hours (gangrene and loss).

C What is the effect on the hand and forearm if the brachial artery is suddenly and totally occluded, where no chronic ischaemic condition exists? Here the judge accepted the evidence of the respondent's vascular surgeon Professor Ruckley, Honorary Professor of Vascular Surgery at the University of Edinburgh and former President of the Vascular Society of Great Britain and Ireland 1993-94 that the effect of the brachial artery being suddenly and totally occluded is that the hand will become critically ischaemic and pain will develop rapidly within a matter of 30 minutes.

D Can a brachial artery which is partially occluded at BCC become totally occluded within a matter of hours? The judge found that all the experts agreed that it could, but they disagreed as to the likelihood of this occurring in this case.

E Can blood pressure be taken from an arm where the brachial artery is totally occluded? The judge made this finding, I conclude, on the evidence that it is less than likely that a blood pressure reading may be taken from an arm where the brachial artery is totally occluded. It follows that the taking of a blood pressure reading implies the patency of the brachial artery beneath it on the balance of probabilities.

F Can a brachial artery which is partially occluded become totally occluded some two weeks later? The judge concluded on the balance of probabilities that it was medically possible, although unusual, for a partial occlusion to become total some two weeks after BCC.

In making his findings on the medical issues, the judge generally preferred the evidence of the respondent's medical experts to that of the experts called on behalf of the appellant. The judge then returned to the questions of fact that he had posed earlier in his judgment answering them in this way.

1 The brachial artery was partially rather than totally occluded at the time of closure of the arteriotomy.

2 The suture picked up the intima or lining of the artery but did not go through the posterior wall of the artery. The significance of that finding was that the judge accepted the evidence of Professor Ruckley that the error would probably have not been visible to the operator once the artery had been closed.

3 and 4 The judge answered the third and fourth questions together and found that although there was no doubt that Mr Joyce was in substantial pain after his return home during the evening of 4 March, that pain was at the site of the BCC and was due to a combination of wound pain and additional pain caused by bleeding into the tissues around the wound and that it was not ischaemic pain. The judge found that the pain was likely to have diminished in intensity with the passage of time. The judge found that, on the balance of probability, Mr Joyce's artery did not occlude totally on the evening of 4 March after his return home.

5 The fifth question, what were the signs and symptoms exhibited and experienced by Mr Joyce on 11 March, was answered by the judge finding that Mr Joyce suffered a transient ischaemic episode about a week after the BCC. That was explained medically on the evidence by thrombus collecting and being washed down to the fingers and then dissipating through network of little veins and arterioles into the capillaries of the fingers. It was likely that those transient ischaemic symptoms were the cause of the visit to the day ward by Mr Joyce when he saw Dr Stewart. He may also have been complaining about continuing pain as he did the next day to his GP, but that was unlikely to have been substantial pain at that stage. As regards what had occurred in the day ward on 11 March the judge made this finding:

'In so far as there is a dispute between Dr Stewart's reported practice and the evidence of Mr Joyce and his daughter Carol Joyce, I prefer the evidence of Dr Stewart. I found him to be a careful and conscientious witness, anxious to assist the court. I do not think it at all likely that he would ignore his training as a doctor, for example by failing to observe Mr Joyce's radial pulse. His career path has been exemplary, and he is spoken of highly by those who have worked with him. He has recently accepted a consultant's appointment in New Zealand. I conclude that it is probably that Mr Joyce still had a radial pulse on 11 March and he was not exhibiting signs or symptoms of ischaemia in his forearm. He may have complained of pain in his arm which he said was not feeling right. He may also have described an incident when his fingers went cold and white for an hour and then fully recovered.'

6 The sixth question the judge answered in these terms:

'I find that on 19 March Mr Joyce was suffering from only minor, if any, ischaemic symptoms. Dr Cameron gave evidence to the court and impressed as a thorough and conscientious houseman. I find that Mr Joyce did not tell Dr Cameron of any symptoms that were worrying him and Dr Cameron did not find any signs that concerned him. I conclude that Mr Joyce's brachial artery was patent and that his brachial pulse present (it would have been noted by Dr Cameron if it were absent). It follows that his radial pulse was also likely to have been present on that day.'

7   The final question was answered by the judge finding that the brachial artery was likely to have become totally occluded between 19 March and 24 March when the appellant attended for a review by Dr Pumphrey and the artery was found to be occluded. By then it was likely that the collateral circulation had developed following the partial occlusion some two weeks before, which prevented critical ischaemia developing when the total occlusion occurred. The judge noted that two of the respondent's medical experts, Professor Ruckley and Dr Hall, suggested that the exercise test might have acted as a trigger for this late occlusion.

The judge then turned to the various allegations of negligence. He noted that Mr de Wilde QC for the appellant had not argued that the suturing of the lining of the back wall of the artery to the front was negligence on Dr Stewart's part, accepting that it could happen in the most competent of hands. The judge rejected the allegations that the error in suturing the artery should have been observed either while the artery was being sewn up or after the artery had been sewn up and was being lowered back into position. The judge said:

'In view of the finding of fact that the stitch was likely to have caught the intima and not the back wall, and that the artery was partially and not totally occluded by the stitch, and in the light of the evidence to which I have referred, I think it probable that the missuturing would not have been apparent to Dr Stewart at the time. I should also record that my view of Dr Stewart is that had the effect of the missuturing been visible on inspection it is highly likely that he would have seen it and would have done something about it.'

With regard to the allegations that Dr Stewart had failed to diagnose a serious occlusion of the artery and had failed to reopen the artery the judge found, having reviewed the evidence of the various medical experts and pointed to a difference between the evidence of the cardiologists on the one hand and the vascular surgeon, Mr Scurr, on the other hand, called on behalf of the appellant, the judge said:

'There is accordingly, on the plaintiff's own case, a divergence of views on the need for immediate re-exploration before the patient was returned to the day ward. So far as the defendant's experts are concerned, they are unanimous. Dr Dawkins (a consultant cardiologist) would not re-open an arteriotomy if there is a weak pulse, nor does he teach his Registrars to do so. Dr Hall (another consultant cardiologist) would only do so if the artery was of normal or large size. He would not do so where the artery was small as in the case of Mr Joyce.'

Later, after reviewing the evidence of Dr Dawkins and Dr Hall in some detail, the judge referred to Professor Ruckley's evidence that he did not think a vascular surgeon should have been called in on the findings as presented in the medical records. Had he been called in he would have operated upon Mr Joyce, provided the patient was otherwise fit and well.

The judge went on to review the medical literature, it being the contention of the cardiologists called on behalf of the appellant that the medical literature indicated that on the medical signs present at the conclusion of the appellant's BCC, there should have been a re-exploration of the appellant's brachial artery. The judge expressed his conclusion in these terms:

'I conclude that the practice that was followed by Dr Stewart in allowing Mr Joyce to proceed to the day ward without re-exploration of the arteriotomy closure or calling for the assistance of others, including a vascular surgeon, was one which was in accordance with the practice of the cardiologists Dr Dawkins and Dr Hall, as well as being the practice of Dr Stewart's mentor, Dr Pumphrey. It was a practice that they regarded as perfectly proper and acceptable. There is nothing in the literature that leads me to believe that the practice was improper, or not part of a broad spectrum of respectable medical opinion. Further, neither vascular surgeon gave evidence that directly supported the approach of Dr Wainwright, who appeared to be in a minority on this allegation. I hold the practice to be in accordance with accepted and proper practice.'

With regard to the decision to discharge Mr Joyce instead of re-exploring or calling in a vascular surgeon, the judge repeated the findings on fact that he had made, namely:

'Around 3.30 pm his radial pulse was present but faint or very faint, measurable at 60 BPM and his right hand was very pale looking but warm. He had no problems with movement of his hand and he was not complaining of pain or pins and needles. His blood pressure was likely to have been monitored since the last timed record at 1300 hours showing measurements between 100 and 110 over 70 on two or three occasions that it had been taken between 1300 and the time of discharge.'

The judge went on to set out Dr Stewart's evidence that he would not have authorised the discharge of Mr Joyce unless he satisfied himself that the radial pulse was present and that there is no ischaemia in the hand. The judge commented that the observations showed that the patient was improving. The judge's conclusion on this aspect of the case was:

'Again there is a spectrum of evidence as to the correct clinical practice that should have been adopted in the day ward and of the time of the decision to discharge. In the light of the evidence, I find that Dr Stewart's actions in not re-exploring the arteriotomy after Mr Joyce had gone to the day ward, in discharging him from the day ward and in asking him to return to see Dr Pumphrey in two weeks for review of his heart disease after an exercise test were in accordance with the practice of Dr Dawkins and Dr Hall. I find this practice to have been a proper practice.'

The judge went on to find on the balance of probabilities that, had Mr Dormandy been the vascular surgeon called in on 4 March, it is unlikely that he, or any of his team, would have operated.

Turning to the alleged failure to inform the plaintiff that he should return to hospital if he were to discover any problems with his right arm, the judge found that the allegation was not made out of the facts. The judge found that the printed discharge instructions were probably given. But whether that was so or not, a warning was given on 4 March in terms that were appropriate, although the written instruction sheet could well have been improved, as indeed it later was.

The judge then turned to the events of 11 March and found that allegations of negligence in the relation to the events of 11 March were not made out on the facts. The judge found that Dr Stewart acted in accordance with proper practice. The judge added that had the allegation of negligence been made out the appellant would still have failed on the ground of causation, by which the judge meant that had it been shown that Dr Stewart had failed to make a proper examination, a proper examination would have revealed a radial pulse and that the appellant was not exhibiting signs or symptoms of ischaemia in his forearm. Had Dr Stewart called in a vascular surgeon, that doctor would have been unlikely to have taken any action. Had he decided to operate, then surgery would have taken place as a planned rather than an emergency procedure. In those circumstances it was unlikely on the evidence that the results of the vascular surgery would have been any better than that actually achieved on 22 April by Mr Pattison.

Finally, the judge subjected to critical examination the practice of Dr Dawkins, Dr Hall and Dr Pumphrey in regard to weak pulses directing himself that what he described as the gloss on *Bolam v Friern Hospital Management Committee* (1957) 1 BMLR 1, [1957] 1 WLR 582 required him to consider whether the non-interventionist clinical practice of those doctors was an unreasonable practice. The judge reviewed the evidence, pointing to the fact that it was common ground between the medical experts on both sides that re-exploration of an arteriotomy can lead to complications. Those could include the risk of fracture of the artery, the risk of the tear extending, the risk of the need for a vein patch or a graft from a donor site, the risk of causing total occlusion, the risk of intimal damage and the risk of thrombus developing. The judge concluded that, on the evidence, there were risks associated with both the interventionist and the conservative approach to the management of weak pulses following BCCs. The risks appeared to the judge to be evenly balanced. The judge ended by saying:

> 'Accordingly I conclude that the plaintiff has not proved negligence by Dr Stewart in his management of Mr Joyce either on 4 March or on 11 March 1987. The evidence of Dr Dawkins and of Dr Hall, honestly held and truthfully expressed, is evidence of a respectable and responsible body of medical men who do not share the view of the plaintiff's expert cardiologists on the appropriate clinical practice that they say should have been adopted. It is not for the court to decide the question of negligence by preferring the evidence of one set of experts for another in the field of diagnosis and treatment. I propose therefore to give judgment for the defendants.'

Early in his submissions, Mr de Wilde for the appellant said:

> 'When Dr Stewart closed the artery, he stitched the posterior wall to the anterior wall. It was never a complete occlusion because of the evidence.'

I understood Mr de Wilde to mean that those acting for the appellant now accept, in the light of all the evidence, that the misplaced suture did not completely occlude the artery until some time after 19 March. If the suture had totally occluded the artery, the radial pulse would have been lost and it was common ground that, if the radial pulse was lost during the procedure, the arteriotomy had to be reopened and the artery re-explored. It was also common ground that reopening and re-exploration of the artery within the first 48 hours following the procedure presented a high prospect of restoring pre-procedure circulation through the artery, whereas the outcome of re-exploration undertaken after that period had expired was uncertain.

A general criticism made by Mr de Wilde of the judge's judgment was that the judge posed and answered too many irrelevant questions, thus distracting his attention from what was the central core of the case, namely that the appellant had, prior to the procedure, enjoyed good circulation in both arms and should have had good circulation in both his arms when discharged from the cardiac unit on 4 March.

In my judgment this criticism is misconceived. Each of the medical issues identified by the judge was an issue that had to be resolved in the process of answering the principal question:

> 'had the appellant's brachial artery been totally occluded by the stitch on 4 March or, rare though such an occurrence is, had there been a lapse of some two weeks or so between the partial occlusion of the artery by the stitch and the total occlusion of the artery by thrombus?'

which was the judge's final medical issue, F.

With respect to the factual questions posed and answered by the judge, the judge having found the total occlusion could follow partial occlusion after a period of some two weeks, these questions had to be asked and answered in order for the judge to decide whether that rare occurrence was what in fact had occurred in the appellant's case.

The first three grounds of appeal in the notice of appeal are allegations that the judge misdirected himself as to the law. I shall return to those grounds later in this judgment. The fourth, fifth and sixth grounds are all matters of fact concerning the events on 4 March. It is said that the judge was wrong on the evidence to find that Dr Stewart had not failed to make a diagnosis that he should have made, namely that there was a serious occlusion of the brachial artery, possibly due to a misplaced suture which called for re-exploration of the arteriotomy. Alternatively, the judge was wrong on the evidence in finding that Dr Stewart was not in breach of duty in discharging the appellant on 4 March. If the clinical sign is, namely a small volume pulse and the pallor of the right hand, did not call for the reopening of the arteriotomy, the judge should have found that they at least called for the retention of the appellant in hospital for further observations during the critical 48-hour period. The sixth ground is that the judge was wrong in failing to find that there was inadequate post-procedure recorded observation of the appellant's condition.

The seventh ground is also based on the events of 4 March and is that the judge's finding that the appellant was given written discharge instructions and adequate oral instruction prior to leaving the day ward was wrong, and in so finding the judge failed properly to address the admitted inadequacies of the written instructions.

The ninth and tenth grounds of appeal are linked and are based on the absence in the medical literature of any support for the respondent's practice of not re-exploring the arteriotomy if the radial pulse is present, albeit that the pulse is of small volume compared with the pre-procedure pulse and compared to the radial pulse in the left arm. The eleventh and twelfth grounds of appeal relate to 11 March and are that the judge wrongly rejected the evidence of the ;appellant and his daughter as to what had occurred on that day; and wrongly accepted the evidence of Dr Stewart, who had no recollection of the appellant's visit to the day ward on 11 March, and who had initially in his written statement of 16 August 1994 stated: ·

'However, I do not remember seeing Mr Joyce on that date. If that had happened I am sure that I would have remembered.'

Dr Stewart had then referred to an incident involving another patient who contacted the hospital approximately one week after catheterisation and then stated:

'I remember this incident and I am sure I would have remembered Mr Joyce returning to the hospital.'

The twelfth ground is that the judge, in accepting the evidence of Dr Stewart as to what he would have done on seeing the appellant at the day ward, ignored the evidence of Dr Hall, one of the respondent's expert cardiologists, as to the steps he would have taken had he been in Dr Stewart's position on 11 March. Dr Hall at this point in his evidence was answering a question put to him by the judge in this way:

'The first thing I would have done would have been to take a more precise history from the patient themselves [sic]. You have already outlined many factors of the history but I would want to know under exactly what circumstances the pain had been occurring; whether it was truly rest pain throughout that period of time, or whether it had been related to use of the arm and exertion; and I would ask about numbness and power as well. We have had some implication from the rest of the history that power may be reduced or the movement is uncomfortable because of raising the hand to shave. But I would really want to know whether this pain was an ischaemic pain or a local pain for some reason that I can't explain. Infection would be one possibility at that stage. Wounds can become infected and become very painful at that time. I would want to find out whether he had had a fever or not. Then I would examine him and examination would be important because if he was having what sounded like ischaemic pain at rest, then I would expect to find some evidence of coldness, the pulse may have disappeared by this stage completely, and I would at this stage see what he could do if he had not got pain at rest, see what happened when he clenched his fist a few times to see whether that produced pain. If I had any suspicion that this pain was vascular in origin, I would have asked a vascular surgeon at that time. Any symptom at any time in this history which can be related to the artery demands a surgical opinion.'

These grounds of appeal relating to 11 March were relied upon by Mr de Wilde as giving rise 'to an inference of fact of the propensity and similar evidence of neglect of Dr Stewart on 4 March 1987'.

Dr Stewart's failure to carry out a full and proper examination of the appellant on 11 March:

'Illuminated the failure by him to perform any or any proper examination on 4 March at which time it is common ground that the plaintiff would have been saved.'

Mr de Wilde relied on those two grounds of appeal in that way because he accepted that had the appellant been properly examined on 11 March and a decision made to re-explore the arteriotomy, it could not be said on the balance of probability that the subsequent tragic events would not have followed.

The judge's finding that the appellant was given a copy of the written instructions and was given the oral instructions by Dr Stewart to get in touch with the cardiac unit or his GP, whichever was the more convenient, if he was aware of any problems to do with the arteriotomy site or to do with his hand, are, in my judgment unassailable before this court because they depend on an assessment of the witnesses and particularly of the evidence of Dr Stewart and Nurse Eugene, who were seen and heard by the judge. The judge has preferred the evidence of these two witnesses to that of the appellant's witnesses, not because anyone suggested that the appellant's witnesses were doing anything other than giving their present recollection as honestly and as accurately as they could, but because of what has befallen the appellant and his family and the lapse of time (some 7 1/2 years) between the events and the hearing, their memories were likely to be at fault. The recollection of Dr Stewart and Nurse Eugene of their normal practices and the judge's assessment of them as reliable, not merely as witnesses, but also in their work making it more likely than not that their normal practices were followed, are not findings which this court can disturb, in my opinion. Before reaching this conclusion, the judge took into account the absence of recorded observations after 1.00 pm, the absence of a recorded time for the appellant's discharge, and the departure of Nurse Eugene from her written statement as to the time at which the observations recorded in the last four lines of the cardex were made, as well as those passages in Dr Stewart's written statement to which reference has been made.

Concerning the instructions given to the appellant both written and oral, this court is, in my view, in as good a position as the judge to assess the adequacy of the instructions which the judge has found as a fact were given to the appellant. In my judgment these were not adequate. The inadequacies of the written instructions were conceded. Shortly after the tragic events of this case those instructions were redrafted. The redrafted instructions read:

'4 If you notice any change in the sensation or colour of your arm/hand, contact your GP or go to your nearest accident and emergency department. If you are worried about any aspect of your recovery, then please contact:
i   Your GP
ii The Cardiac Day Ward (telephone number given) who will be pleased to advise you.
iii The Cardiac Help Line (telephone number given).'

Even the adequacy of these instructions is doubtful in my opinion because the problem which can arise from instructing the patient to contact his GP is that the notes of the BCC and the record of the observations kept in the day ward will not be available to the GP. Further, the GP's knowledge of potential complications following a cardiac catheterisation and the warning signs of such complications likely to be seen in the particular patient may be limited. Adequate instruction, in my opinion, requires the patient to be told that if he is concerned about any aspect of his recovery he should contact the hospital's cardiac day ward or the cardiac help line. As Dr Hall said in his evidence:

'I would take it further than you would, in fact. I do not say come back within 24 hours. I would say come back immediately should there be a problem or make contact. Phoning the GP is unlikely to be as effective as phoning the unit.'

The oral instruction given by Dr Stewart, as found by the judge, suffered from the same shortcomings. Further, there is the added difficulty that oral warning to a patient who has reacted badly to the procedure may for that very reason not be understood and remembered by the patient. The evidence in this case was that the appellant had reacted badly to the procedure.

Consequently, I would disagree with the conclusion of the judge. Nevertheless, there remains the question:

'if the appellant had returned to the cardiac unit within 48 hours of the procedure what signs and symptoms would have been found and what action, if any, would have been taken to re-explore the arteriotomy?'

This question is linked to the fourth, fifth and sixth grounds, namely that the judge's findings that Dr Stewart had not failed to make a diagnosis that he should have made on 4 March, that Dr Stewart had not discharged the appellant prematurely and that there were adequate post-procedure observations kept, were findings that the judge should not have made on the evidence.

Once the judge accepted Nurse Eugene's evidence that the last four lines in the cardex represent a recording by her in summary of two or three observations kept between 1.00 pm, and the appellant's discharge at about 3.30 pm, the judge was entitled to find that adequate post-procedural observations had been kept in the day ward. Again, in my opinion, this court, not having seen and heard the evidence of Nurse Eugene and bearing in mind there was no direct evidence from the appellant that regular observations were not kept on his condition in the day ward, cannot say that this finding of fact was wrong. The evidence of Dr Stewart was that he would have been aware, because of the small volume pulse and the paleness of the appellant's right hand, that the flow of blood through the brachial artery had been significantly reduced and that such reduction in flow could be due to one or more of several reasons, one of which might be a misplaced suture. The decision not to reopen the arteriotomy was not the result of any failure to make a proper diagnosis, but a deliberate decision taken on the basis that the chances of adequate circulation being re-established in the disappearance of a temporary constriction in the brachial artery or alternatively by the development of the collateral arteries in the arm, were good, and the risk of some complication arising was counterbalanced if not outweighed by the risk of serious damage to the artery if it was re-explored. With respect to Dr Stewart's decision to discharge the appellant from the day ward, the judge made findings of fact as to the signs and symptoms present in the appellant's right arm at about 3.30 pm on 4 March, namely that the appellant's radial pulse was present and there was no ischaemia in the hand or forearm. The judge found that Dr Stewart's decision to wait and see rather than re-explore, and his decision to discharge in the light of the condition of the appellant's right arm at about 3.30 pm, were both in accordance with the practice accepted at the time as proper by a responsible body of medical opinion skilled in the particular form of treatment in question. If the judge was correct in that finding, then the allegation that Dr Stewart was negligent in deciding to wait and see and in deciding to discharge the appellant are not made out.

Grounds 9 and 10 of the appeal are directed to this aspect of the judge's decision. The respondent's medical evidence included the evidence of Dr Pumphrey and Mr Dormandy, because both were permitted to give evidence of an expert nature. It has to be remembered that the cardiac unit at St George's Hospital is one of the larger cardiac units. The evidence of Dr Pumphrey made it clear that Dr Stewart had acted in accordance with the practices taught at that cardiac unit. Both consultant cardiologists called on behalf of the respondents were highly qualified and held major posts. Dr Dawkins with the Wessex Cardiac Unit at Southampton University Hospital and Dr Hall at the University Hospital of Wales in Cardiff. Both taught cardiology. Both those doctors supported the practice of waiting and seeing in cases where the radial pulse was not totally lost following a BCC. The views of the cardiologists received strong support from the two vascular surgeons, Mr Dormandy and Professor Ruckley.

The only ground on which it could be said that the judge's acceptance that the evidence of the respondent's experts represented a responsible body of medical opinion skilled in the particular form of treatment in question was mistaken, is the accepted absence in the medical literature of any reference to the practice of waiting and seeing after a BCC in cases where the radial pulse is markedly reduced in following the procedure volume.

The judge gave careful consideration to this point and examined the medical literature with great care. This court was taken to the medical literature and in my judgment the judge's view that the medical literature was not as strongly supportive of the views of the appellant's cardiologist as might appear at first glance was a proper view for the judge to take. Only one author states in terms that the artery should be re-opened if the radial pulse is markedly reduced and that is Dr Grossman, the author of the chapter on cardiac catheterisation in the American textbook Grunwald on Heart Disease. Even with regard to that work, it is noticeable that whereas there are references to other medical authorities as support for many of the statements in that chapter, there is no such footnote with regard to this particular statement. Although there was a reference in another work by Karmody to diminished wrist pulses after catheterisation, the continuation of that passage referred only to patients with absent wrist pulses. If absent means totally missing, then the article provides very limited support for the views of the consultant cardiologists called on behalf of the appellant.

In any event, the existence of a body of medical opinion that considered that a markedly reduced radial pulse should result in re-exploration of the arteriotomy, does not mean that there cannot and does not exist a responsible body of medical opinion holding the contrary view.

During the course of the hearing of this appeal Miss Ritchie took us to the evidence of the medical witnesses who gave expert evidence on behalf of the respondents, and it is clear that they gave persuasive and compelling evidence on this issue.

Finally, I turn to the first three grounds of appeal which allege that the judge misdirected himself as to the law.

The first misdirection alleged is that the judge failed to appreciate the distinction between a medical issue such as medical issue F — 'can a partially occluded brachial artery become totally occluded by thrombus some two weeks later?' — where it has to be shown that this is more likely than not on all the evidence in the case relating to that issue and the question whether the conduct of a doctor has been negligent. Medical issues are not answered either by simply accepting the opinion or belief of a witness, however eminent, that that event could or could not happen, nor are they answered by showing that there is a respectable and responsible body of medical opinion that that event could or could not happen. The complaint is that the judge used the respectable and responsible body of medical opinion approach to answer such questions. This complaint, in my opinion, is unfounded. The judge's approach to medical issues can be seen where, in relation to issue F, he reviewed the relevant evidence in the case, setting out, inter alia, the evidence of Dr Hall describing one of his cases where this had occurred, and the evidence of Professor Ruckley that he had had experience of late total occlusions occurring after partial occlusions. The judge accepted the evidence of Professor Ruckley and rejected the contrary evidence of the vascular surgeon called on behalf Mr Joyce, Mr Scurr. The judge's approach in my estimation was precisely that which Stuart-Smith LJ, sitting as a judge of first instance, said was the correct approach in *Loveday v Renton* [1990] 1 Med LR 117 at 182.

The second misdirection of which complaint is made is the passage in the judgment which is set out in the skeleton argument of counsel for the appellant as:

'In the field of diagnosis and treatment, a defendant is not guilty of negligence if his acts or omissions were in accordance with accepted clinical practice.'

Had that been the totality of the judge's direction to himself on the law I would have agreed that it amounted to a misdirection. However, the judge added these words:

'Provided that clinical practice stood up to analysis and was not unreasonable in the light of the state of the medical knowledge at the time.'

The addition is very important because, without it, it leaves the decision of negligence or no negligence in the hands of the doctors, whereas that question must at the end of the day be one for the courts. In my view, the judge's direction would have been better phrased if, instead of the words 'if his acts or omissions' he had used the words 'if his acts or decision not to act' because it is to be hoped that an omission would never be part of accepted clinical practice. In the present case, the question was not whether Dr Stewart had omitted to re-explore the artery but whether his decision not to re-explore because there was a palpable pulse, albeit of small volume, was in accordance with accepted clinical practice and whether that clinical practice stood up to analysis.

Next, it is said that the judge approached the question whether the accepted clinical practice stood up to analysis in the wrong way. He should have considered the literature including textbooks and scientific publications; then the medical evidence, records, results of tests, observations and actual treatment, and finally the evidence from expert medical witnesses. The appellant's counsel in their skeleton argument accept that:

'The body of opinion can be small provided that it is in a qualitative sense, substantial. The relevant body of medical opinion must be that of the defendant's specialisation.'

In my judgment the judge cannot be criticised for treating the views of vascular surgeons as being relevant to the medical issues he had to determine nor for the fact that he took account of the views of Mr Dormandy, Professor Ruckley and Mr Scurr when deciding if the practice followed at the cardiac unit at St George's Hospital of non-intervention where there was a palpable pulse was a clinical practice accepted by a responsible body of medical opinion skilled in the particular form of treatment in question. In my view the expertise and experience of vascular surgeons is so closely linked to a procedure which involves entering an artery that the judge was correct to take their practices and views into account. The judge reviewed and took account of the medical literature both in relation to the question whether there existed a reputable and responsible body of medical opinion in favour of non-intervention and when analysing the clinical practice of non-intervention. The judge was not, in my opinion, obliged to reject the non-interventionist practice or to find that there was no responsible body of medical opinion who applied such a practice by the mere fact that such a practice found no place in the medical literature.

Finally, the judge is criticised for applying the dicta of the majority of this court in the case of *Bolitho v City and Hackney Health Authority* (1992) 13 BMLR 111, [1993] 4 Med LR 381 on the basis that the judge in this case applied those dicta to the issue of breach of duty whereas in *Bolitho* the question was one of causation, the negligence of the doctor, Dr Horn in failing to attend the patient, being accepted.

This is not, in my view, the way in which the judge applied the decision of the majority of this court in *Bolitho*. The judge looked at the issues which would arise if he should have found that Dr Stewart had been negligent in not retaining the appellant in hospital and continuing regular recorded observations for a period of 48 hours, or that the respondents had been in breach of duty in failing to have a system whereby day patients undergoing BCCs are given clear and adequate instructions to contact or return to the cardiac unit if they notice any change in the sensation or colour of their arm or hand. The judge, if such were the correct findings, had to consider what signs and symptoms the appellant would probably have exhibited in that 48-hour period and what action would and should have been taken in the light of those signs and symptoms. That is, as I understand the decision in *Bolitho*, what this court has held that the law requires a judge of first instance in a medical negligence case to do. That, in my judgment, is what the judge did in this case and I detect no misdirection.

In the first ground of appeal there is reference to the decisions of the House of Lords in *Hotson v East Berkshire Health Authority* [1987] 2 All ER 909, [1987] AC 750 and *Wilsher v Essex Area Health Authority* (1988) 3 BMLR 37, [1988] AC 1074. In both those cases the issue was whether the evidence established on the balance of probabilities that the plaintiff's condition for which compensation was sought was attributable to the established negligence of the doctors. The House of Lords held that the burden of proving on the balance of probabilities that the plaintiff's condition had been caused by the doctor's negligence was on the plaintiff. The House of Lords were not directly considering the question that arose in the present case, namely that where the physical causal link is conceded between the failure to intervene and the condition for which the plaintiff seeks damages, nevertheless there is no causal link in law because even if the doctors had acted properly, the outcome would have been the same. This is, in my opinion a different situation from those which arose in *Hotson* and *Wilsher*. In *Bolitho* it was accepted that intubation would have averted the child's collapse. In this case it was accepted that re-exploration of the artery within 48 hours of the BCC would have re-established circulation in the arm and consequently there would have been no aortogram and no cerebral accident.

The significance of the decision in *Bolitho* is that in such cases as these this court has said that the burden of proof that, had the doctor not been negligent, the child would have been intubated or the artery would have been explored, and that a failure to intubate or a failure to re-explore would have been negligent remains on the plaintiff. I can see arguments for the burden of proof in such cases being upon the defendants, but at present we, like the judge below, are bound by the decision of this court in *Bolitho*. For the purposes of this appeal, it suffices to say that in my view the judge correctly understood and applied the decision of this court in *Bolitho* to the facts of this case. Moreover, had the burden of proof rested on the respondents, I have no doubt that the judge's resolution of these issues would have been the same.

Conclusion

This has been a difficult and anxious case. Although I would reverse the judge's finding that the instructions given to the appellant on his discharge from the day ward were adequate and hold that they were inadequate and a breach of the respondents' duty of care, that cannot lead to the granting of this appeal, in my judgment, because of the findings of fact that cannot be disturbed as to the signs and symptoms that the appellant exhibited during the initial 48-hour period and that, on these signs and symptoms, no re-exploration of the appellant's arteriotomy would or should have been made.

HOBHOUSE LJ: I agree. On 4 March 1987 the appellant, Cyril Joyce, then aged 49 attended St George's Hospital, Tooting where a brachial cardiac catheterisation was carried out as a diagnostic aid to the treatment of a heart condition. He had had a mild heart attack the previous September and been referred to Dr Pumphrey, the consultant cardiologist at St George's, who had advised the catheterisation. This is an invasive diagnostic procedure, carried out under a local anaesthetic which involves the introduction of a catheter into the patient's brachial artery so that it can then be fed up the arterial system to the area of the patient's heart and radio-opaque dye introduced so that the state of the relevant vessels can be observed. At the conclusion of the procedure the catheter is withdrawn and the aperture which has been made in the patient's brachial artery immediately above the elbow is stitched up and the wound closed.

Mr Joyce was a day patient and the procedure was carried out by Dr Stewart, who was a registrar in training at St George's, using Mr Joyce's right brachial artery as the point of entry. In closing the incision he inadvertently sutured part of the posterior wall of the artery to the anterior wall. He did not observe the error that he had made and Mr Joyce was discharged home later on the same day. This error of Dr Stewart's set in train a chain of events which eventually led, on 22 June 1987, to Mr Joyce suffering a catastrophic stroke as a result of a blood clot lodging in his brain stem, leaving him totally paralysed except for his eyes. This action is concerned with whether the defendant health authority is liable for that consequence. In order to succeed in the action the appellant has to prove both that there was negligence on the part of those for whom the respondent health authority was responsible and that the terrible injury which he suffered was caused by the proved negligence.

The trial took place before Overend J during some three weeks in November and December 1994. On 14 December Overend J handed down his judgment. He decided in favour of the respondent both on the issue of negligence and on the limited remaining issue on causation. At the trial it had been conceded on behalf of the respondent that no issues of causation was raised with regard to anything that occurred after 11 March but it was in issue whether any negligence which might be proved against Dr Stewart and the staff of the hospital in relation to 4 March and the days immediately following had a causative relevance to the subsequent history of events. It was accepted that the initial error of Dr Stewart in suturing part of the posterior wall to the anterior wall of the artery was not itself negligent. It is the type of mishap that can occur when even a competent and careful surgeon is suturing an empty artery particularly, as was the case with Mr Joyce, a small artery. It is one of the recognised complications that can occur in a procedure of this kind even when carefully carried out.

At the time the trial commenced the appellant was entitled to believe that he had a very strong case. The respondent had served the signed statement of Mr Paterson, the surgeon who had, on 22 April, performed the operation during which Mr Joyce's brachial artery had been explored and the misplaced suture found. His statement said:

'Having made an incision into the right arm with the distal end over the anti-cubital fossa I noted that the brachial artery appeared completely occluded by a suture at the site of the catheterisation. The suture was incorporating the anterior and posterial wall of the artery'

This evidence was in accordance with the notes which he had made at the time (which had also been disclosed to the appellant). This evidence, if it was to be taken at face value, was highly significant. If the effect of Dr Stewart's error had been to occlude the artery completely and if it had incorporated both walls of the artery, Dr Stewart should probably have observed this from the external appearance of the artery before he closed up the operating wound and he should further have been able to detect subsequently that the artery was completely occluded. If this was the state of the artery at the completion of the procedure, the case of negligence, and its causative relevance, against those responsible for the care of Mr Joyce on 4 March was very strong indeed. The artery should have been re-opened immediately; the cause of the complete occlusion indentified and remedied.

However, shortly before the trial, the consultation vascular surgeon at St George's, Mr Dormandy, produced a photograph which he had caused to be taken on 22 April 1987 of the opened-up artery but which had not previously been disclosed to the appellant or his advisers. This photograph was put in evidence at the trial and it was accepted by the experts, including the appellant's experts, that it showed that the suture did not completely occlude the artery and that what was blocking the artery was the build-up of thrombus at the site of the partial occlusion. Accordingly the judge found:

'On this basis alone, I find that it is probable that the artery was partially, rather than totally, occluded at the time of the closure of the arteriotomy.'

Also, the vascular surgeon, Mr Scurr, called by the appellant, agreed that the photograph showed that the suture had caught only the lining of the wall of the artery (the intima) and that the surgeon carrying out the procedure might not be able to see this externally. The vascular surgeons called by the respondent gave similar evidence. Therefore, the appellant was unable to prove at the trial that Dr Stewart ought to have been able to observe that he had missutured the artery. Also, since the case had become one of partial not complete occlusion, the assessment of what had occurred and its seriousness became very different. The evidence of Mr Scurr was that: 'It is possible to narrow the artery by 85% without significantly altering the haemodynamics.'

The other evidence given at the trial made the finding of partial not complete occlusion inevitable. There was no evidence that at any time prior to 24 March was Mr Joyce's pulse observed to be absent. Further, on 19 March, he had undertaken an exercise test at the hospital with Dr Cameron, who had used Mr Joyce's right arm for the purpose of measuring his blood pressure and taking his pulse. The evidence of what occurred on 19 March was conclusively inconsistent with Mr Joyce having a wholly occluded artery on 19 March and, therefore, with Dr Stewart having wholly occluded the artery whilst suturing it on 4 March.

Therefore, the case of the appellant had to be re-assessed and presented on the basis that the symptoms and signs available to be observed from a partially occluded artery on and shortly after 4 March were such as to call for some intervention which would have discovered the misplaced suture and have caused the situation to be remedied before it was too late. For the purpose of this appeal, the appellant has accepted that this opportunity existed only for about 48 hours after the artery had been closed. He accepted, through this counsel, that after that period had elapsed he could not show that any intervention would have been any more successful than that which followed upon the diagnosis of a blocked artery by Dr Pumphrey on 24 March.

This meant that the appellant had to make out his case by reference to what occurred on 4 March and at the time of his discharge. After discharge he was not at the hospital again until 11 March, by which time the opportunity had passed. On the evidence of Mrs Joyce, she rang the hospital on Friday 6 March and complained that her husband was in pain. She was told that her husband should keep taking the pain killers and that if the pain remained bad he should go back to the hospital. She said that it was a result of this and his continuing pain that Mr Joyce went back to the hospital on 11 March. The hospital had no record that she had telephoned, nor did they have any record of the visit of Mr Joyce on 11 March. No separate case has been made by the appellant on the basis of what Mrs Joyce was told on 6 March.

The other radical change that occurred related to the evidence of Nurse Eugene. She was in charge of the cardiac day-care ward at St George's and was on duty on 4 March 1987. Her duties included organising patients' admission and discharge and the day-to-day management of the ward. She was also responsible for assessing patients and escorting them to the catheter laboratory and recording the observation of those patients after they returned to the ward. She had other nurses to assist her in looking after the patients on her ward.

She had no recollection whatsoever of the day in question and her evidence had to be guided by the practice which a nurse in her position would normally follow and the notes which she had made. These notes consisted of two documents, the 'cardex' and the record of observations. Mr Joyce had been taken from the ward to the catheter laboratory at about 10.30 am and returned to the ward at about 11.30 am. Entries were made on the observations sheet at 1.30 am, 12 noon and 1.00 pm. The 1.00 pm entry recorded a pulse that was faint and a hand that was pale and warm and which could be moved. It also recorded a blood pressure of 90 over 66 and a pulse rate of 56. There were no later entries. The cardex reads:

'On return very pale looking.
Observations b/p 100–110/70 pulse 60 bpm very faint.
No oozing.
Radial pulse present, hand very pale looking.
Seen by Dr Stewart OPD 2 wks with EX test.'

Nurse Eugene's signed statement said:

'Mr Joyce's medical record suggests the normal routine was followed in his case. When he returned to the ward from catheterisation I examined him and found him 'very pale looking'. This was not unusual for a post-catheterisation patient. His bp was 100–110/70 and the pulse was present (60 bpm) although very faint. Over the next three hours I carried out the observations of the patient, checking his bp, pulse and colour and temperature of the hand. These observations improved in that the hand which was cool to start became warm by 1300. Radial pulse was present throughout. It was faint but it was there . . .'

On this evidence the last recorded observation was that at 1.00 pm. This statement was a signed statement and Nurse Eugene said that it was in accordance with the statement which she had made to the respondent's solicitor in the present of a medical officer. When she attended the trial Nurse Eugene changed her evidence. She said that the observation recorded on the cardex was not an observation made between 1.00 pm and the time he was discharged from the ward. She thus used it as a basis for justifying the decision to discharge Mr Joyce rather than ask him to stay in the ward longer or overnight. Had she not changed her evidence it would have been well nigh impossible for the judge to conclude that the care of Mr Joyce on the afternoon of 4 March was satisfactory. But it remained the fact that there were no time and recorded observations after 1.00 pm.

The judge's judgment contains a masterly summary of the evidence and the issues and clear statements of his decisions upon those issues with his reasons. The case was a complex one which raised many more factual issues than have been raised on this appeal. One of the reasons for this was that the appellant's expert evidence had been prepared on the basis of factual evidence served by the respondent which was later departed from. His treatment of the expert evidence cannot be criticised. But there is one aspect, an important aspect, upon which I consider that his judgment can and should be criticised.

The trial was taking place in 1994 and concerned what had happened in 1987, 7 ¹/₂ years earlier. Neither Dr Stewart nor Nurse Eugene had any recollection of Mr Joyce at all. They therefore had to give evidence which was solely based upon their notes and what they said was their ordinary practice. This presentation of the factual evidence of the respondent was further emphasised by the fact that it was Dr Pumphrey who gave evidence first and who said what was the practice that he had taught Dr Stewart to follow. The findings of fact which the judge made in relation to what Dr Stewart and Nurse Eugene had done adopted the evidence of those two witnesses as to what they said they would have done. This is an approach which in my judgment should be adopted with a considerable degree of circumspection where there is evidence that proper practices have not been followed. I have already referred to the evidence that on 4 March Nurse Eugene manifestly did not keep, or cause to be kept, a proper record of the observations of Mr Joyce. The making of recorded observations is an important part of the management and care of a patient. Mr Joyce was displaying symptoms and signs which required that he be carefully observed. He had not reacted well to the procedure. His pulse was no better than faint, which indicated that there might well be some obstruction of his brachial artery. The records kept show the proper procedure was not followed in the making of recorded observations. It is therefore wrong to assume or infer that the proper procedure was necessarily followed in all other respects. It is equally legitimate to infer the reverse.

The same point can be illustrated in relation to what happened on 11 March. It was the appellant's pleaded case that he had returned to the day-care ward at the hospital at 11 March, had complained to Dr Stewart of severe pain in his right arm and that Dr Stewart had not examined his arm. In his signed statement Dr Stewart referred to this allegation and continued:

> 'However I do not remember seeing Mr Joyce on that date. If that had happened I am sure that I would have remembered. To date I can remember only one patient who contacted the hospital approximately one week after catheterisation, because he was slightly worried about the state of his arm, and he did so by telephone. (He subsequently saw his general practitioner and the problem with the arm disappeared.) I remember this incident and I am sure that I would have remembered Mr Joyce returning to the hospital.'

This confident evidence turned out to be completely wrong. The evidence called by the appellant established beyond any reasonable doubt that he been in the ward on that day. It is also accepted now that he had by then probably had a transient ischaemic episode in his hand and the Judge found that it was likely that these transient ischaemic symptoms may have been the cause of his return to the hospital. It was the evidence of the appellant and his daughter Carol that he received from Dr Stewart at best only a cursory examination and was sent away with remarks that were dismissive of his complaints. It also emerged that on that day Dr Stewart had to carry out no fewer than 11 catheterisation procedures. No note was made by anyone at the hospital that Mr Joyce had returned, nor was any history taken, nor was any record made of any observation of his condition or what advice he was given.

In my judgment it is clear beyond argument that proper procedures were not followed by Dr Stewart and whatever nurse was in charge of the ward that day. It also shows that Dr Stewart's evidence about what he would and would not have remembered and what he should be regarded as significant and what practices he would have followed was unreliable. It is against this background that the other evidence of Dr Stewart must be assessed. For example a few paragraphs earlier in his signed statement he said: 'The fact that I discharged him means that he was in an appropriate condition to be discharged.'

This statement is typical of a number that he made of various answers that he gave during his oral evidence. Sometimes a professional man who is accused of malpractice may only be able to defend himself by referring to what his normal practice was and statement his belief that he did not depart from his normal practice on the occasion in question. Such evidence is evidence to be taken into account and given appropriate weight. But when there is evidence from the aggrieved party or other witnesses that he did not follow what he says was his normal practice and, furthermore, the documentary evidence shows that proper practices were not followed on the occasion in question, then the weight that can be given to such evidence must be limited. It is a truism that even competent and experienced practitioners can on occasions make careless errors.

The criticism that I would make of the judgment is that the judge was too impressed by the reputation, at the time of the trial, of Dr Stewart and Nurse Eugene and placed inappropriate weight on it in the face of the documentary evidence which could not be gainsaid and the evidence of the appellant's witnesses which, whilst in certain respects understandably confused or overlaid by the tragic situation of Mr Joyce, nevertheless included evidence which was corroborated and not seriously contradicted. For example, why should Mr Joyce's evidence that on 4 March those at the hospital had had difficulty in finding his pulse be regarded as unreliable when the records themselves showed that his radial pulse was faint? Why should his evidence and that of his daughter that he was not properly examined on 11 March be rejected when it is clear from the other evidence that his return to the ward on that day was not regarded as significant? No record was made; it was not remembered. Even his at first sight surprising evidence that the word 'gunge' was used is not strikingly different from the word 'debris' which is used elsewhere by the doctors.

In his oral evidence about 11 March, faced by the cogency of the evidence of the appellant's witnesses, Dr Stewart accepted that Mr Joyce must have come back to the hospital on that day complaining of pain, including ischaemic pain. He then stated his confidence that he gave him a proper examination and proper advice before he allowed him to leave. The judge accepted this evidence of Dr Stewart. He gave his reasons:

> 'I found [Dr Stewart] to be a careful and conscientious witness, anxious to assist the court. I do not think it at all likely that he would ignore his training as a doctor, for example by failing to observe Mr Joyce's radial pulse. His career path has been exemplary and he is spoken of highly by those who have worked with him. He has recently accepted a consultant's appointment in New Zealand.'

In my judgment in this passage and in similar passages elsewhere in his judgment the judge has fallen into the error which I have described. He has based his findings not upon evidence regarding what actually occurred on the occasions in question but rather upon criteria of subsequent reputation and how the witness impressed him at the trial over seven years later. The scope for error in adopting this approach is particularly obvious where the person concerned was at the time in training and relatively inexperienced. Besides, this is not a case where dishonest or deliberately reckless conduct was alleged. It is a case where the allegation is want of reasonable skill and care in connection with properly ascertaining the relevant facts of a patient's condition, properly assessing the relevant risks, and taking the appropriate steps.

Having carefully considered the judgment and reviewed the evidence given in the case with the assistance of counsel on both sides, I, like the other members of this court, have come to the conclusion that the judge ought to have found that there was a want of reasonable care on the part of Dr Stewart and, probably, Nurse Eugene on 4 March. This want of care culminated in the decision to discharge Mr Joyce and to do so without a warning or advice that was appropriate to his case. It was preceded by inadequate observations of his condition and an inadequate recognition of the risk category into which he was, on the evidence, to be placed. The inescapable facts in this case are that the mishap which caused Mr Joyce's problems was a known and recognised risk of the procedure which Mr Stewart had carried out. It was a risk which was aggravated by the fact that Mr Joyce's brachial artery was of small size. The fact that he had a faint pulse showed that his artery was not totally occluded but raised more than a possibility that his artery was partially occluded. Dr Stewart himself explained that faint pulse could mean occlusion of the order of 90% of the available capacity of the artery. This fitted in with the evidence of Mr Scurr, to which I have already referred, that 85% occlusion would not significantly affect the blood flow. This observation alone put Mr Joyce into a risk category which was said by some witnesses to be occupied by only 5% of all patients (although others gave a higher percentage). The risk was a risk of ischaemia as a result of damage which had been done to the artery during the procedure, possibly with the build-up of thrombus adjacent to the constriction.

In his evidence Dr Stewart sought to suggest that there could have been other possible explanations for the faintness of Mr Joyce's radial pulse. This evidence was unimpressive. The suggestion that it was caused by spasm in the artery was, on the evidence, possibly sufficient in relation to the period shortly after the completion of the procedure but, on the evidence, was not sufficient as a likely explanation of what was to be observed some hours later. Dr Stewart's evidence was unimpressive for two particular reasons. First, his suggestion of other possible causes of a weak pulse did not negative the partial obstruction of the artery as being a possible, indeed more likely, explanation; his reasoning was disturbingly deficient. Secondly, his evidence was that he did not concern himself with any comparative assessment of the patient's radial pulse distal to the site of the incision with either that pulse prior to the carrying out of the procedure or to the patient's radial pulse in his other arm. Since the purpose of the observation of the distal pulse was primarily to enable Dr Stewart to make an assessment of the condition of the brachial artery in that arm, the making of such comparisons would appear to be elementary; this was indeed the evidence of the appellant's expert witnesses which there was no reason to reject and which the judge does not appear to have rejected. Dr Stewart's attitude to a patient such as Mr Joyce appears, on his own evidence, to have been inadequate.

It is also clear that Mr Joyce was not treated as being in a risk category of any kind. The observation period was certainly no longer than the minimum acceptable and may indeed have been shorter. The advice which was given to Mr Joyce on his discharge in no way departed from the standard advice given by the hospital to all day case cardiac catheter patients who were being discharged from that ward. The lack of recorded observations after 1.00 pm and the absence of any record of the discharge decision or even its time confirm the overall picture.

In my judgment, given that it is now accepted that it cannot be proved that the missuturing was itself observable, Dr Stewart was not at fault in treating the faint pulse as justifying him in closing up the wound and returning Mr Joyce to the ward. A faint pulse at that stage was not inconsistent with a successful operation although others, including the appellant's experts, would have shown more concern about it than did Dr Stewart. Thereafter there was, in my judgment, a want of reasonable care in that after 1.00 pm proper recorded observations of Mr Joyce's condition were not made. It appears that his condition was not properly evaluated. On the evidence, including that of the respondent's expert, Dr Hall, it would have been prudent to have kept Mr Joyce under observation in the ward for a longer period so that the stability of his condition could be better assessed, particularly in view of the fact that the drugs which he had been given would be wearing off. He had, as an ordinary incident of the procedure, been given substantial doses of heparin, which affects the consistency of the blood, and he had also been given pain killers. When these drugs ceased to affect him more revealing observations, including complaints of pain, would be possible. By discharging Mr Joyce at or before 3.30 pm, the respondent health authority deprived itself of that advantage.

At the time of his discharge, which the judge put at about 3.30 pm (although this finding may have been too favourable to the respondent), Mr Joyce was in my judgment given no adequate warning which recognised that he was in a risk category and that he had not been detained long enough in the ward to provide a basis for confidence that his condition would not deteriorate. If he was to be discharged at that time, there was, in my judgment, a want of reasonable care in not setting up a clear procedure whereby he would return to the hospital and be properly reassessed if there was any deterioration in this condition. This was not done.

The want of reasonable care on the part of the respondent in relation to Mr Joyce was that he was discharged from the hospital when he was at risk and without any steps being taken to deal with that risk. The next question then is whether there were relevant consequences of that breach of duty. What the appellant has to prove is that it was as a result of that breach of duty that no steps were taken to re-open the artery during the next 48 hours and deal with the missuturing and consequent obstruction. Here again I agree with my Lords that the appellant has not discharged this burden of proof. In my judgment the judge's findings of fact on this aspect are unassailable.

The expert evidence was that any decision to re-open the brachial artery involves risk. Where the artery is only partially occluded there is a risk that further intrusion may simply make the position worse. As regards these risks, the judge said:

'On the other side of the coin it is also common ground that re-exploration of an arterotomy can lead to complications. They include risk of fracture of the artery, the risk of a tear extending, the risk of a need for a vein patch of graft from a donor site, the risk of causing total occlusion, the risk of internal damage and the risk of thrombus developing. Mr Scurr said that both risks happened in one case out of every 100. On the evidence it would appear that there are risks associated with both the interventionist and conservative approach to the management of weak pulses. They appear to be evenly balanced.'

Although any decision about re-opening the artery at the conclusion of the procedure or possibly very shortly thereafter would be a matter for the cardiologists, at any later stage it would be a matter for a vascular surgeon. Therefore, the question is whether a vascular surgeon, if called in during the 48-hour period to assess whether a further operation should be performed on Mr Joyce would have decided that his signs and symptoms justified re-opening the artery. It is not in dispute that if the vascular surgeon had decided to do this he would in fact have discovered the missuturing and, given that he was operating within the period of 48 hours, probably have been able to remedy the position satisfactorily.

Any decision by a vascular surgeon would have to be taken in the light of the symptoms and signs which Mr Joyce was presenting during this period. At the time of his discharge it is accepted that on the balance of probabilities a pulse was present, albeit faint. Mr Joyce was able to move his hand and was not at that time complaining of pain. His hand was probably warm but of a poor colour. There was an issue as to what pain he suffered on the evening of 4 March and the following day. It is accepted that he did suffer pain. The judge found that this was wound pain, not ischaemic pain. The two types of pain would differ in their intensity and location. Ischaemic pain would be found in the lower arm, wrist and hand because that is the area which would be being deprived of blood by the obstruction and would therefore be the site of the ischaemic pain. Ischaemic pain would also be of a greater intensity than wound pain.

The evidence of Mr Joyce was that the pain which he suffered after his return from hospital was in the location of his elbow, that is to say in the location where wound pain would be felt. The evidence of the intensity of the pain was also not such as clearly to lead to the inference that it was ischaemic pain. Later in March and in April, Mr Joyce was twice asked to give a history of his symptoms. The history he gave was recorded and the notes were in evidence. That history suggested that the first time that he suffered ischaemic pain was about a week later when a specific episode of transient ischaemia occurred. The judge found, in my judgment in accordance with the evidence, that this probably occurred shortly before Mr Joyce returned to the hospital on 11 March.

In my judgment the judge was right to find that the only deterioration of Mr Joyce's condition during the 48 hours after the procedure was the wound pain and that it was not proved that there was probably any signs or symptoms which would have justified a cardiologist or a vascular surgeon in concluding that his condition had worsened or that there was ischaemia. Under these circumstances it would have been proper for a cardiologist not to call in a vascular surgeon and for a vascular surgeon, if consulted, to decide that it was not appropriate to operate. It follows that even if Mr Joyce had been kept in the ward for further observation or had returned within the 48-hour period, the position would have been the same: his artery would not have been re-opened.

The expert evidence is summarised in the judge's judgment and has been reviewed by Roch LJ. The judge correctly found that there was a balance of risk. Mr Scurr accepted that if he had been called in he would have continued to observe the patient and that the evidence justified at that stage a conclusion of arterial sufficiency. The respondent's experts expressed similar views. Further, it was the evidence of Dr Pumphrey and Dr Stewart that they would not have considered it necessary to call in a vascular surgeon and the evidence of Mr Dormandy was that if he had been called in he would definitely have declined to operate. The judge said:

'On the evidence and the balance of probabilities, I find that it is unlikely that Dr Dormandy would have operated had he or any one of his team been called in on 4 March. So far as it may be relevant, I also find that it is unlikely that any other vascular surgeon would have operated in similar circumstances.'

The conclusion on causation is based upon three factual findings made by the judge, findings which were in accordance with the evidence. First, there was no relevant deterioration in the condition of Mr Joyce during the 48 hours following the procedure.

Secondly, it was not improper to take the view that his condition, whilst requiring that he be watched, did not call for the intervention of a vascular surgeon or the re-opening of his brachial artery. Thirdly, all the cardiologists and vascular surgeons working at St George's in March 1987 would in fact have adopted the cautious approach and would not in fact, on the signs and symptoms which Mr Joyce was displaying during the material period, have re-opened the artery. It follows that, on the evidence, the correct conclusion is that the want of care that occurred on 4 March did not cause the appellant's injuries which are the subject of this action.

This conclusion means that this appeal must fail on the facts. However, we have been referred to *Bolitho v City and Hackney Health Authority* (1992) 13 BMLR 111, [1993] 4 Med LR 381 and what Overend J said about the burden of proof has been criticised.

It is therefore appropriate to say, briefly, something about the law applicable to this part of the case.

A plaintiff must prove that the defendant was at fault and that the defendant's fault was a cause of ('materially contributed' to) the plaintiff's injury or loss. Medical negligence cases are no exception to this rule. The general burden of proof remains on the plaintiff although he may be able to rely upon inferences from the evidence which, if not rebutted by the defendant, lead to the conclusion that the plaintiff has proved his case. Where the fault consists of an act which is alleged to have had physical consequences, the question to be asked is straightforward even though its answer may not be: was the act a cause of the injury? Where the fault consists of an omission, or an act which does not in itself have physical consequences, identifying the correct question to ask may be less easy. The present case comes into this category since the fault proved was, critically, discharging Mr Joyce on the afternoon of 4 March and doing so without prior proper instructions and advice.

Such cases can be further subdivided into cases where the question is what steps would have been taken if proper care had been taken and cases where the question is what would have been the outcome of any further steps that ought to have been taken. The present case is not of the latter type. It is accepted that had a vascular surgeon decided to re-open his artery within the 48-hour period, Mr Joyce's injury would probably have been avoided. What the appellant had to seek to prove was that a vascular surgeon would (or should) have been called in and would (or should) have operated.

This is the same type of question as was raised by *Bolitho*. There, a hospital registrar (Dr Horn) negligently failed to attend a child suffering a cardiac arrest. The child then suffered serious brain damage which could have been avoided if he had been intubated by a doctor. The case of the health authority was that even if the registrar had attended she would not have intubated the child and that a prudent doctor would likewise not have done so. The Court of Appeal picked up the two aspects of the issue: per Farquharson LJ (1992) 13 BMLR 111 at 120, [1993] 4 Med LR 381 at 386:

> 'It was for the [plaintiff] to prove that she would probably have intubated and further that if she did do so [her] "failure was contrary to accepted medical practice".'

and per Dillon LJ (1992) 13 BMLR 111 at 130–131, [1993] 4 Med LR 381 at 391:

> '... if the starting place is the evidence of Dr Horn, as the doctor who ought to have attended, as to what she would have done, that could only be displaced by showing that if she had done that she would have been negligent...'

These statements formed part of the ratio decidendi of the majority.

Thus, a plaintiff can discharge the burden of proof on causation by satisfying the court either that the relevant person would in fact have taken the requisite action (although she would not have been at fault if she had not) or that the proper discharge of the relevant person's duty towards the plaintiff required that she take that action. The former alternative calls for no explanation since it is simply the factual proof of the causative effect of the original fault. The latter is slightly more sophisticated: it involves the factual situation that the original fault did not itself cause the injury but that this was because there would have been some further fault on the part of the defendants; the plaintiff proves his case by proving that his injuries would have been avoided if proper care had continued to be taken. In *Bolitho* the plaintiff had to prove that the continuing exercise of proper care would have resulted in his being intubated.

Properly viewed, therefore, this rule is favourable to a plaintiff because it gives him two routes by which he may prove his case — either proof that the exercise of proper care would have necessitated the relevant result, or proof that if proper care had been exercised it would in fact have led to the relevant result.

In assessing what the exercise of proper care necessitates, no different test is to be applied to that to be applied in any case where professional negligence is alleged, essentially the so-called Bolam test (*Bolam v Friern Hospital Management Committee* (1957) 1 BMLR 1, [1957] 1 WLR 582). This is because it is the same question as is involved in the initial allegation of fault; the causation question merely extends the ambit of the allegation of fault. The plaintiff's case is still based upon saying what the exercise of proper care required and saying that if proper care had been exercised in all respects and had continued to be exercised, the plaintiff would not have suffered the injury. Nor do any different principles of burden of proof apply; the plaintiff has the same general burden but can rely upon evidential inferences to assist him to discharge that burden. In my judgment (pace Dillon LJ *Bolitho v City and Hackney Health Authority* (1992) 13 BMLR 111 at 132, [1993] 4 Med LR 381 at 392), it does not assist to introduce concepts from administrative law such as the *Wednesbury* test (*Associated Provincial Picture Houses Ltd v Wednesbury Corpn* [1947] 2 All ER 680, [1948] 1 KB 223); such tests are directed to very different problems and their use, even by analogy, in negligence cases can, in my judgment, only serve to confuse.

Bolitho and similar cases confirm that, to succeed on causation, Mr Joyce had to satisfy the court that either the vascular surgeon at St George's Hospital would in fact have re-opened his artery or that it would have been negligent for him not to have done so. Overend J carefully considered both aspects and concluded, in my judgment in accordance with the evidence, that Mr Joyce had not proved his case on either alternative.

This appeal accordingly fails.

NOURSE LJ: I agree that this appeal must be dismissed for the reasons given in the judgments of Roch and Hobhouse LJJ, to which I cannot usefully add anything of my own.

APPENDIX 7

Glossary of medical terms

Abdomen – The cavity of the body which extends from the diaphragm to the floor of the pelvis.

Abdominal claudication – Abdominal pain after eating, due to chronic mid-gut ischaemia.

Abducent nerve – The 6th cranial nerve.

Abduction – Moving a limb outwards from the medial line.

Abductor – A muscle which tends to pull a limb away from the middle line, or one part from another.

Ablation – Cutting away tissue or abnormal growth.

Abortion – Premature or untimely expulsion of the fetus.

Abrasion – A portion of surface from which the skin or mucous membrane has been removed by rubbing.

Abscess – A collection of pus circumscribed in a cavity produced by tissue disintegration and displacement.

Acanthosos – A condition seen typically in psoriasis and eczema: proliferation of the prickle-cell layer of the epidermis without destruction of the intercellular fibrils.

Accessory nerve – The 11th cranial nerve.

Accommodation – Adjustments of the eye to provide clear and distinct pictures of objects at various distances.

Acetabulum – Socket on the lower part of the pelvic bone in which the head of the femur (hipbone) is situated and attached by ligaments.

Achilles tendon – The common tendon of insertion of the calf muscles.

Acidosis – Decrease in pH of the blood below 7μ36.

Acrocyanosis – Slow blood circulation causing bluish discolouration of hands and feet.

Acromioclavicular joint – The plane joint between the acromial end of the clavicle and the medial margin of the acromion.

Acromion – A flat plate of triangular shape which is continuous with and projects beyond the outer end of the spine of the scapula.

Acroparaesthesia – A tingling sensation in hands and feet.

Acuity – Sharpness or clearness of vision.

Acute – Severe symptoms, brief in duration.

Adduction – The drawing of any limb towards the medial line.

Adductors – Any muscle which adducts or draws a part towards the median line or the axis of the body.

Adenitis – Inflammation of a gland.

Adenocarcinoma – A malignant or carcinomatous adenoma.

Adenoidectomy – An operation for excision of adenoids.

Adenoids – A mass of lymph tissue located at the back of the mouth.

Adenoma – A benign tumour or swelling of the glandular tissue.

Adenopathy – A diseased gland.

Adhesion – The union of normally separate parts by new tissue produced as a result of inflammation.

Adnerval – Near a nerve.

Adrenal glands – The glands of the endocrine system which are located above the kidneys.

Adventitia – Loose connective tissue on the outer surface of a blood vessel.

Aerobic – Requiring gaseous oxygen in order to live.

Aerogenic – Giving rise to gas annulus: any ring-shaped structure.

Aetiology – The science of the investigation of the cause or origin of disease.

Agnosia – In this condition there is inability to recognise objects and lack of the perceptive faculty in general.

Aids – Acquired Immune Deficiency Syndrome.

Akathisia – A form of restlessness in which the subject is unable to remain seated for any length of time.

Akinesia – Loss of muscular response.

Alexia – Difficulty in reading.

Alopecia – Loss of hair.

Alveolar process – One of the four projections which make up each jaw bone.

Alveolus – The part of the upper or lower jawbone that holds the roots of the teeth.

Amblyopia – Deterioration of vision without structural abnormality of the visual pathway and uncorrectable by optical means.

Amniocentesis – Transabdominal or transvaginal puncture of the amniotic sac to drain or sample amniotic fluid.

Anaerobic – Growing most vigorously in an atmosphere which is free from oxygen.

Analgesic – A medication to relieve pain.

Anastomosis – Joining up two ends of a hollow organ.

Andexa – Appendages, adjoined parts.

Androgen – The name given to the group of steroids, both natural and artificial, which promote growth in, and maintain the function of, the secondary sexual structures of the male.

Aneurysm – A localised dilatation of the walls of a blood vessel, usually an artery, due to weakening through infection, injury, degenerative conditions or congenital defects.

Angina pectoris – Literally angina of the chest; a substantial pain or sense of constriction or oppression.

Angiocardiogram – A series of X-ray films of the heart after the intravenous injection of a radio-opaque substance.

Angiogram – X-ray picture of artery (same as arteriogram).

Angioma – A simple tumour composed of blood vessels or of lymphatic vessels.

Angiomatous – Resembling, relating to or of the nature of angioma.

Anisometropia – A difference in refractive measurement between the two eyes or because of poor clarity in the media of one eye.

Anisopia – Inequality of power of vision as between one eye and the other.

Ankylosing spondylitis – A gradual loss of mobility in the joints between the vertebrae. Disease of the spine.

Ankylosis – Complete immobility of joint resulting from pathological changes in that joint or of the structures associated with it.

Anodontia – The absence of teeth.

Anodyne – Treatment to ease pain.

Anopia – Defection or lack of power of seeing; anopsia (quadrantic anopia: a defect of a quarter of the visual field bounded by vertical and horizontal radii).

Anosmia – Loss of sense of smell.

Anoxia – Without oxygen.

Anterior – Front part of the body of an organ.

Anteroposterior – Extending from the front to the back.

Anthropoid – Descriptive of apes who most nearly resemble man in form and structure.

Antibiotic – A substance used to inhibit the growth action of micro-organisms.

Antibody – Serum protein with the molecular properties of an immunoglobulin.

Antipyretic – Fever reducing drug.

Antrectomy – Operation for the removal of part of the stomach.

Antum – A cavity or hollow, commonly used for a cavity surrounded by bone.

Anuria – Complete cessation of the secretion and excretion of urine; a symptom of kidney failure.

Anus – The opening of the terminal part of the alimentary canal in the posterior part of the perineum.

Aorta – The largest blood vessel in the body beginning at the left ventricle of the heart and ending opposite the body of the 4th lumbar vertebra by dividing into the two common iliac arteries.

Apgar score – A system for rating an infant's physical condition one minute after birth.

Aphacia – Condition where lens of eye is absent.

Aphacic – Term applied to an eye devoid of the lens.

Aphasia – A disorder affecting the comprehension or expression of language, implying damage to left frontal and temporal regions of the brain. More specifically, a defect or loss of the power to produce or to understand spoken or written speech, due to pathological interference with the speech centre or speech region in the brain.

Apical – Located at or appertaining to the apex of any structure.

Apnoea – A cessation of breathing.

Appendectomy – Surgical removal of the appendix.

Appendicitis – An inflamed condition of the vermiform appendix.

Appendix – The small structure (worm like) which is attached to the first portion of the large intestine.

Apraxia – Failure of brain to utilise some object in its normal context.

Apyrexia – Absence or temporary cessation of fever.

Arachnoid mater – A delicate membrane enveloping the brain.

Arachnoiditis – Inflamation of the arachnoid mater of the brain. Inflammation of the membrane which surrounds the spinal cord and brain.

Arrhythmia – Absence of rhythm: irregularity; variation in either the force or rate of the heart beat.

Arteriography – The visualisation of arteries by means of X-rays after injection of radio-opaque material.

Arteriorrhexis – Rupture of an artery.

Arteriosclerosis – Narrowing of the lumen of arterioles due to duplication of the internal elastic lamine and fibrosis of the media; it is the arteriolar lesion found in essential hypertension.

Arteriovenous – Venous as well as arterial; affecting or referring to an artery as well as a vein.

Artery – A vessel carrying blood from the heart to different parts of the body.

Arthralgia – Pain of any kind affecting a joint.

Arthritis – Inflammation of a joint.

Arthro – Prefix meaning joint.

Arthrodesis – Operation to fuse joints.

Arthropathy – Disease of a joint.

Arthroplasty – Operative restoration of the functional part of a joint either by re-construction or by prosthetic replacement.

Arthropneumography – Radiography of joint after injection of air or oxygen into the joint space in order to visualise cartilage and limits of the joint cavity.

Arthroscopy – Examination of a joint with an endoscope.

Arthrotomy – The surgical procedure of cutting into or puncturing a joint.

Articular – Having reference to a joint.

Articulation – A joint between two skeletal elements, bones or cartilages.

Asbestosis – Form of pneumoconiosis caused by inhalation of asbestos.

Asepsis – The condition of being free from infection or from the presence of living pathogenic organisms.

Aspiration – Withdrawal of fluid from the body by means of suction.

Asthenia – Being weak.

Asthma – The term used for a syndrome characterised by paroxysmal attacks of dyspnoea of expiratory type.

Astigmatism – A condition in which a point source of light cannot be brought to a point focus on the retina by the use of spherical lenses.

Astragalus – An obsolete term for the talus, the bones of the tarsus with which the tibia and fibula articulate.

Asymptomatic – Without symptoms.

Ataxaphasia – A state in which disconnected words may be used without understanding but there is inability to form a connected sentence.

Ataxia – Loss of co-ordination.

Atelectasis – Collapse of the lung.

Atheroma – Degeneration of artery walls with fatty deposits sometimes leading to thrombosis.

Atherosclerosis – Disease of arteries in which calcarious plaques develop; hardening of the arteries.

Atopic – Referring to or characterised by atopy.

Atopy – Constitutional tendency in certain persons to develop immediate hypersensitivity states such as asthma or hay fever.

Atria – The plural of atrium.

Atrial – Referring to an atrium.

Atrioventricular – Belonging to an atrium and a ventricle of the heart.

Atrium – Literally, an entrance hall or vestibule, in anatomy, a cavity into which one or more other cavities open.

Atrophy – To waste away: a condition of general malnutrition from whatever cause, the signs of which are wasting or shrinking of the tissues of the whole body or part of it; wasting of a tissue or organ.

Audiogram – A graph recording level of hearing, pursuant to tests carried out on an audio meter.

Auditory nerve – The 8th cranial nerve, providing equilibrium and the sense of hearing.

Auditory ossicles – The bones of the middle ear.

Auricle – The expanded portion of the external ear.

Ausculation – The art of listening and interpreting the meaning of sounds produced within the body.

Autism – A condition in which the individual tends to be morbidly self-centred.

Autonomic – Spontaneous, existing independently, being functionally independent.

Avascular necrosis – Death of bone or tissue through interruption of blood supply.

Avulsion – A tearing, such as of skin from underlying tissue.

Axilla – The armpit.

Axon – A nerve fibre.

Axonal – Disruption of inter-connecting fibres.

BS – Blood sugar.

Babinski's combined flexion phenomenon – A sign seen in hermiplegia of organic origin: the supine patient attempts, with arms folded across the chest, to rise to the sitting position. There is flexion at the hip joint with raising of the heel on the paralysed side, but the unaffected side remains stationary.

Babinski's phenomenon or reflex – The extensor plantar response which occurs in pyramidal-tract disease: on stroking the lateral aspect of the sole of the foot there is spontaneous dorsiflexion of the great toe with plantar flexion and 'fanning' of the other toes.

Babinski's reflex – Upon stimulation of the sole of the foot, a movement of the great toe towards the sole of the foot.

Babinski's sign – The extensor plantar response; usually called the Babinski reflex. Absence of the ankle jerk in sciatica.

Bacillus – Aerobic, spore-bearing, rod shaped organisms, most species of which are mobile.

Bacteraemia – A condition in which there are bacteria in the circulating blood.

Barbiturates – Effective sedatives.

Baritosis – A form of lung disease (from barium dust).

Barotitis – Earache when eg climbing or descending in an aeroplane.

Barotrauma – Injury to the middle ear after eg climbing or descending in an aeroplane.

Basal – Referring to a base.

Basal ganglia – Masses of grey matter within the cerebral haemispheres biparietal: relating to the two parietal bones or eminences.

Basal metabolic rate (BMR) – Used as a test of thyroid function.

Beclamide – A drug used to test epilepsy, by quelling convulsions.

Bells palsy – Acute peripheral facial nerve paralysis.

Biceps – A muscle that has two heads.

Bicuspid – A premolar tooth; a valve with two cusps.

Bicuspid teeth – Four premolars on the upper and lower jaw.

Bilateral – Occurring on both sides (eg bilateral black eyes).

Bilateral carotid bruits – Noises which suggest narrowing of the carotid arteries by atheroma.

Bilirubin – Red pigment occurring in human bile and as the calcium salt in gall-stones. Its concentration in the blood is greatly increased in jaundice.

Binocular – Involving both eyes.

Biopsy – Removal and examination of living tissue for diagnostic purposes (tissue sampling).

Bladder – The sac situated in the anterior part of the pelvis which serves as a storage tank for urine before it is discharged.

Blepharitis – Inflammation of the eyelids.

Blood pressure – The pressure of the column of circulating blood within the vascular system.

Bowel – The intestine.

Brachial – Referring or relating to the arm.

Brachioradialis muscle – A superficially placed muscle on the radial side of the forearm.

Bradyarrhythmia – A slow abnormal cardiac rhythm.

Bradycardia – Slowing of the heart rate.

Bright's disease – Nephritis.

Bronchitis – An inflammation of the mucous membrane of the larger and medium-sized bronchi.

Bronchus – Any part of the air passages between the bifurcation of the trachea and the bronchioles in the lungs.

Buccal – Involving the cheek or mouth.

Bunion – An inflammatory swelling of the bursa of the metatarsophalangeal joint of the big toe with abduction of the toe.

Bursa – Natural hollows in fibrous tissues lined by smooth cells and containing a little fluid. Situated at points where there is pressure or friction, they try to allow free movement, without straining tissues.

Bursitis – Inflammation of a bursa (eg housemaid's knee).

Byssinosis – A form of lung disease, resulting from inhalation of cotton flax or hemp dust.

Cacosmia – Irregularity in the sense of smell caused by brain damage.

Calcification – The deposition of calcareous matter within organic tissue so that it becomes hardened.

Callus – Bony material grown around and between two ends of a fractured bone in healing.

Cancer – A malignant tumour arising from epithelial cells. Any malignant growth.

Canthus – The corner, eg of the eye.

Capitate bone – The largest of the carpal bones, placed in the distal row opposite the base of the 3rd metacarpal bone.

Capsulitis – Inflammation about a joint.

Carbon dioxide – CO2, a gas which dissolves readily in water to form carbonic acid; it is one of the end-products of the tissue oxidation of carbohydrates and fats.

Carbon monoxide – CO, a colourless gas, the chief constituent of coal gas.

Carcinogen – Any substance which causes living tissues to become carcinomatous.

Carcinoma – A malignant epithelial tumour which tends to spread locally.

Cardiac – Of the heart.

Cardiac tamponade – The compressive effect upon the heart of blood or fluid that has accumulated in the pericardium.

Cardiologist – A heart specialist and consultant.

Cardiomyopathy – Disease of the heart muscle; usually restricted to diffuse myocardial disease not resulting from coronary arterial disease and sometimes only to disease of unknown aetiology.

Caries – Tooth or bone decay.

Carotid – Relating to or situated near one of the carotid arteries.

Carotid arteries – The main artery of the neck.

Carpal – Of the wrist.

Carpal bones – The eight bones which form the wrist.

Carpopedal – Relating to the wrist and foot.

Carpus – Bones of wrist.

Cartilage – A skeletal or connective tissue which is firm, flexible and slightly elastic.

Cataract – Opacity in the crystalline lens of the eye which may be partial or complete.

Catharsis – Cleansing the bowels; purgation; the relief of strong feelings or tension.

Cauda equina – A sheaf of roots which runs down through the lower part of the spinal canal.

Causalgia – Burning pain, intense hypersensitivity and trophic changes in the cutaneous distribution of an injured peripheral nerve, especially the median and sciatic nerves.

Cauterization – The process of burning a part with a cautery.

Cecum – or Caecum –The blind pouch in the right iliac fossa which forms the beginning of the large intestine.

Cellulitis – A diffuse inflammation of connective tissue, especially of subcutaneous tissue.

Cephalalgia – Pain in the head.

Cephalic – Of the head.

Cerebellum – The largest part of the hind brain.

Cerebral – Relating to the cerebrum.

Cerebrovascular accident – Stroke.

Cerebrum – The celebral hemispheres and their commissure, the corpus callosum.

Cervical – Of the neck.

Cervical spondylosis – A certain degeneration of bones of the neck.

Cervix – A neck, or any part resembling a neck.

Chalarion – Swelling and congestion of a tarsal gland of the eyelid, with retention of the secretion, the result being a hard tumour about the size of a pea on the eyelid, generally the upper eyelid.

Chemotherapy – Specific treatment with drug of parasitic infections.

Chest – The thorax.

Chiasma – An x-shaped crossing.

Cholecystectomy – Excision of the gall bladder. Cytology: science of form and functions of the cells.

Chondritis – A condition of inflammation in cartilage.

Chondrocyte – A mature cartilage cell.

Chondrolysis – A destruction of cartilaginous tissue which takes place during the process of calcification.

Chondromalacia – A condition of abnormal softness of cartilage.

Choroid – The main part of the vascular coat of the eye, lining the sclera and composed of two main layers, the suprachoroid lamina and the choroid proper.

Chronic – Slowly developing, long lasting.

Chvostek's sign – In tetany, eg after total parathyroidectomy, tapping the seventh nerve results in twitching of the facial muscles.

Cicatrix – The scar of a healed wound.

Cirrhosis – Chronic disease of the liver.

Claudication – Pain which develops after a certain amount of exertion; can cause limping. Lameness, limping, an obstruction.

Clavicle – The long bone of the shoulder girdle shaped like the italic letter f.

Clawfoot – A deformity of the foot caused by paralysis of the muscles.

Clawhand – Deformity of the hand characterised by a bending forward of the fingers.

Cleft – A fissure, notch, gap, depression, or incisura.

Clitoris – A small erectile organ in the female homologous to the penis in the male.

Clivus – A sloping surface, particularly of bone.

Coccydynia – Pain in the coccyx and surrounding area.

Coccygeal – Belonging or relating to, or involving the coccyx.

Coccygectomy – Excision of the coccyx.

Coccyx – Vestigial human tail; small triangular bone attached to the lower part of the sacrum.

Colitis – Inflammation of the colon.

Collapsed lung – A condition existing when the lung contains no air.

Collarbone – The clavicle.

Colles' fracture – Fracture across the lower end of the radius.

Colon – Large intestine.

Colostomy – A temporary or permanent artificial opening made through the abdominal wall into the colon.

Colour blindness – The inability to perceive one or more colours (primary ones).

Colposcopy – Examination of the cervix through a microscope.

Coma – A state of unconsciousness from which the person cannot be roused by external stimuli.

Comminuted – Bone fractured into several pieces.

Compound fracture – A fracture associated with a skin wound.

Compression fracture – A fracture of a vertebral body by vertical crushing.

Computerised axial tomography (CAT scan) – A computerised analysis of X-rays focused at different levels which produce detailed images of a particular structure. Useful in studies of the brain.

Concussion – An injury resulting from a blow or impact.

Condyle – Rounded bulge at the end of some bones.

Congenital – Present at birth.

Conjunctivitis – Inflammation of the mucous membranes lining the eyelids.

Contraceptive – Any agent or measure used to prevent conception.

Contusion – A bruise.

Cordectomy – The operation to remove a vocal cord.

Cordoma – A neoplasm made up of notochordal tissue; a small malignant neoplasm composed of notochordal tissue, which may occur at the union of the occipital with the sphenoid bone.

Cornea – The transparent anterior part of the fibrous coat of the eyeball, of which the posterior part is the sclera.

Coronary arteries – Arteries supplying blood to the walls of the heart.

Coronoid process – The protuberance towards the top of the ulna.

Corpus lutea – Yellowish or orange bodies found in the ovary after rupture of graafian follicles and derived from the granulosa and theka cells.

Cortex – Outer part of an organ.

Costal – Of the ribs.

Costavertebral – Having reference or belonging to a rib and a vertebra, or ribs and vertebrae.

Coxa – The hip joint.

Coxa valga – Deformity of the femoral neck in which the angle between the neck and the shaft is increased.

Coxa vara – A deformity of the femoral neck in which the angle between the shaft and the neck is decreased.

Cranial – Relating to the cranium.

Cranial nerves – The nerves arising from the brain.

Craniectomy – The cutting away of a portion of the skull.

Craniopharyngioma – A neoplasm originating in the remnants of the hypophyseal duct. These are chiefly supresellar tumours occurring mainly in children and adolescents.

Cranioplasty – Surgical correction or restoration of defects of the skull.

Craniosacral – Relating to the skull and the sacrum.

Craniotomy – Any operation on the skull; the cutting away of part of the skull.

Cranium – The skull.

Crepitations – Crackling noises caused by congestion or inflammation of the lungs.
Crepitus – Grating caused by bone running against bone or roughened cartilage (usually associated with movement of arthritic joint).
Cruciate – Shaped like a cross.
Crural – Of the leg or thigh.
Cubitus – Elbow.
Cuboid bone – An irregular cuboidal bone on the lateral side of the foot, and in front of the heel bone.
Cuneiform bone – One of the bones of the ankle forming the bottom portion of the foot, located behind the 1st, 2nd and 3rd metatarsal bones.
Cutaneous – Affecting or associated with the skin; superficial.
Cyanosis – Blueness of skin owing to circulation of imperfectly oxygenated blood.
Cyclitis – A form of inflammation of the eye.
Cycloplegia – A form of paralysis of the eye muscle.
Cyst – A cavity lined by a well defined epithelium of fibrous tissue or degenerating, inflamed or neoplastic tissue.
Cystic duct – The normal drainage channel for the gall bladder.
Cystitis – A condition which is characterised by an inflammation of the bladder.

D & C – Dilation of the cervix and uterine curettage.
Dactylitis – When a digit (eg toe, finger) becomes inflamed.
Daltonism – Loosely used to mean colour blindness. Accurate meaning: inability to distinguish between red and green.
Debridement – Excision from a wound of dead tissue or tissue the blood supply of which has been so seriously interfered with that it is likely to die, in order to remove food on which organisms can grow.
Debriding – The removal of alien matter in a wound (such as dirt, dead tissue, etc) thereby to clean the wound to facilitate healing.
Decubitus ulcer – Bedsore.
Defibrillation – Restoration of heart rhythm by means of an electric shock.
Degeneration – A breaking down of an organised structure into one less organised in form or function.
Dehydration – The restriction of water in the dietary.
Deltoid muscle – The large muscle covering the shoulder region and running from the scapula and clavicle to the middle of the humerus.
Demyelination – Removal and destruction of the myelin of nerve tissue.
Depression – In psychiatry, the effective attitude of unhappiness and hopelessness.
Dermal – In respect of the skin.
Dermatitis – Inflammation of the skin.
Dermatome – An instrument for cutting split-skin transplants.
Dermatoplasty – General generic term covering skin grafting, plastic surgery, etc.
Dermis – The skin.
Detached retina – A condition where the retina in part or whole, becomes separated from the choroid.
Devitalise – To remove the 'nerve' of a tooth or an organ.
Diabetes – Any of a group of diseases in which there is polyuria and/or an error of metabolism, especially of carbohydrate metabolism.
Diaclasia – The deliberate surgical fracture of a bone – to reset deformity.
Dialysis – The removal of harmful chemicals from the blood by operation of an artificial kidney.
Diaphoresis – Increased perspiration.

Diaphragm – In anatomy, a thin layer of tissue stretched across an opening.

Diaphysis – The central shaft of a large bone.

Diastasis – Forcible simple separation of parts that normally are joined.

Diastem/Diastema – In dentistry, a space between two teeth not produced by loss of the tooth or teeth normally lying between them.

Diastole – The period of the cardiac cycle from the closure of the aortic and pulmonary valves to the beginning of the next ventricular contraction. The period when the heart fills with blood and dilates.

Diastolic – Referring or belonging to diastole.

Diplegia – Paralysis of both sides of the body.

Diplopia – Double vision.

Disarticulation – To separate the joints (by injury or surgery).

Disc – A flat, circular; coin shaped structure.

Discography – Demonstration of a disc of a joint by the injection of a radio-opaque medium.

Dislocation – Displacement of one part upon another, usually confined to the abnormal displacement of one bone upon another at a joint.

Distal – Extremity of a limb or organ. Furthest from centre of body.

Diuresis – Excretion of urine, usually meaning an excessive quantity.

Diuretic – Producing an increase in the amount of urine.

Diverticulitis – A condition of inflammation of the diverticulum or diverticula in the colon which may lead to colic and constipation and eventually to intestinal obstruction.

Dorsal spine – Part of the spine where ribs join.

Dorsiflexion – Backward movement of joints.

Dorsum – Back or outer surface.

Duodenal – Relating or belonging to the duodenum.

Duodenitis – A condition of inflammation of the duodenum.

Duodenum – Name applied to the first 20–25 cm of the small intestine.

Dura mater – The outermost membrane of the brain, thick, dense and inelastic.

Dys – (prefix) Difficult, abnormal, impaired.

Dysaethesia – Impairment, not to the point of anaesthesia, of any of the senses, particularly the sense of touch.

Dysarthria – Difficulty in articulating words caused by disease of the central nervous system. Implies a disorder of the brain stem functions regulating the speech musculature.

Dysgenesis – Impairment or loss of power to procreate; lack of proper development.

Dysmorphia – Ill-shaped; deformed.

Dyspareunia – Difficulty or pain in coitus.

Dysphagia – Difficulty in swallowing.

Dysphasia – Difficulty in speaking with inability to co-ordinate words and arrange them in correct order.

Dyspnoea – Difficulty in breathing, breathlessness.

Dyspraxia – Impairment of the ability to perform co-ordinated movements.

Dysthesia – A condition of ill-health or of illness; (applied particularly to a condition caused by a non-febrile vascular disorder); impatience or bad temper engendered by illness.

Dystocia – Difficult childbirth.

Dystrophy – The deterioration or degeneration of an organ or body tissues.

Dysuria – Pain during urination.

Eburnation – The final result of osteoarthritis, when the cartilage at the articulating surface of a bone is totally worn down.

Ecchymosis – An extravasation of blood.

Ecdysis – The shedding of skin.

Eclampsia – a type of epileptic convulsion, to which pregnant women are particularly susceptible, caused by collection of harmful chemicals in the brain which irritate the brain substance.

Ectropion – Eversion, usually of the eyelids, especially of the lower.

Eczma – A type of inflammation of the skin.

Edentulous – No teeth.

Effusion – The escape of fluid (eg pus, blood etc) into a body cavity.

Electrocardiogram – A record of the electrical potentials generated by the activation process of the muscles of the heart.

Electro-encephalogram – A graph derived from a recording of brain activity, used for example in the diagnosis of epilepsy. (Also note: computered tomography of the brain – CT brain scan.)

Electrolytes – The ionised salts in the blood.

Electromyogram – The graphic record after amplification of muscle action potentials.

Embolism – Plugging of blood vessels by material carried through larger blood vessels in the blood stream.

Embrasure – The gaps existing between neighbouring teeth.

Embryo – In man the term is usually restricted to the first 8 weeks of intrauterine life, the term fetus being employed after that.

Emetic – Causing vomiting. Any substance that causes vomiting.

Eminence – A projection – usually describing that on a bone.

Emphysema – Collection of air in certain parts of the body where it is not usually present.

Enarthrosis – A joint, such as the hip or shoulder, which operates by way of a ball and socket.

Endocarditis – Inflammation of the lining of the heart, caused either by microbial infection (bacterial endocarditis) or by a generalised inflammatory disorder such as rheumatic fever or a collagenvascular disease = subacute endocarditis.

Endocardium – The smooth thin endothelial membrane which lines the chambers of the heart and is continuous with the endothelium of the large blood vessel.

Endocervix – The endometrium of the cervix uteria.

Endocrine – Of or pertaining to internal secretions; relating to a gland secreting directly into the blood stream and not into a duct.

Endocrinology – The science of the endocrine glands and their secretions.

Endometrium – Mucous membrane which lines the uterus.

Enema – An injection of fluid into the rectum for cleaning, healing, sedative, diagnostic or nutritive purposes.

Endoscope – An instrument with which the interior of a hollow organ can be examined.

Endoscopy – Examination of hollow organs of the body by means of an endoscope.

Enophthalmos – Recession of the eyeball into the cavity of the orbit.

Enteritis – Inflammation of the mucous membrane of the intestine.

Enterocentesis – The removal of an undue quantity of fluid from the stomach (or intestine) by use of a hollow needle.

Enucleate – To remove an eye.

Enuresis – Bed wetting.

Enzyme – A protein substance which will catalyse a biochemical reaction.

Eosinophila – The condition in which there is abnormal increase in the number of eosinophil leucocytes in the blood; it may be a relatively benign eosinophilic leucocytosis of ideopathic aetiology, a secondary to an allergic condition in the patient, a concomitant of parasitic infestation, skin lesions, acute infections or Hodgkin's Disease, or more serious but rare acute or chronic eosinophilic leukaemia of unknown cause.

Epicondyle – Protuberance above a condyle at the end of a bone which articulates with another bone.

Epicondylitis – Inflammation of the epicondyle of the humerus or of the area immediately surrounding it.

Epicranius – The scalp muscle.

Epidermis – The outer protective layer of the skin, composed of stratified pavement epithelium of ectodermal origin, fused to the underlying dermis of the skin.

Epidural – Relating to the outermost membrane covering the spinal cord.

Epigastric – Referring to the epigastrium.

Epilepsy – An affection of the nervous system characterised by recurrent paroxysmal symptoms, the epileptic fit.

Epiphysis – The growing part of a bone – at the end of the bone (epiphysitis: inflammation of the epiphysis). Secondary bone-forming centre attached to a bone and separated from it by cartilage.

Epistaxis – Nose bleed.

Epithelial – Pertaining to or composed of epithelium.

Epithelium – A closely packed sheet of cells arranged in one or more layers, the component parts of which usually adhere to each other along their edges and surfaces. It covers the external surface of the entire body and lines all hollow structures within the body with the exception of blood cells and lymphatics.

Erb's palsy – The upper plexus type of birth injury to the brachial plexus; a traction injury to the fifth and perhaps the sixth cervical root. There is paralysis of the deltoid, brachialis, biceps and brachioradialis muscles, giving inability to abduct the arm or to flex or supinate the forearm.

Erythema – Redness of the skin due to hyperaemia.

Erythrocyte – A mature non-nucleated, red blood cell.

Eschar – The slough or dry scab, eg that forms on an area of skin that has been burned.

Esophagos – See oesophagos.

Ethmoid bone – An unpaired cranial bone lying in front of the sphenoid bone and composed of a perpendicular plate, forming the upper part of the nasal septum, and a lateral mass on either side filled with air cells and lying between the nose and the orbit.

Eutocia – Normal labour and childbirth without complications.

Eversion – The bending outwards of a joint.

Exacerbation – Increase in severity of a disease or in violence of symptoms.

Excise – To cut tissue away surgically.

Euthyroidism – The condition in which there is normal healthy function of the thyroid.

Exophthalmos – Prominence or protrusion of the eyeball, due to disease, to such an extent that the eyelids will not cover it.

Exostosis – Any growth of bone from the surface of a bone.

Expection – The period during which the reproductive organs are returning to their normal condition following labour. The duration is about six weeks.

Exploratory operation – An operation to investigate and decide upon the cause of symptoms.

Exsanguinated – Partial blood loss to a dangerous degree.

Extension – Straightening out of a joint.

Extensor – An extensor muscle, to stretch out.

External Os – The outer most visible part of the cervix.

Extradural – Situated on the outside of or lying outside the dura mater.

Extra-ocular – On the outside of, or outside, the eyeball.

Extravasation – The act of forcing a fluid out of, or allowing it to escape from its proper duct or vessel.

Exudate – An exuded substance.

FNA – Fine needle aspiration.

Facet – That surface on a bone which is small and flat (analogous to the facet of a precious stone).

Fauces – Structures at the back of the throat.

Fibrosis – Thickening of tissue.

Fistula – Abnormal communication.

Flexion – Bending of a joint.

Flexor – The bending movement of a joint.

Focal brain damage – Direct damage from blunt injury.

Foramen – A hole or aperture.

Foramen Magnum – The hole in the base of the skull through which the spinal chord exits.

Foramen Ovale – Of the heart; an aperture in the interatrial septum of the heart which normally closes at or shortly after birth.

Foramen Ovale, patent – Persistence of the foramen ovale after birth.

Frenum/Frenulum/Frenus – A term originally denoting the folds of mucous membrane running from the gums to the lip or tongue and limiting undue movement; now applied to many other structures similar in appearance.

Friable – Easily reduced to powder, easily crumbled. In bacteriology, term applied to a culture which is dry and brittle and falls to powder when it is shaken or touched.

Frigidity – Want of generative heat, lack of warmth of feeling.

Frontal – Relating or belonging to the forehead.

Frontal bone – An unpaired cranial bone forming the forehead and the greater part of the orbital roof, and lying in front of the parietals.

Funduscopy – Ophthelmoscopic examination of the ocular fundus.

Fusion – The joining together, normally of two bones.

Gall-bladder – A pear shaped sac on the inferior surface of the right lobe of the liver in which bile is stored and concentrated.

Gallstone – A concretion which may form in the gall-bladder or bile-duct.

Ganglion – A group of nerve cells with a common function, especially applied to a collection outside the central nervous system.

Gangrene – Necrosis and putrefaction of tissue due to cutting off the blood supply.

Gastrectomy – The surgical removal of the stomach in whole or part.

Gastric – Relating or belonging to the stomach.

Gastritis – Inflammation of the gastric mucous membrane.

Gastrocnemius muscle – The most superficial of the calf muscles.

Gastro-enteritis – Inflammation of the mucous coat of the stomach and intestines as a result of infection with a bacterium of the salmonella genus.

Gastro-intestinal – Relating or belonging to the stomach and the intestine.

Gastrostomy – The establishment by abdominal operation of a communication between the interior of the stomach and skin surface for tube feeding in patients with complete inability to swallow.

Gastrotomy – The surgical opening of the stomach.

Genioplasty – Plastic surgery to build up cheek bone.

Genital – Relating or belonging to the generative organs, or to reproduction.

Genu – Knee.

Germinal – Relating to or belonging to a germ.

Gibbus – An angular and sharp backward curvature of the spine usually the result of a disease or tumour.

Gingivitis – Gum inflammation.

Ginglymus – A hinge joint.

Glaucoma – A term signifying increased intra-ocular pressure and its consequences. The end result if untreated, the eye being completely blind.

Glenoid cavity – A socket or a smooth hollow depression, located on the upper, outer portion of the shoulder blade.

Gliosis – A proliferation of astocytes which may be diffuse or local, often seen as a reparative process following cerebral injury.

Glomerular – Relating to or belonging to or having the character of a glomerulus of the kidney.

Glomerulonephritis – Nephritis which is characterised primarily by inflammation of the glomeruli of the kidney and which may appear in acute, subacute or chronic forms.

Glomerulus – A compact tuft or tangled mass of branching process.

Glomus – A cluster of blood cells gloserulonephricis Nephritis which is characterised primarily by inflammation of the glomeruli of the kidneys.

Glossopharyngeal nerve – The 9th cranial nerve which controls the muscles of the back portion of the roof of the mouth; soft palate.

Gluteal – Of the buttock.

Gluteus maximus – A large muscle arising from the iliac bone, the sacrum and the sacrotuberous ligament.

Goitre – An enlargement of the thyroid gland. It is usually taken to mean a visible enlargement.

Goodpasture's syndrome – A rare condition leading to renal failure.

Grain – A unit of weight equal to 64.798 mg: equivalent to 0.0648 gramme.

Gramme – A thousandth part of a kilogramme.

Granulation – The formation of small rounded masses of tissue.

Granulomatosis – A chronic inflammatory process leading to the formation of nodules or tumour-like masses.

Groin – The external groove or depression that marks the junction of the lower part of the anterior abdominal wall and the thigh.

Guillaine-barre syndrome – Acute infective polyneuritis.

Gustatory – Relating to taste organs.

Gynaecological – Relating or belonging to gynaecology.

Gynaecologist – A physician who specialises in the diagnosis and treatment of diseases peculiar to women.

Gynaecology – Broadly speaking the study of disease in the female.

Gynaecomastosis – A condition in the male in which the mammary glands are excessively developed.

Haemangioma – An innocent tumour composed of dilated blood vessels.

Haemarthrosis – The swelling and pain resulting from bleeding into a joint.

Haematology – The science which is concerned with the blood and blood-forming tissues.

Haematoma – Collection of blood forming swelling.

Haematuria – The presence of blood in the urine.

Haemoglobin – The respitory pigment of vertebrates which occurs in the red blood cells.

Haemomangioma – An innocent tumour composed of dilated blood vessels.

Haemopericardium – Accumulation of blood in the pericardial sack, usually from rupture of a diseased heart muscle or from rupture of the ascending aorta.

Haemophilous – A genus of bacteria.

Haemopneumothorax – An accumulation of blood and gas in the pleural cavity.

Haemoptysis – The expectoration of bright red blood from the lungs of bronchia and trachea.

Haemorrhage – Bleeding; the escape of blood from any part of the vascular system.

Haematosis – A slowing of the movement of the blood; the arrest of haemorrhage by eg ligation of an artery.

Haemothorax – Effusion of blood into the pleural cavity.

Halitosis – Bad breath.

Hallux – Great toe.

Hamate bone – The most medial bone in the distal row of carpal bones.

Hamstring – A tendon at the back of the knee.

Hemianopia – Loss of half the vision in each eye.

Hemiparesis – Unilateral muscular paralysis.

Hemiplegia – Paralysis of one side of the body.

Heparinised – The effect of the use of a drug to prevent clotting.

Hepatiscostomy – The making of a surgical opening in the main bile duct.

Hepatitis – Inflammation of the liver.

Hernia – The protrusion of an internal organ through a defect in the wall of the anatomical cavity in which it lies, or into a subsidiary compartment of that cavity.

Herniation – The process of formation of a hernia or a protrusion.

Hernioplasty – The surgical repair of a hernia.

Herpes – Inflammation of the skin or mucous membrane, with clusters of deep-seated vesicles.

Hiatus – An opening.

Histiocyt – Plays an important role in the tissue defences as a scavanger.

Histiocytosis – A condition in which histcytes are present in the blood.

Histogenesis – Tissue formation.

Histology – Study of structure of tissues by means of special straining techniques together with light and electron microscopy.

Histiopathology – Histological description or investigation of diseased tissues.

Hodgkin's disease – A disease of unknown aetiology characterised by enlargement of the lymph glands, hyperplasia of the lymphoid tissue in the spleen, liver and other organs, and anaemia.

Homeostasis – The system whereby body functions (temperature, blood pressure, etc) remain in equilibrium whatever the outside environment).

Homoplasty – Repair of damaged tissue by grafting on similar tissues from another of the same species.

Horner's syndrome – Slight enophthalmos, miosis, and slight ptosis, with narrowing of the palpebral fissure, with sometimes decrease of sweating vasadilatation of the conjunctival, retinal and facial vessels, and rise in the skin temperature.

Humerus – The longest and largest bone of the arm.

Hyalitis – A form of eye inflammation.

Hydramnios – Excessive amniotic fluid.

Hydrocele – A circumscribed collection of fluid, particularly a collection of fluid in the tunica vaginalis testis.

Hydrocephalus – Distension of the cerebal ventricles by the accumulation of fluid.

Hydrogen – The lightest of the chemical elements, gaseous, colourless, odourless and tasteless.

Hydrosalpinx – A uterine tube distended with fluid. This is now held to be the end result of perions inflammation.

Hyoid bone – A V shaped bone situated at the base of the tongue.

Hyper – (prefix) Over, to excess, above normal.

Hyperacusis – Excessive sensitivity to sight, sound, taste and smell.

Hyperaesthesia – Excessive sensitivity to sound, taste, smell or feeling.

Hyperextension – Abnormal movement of a limb beyond its limit.

Hypermesis – Excessive vomitting.

Hypermethripia – A condition in which the image of an object viewed by the eye is formed behind the retina.

Hypermetropic – Long sighted.

Hyperpathia – Excessive sensory sensibility. A condition of extreme illness.

Hyperplasia – Any condition in which there is an increase in the number of the cells in a part.

Hypertension – High arterial blood pressure.

Hypertonia – Excessive tension, as of arteries or muscle. Excessive activity as of muscles. State of increased intra-ocular tension.

Hypertrophy – Enlargement of cells generating increase in size of organ or tissue.

Hyperventilation – Abnormally fast or deep breathing.

Hyphaemia – Effusion of blood into the anterior chamber.

Hypo – (prefix) Below normal, decreased.

Hypoaesthesia – Diminished sensibility of touch.

Hypocalcemia – Metabolic disturbance with a drop in the serum level of calcium.

Hypoglossal nerve – The 12th and last cranial nerve.

Hypohidrosis – Failure to sweat sufficiently, for environmental temperature/physical exertion.

Hypophysis – An outgrowth.

Hypopituitarism – Sparse facial hair.

Hypoplasia – Failure of tissue to develop fully.

Hyposecretion – Secretion in quantity below the normal.

Hypotension – A fall in blood pressure below the normal range.

Hypothalamus – The part of the diencephalon which lies below the thalamus and forms the floor and the side walls of the 3rd ventricle below the hypothalamic sulcus.

Hypothyroidis – A condition caused by under activity of the thyroid gland; thyroid deficiency.

Hypotonia – Lessened tone or tension generally, or applied to any body structure.

Hypotropia – Squint.

Hypoxaemia – A condition in which the blood contains too little oxygen.

Hypoxia – A supply of O2 to the tissues which is inadequate to maintain normal tissue respiration.

Hypsarrhythmia – A severe generalised disorganisation of the electro-encephalogram in children.
Hysterectomy – Removal of the womb (uterus). (Vaginal hysterectomy – removal of womb from below.)
Hysteria – A neurotic disorder the symptoms of which may take any imaginable form.
Hysterosalpingogram – Injection of radio-opaque material into the uterus and uterine tubes and subsequent X-ray examination of the organs.

Ileostomy – Surgical incision of the ileum through the wall of the abdomen.
Ileum – Small intestine.
Ilium – Superior bone of pelvis (hip bone).
Immunisation – The production of immunity by specific means.
Immunoglobulins – Proteins endowed with known antibody activity and certain other proteins related to them by chemical structure.
Impacted – Wedged closely together, as calculi or unerupted teeth.
Implant – In dentistry, the plate to which false teeth are attached.
Impotence – Male sterility.
Incisor – Any one of the four front teeth in each jaw.
Incontinence – The lack of voluntary control over the discharge of faeces or urine.
Incus – The bone situated in the middle ear between and articulating with the malleus and stapes, ie the central one of the three auditory ossicles.
Induration – Excessive toughening of an organ or tissue.
Infarction – Death of whole or part of organ, caused by obstruction of relevant artery (eg myocardial infarction).
Infertility – Barrenness; inability to produce offspring.
Inflammation – The reactive state of hyperaemia and exudation from its blood vessels, with consequent redness, heat, swelling and pain, which a tissue enters in response to physical or chemical injury or bacterial invasion.
Infra-orbital – Situated below the level of the floor of the orbit.
Inguinal – Of the groin.
Injection – The act of propelling a fluid into the body, especially by the use of a hollow needle.
Innominate bone – The hip bone.
Inotrophic – Of nerve fibres influencing the contracting of muscles and muscular tissue, particularly of the heart.
Insomnia – The condition of being unable to sleep.
Intercostal – Situated between ribs.
Interfrontal – Situated between the two hearts of the frontal bone before they have fused.
Internal rotation – Rotating a limb inwards.
Interstice – Any small space or crevice present between parts of the body.
Intervertebral – Between two adjacent vertebrae.
Intervertebral disc – Disk-like flattened cartilagenous structure between two vertebrae.
Intestine – The part of the digestive tract that extends from the stomach (pylorus) to the anus.
Intracranial – Inside the skull.
Intraduct – Within a duct or the ducts of a secreting gland.
Intramuscular – Occurring within the substance of a muscle.
Intraneural – Within a nerve.
Intrathecal – Within a sheath.

Intravenous – Within or introduced into a vein.

Intravenous injection – An injection into the vein.

Introitus – The entrance into any hollow organ or canal; an aperture.

Iridoplegia – The paralysis of the iris in the eye.

Iris – A thin circular disc, perforated, usually a little to the nasal side, by the pupil.

Iritis – Inflammation of the iris.

Iritomy – Surgical incision of the iris.

Irradiation – A spread from a common centre; treatment of disease by various forms of radiant energy.

Ischaemia – Deficiency of blood in part of body.

Ischium – Of the three fetal pelvic bones, the one that after fusion forms the inferior and posterior portion of the hip bone.

Isometric – Having equal dimensions.

–Itis (suffix) Inflammation.

Jaundice – Yellowing of skin through accumulation of bile products in the blood.

Jejunum – The proximal two-fifths of the small intestine extending from the end of the duodenum to the ileum.

Jugular vein – The chief vein of the head and neck, carries blood from the head to the heart.

Juxta-articular – In close proximity to a joint; in the neighbourhood of a joint.

Keloid – Overgrowth of fibrous tissue usually on site of scar of previous injury.

Keratectomy – The surgical removal of a superficial layer of the cornea.

Keratic – Horny, belonging to the cornea.

Keratitis – Inflammation of the cornea.

Keratoplasty – Corneal graft.

Ketosis – The presence of excessive quantities of ketone bodies in the tissues.

Kidney – One of the paired organs, right and left in the lumbar region below the diaphragm, lateral to the spine in the retroperitoneal tissue plane.

Kirschner wire – Wire used in skeletal traction.

Knuckle – A prominence produced by the head of any of the metacarpal bones.

Kocher's incision – For exposure of the gall-bladder; an incision from the tip of the xiphoid process to the tip of the ninth costal cartilage parallel to the rib margin and 25mm below it.

Kyphoscoliosis – Forward and lateral curvature of the spine.

Kyphosis – Forward curvature in the vertebrae; in mild form, can cause neck to lean forward (the hunch-back condition).

Labial – Of the lips either of the mouth or the vulva.

Labioplasty – Surgical repair to the lips either of the mouth or the vulva.

Labyrinth – An interconnecting system of cavities applied especially to the inner ear.

Labyrinthitis – Otitis interna; a condition of inflammation of the labyrinth (ear).

Laceration – A rent or tear.

Lachrymal – Relating to the production of tears.

Lacrimal bone – A small delicate bone forming the anterior part of the medial wall of the orbit and part of the side wall of the nose.

Lamella – A thin plate or layer.

Laminectomy – Operation to the backbone to reach the spinal cord.

Laparoscope – A type of trocar provided with an illuminating mechanism with which the cavity of the peritoneum, the abdominal viscera and in particular the surface of the peritoneum and liver can be examined.

Laparoscopy – Technique to inspect pelvic organs by distending abdominal cavity with gas, and then inserting a laparoscope below the umbilicus.

Laparotomy – Incision into abdomen to explore for the possibility of some disease.

Laryngeal – Pertaining to the larynx.

Laryngectomy – The removal of part of the larynx.

Larynx – The organ situated at the upper end of the trachea and concerned with the production of the voice.

Lateral – To the side, external.

Lesion – Damage, injury, harmful change in functions or texture of organs.

Leucocytosis – Increase in the total number of leucocytes in the blood above the normal.

Leukaemia – A malignant neoplasm of blood-forming organs characterised by diffuse replacement of bone marrow with proliferating leucocyte precursors, abnormal numbers and forms of immature white cells in circulation, and infiltration of lymph nodes, spleen, liver and other sites.

Ligament – Short, flexible fibrous tissue binding together bones of the body.

Lithium – An element of the alkaline metals group.

Liver – The largest gland in the body, situated on the right side of the upper abdomen below the diaphragm.

Lordosis – Forward curvature of the spine (the opposite of 'Kyphosis').

Lumbago – Pain in the lower part of the back. (Note – not a diagnosis; similarly fibrositis and sciatica.)

Lumbar – Applying to the lower back in the region of the lumbar spine or adjacent muscles.

Lumbosacral spine – Spine composed of lumbar vertebrae and sacrum.

Lunate bone – A bone of the wrist which articulates with the radius and ulna to the rear and the capitate bone to the front.

Lung – The paired organ of respiration situated on each side of the mediastinum.

Lymph – A pale yellow clear or cloudy fluid that flows in the lymphatic channels.

Lymphodermia – Any morbid condition affecting the lymph glands or associated lymph vessels of the skin.

McMurray's test – Test for tear of knee cartilage.

Macrocytosis – Red blood corpuscles being larger than normal.

Macrophage – A large phagocytic cell found in connective tissues especially in areas of inflammation.

Macula – A transient or permanent, congenital or acquired, small or large, circumscribed alteration in the colour of the skin without any change in the consistency of the skin or disturbance of its surface.

Malacia – Pathological softening of an organ or tissue.

Malar – Relating to the cheek or cheek bone.

Malignant – Threatening life or tending to cause death; the opposite of benign.

Malingerer – An individual who feigns disease or illness.

Malleolus – A rounded bony prominence on either side of the ankle joint.

Malocclusion – The lack of occlusion, or the abnormal occlusion existing between the teeth of opposite jaws either when the jaws are at rest or during their physiological movements.

Malunion – The failure of bones properly to align after fracture resulting in deformity.

Mammary – Belonging or relating to the mammary gland.

Mammary gland – The breast.

Mammogram – A radiograph of the mammary gland.

Mammoplasty – Operation to reduce the size of the female breasts.

Mandible – Lower jaw.

Mania – A loose term frequently applied to any form of mental disorder.

Manipulation – The procedure whereby a joint is moved to reduce or eliminate stiffness; can be used to replace a dislocation.

Mastectomy – Removal of breast.

Mastication – Chewing food.

Maxilla – Either of the pair of bones constituting the upper jaw.

Medial – Middle, internal.

Median – Placed in the middle, mesial.

Median nerve – One of the main nerves of the forearm and hand.

Mediastinum – The space between the two pleural sacs.

Medulla – The marrow of bones.

Medulla oblongata – The tapering candal portion of the hind brain, extending from the posterior border of the pons to the first segment of the spinal cord.

Melanoma – A skin tumour consisting of darkly pigmented cells.

Membrane – A thin layer of tissue which covers a surface or divides a space or organ.

Meningioma – A benign meningeal tumour.

Meningitis – Inflammation of the membranes of the brain or spinal cord.

Meniscetomy – Removal of cartilage in knee (to ease pain and locking of joint).

Meniscus – Semi-lunar cartilage as in wrist or knee joints.

Menorrhagia – Excessive discharge of the menses or excessive prolongation of menses.

Mesothelioma – A tumour of the lining of the lung which enlarges slowly and insidiously to encase the lung gradually in a fixed unmoving cocoon of tumour tissue. The lung, thus enclosed, ceases to function and there is therefore a gradual increase in breathlessness. Almost invariably the result of exposure to asbestos.

Metabolism – The chemical processes participating in the essential for the phenomena of life.

Metacarpal bones – Any of the bones of the palm.

Metaphysis – That part of the bone which is growing, between the ends and the shaft. The region of a long bone corresponding to the termination of the epiphysis and the beginning of the diaphysis.

Metastasis – The transfer of disease from its primary site to distant parts of the body by way of natural passages, blood vessels, lymphatics, or direct continuity.

Metatarsal bones – Five long bones forming the skeleton of the anterior part of the foot.

Metatarsalgia – Aching pain in the region of the metatarsal bones of the foot.

Metrorrhexis – Rupture of the womb.

Miscarriage – Abortion, expulsion of the fetus before it is viable.

Mitosis – Cell multiplication.

Molar – A broad topped tooth used for grinding; one of the two back teeth in the deciduous dentition, or one of the three back teeth in the permanent dentition situated on each side of the jaws.

Monoplegia – A paretic condition affecting one muscle or group of muscles, one limb or one part of the body only.

Morphology – That aspect of biology which deals with the structure and form of living organisms.

Morton's neuralgia – A condition associated with falling of the metatarsal arch and pressure on the digital branches of the lateral plantar nerve.

Mucocele – A dilated cavity containing an accumulation of mucoid substance.

Muscle – Muscular tissue.

Muscular – Relating to the muscles.

Myasthenia – Weakness of muscles from whatever cause.

Mydriatic – Any drug causing dilation of the pupil.

Myectomy – The surgical removal of part of a muscle.

Myelitis – Inflammation of bone marrow; osteomyelitis inflammation or degeneration of the spinal cord.

Myelogram – X-ray of the spinal canal after injection of a radio-opaque contrast medium into the subarachnoid space.

Myocardial – Relating to the myocardium.

Myocarditis – Inflammation of the myocardium.

Myocardium – Middle of the three layers which go to form the walls of the heart.

Myoclonus – A sudden shock-like muscular contraction which may involve one or more muscles or a few fibres of a muscle.

Myodynia – Muscle pain.

Myodystonia – Any disorder affecting muscle tone.

Myopathy – Any diseased condition of the muscles.

Myositis – Inflammation of voluntary muscles.

Myotasis – Muscular extension, as in stretching.

Myotomy – Operation to divide a muscle.

Naevus – A birth mark.

Narcotic – A drug that induces a stuporous condition or sleep.

Nares – Nostrils.

Nasal – Of the nose.

Nausea – A feeling of sickness with a desire to vomit.

Navicular bone – An irregular tarsal bone situated on the medial side of the foot, between the talus and the three cuneiform bones.

Necrophilism – Unnatural pleasure in corpses and in being in their presence.

Necrosis – Death of tissue, mortification of bones.

Neoplasia – Growth of a new tissue.

Neoplasm – Any new and morbid formation of tissue; a tumour.

Nephritis – Inflammation of kidneys.

Nephrotomy – Operation into the kidney.

Nerve – A bundle of nerve fibres along which impulses pass from one part of the body to another, each fibre being the axon of a nerve cell (neuron) surrounded by a neurilemma and often a myelin sheath.

Neuralgia – A painful affection of the nerves due to functional disturbances or to neuritis.

Neurasthenia – Irritability, headache, dizziness, anxiety, impatience – being a condition caused by injury to the skull or neurosis.

Neuritis – Inflammation of a nerve, with pain and tenderness and diminution or loss of function in its distribution ie of sensation or motor power.

Neurectomy – Removal of nerve (eg neurotomy – severing a nerve).

Neuro-anastomosis – The surgical formation of an anastomosis between nerves.

Neurocranium – That part of the skull in which is situate the brain.

Neurofibromatosis – A familial disorder in which developmental changes occur in the skin, nervous system, bones and viscera.

Neurogenesis – Development and growth of nerves and nervous tissue.

Neurogenic – Producing nerve tissue. Rising in a nerve; caused by some disordered condition of the nerves or nervous system.

Neurology – The section of medicine that deals with the study and treatment of diseases of the nervous system.

Neuroma – Benign tumour made up of nerve cells, caused by cutting into a nerve.

Neuropathy – Any disorder of peripheral nerves (the symptoms being usually numbness and weakness).

Neuropraxia – Failure or impairment of functions due to a neurological condition (only temporary; condition permits full recovery).

Neuroretinitis – Inflammation of optic nerve and retina.

Neurosis – A pathological emotional state, eg anxiety state, phobic state, hysteria state.

Neurovascular – Relating to the nervous and vascular systems.

Nitrogen – A colourless tasteless gas making up 78% of the atmosphere.

Node – A small knot of tissue.

Nucleus pulposus – The soft pulpy centre of an intervertebral disc.

Nulliparous – Never having given birth to a child.

Nutation – Involuntary nodding the head.

Nystagmus – A condition in which the eyes are seen to move in a more or less rhythmical manner, from side to side, up and down or in a rotary manner from the original point of fixation.

Obesity – An excessive accumulation of fat in the body.

Obsessive compulsive – Characterised by the occurrence of thoughts and actions against the will of the subject and with his recognition of their apparent irrationality.

Obstetrician – One who is practised in obstetrics; an accoucher.

Obstetrics – That branch of medicine and surgery dealing with the care of women during pregnancy, childbirth and puerperium.

Occipital – Referring to the occiput (the back part of the head or skull).

Occipital bone – The composite bone at the posterior and inferior part of the skull, articulating anteriorly with the temporal, parietal and sphenoid bones, and containing the foramen magnum.

Occiput – Back of skull.

Occupational therapy – A recognised procedure whereby a person is given something practical to do to facilitate recovery from illness.

Ocular – Relating to the eye.

Oculomotor nerve – The 3rd cranial nerve, arising from cells in the mid-brain. Supplies all the extrinsic muscles of the eye except the superior oblique and the lateral rectus. Also carries the nerves of supply to the sphincter of the pupil and the ciliary muscle.

Odont – (prefix) To do with a tooth.

Oedema – Swelling due to accumulation of fluid in tissue.

Oesophagectomy – Exclusion of part of the oesophagus.

Oesophagitis – Inflammation of the gullet.

Olfaction – The sense of smell.

Olfactory nerves – The nerves of smell.

Oligaemic – Relating to deficiency in the blood.

Oligo – (prefix) Small, few.

Oliguria – Daily output of urine below normal levels.

Omentum – A double layer of peritoneum connecting two viscera; usually applied only to those layers which connect the stomach with other viscera.

Omphalic – Referring to the umbilicus.

Onych – Of the nails.

Onychalgia – A painful condition affecting the nails.

Oophorectomy – Excision of an ovary.

Ophthalmectomy – Surgical removal of eye.

Opthalmia – Usually conjunctivitis but sometimes used loosely for inflammation of the whole eye.

Ophthalmic nerve – The first division of the trigeminal nerve, supplying the eyeball, through its nasociliary branch, the lacrimal gland, conjunctiva and eyelids through its lacrimal and frontal and nasociliary branches, and the forehead and scalp by the frontal nerve.

Ophthalmitis – Inflammation of eye.

Ophthalmologist – A specialist in the investigation and treatment of eye diseases and defects.

Ophthalmorrhexis – The bursting open of the eye ball.

Ophthalmoscopy – Inspection of the back of the eye with an ophthalmoscope.

Optic nerve – The nerve of sight.

Optometrist – One who practises optometry.

Optometry – The process of assessment of the visual acuity, and the correction of visual defects by the fitting of spectacles.

Orbit – The large bony cavity which contains the eyeball, its associated vessels, nerves, muscles etc formed by parts of the frontal, sphenoid, zygomatic, maxillary, ethmoid, palatine and lacrimal bones – the eye socket.

Orchidectomy – Surgical removal of the testis.

Orchitis – Inflammation affecting the testis and characterised by hypertrophy, pain and the sensation of weight.

Organic – Relating to a body organ.

Orthodontist – One who corrects the malocclusion of teeth.

Orthopaedic – Relating to or employed in orthopaedics, ie surgery.

Orthosis – The procedure of adjusting or otherwise correcting deformity.

Os calcis – Calcaneum, heel bone.

Ossification – The process by which bone is formed.

Ostectomy – Removal of bone.

Osteitis – Bone inflammaton.

Osteoarthritis – Degenerative disease of joint involving joint cartilage (ie when it wears out).

Osteoarthrotomy – Operation to excise bone adjoining joint.

Osteochondritis – A degenerative change in one or more epiphyses commencing with necrosis and fragmentation followed by repair and regeneration.

Osteomyelitis – Inflammation of the interior of a bone, especially affecting the marrow spaces.

Osteopath – One who is expert in the practice of osteopathy.

Osteopathy – A system of treatment of disease by manipulation.

Osteoporosis – Loss of bony tissue causing bones to become softer and liable to bend or to fracture.

Osteorrhaphy – The operation of suturing or wiring together the fragments of a fractured bone.

Osteotomy – The operation of cutting through a bone.

Otology – The branch of medicine which deals with the science and treatment of aural diseases.

Otoscope – A tube or funnel used for examination of air.

Otoscopy – Inspection of the air and particularly the tympanic membrane with the aid of the otoscope.

Otitis – Inflammation of the ear.

Otosclerosis – A thickening of the bone of the middle and internal ear producing deafness.

Otoplasty – Surgical repair to the ear.

Ovary – The female gonad, one of a pair of organs attached to the posterior surface of the broad ligament by a mesovarium.

Ovulation – The development and discharge of an ovum from the vesicular ovarian follicle.

Ovum – A female germ cell or egg.

Paget's disease – Osteitis deformans.

Palate – The roof of the mouth.

Palmar – Palm of hand (see volar).

Palmarflexion – Bending of wrist towards arm.

Palpate – To examine or explore by feeling or pressing with the palms or fingers.

Palpitation – Undue awareness of the heart beat occasioned by anxiety, rapid heart action, premature contractions, or paroxysms of abnormal rhythm.

Palsy – Paralysis.

Pancreas – A large compound racemose gland lying transversely on the posterior abdominal wall in the epigastric and left hypochondriac regions of the abdomen.

Pancreatitis – Inflammation of the pancreas.

Papanicolaou's stain or smear – A method of staining smears of various body secretions to detect the presence of a malignant process.

Papillodema – Odema of the optic nerve head. The commonest cause is raised intra-cranial pressure from cerebral tumour.

Papilloma – An innocent stalked tumour of surface or lining of epithelium.

Para – (prefix) Alongside of, abnormality of, beyond.

Paraesthesia – Pins and needles.

Paralysis – Loss of motor power due to a functional or organic disorder of neural or neuro-muscular mechanisms; also called palsy.

Paranoia – A mental disorder, characterised by delusions of persecution.

Paraparesis – An incomplete paralysis affecting the lower extremities.

Paraplegia – Paralysis of both legs resulting from an injury to the dorsal and lumbar cord.

Parasympathetic – The craniosacral subdivision of the autonomic nervous system, functionally antagonistic to the sympathetic division.

Parathyroidormone – The hormone secreted by the parathyroid glands, the function of which is the control of the calcium level in the blood.

Parathyroid glands – These consist of an upper and lower pair of small flattened reddish discs of glandular tissue about 5mm in diameter, though one or both of the lower pair may be found in the mediastinum. They are concerned with calcium metabolism, mobilising calcium from the bone into the blood and thence into the urine and diminishing the output of phosphate from bone.

Paravertebral – Situated alongside of the spinal column, or the vertebra.

Parenteral – Introduced intravenously or by a route other than by way of the digestive tract.

Paresis – Partial paralysis.
Parietal – Referable to the outer lining of membrane of each organ in the peritoneum, pericarduim and pleura.
Parietal bone – One of the bones forming the top of the skull.
Parkinson's disease – Paralysis agitans.
Parosmia – Experience of a smell which is not there; sometimes associated with a feeling of 'other-worldliness'.
Paroxysm – A sudden attack or exacerbation of a disease or of symptoms, particularly recurrent symptoms.
Parturition – The process of childbirth.
Patch testing – The application of a number of substances to the body to establish which are responsible for an allergy.
Patella – Knee cap.
Patellectomy – The operation of removing the patella.
Patellofemoral – Relating to the patella and to the femur.
Pathogenic – Disease producing.
Pathology – The science of disease.
Patulous – Freely expanded, patent.
Pelvimetry – Measurement of the pelvic shape or dimensions.
Pelvis – The basin-shaped ring of bone at the lower end of the trunk.
Penicillin – An antibiotic.
Penis – The male organ of copulation.
Percussion – The art of striking the thoracic or abdominal wall in order to produce sound vibrations from which the nature of the underlying structures can be deduced.
Peri – (prefix) Around.
Periarthritis – Inflammation of tissue around a joint.
Pericapsular – Occurring around a capsule.
Pericardial – Situated around or surrounding the heart.
Pericarditis – Inflammation of the pericardium, visceral, parietal or both.
Pericardium – The membrane which encloses the heart.
Peridentitis – Periodontitis.
Perineum – The area between the medial sides of the thighs laterally, the scrotum anteriorly, and the buttocks posteriorly.
Periodontitis – Inflammation of the periodontal membrane.
Periostitis – Inflammation of the membrane on surface of bone.
Peripheral – Relating to or belonging to the periphery; occurring at or near the periphery, or near the surface of an organ or of the body.
Peritoneoscope – An endoscope, or surgical periscope, for surgical inspection of the contents of the abdomen through a stab incision in the abdominal wall.
Peritoneum – The serous membrane which lines the whole abdominal cavity.
Peritonitis – Inflammation of the peritoneum caused by bacterial infection.
Peroneal nerves – Lateral popliteal nerve. Anterior tibial nerve. Musculo-cutaneous nerve of the lower limb.
Pertussis – Whooping cough.
Petechia – A small spot, generally reddish or purple and ranging in size from a pinhead to a pinpoint, appearing under the epidermis and caused by extravasation of blood.
Petit mal – A form of epileptic fit beginning in childhood and characterised by abrupt loss of consciousness without falling or convulsion, with rapid recovery.
Phalanges – The main bones of the digits of both the hand and foot. There are three, the proximal, middle and distal.

Phenylketonuria – A heriditary disorder that produces brain damage resulting in severe mental retardation.

Phlebitis – Inflammation of a vein.

Phlebotomy – Venesection.

Phobia – Fear.

Photocoagulation – Coagulation of tissue produced by an intense beam of light used in treatment of retinal disease.

Photosensitivity – Abnormal or excessive sensitivity to light.

Phrenic arteries – Branches of the abdominal aorta, given off as the aorta passes between the diaphragmatic crura.

Phrenic nerve – A paired nerve, one of the branches of the cervical plexus, supplies the diaphragm, pericardium and pleura.

Physiotherapy – Treatment to restore full movement of a limb, including massage, infrared/ultra-violet rays. Manipulation, exercise, etc.

Pilosis – A condition in which the growth of hair is excessive or present in unusual places.

Pisiform – The pisiform bone in the wrist.

Pituitary – An endocrine gland situated in the pituitary fossa of the sphenoid bone; the hypophysis cerebri.

Placenta – A complex structure, peculiar to pregnancy.

Plantar – Of sole of foot.

Plantar flexion – Flexing foot.

Plantaris – The plantaris muscle. Sole of the foot.

Plaques – Raised patch of skin, sometimes due to infection.

Plasma – The fluid portion of the blood in which the blood corpuscles are suspended.

Platelet – A very small cell in the blood.

Plegia – (suffix) Paralysis.

Plerosis – The replacement of tissue which has been lost during a spell of bad health.

Pleural cavity – The space between visceral and parietal pleura, pleura being the covering of the lungs (visceral pleura) and of inner surface of chest wall (parietal pleura).

Pleurisy – Inflammation of the pleura.

Plexus – An interwoven network of blood vessels, nerves or lymphatics.

Pneumocardial – Relating to the lungs and the heart.

Pneumocentesis – Lung puncture in order to aspirate the contents of a cavity.

Pneumoconiosis – Lung disease caused by inhalation of dust.

Pneumonia – A general disease in which the essential lesion is an inflammation of the spongy tissue of the lung with consolidation of the alveolar exudate.

Pneumonitis – Inflammation of the lung.

Pneumopericarditis – Pericarditis associated with the presence of air or gas in the pericardial sac.

Pneumothorax – Collection of air in pleural cavity (through lesion in lung or wound in chest wall).

Podiatrist – A chiropodist.

Poliomyelitis – An acute inflammation of the anterior horn cells of the spinal cord due to an enterovirus infection.

Pollux – Thumb.

Polyarteritis nodosa – A collagen disease characterised pathologically by inflammatory changes and fibrinoid necrosis in the walls of medium sized and small arteries.

Polycystic – Composed of or containing many cysts.

Polydipsia – An excessive degree of thirst often associated with diabetes insipidus.

Polydisplasia – The condition of possessing multiple developmental abnormalities.

Polyhydramnios – An abnormality of pregnancy in which liquor amnii exists in excessive quantity.

Polyp – A tumour with a stalk arising from the mucous membranes or the body surface.

Polypectomy – The operation of removing a polyp.

Polypus – Tumour attached by stalk to surface.

Polyuria – Increase in the amount of the urine excreted, usually due to diabetes insipidus.

Pompholyx – An acute vasicular type of eczema which attacks the palms and sides of the fingers and soles of the feet, particularly in individuals who perspire freely.

Pons – A bridge; any tissue which bridges across some space or structure.

Popliteal artery – A continuation of the femoral artery in the popliteal fossa.

Posterior – Behind a part; the back of a part; dorsal.

Postero-anterior – From the back to the front.

Postnatal – Relating or belonging to the period immediately following birth.

Postpartum – Relating to the period immediately following childbirth.

Postural hypotension – A feeling of faintness and light headedness.

Potassium – A soft white metal related to sodium and even more highly reactive.

Pott's disease – Tuberculosis of the spine.

Pott's fracture – Fracture of the lower end of the fibula, with outward displacement of the ankle and foot.

Pouch – A small sac-like appendage or pocket whose cavity communicates with that of a larger parent structure.

Precordium – The part of the anterior aspect of the thorax which overlies the heart.

Pre-eclampsia – A condition arising in pregnancy and characterised by the presence of any two of the following: hypertension, oedema, proteinuria.

Prenatal – Preceding birth; antenatal.

Previable – Before the point at which extra-uterine existence is possible.

Priapism – Persistant erection of the penis.

Process – A course of action or of events.

Proctitis – Inflammation of the rectum.

Proctologist – One who makes a special study of diseases of the anus and rectum and their treatment.

Prolactin – A polypeptide hormone produced by the anterior pituitary and responsible for the stimulation of milk production.

Prolapse – Slipping down or displacement of organ or structure (eg prolapsed intervertebral disc).

Pronation – Rotational movement of forearm so that the palm faces downwards.

Proprioception – Joint position sense.

Proptosis – Forward displacement of the eye.

Prostate – A gland confined to the male, which surrounds and is continuous with the neck of the bladder.

Prostatectomy – Removal of the prostate gland by surgery.

Prostatitis – An inflammatory condition of prostate gland.

Prosthesis – An artificial part, eg a leg or arm.

Proteinuria – A condition marked by the presence of blood in the urine.

Proximal – Nearer centre of body.

Prudendum – The external genitalia.

Pseudo-arteriosclerosis – The arteries become tortuous and signs are therefore produced which simulate those occurring in cases of true arteriosclerosis.

Pseudoneuroma – A tumour present in a nerve trunk, but not composed of nerve substance.

Psychiatrist – A medically qualified person who has undergone post graduate training extending over many years in psychiatry.

Psycho-analysis – A procedure developed by Freud for the investigation of unconscious mental processes in particular by the use of free association and the study of dreams.

Psycho-analyst – One who practises psycho-analysis.

Psychoneurosis – A group of mental disorders characterised by a faulty emotional response to the stresses of life.

Psychosis – A term applied generally to any kind of mental disorder.

Pthisis bulbi – Shrivelling of the eye.

Ptosis – The prolapse or dropping of an organ, drooping of the upper eyelid.

Pubis – The anterior portion of the hip bone, joining its fellow to form the pubic symphysis in the median plane.

Puerperium – The period during which the reproductive organs return to their normal condition following labour. The duration is about six weeks.

Pulmonary – Of the lung.

Pulse – A regularly recurring variation in quantity, usually referring to the change of arterial tension caused by the heart beat.

Purgative – Laxative.

Pyelonephritis – Inflammation affecting the kidneys and the pelvis of the ureter.

Pyorrhoea – A discharge of pus.

Pyrexia – Fever.

Pyrophobia – Morbid fear of fire.

Pyrosis – Heartburn.

Quadrant – One quarter of a circle. A division of any anatomical area that can be divided by the imaginary bisecting lines, one vertical the other horizontal.

Quadrantanopia – Loss of a quadrant of visual field.

Quadriceps femoris muscle – The mass of muscles on the front of the thigh which have a common insertion into the patella.

Quadriplegia – (Also called tetraplegia) Weakness (at worst, paralysis) of upper limbs including hands and loss of function of trunk and legs, resulting from a cervical cord injury.

Rabies – Hydrophobia; a virus disease of warm-blooded animals particularly foxes, wolves, bats and dogs, fatal to humans.

Rachialgia – Any painful infection of the vertebral column, particularly Pott's disease.

Radial nerve – The largest branch of the posterior cord of the brachial plexus (root value C5, 6, 7, 8 and possibly T1).

Radiation – The emission of energy in the form of electro-magnetic waves, or of particles charged or uncharged with electricity.

Radiculitis – Inflammation affecting the root of a spinal nerve.

Radiculopathy – Any diseased condition of the roots of nerves.

Radiopaque – Radio-opaque.

Radius – The lateral bone of the forearm, articulating above with the capitulum of the humerus, below with the scaphoid and lunate bones and medial with the ulna.

Raynaud's Disease – 'Vibration white finger'. A condition in which the arteries of the fingers are unduly reactive and enter spasm: primary when it occurs without any apparent cause, secondary when it is caused by use of machinery or drugs.

Rectal – Relating or belonging to the rectum.

Rectocele – Protrusion of the wall of the rectum into the perineum or vagina.

Reduction – Bringing back to normal position.

Reimplantation – The reinsertion in its original situation of an organ or part which has been removed.

Renal – Of the kidneys.

Resection – Any surgical removal of a portion of the body.

Respiration – The complex process by which the gaseous interchange between the tissues and the external atmosphere is effected.

Retardation – Mental backwardness.

Retina – The innermost coat of the eyeball.

Retinal – Pertaining to the retina.

Retinitis – Inflammation of the retina.

Retinopathy – Any diseased condition of the retina, usually associated with impairment of vision, distortion of objects.

Retrenchment – A plastic procedure for the removal of redundant tissue.

Rhesus – A blood group system which is clinically important because incompatibilities between mother and child can result in the immunisation of the mother to produce antibodies that react against the fetal red cells.

Rheumatoid arthritis – Progressive inflammatory disease of joints with considerable disfiguration.

Rhinitis – An inflammation of the nasal mucous membrane.

Rhinoplasty – The operative correction of a deformity of the nose resulting from injury, disease or congenital defect.

Rhinorrhoea – Profuse discharge of thin mucus from the nose.

Rhizotomy – The cutting of a nerve root, for the relief of pain.

Right homonymous hemianopia – Visual loss of the right field of vision.

Rigor mortis – Stiffening ensuing soon after death.

Romberg's sign or test – With the feet together the patient closes his eyes; swaying or falling is indicative of sensory ataxia due to loss of appreciation of position sense in the lower limbs. It is seen in tabes dorsalis and subacute combined degeneration of the cord.

Rubella – German measles.

Sacral – Relating or belonging to the sacrum.

Sacrolumbar – Relating or belonging to the sacrum and the lumbar region.

Sacrum – Curved triangular element of backbone consisting of five fused vertebrae (sacral vertebrae).

Sacrodynia – pain in sacrum.

Saline – Salt; pertaining to or having the characteristics of common salt.

Salpingectomy – Excision of a uterine tube.

Salpingitis – Inflammation of the uterine (fallopian) tubes; sometimes applied also to inflammation of the pharyngotympanic (eustachian) tubes.

Saphenous – Applied to certain structures in the leg, eg nerve vein.

Saphenous vein – Superficial veins of the foot and leg.

Sarcoma – A malignant tumour of connective tissue or its derivatives.

Sartorius muscle – A long strap like muscle arising from the anterior superior spine of the ilium and passing obliquely across the front of the thigh to its insertion into the upper part of the medial surface of the tibia.

Scaphoid bone – The largest bone in the proximal row of carpal bones, on the lateral side.

Scapula – The flattened triangular bone lying on the posteriolateral aspect of the chest wall.

Schizophrenia – A mental disorder characterised by a special type of disintegration of the personality.

Sciatica – Pain in distribution of sciatic nerve down back of leg. (Note – not a diagnosis.)

Sciatic nerve – The largest nerve in the body, running from the lower spine to the pelvis and down the back of each thigh.

Sclera – The outer, opaque fibrous coat of the eyeball.

Sclerosis – Hardening of a tissue due to inflammation.

Scoliosis – When vertebrae become ``S'' shaped, eg twisted sideways.

Scrotum – A pouch of skin and subcutaneous tissue divided into two by a median septum containing the testes, epididymides and the lower parts of the spermatic cords; situated below the root of the penis.

Sellar – The part of the sphenoid sinus in which the pituitary gland lies.

Semen – A seed.

Sepsis – A term originally used to denote a putrefactive process in the body but now usually referring to infection with pyogenic micro-organisms.

Septicaemia – The severe type of infection in which the blood stream is invaded by large numbers of the causal bacteria which multiply in it and spread.

Septum – A thin partition within or between anatomical structures or organs.

Sequestrectomy – Removal of necrosed bone by surgical means.

Sequestrum – A portion of dead bone which has become detached from the healthy bone tissue, as occurs in necrosis.

Serology – A branch of medical science which is concerned with the study of blood sera.

Serum – The yellowish fluid that remains after whole blood or plasma has been allowed to clot.

Shoulder blade – The scapula.

Sigmoidoscopy – Inspection of the pelvic colon with the sigmoidoscope.

Sign – What a doctor sees (compare symptom).

Silicosis – A form of lung disease in the nature of pneumoconiosis, caused by inhalation of silicon dust.

Sinus – An air sinus; a mucus-lined cavity in one of the bones of the face or skull which communicates with the nose (frontal, sphenoid, ethmoid, maxillary).

Sinusitis – Inflammation affecting the mural epithelium of a sinus, particularly of the paranasal sinuses.

Sinusoid – Having resemblance to a sinus, a small terminal blood vessel to be found in certain organs.

Sodium – A metallic element used in medicine, chemical symbol Na (Natrium).

Soleus muscle – A muscle of the calf.

Spasm – A sudden, powerful, involuntary contraction of a muscle.

Speculum – Any instrument used in the inspection of a normally closed tube or passage.

Speroid bone – A complicated unpaired bone forming the central part of the base of the skull.

Sperm – The semen.

Sphenoid bone – A complicated unpaired bone forming the central part of the base of the skull.

Sphincter – Any anular muscle closing an orifice.

Spina bifida – A defect in development of the vertebral column in which there is a central deficiency of the vertebral lamina. Most common in the lumbar region.

Spinothalmic – Pertaining to the spinal cord and the thalmus.

Spirometer – An apparatus used to determine the sum of the tidal, complemental and supplemental air (vital capacity) of the lungs.

Spleen – The largest endocrine (ductless) gland.

Splenectomy – The operation of excising the spleen.

Splenomegaly – Enlargement of the spleen.

Spondylitis – When synovial joints of backbone are inflamed, ie inflammatory disease of spine.

Spondylo-listhesis – The slipping forward of one vertebra onto another, usually due to the degenerative changes of osteoarthritis; occasionally due to a congenital effect.

Spondylolysis – The breaking down of a vertebrae.

Spondylosis – Osteoarthritis of spine.

Sprain – Injury by sudden traction to the muscles, ligaments or articular capsule of a limb, not sufficient to produce rupture of these structures.

Spur – A projecting portion of bone.

Squamous – Resembling a scale, platelike, subcutaneous: beneath the skin.

Stapes – One of the chain of three movable ossicles in the tympanic cavity of the ear which has a resemblance to a stirrup.

Staphylococcus – A bacterial genus in the family of Micrococcaceae.

Stenosis – Narrowing of an opening or passage in abnormal circumstances.

Sterilisation – The production of sterility.

Sternum – Breast bone; a long flat bone forming the anterior wall of the thorax in the middle line articulating with the clavicles above and with the other seven pairs of costal cartilages marginally.

Stillbirth – The lifeless state of birth.

Strain – To overtax a faculty or part of the body; the result of such an overtaxing.

Streptococcus – A bacterial genus in the family lactobacillaceae.

Stroke – A sudden seizure; the commonly used lay term for apoplexy. Malady arresting powers of sense and motion, usually caused by effusion of blood or serum in brain.

Subcutaneous – Beneath the skin.

Subcuticular – Beneath the epidermis.

Subluxation – Partial dislocation of a joint, so that the bone ends are misaligned but still in contact.

Supination – Outward rotation movement of forearm, so that the palm lies upwards and the thumb lies laterally.

Supracondylar – Above a condyle.

Supra-orbital – Above the orbit, relating to the supra-orbital nerve.

Supraorbital nerve – The larger and more lateral of the branches of the frontal nerve.

Suprapubic – Above the pubic arch.

Suprasellar – Above the sella turcica.

Sural nerve – A branch of the medial popliteal nerve to the skin of the lateral and posterior sides of the lower part of the leg.

Suture – A surgical stitch.

Sympathectomy – The operation for the removal of the dorsal and lumbar sympathetic trunk or parts thereof.

Symphysis – Where fibrocartilage separates bones in a joint, minimising movement and making long structure rigid.

Symptom – What the patient describes (compare 'sign').

Syncopal – Relating to or resembling syncope.

Syncope – Transient loss of consciousness due to inadequate cerebral blood flow.

Syndesmosis – A fibrous joint in which the opposing surfaces are held together by a ligament.

Syndrome – A distinct group of symptoms or signs which, associated together, form a characteristic clinical picture or entity.

Synosteosis – Synostosis.

Synostosis – Bony ankylosis; the joining of bones by the ossification of the connecting tissues.

Synovectomy – The cutting away of part or all of a synovial membrane.

Synovia – The viscous fluid secreted by synovial membranes.

Synovial effusion – Extra fluid generated in a synovial cavity near a joint.

Synovitis – Inflammation of membrane lining joint.

Syringomyelia – The presence in the spinal cord, particularly the cervical region, of elongated central fluid-containing cavities surrounded by gliosis and probably resulting from congenital partial obstruction of the flow of cerebrospinal fluid.

Systemic – Systematic; relating to the body as a whole – rather than its individual parts.

Systole – The period during which the heart contracts.

Systolic – Relating to or resulting from a systole supernatant: floating born upon the surface of a liquid.

Tachycardia – Rapid heart rate.

Tachypnoea – Unduly rapid breathing.

Talus – The ankle bone; the bone connecting the bones of the foot with those of the leg, forming the ankle joint.

Tangential thinking – An inability to express ideas precisely, often characterised by a garrulous style of conversation.

Tarsal – Relating to the tarsi of the eyelids, or the foot.

Tarsalgia – Aching pain in the sole of the foot.

Tarsus – Bones of foot between metatarsals and ankle.

Tay-sachs disease – Amaurotic family idiocy, cerebromacular degeneration; a familial disease of infancy in which there is a progressive degeneration of nerve cells throughout the whole nervous system and in the retina.

Temporal – Located in the region of the temple or pertaining to the temporal bone.

Temporal bone – One of a pair of bones lying in the side wall of the vault and base of the skull and housing the middle and internal ear.

Temporomandibular – Connecting the temporal bone and the mandible; pertaining to the articulation of the lower jaw.

Tendinitis – Inflammation of the tendon.

Tendon – A discrete band of connective tissue mainly composed of parallel bundles of collagenous fibres by which muscles are attached, or two muscle bellies joined.

Tenodesis – Fixation of a tendon; the suture of the end of a tendon to a new point.

Tenoplasty – Operation to repair a damaged tendon.

Tenorrhaphy – An operation to unite the ends of a severed tendon.

Tenosynovitis – Inflammation of the sheath through which the tendon moves, producing pain, swelling and sometime an audible creaking on movement (also peritendinitis).

Tenotomy – The cutting of a tendon by surgery.

Tensor – A muscle that stretches or tightens some part of the body.

Tentorial – Relating to the tentorium cerebelli.

Testicle – The male gonad, where in adult life, spermatozoa develop; the testis.

Tetanus – An infectious disease due to the toxins of the clostridium tetani, the organisms entering through an abrasion or wound of the skin.

Tetany – A disease caused by a decrease of calcium in the blood serum and marked clinically by a hyperexcitability of the neuromuscular system.

Tetraplegia – See quadriplegia. Tetraplegia is the better expression since quadriplegia is a hybrid.

Thalassaemia – A chronic, progressive anaemia of congenital, familial, and racial incidence, showing splenomegaly, tone changes, mongoloid facies and typical target cells or thin, poorly staining red cells in the circulating blood.

Theca – A sheath or envelope.

Thenar – Relating to the ball of the thumb.

Thoracic – Of the chest (the part of the body cavity between the neck and the diaphragm).

Thoracotomy – The operation of incising the wall of the thorax.

Thorax – The part of the trunk between the neck and the abdomen; the chest.

Thrombolytic – Having the effect of breaking up a thrombus.

Thrombophlebitis – Phlebitis following the formation of an intravascular clot, caused by an alteration of the blood.

Thrombosis – Formation of blood-clot within vessels or heart.

Thrombus – A blood clot formed in and remaining in a blood vessel or the heart.

Thyroid gland – A highly vascular ductless or endocrine gland situated in the front of the neck and composed of two conical lobes lying on either side of, and moulded to, the larynx and lower pharynx above and the upper four or five rings of the trachea and oesophagus below.

Thyrotoxicosis – Any toxic condition attributable to hyperactivity of the thyroid gland.

Tibia – The long bone on the medial and pre-axial border of the leg, articulating with the fibular laterally, the femur above, and the talus below.

Tibial nerves – Nerves that constitute the main nerve supply of the leg and foot.

Tinnitus – Noise heard in ear without external cause.

Tonsil – A mass of lymphoid tissue, in particular the palatine tonsil.

Tonsillectomy – Surgical excision of a tonsil.

Torticollis – Spasm of the neck muscles, drawing the head to one side and twisting the neck.

Trabeculae – Bands of tissue which pass from the outer covering of an organ to the interior.

Trachea – The windpipe, a rigid tube 10 cm long.

Tracheostomy – Operation to open windpipe so that air may obtain direct entrance into lower air passages.

Tracheotomy – The surgical establishment of an opening from the exterior into the interior of the trachea.

Traction – Drawing or pulling of limb or spine as part of treatment.

Transurethral – Passing through the urethra, or describing any operation performed via the urethra.

Trapezium – The carpal bone on the radial side of the distal row, articulating with the base of the metacarpal bone of the thumb.

Trapezius muscle – A large flat muscle of the back located in the upper portion.

Trapezoid – Trapeziform.

Trauma – Fracture or blow; overwhelmingly stressful event; often used in psychological sense.

Trendelenburg test – Test for function of hip muscles.

Trephination – The surgical operation of removing a circular disc of bone or other tissue with a trephine (surgeon's cylindrical saw).

Triceps – Three-headed.

Trigeminal – Triple, divided into three, referring to the trigeminal nerve (which is the fifth cranial nerve).

Trigeminal nerve – The 5th cranial nerve.

Triquetrum – Bone in wrist.

Trismus – Inability to open the mouth due to chronic contracture of the muscles of the jaw.

Trochanter – Either of the two bony prominences at the upper end of the femur.

Trochlear nerve – The 4th cranial nerve.

Trousseau's phenomenon – A sign of latent tetany; spasm of the hand and wrist with adduction of the thumb, bunching of the fingers, and flexion of the wrist, produced by compression of the forearm in subjects having undue neuromuscular excitability as a result of deficiency of ionised calcium.

Trousseau's sign – A streak of congestion caused by scratching the skin. It occurs in a variety of cerebral diseases.

Tuberculosis – The disease caused by infection with the Mycobacterium tuberculosis.

Tuberosity – A rounded protuberance on the surface or side of a bone.

Turbinate – Scroll-like, or shaped like an inverted cone.

Tympanic cavity – Middle ear.

Ulcer – Breach on surface of skin or membrane which does not tend to heal quickly.

Ulna – The inner bone of the forearm (adjective – ulnar).

Ulnar nerve – One of the primary nerves in the arm.

Ungual – Of the nails.

Urea – A colourless crystalline, solid, soluble in water and alcohol, insoluble in ether (BP 1958). Occurs in the blood and tissue fluids of all vertebrates.

Ureter – Tubes which take urine from the pelvis of the kidney to the bladder.

Urethra – The canal through which the urine passes on its way from the bladder to the exterior.

Urethritis – Inflammation of the urethra, associated with a purulent discharge from the external meatus.

Uterus – A hollow, thick-walled, muscular organ in which the impregnated ovum is developed into the child.

Vaccination – The process or act of immunising for preventive purposes, less commonly for the treatment of disease.

Vagina – Any structure resembling a sheath, the female genital canal.

Vaginitis – Inflammation of the vagina or of a sheath.

Vagus nerve – The 10th and longest of the cranial nerves.

Valgus – Disease in outer angle of a joint. (Valgus deformity means bow-legged.)

Valvotomy – Surgical severing of a valve.

Varicocele – Variosity of the testicule producing swelling of the scrotum.
Varus – Increase in outer angle of a joint.
Vascular – Concerned with a vessel or vessels.
Vasculitis – Inflammation of a blood vessel.
Vasospasm – The condition of small arteries going into spasms.
Vein – A vessel conducting blood from the capillary bed to the heart.
Venography – Radiographic visualisation of veins after injection of a radio-opaque contrast medium into the lumen.
Ventral – Referring to the belly.
Ventricle – A small cavity, chamber, or compartment.
Vertebra – A bony unit of the segmented spinal column, typically composed of an anterior part [corpus vertebrae (NA)].
Vertigo – Giddiness, swimming in the head, a sense of instability, often with a sensation of rotation.
Visceral – Concerned with the internal organs, inwards including the heart, lungs, liver, stomach, entrails.
Visual acuity – Sharpness of the vision.
Volar – Palm of hand (see palmar).
Volkmann's contracture – Fixed deformity due to fibrosis of muscle following injury to its blood supply, usually affecting the hand.
Vomen – The thin bony inferior part of the septum of the nose extending from the sphenoid bone to the palatine bone.
Vulva – The female external genitalia: pudendum.

Watershed infarction – A stroke affecting the boundary between the parietal and occipital lobes of the brain on both sides.
Whiplash – A violent forward and backward movement of the head upon the neck, occurring in sudden acceleration or deceleration involving passengers in motor and other vehicles upon impact.
Windpipe – The trachea.
Wrist drop – Paralysis of the extensor muscles of the hand and digits.

Xerosis – Abnormal dryness, especially of eyes.

Zygoma – The zygomatic or malar (cheek) bone.

Index

333